Comparative criticism
A yearbook
1

Comparative criticism

A yearbook

1

Edited by

ELINOR SHAFFER

READER OF COMPARATIVE LITERATURE
SCHOOL OF MODERN LANGUAGES AND EUROPEAN HISTORY
UNIVERSITY OF EAST ANGLIA

CAMBRIDGE UNIVERSITY PRESS

CAMBRIDGE

LONDON · NEW YORK · MELBOURNE

Published by the Syndics of the Cambridge University Press
The Pitt Building, Trumpington Street, Cambridge CB2 IRP
Bentley House, 200 Euston Road, London NWI 2DB
32 East 57th Street, New York, NY 10022, USA
296 Beaconsfield Parade, Middle Park, Melbourne 3206, Australia

© Cambridge University Press 1979

First published 1979

Printed in Great Britain at the
University Press, Cambridge

ISBN 0 521 22296 6

CONTENTS

List of contributors   *page* vii
Acknowledgements   viii
Editor's note: Comparative literature in Britain   ix

Part I The literary canon

J. P. STERN Living in the metaphor of fiction (opening
address)   3
RENÉ WELLEK The critical realism of Francesco De Sanctis   17
M. A. MANZALAOUI Tragic ends of lovers: medieval Islam
and the Latin West   37
PETER W. HURST The encyclopaedic tradition, the
cosmological epic, and the validation of the medieval
romance   53
DAVID WILLIAMS Of diamonds and dunghills: Voltaire's
defence of the French classical canon (a bicentennial essay)   73
MARTIN SWALES The German *Bildungsroman* and 'The
Great Tradition'   91
CHRISTOPHER HEYWOOD French and American sources of
Victorian realism   107

Part II Translation in the canon of W. H. Auden

W. H. AUDEN A translation of 'The Sun Song'   129
PETER H. SALUS Englishing the *Edda*   141
W. H. AUDEN AND LEIF SJÖBERG A translation of three
poems by Erik Lindgren   153
GÖRAN PRINTZ-PÅHLSON The canon of literary modernism:
a note on abstraction in the poetry of Erik Lindegren   155

HARALD H. OHLENDORF W. H. Auden: 'In Memory of
Ernst Toller'   *page* 167
LEIF SJÖBERG Translating with W. H. Auden: Gunnar
Ekelöf's last poems   185

MURIEL RUKEYSER AND LEIF SJÖBERG A translation of
Gunnar Ekelöf, *A Mölna Elegy*, with an introductory essay
by Leif Sjöberg: The attempted re-construction of a
moment   199

Part III Essay reviews

MICHAEL HAMBURGER Goethe in English. On recent
translations: Randall Jarrell, *Faust* and David Luke, *The
Roman Elegies*   273
RICHARD GORDON Reason and ritual in Greek tragedy: On
René Girard, *Violence and the Sacred* and Marcel Detienne,
The Garden of Adonis   279
ELINOR SHAFFER The longest way with the dissenters: A
review of Donald Davie's Clark Lectures   311

Books received   317
*Bibliography of comparative literature in Britain: 1975 and
1976*   320

CONTRIBUTORS

Richard Gordon, Lecturer in Interdisciplinary Studies, School of Modern Languages and European History, University of East Anglia

Michael Hamburger, Poet, critic, and translator

Christopher Heywood, Senior Lecturer in English, Sheffield University

Peter W. Hurst, Lektor, Englisches Seminar, Universität zu Köln, Cologne, Germany

Mahmoud Manzalaoui, Professor of English, University of British Columbia, Canada

Harald H. Ohlendorf, Assistant Professor of German, Scarborough College, University of Toronto, Canada

Göran Printz-Påhlson, Lecturer in Swedish, Department of Scandinavian Studies, Faculty of Modern and Medieval Languages, Cambridge University

Muriel Rukeyser, Poet, critic, and translator

Peter H. Salus, Professor of German, Scarborough College, University of Toronto, Canada

Elinor Shaffer, Reader of Comparative Literature, School of Modern Languages and European History, University of East Anglia

Leif Sjöberg, Professor of Swedish, Department of Germanic Languages, State University of New York at Stony Brook

J. P. Stern, Professor of German, University College, London

Martin Swales, Professor of German, University College, London

René Wellek, Sterling Professor of Comparative Literature (Emeritus), Yale University

David Williams, Professor of French, Sheffield University

ACKNOWLEDGEMENTS

Acknowledgements are made to Albert Bonniers Förlag (Stockholm) for permission to quote from the published works of Gunnar Ekelöf; and to Mrs Ingrid Ekelöf, the poet's widow, for permission to publish a translation of *En Mölna-elegi*.

Thanks are owing to Professor Edward Mendelson for his generous help, and to him and the Estate of W. H. Auden for permission to quote from published and unpublished works of Auden. We are grateful to Professor John Matthias for supplying us with the draft translations by W. H. Auden of poems by Erik Lindegren.

Acknowledgements are made to the University of Texas for permission to quote from unpublished draft typescripts by W. H. Auden of his poem 'In Memory of Ernst Toller'.

We should like to express our gratitude to Mr Ove Svensson, the Cultural Attaché of the Swedish Embassy in London, for the interest he has taken in this volume, and the Swedish Institute in Stockholm for their support.

Comparative literature in Britain

Our intention in this first volume of *Comparative Criticism* is to explore the notion of literary canon as it relates to the present situation within literary studies in Britain. The traditional syllabus of literary studies – confined primarily to one national literature, or to two studied for the most part in isolation from one another and ordered mainly by reference to chronology, is clearly in the process of transformation. If the dominant literary culture of our century is international modernism, it follows that literary studies will move in the same direction. This fact by no means implies a bias towards modern studies, but suggests a concern with the impingement of cultures and languages upon one another throughout literary history, leading to a more synchronically oriented literary history; or the release of texts from their specific environment, leading to a more theoretically oriented literary history. In this situation, the methods of comparative literature, past and present (for it is far from a new subject) may prove helpful.

Although English literature has absorbed many foreign influences in the course of its long history, the emphasis on native tradition in the most extensive and powerful literature in the world has sometimes seemed to impede the recognition of foreign literature. As Matthew Arnold wrote to his sister in May 1848: 'How plain it is now, though an attention to the comparative literatures for the last fifty years might have instructed anyone of it, that England is in a certain sense far behind the continent.' Arnold, with his immersion both in the classics and in contemporary European literature, was, not surprisingly, responsible for the phrase 'comparative literatures', adapted from the French, 'littér-ature comparée'. As René Wellek has pointed out, this locution originated in the eighteenth century, at a time when 'literature' still meant 'erudition', or 'knowledge of letters', and had not taken on its modern sense of 'a body of writing' (whether of special aesthetic merit, or what Lamb called 'things in books' clothing'); the phrase signified simply the comparative study of literature ('The Name and Nature of Comparative Literature', *Discriminations* (Yale University Press, 1970); see also Wellek, 'What is Literature?' in the volume of the same title, edited by Paul Hernadi (University of Indiana Press, 1978).

Before Arnold used the phrase, Henry Hallam had already attempted to put it into practice on a large scale in his *Introduction to the Literature of Europe in the Fifteenth, Sixteenth, and Seventeenth Centuries* (1837–9). Hallam pointed out that 'France has no work of any sort, even an indifferent one, on the universal history of her literature; nor can we (Englishmen) claim for ourselves a single attempt of the most superficial kind.' George Saintsbury later acclaimed him for his *History of Criticism*: 'for Hallam was our first master in English of the true comparative-historical study of literature – the study without which. . .all criticism is now unsatisfactory and the special variety of criticism which has been cultivated for the last century most dangerously delusive' (III, 294). It must be said that Saintsbury's judgement of Hallam in his *Nineteenth Century Literature* was altogether more moderate (1908, pp. 212–14).

It was Arnold himself, of course, who attended to the 'comparative literatures' most comprehensively and diversely; by this one does not simply mean his own essays on Heine, the Guérins, or Joubert ('A French Coleridge'), nor his *Study of Celtic Literature*, nor his wide acquaintance with Continental education, nor even the whole range of such writings, but his grasp of the sense that had been given to 'culture':

Let us conceive the whole group of civilised nations, as being, for intellectual and spiritual purposes, one great confederation bound to a joint action and working towards a common result. This was the ideal of Goethe, and it is an ideal which will impose itself upon the thoughts of our modern societies more and more.

(Preface to Wordsworth's *Poems*)

Most of Arnold's characteristic critical conceptions are grouped round this centre: the notion of the critic as one so deeply conversant with the 'touchstones' of literature of the past that he is liberated from the class into which accident has thrust him and enabled to discern the living ideas of the present.

Arnold's influence was great, and probably decisive; but towards the end of the century other voices were raised in Britain to define 'comparative literature'. H. M. Posnett published *Comparative Literature* in 1886 in 'The International Scientific Series', a series devoted to post-Darwinian developments in all the sciences, and including such distinguished works as Walter Bagehot, *Physics and Politics*; Herbert Spencer, *The Study of Sociology*; J. W. Draper, *The History of the Conflict between Religion and Science*; H. Morselli, *Suicide: an Essay on Comparative Moral Statistics*; and Alexander Bain, *Education as a Science*, as well as many books in the natural sciences. Posnett had begun his work while an undergraduate at Trinity, Dublin; a barrister and afterwards Professor of Classics and English Literature at University College, Auckland, New Zealand, he was a follower of Herbert Spencer and Sir Henry Maine, what we should now call a sociologist of literature. 'Comparative' for him meant keeping 'the varying relations of social development to literary growth steadily in view' (p. 8), rather than comparing one national literature to another. He accordingly discussed first the nature and relativity of literature, and the comparative method; and then entered upon a consideration of the different forms of social organization with which literature is associated: 'clan literature', and the evolutionary fusion of clans into ever larger social groups, 'the city commonwealth', national literature, and world literature. Although he belongs so clearly to his time, the book is not a mere historical curiosity, and he puts his views vigorously:

Thus, by neglecting the influences of social life on literature, Greek criticism fostered the deadly theories that literature is essentially an imitation of masterpieces, that its ideals are not progressive but permanent, that they have no dependence on particular conditions of human character, on the nature of that social instrument language, on circumscribed spheres of time and place. (p. 10)

In short, we cannot by the 'science' of comparative literature mean 'a body of universal truths', for 'the very evolution of literature is fatal *per se* to any such literary "science"'. But rather the limited truths of literature must be 'grouped round certain central facts of. . . permanent influence, such as 'the climate, soil, animal and plant life of different countries', 'and the principle of evolution from communal to individual life' (p. 20). Despite his use of Coleridge as whipping-boy throughout – Coleridge, with his subjectivism, his idealism, his yearning for universals – Posnett sounds remarkably like him in his invocation of 'the principle of literary growth': 'How vast and intricate this two-fold process of individuality deepening in the separate units while expanding in the number of units it includes!' (p. 71). (In a later article, 'The Science of Comparative Literature', *Contemporary Review*, 79 (June 1901), Posnett was prepared to admit that some of the Romantics –

Mme de Staël, A. von Humboldt, and the Schlegels – had 'touched the borders of Comparative Literature'.)

What Posnett finally valued was not the communal, the clan principle, but those 'adult ideas of personality [which] have long formed for us the centre of all our creative art, of all our criticism' (p. 68). Indeed, 'individual inquiry' is concomitant with 'comparative thinking' (p. 75). It follows, then, that 'the more advanced the country, the more the individual must look beyond her sea-washed shores':

> Does he accompany Chaucer on his pilgrimage and listen to the pilgrims' tales? The scents of the lands of the South fill the atmosphere of the Tabard Inn, and on the road to Canterbury waft him in thought to the Italy of Dante and of Petrarch and Boccaccio. Does he watch the hardy crews of Drake and Frobisher unload in English port the wealth of Spanish prize, and listen to the talk of great sea-captains full of phrases learned from the gallant subjects of Philip II? The Spain of Cervantes and Lope de Vega rises before his eyes, and the new physical and mental wealth of Elizabethan England bears him on the wings of commerce or of fancy to the noisy port of Cadiz and the palaces of Spanish grandees.   (p. 79)

And so on, through coffee-houses and theatres and the perfuming of licentious wit with 'French *bouquet*', until the enlightened individual arrives at Weimar and his proper cosmopolitan humanity.

But the accomplished comparatist must turn back from these external influences to 'the comparative study of internal developments', the intimate association of its literature with its corporate life (p. 81). This sense of the domestic focus of literature led him to reverse the expected pattern of his evolutionary account, and to treat 'World Literature' before 'National Literature', a reversal he justifies by the historical (and, we may suspect, Hegelian) consideration that the true world literatures are the Alexandrian and Roman, the later Hebrew and Arab, the Indian and Chinese, in which literature is universalized, severed from defined social groups, and becomes reflective and critical in spirit (p. 236). After all, Posnett felt, the national literatures of Western Europe held the best expressions of individual life. 'Provincialism is no ban in truly national literature', he insisted (p. 345). On account of this sturdy insistence on native roots to which his sociological science returned him, chroniclers of comparative literary studies have tended to be rather dismissive about him. (See, for example, the standard history, Ulrich Weisstein, *Einführung in die vergleichende Literaturwissenschaft* (Stuttgart, 1968); translated as *Comparative Literature and Literary Theory* (Indiana University Press, 1973). For a brief account of the reception of Posnett's book, see the useful article by Frederick C. Roe, 'Comparative Literature in the United Kingdom', *Yearbook of Comparative and General Literature* (1954), pp. 1–12.) Only the following description of the 'Herculean labour' of the comparative historian is held to salvage his claim:

To watch the internal and external development by which local and national differences give way in turn to national and cosmopolitan ideals – this is one line of study open to students of national literatures; another is the deepening and widening of personal character which accompany such social expansion; a third is the changing aspect of physical nature which this social and individual evolution likewise involves. But to chronicle the rise of new forms, new spirits, of verse and prose in each European nation, and the gradual separation of science from literature; to trace such growth to its roots in social and physical causes; finally, to compare and contrast these causes as producing the diverse literatures of England and France and Germany, of Italy and Spain and Russia; this, truly, were the task of a literary Hercules. (p. 346)

The main line of development of comparative studies in Britain passed not through Posnett (Roe held), but directly from Arnold to 'an impressive harvest of studies in European literature undertaken by men born around the mid-century and consequently fully open to the influence of Arnold in their formative years': J. Addington Symonds' *History of the Renaissance in Italy*; Walter Pater's *Studies in the History of the French Renaissance*; J. Paget Toynbee's *Dante in English Literature* (1909). The story is surely more complicated than that, and indeed, needs to be unfolded 'comparatively'; for on Posnett as on the others, the influence of German historical thinking was strong, and by the later nineteenth century was directly as well as indirectly available to them. Whatever the full story, however, a formidable number of the new professors of English followed suit: Saintsbury with his *History of Criticism and Literary Taste in Europe from the Earliest Texts to the Present Day*; Edward Dowden, *The French Revolution and English Literature*; C. H. Herford, *Studies in the Literary Relations of England and Germany in the Sixteenth Century*; W. P. Ker, *Epic and Romance*; J. Churton Collins, *Voltaire, Rousseau, and Montesquieu in England*; Sir Sidney Lee, *Shakespeare and the Italian Renaissance*. (This is the merest sampling; see Roe, pp. 3–5, for a somewhat fuller list, which could certainly be much extended.)

The interest in Scandinavian literature had been strong throughout the century. The Romantic taste for ballads, sagas, and folklore had dictated the first wave; the new Scandinavian modernism of the 1880s was imported almost immediately, in the form of the enthusiasm for Ibsen. Sir Edmund Gosse published his *Studies in the Literature of Northern Europe* in 1879, and claimed he had been the first to mention Ibsen's name in English, in an essay in the *Spectator* in 1872. The role played by G. B. Shaw, A. B. Walkley, and Henry James is much better known. (For an account of the reception of Ibsen and Strindberg in England, see Malcolm Bradbury and J. W. McFarlane, *Modernism: European Literature 1890–1930* (Harmondsworth, 1979).

The development of comparative literary studies as an academic subject on the Continent began to make its influence felt, as the first chairs were founded, for Francesco de Sanctis in Italy (1871) and Joseph Texte in France (1897). G. Gregory Smith discussed the French developments in two articles, one reporting on the Paris Congress of Comparative History held in July 1900, in *Blackwood's Magazine* (January 1901), and the other, 'Some Notes on the Comparative Study of Literature', generalizing his critical position, in the first issue of the *Modern Language Review* (1906), edited by J. G. Robertson, who himself contributed an article on 'The Knowledge of Shakespeare on the Continent at the Beginning of the Eighteenth Century'. Gregory Smith is as interesting a case as Posnett, for while he was a whole-hearted supporter of comparative studies, he was distinctly critical of French orthodoxy, especially as represented by Ferdinand Brunetière (the author of another post-Darwinian essay, *L'Evolution des genres*). He is critical of its scientific pretensions – 'the "evolution" of poetic form as well as of marsupials' – and of its equal but opposite tendency (as represented by Texte's *Jean-Jacques Rousseau et les origines du cosmopolitisme littéraire*, translated into English by J. W. Matthews in 1899) to expect 'the rise of an ideal literature which shall be a beneficent blend of all the national aspirations in the common culture of the "United States of Europe"' (p. 39). Despite his asperities, however, he concludes by calling on the universities to take up the new study and produce critics worthy of the name, rather than the journalists who 'expound the Ptolemaic system of criticism as it has always appeared to the good folks of Little Pedlington' (p. 48). As Texte had written, 'Le XIXe siècle aura vu se developper et se constituer l'histoire nationale des littératures; ce sera sans doute la tâche du XXe siècle d'en écrire l'histoire comparative.' This task the International Comparative Literature Association is currently attempting to carry out in the *Comparative History of European Literature*, comprising a number of collaborative volumes. But Gregory Smith was sceptical; he felt that this approach was ruled by antiquarianism and genealogy. He wanted a 'critical branch' of comparative literature, concerned with 'the fundamental doctrines of criticism', as he put it in his later article.

It is perhaps worth noting that academic criticism was, in its earlier stages, strictly comparative. The evidence of Greece and Rome is clear on this point; and sixteenth-century Italy, the birthplace of the new criticism, worked by this method and passed on the lesson to the rest of Europe. Example and Comparison were of course essential to Classicism, with its doctrine of the Model, the Ancients, etc., but there the main purpose was the collection of material and precedents for the establishment of a literary Canon. The application of the Method to individual experience and effort has been left to the Moderns. (p. 4)

Gregory Smith's essay is sketchy; but it is clear that, like Posnett, he was adumbrating a 'national' stance, in which the authority of universalism, whether of traditional precept or 'scientific' fact-mongering, was not acceptable. (Posnett had taken Mathew Arnold to task for advocating an Academy on French lines.) If for Posnett 'comparative literature' pointed towards the social relations of literature, and for Gregory Smith towards the intricate relations of critical problems, both prized the individual, highly 'evolved' expression of collective literary knowledge and experience. Only comparative studies could fit the critic for this.

In the twentieth century, Arnold's legacy continued to bear fruit; and the increasing professionalization of comparative studies abroad exerted an influence, as post-graduate students went to France to work for their degrees under Fernand Baldensperger, Paul Hazard, or Jean-Marie Carré. It has been claimed, rather artificially perhaps, that comparative literature was 'officially' recognized when Baldensperger was invited to give a series of lectures on eighteenth century comparative themes at Aberystwyth in 1921. Scandinavian modernism was succeeded by the more powerful presence of Pound and Eliot, whose fresh canons served to graft American literature onto the English and European, while transforming all of them. Henry Gifford's lively book *Comparative Literature* (1969) starts from the studied internationalism of Pound and Eliot.

All of the English advocates of comparative literary studies had called for some form of institutional arrangements. These were late in coming; in Italy, Hungary, and Germany, the first comparative journals were founded in the nineteenth century; in France, the *Revue de littérature comparée* first appeared in 1921. The first English journal was *Comparative Literature Studies*, edited by Marcel Chicoteau and Kenneth Urwin as a war-time effort to keep the subject alive despite the suspension of the publication of the *Revue*; published from 1940 to 1945 in Cardiff, and in 1946 in Liverpool, it had formidable patrons both in and out of the universities ('The Late Sir Hugh Walpole, C.B.E. and

Mr Walter de la Mare, Mr Hilaire Belloc, and Sir William Rothenstein'). But the crisis over, it quietly disappeared from the scene.

The establishment of posts in the subject waited until the post-war period: in 1953 a Lectureship in Comparative Literary Studies was established at the University of Manchester. Roe, estimating in 1954 that about ten per cent of post-graduate work being done in French departments was comparative in nature, was nevertheless not sanguine about the prospects for further posts. The advent of the new universities, however, created a certain enthusiasm for novelty and interdisciplinary ventures, and it was in this climate that Essex University formed in 1963–4 a School of Literature, appointing Donald Davie as professor of Literature. Sussex and the University of East Anglia formed Schools of European Studies: at East Anglia in 1963 J. W. McFarlane was appointed professor of European Literature; at Sussex in 1967 A. K. Thorlby became the first professor of Comparative Literature. There are at present three chairs of comparative literature in the U.K., one at Sussex, and two at the University of East Anglia, established in 1969 and 1975 respectively. The only undergraduate course leading to a B.A. in Comparative Literature is offered at East Anglia; the Universities of Essex, Sussex, Warwick, and York have undergraduate programmes with strong comparative elements. In view of the long-standing conviction that comparative studies were best conducted at a post-graduate level, a number of new degree courses were established: Manchester University's Department of Comparative Literary Studies offers an M.A., as do East Anglia, Essex, Sussex, and Warwick. East Anglia and Warwick stress literary theory and translation studies, but offer a considerable range of options; Essex offers two, more specialized M.A. courses, one in literary translation, one in the sociology of literature. The Oxford B.Phil. in general and comparative literature is a more advanced degree; and all of these universities offer the degree of M.Phil., Ph.D., or D.Phil. There are other post-graduate degree courses with a comparative bias, though without the title. More important perhaps than the appearance of specifically comparative degrees, departments, and schools of studies, is the increase in comparative interests within English departments, partly through the greater weight being attached to nineteenth- and twentieth-century studies, partly through the impact of recent Continental and American critical theory. The proportion of post-graduate research devoted to comparative study in both English and modern language departments merits investigation.

1975 a conference on comparative studies was held at the

University of East Anglia; on that occasion the British Comparative Literature Association was founded, and a steering committee elected. Since then, at the Warwick conference held in 1977, the Association has elected its first president and become an affiliate of the International Comparative Literature Association.

In our present enterprise, the first volume of *Comparative Criticism: A Yearbook*, published for the British Comparative Literature Association by Cambridge University Press, it is a particular pleasure to have an article by René Wellek on Francesco de Sanctis, the first holder of a chair in comparative literature in Europe, and a critic whose work on realism (as well as his history of Italian literature) is still too little known in this country.

In the present period, recent English literature is increasingly being considered 'minor'; yet literature in the English language is more than ever the major literature in the world. If this implies an interest in Irish, Scottish, and Welsh, as well as in Commonwealth and American, it also offers fresh opportunities to reconsider English literature of the past in relation to its foreign counterparts. The novel has come to be the major modern European genre, and Friedrich Schlegel's original perceptions as to its nature and derivation are borne out by Martin Swales' vigorous revaluation of the significance of the German *Bildungsroman* for the English and European novel tradition, and by Christopher Heywood's demonstration of the interweaving of French, American, and English theory and practice of the novel in the nineteenth century.

Another traditional comparative topic is of course the history of the reception of Shakespeare in Europe and elsewhere. David Williams shows how Voltaire, even in the act of defending the French neo-classical theatre of Corneille and Racine against the inroads of Shakespeare, found himself unable any longer to accept it fully. We are especially glad to be able to publish this essay as a contribution to the celebration of the Voltaire bicentenary.

Medievalists have long been indisputable comparatists, and on the basis of just that cosmopolitan Latin culture for which Herder and Goethe, preparing the ground for the formal study of comparative literature, sought a modern equivalent in *Weltliteratur*. Professor Manzalaoui's article, in showing the use of the authority of pseudo-canonical sayings of the Prophet in the founding of the service of love, has broad implications for the relation of literary to religious canon and for the theory of tragedy. The Arabic material is here translated for the first time. Peter Hurst's paper too shows how the authority of learned tradition was used to justify the genre of romance, and has general implications for interdisciplinary studies. Richard Gordon goes to the root of the question in his discussion of the work of French anthropological critics on the relation between ritual religion and Greek tragedy.

For this first volume we are very pleased to have a number of W. H. Auden's unpublished translations and several articles touching in various ways on the relation of his translations to the canon of his poetry. This is of particular importance because the editions we have and those in prospect do not include his translations. Yet it is clear not only that some of the unpublished and uncollected translations are distinguished poems, such as the resplendent 'Sun Song' which we offer here, but that they often throw fresh light on his work as poet and critic. The Scandinavian element in his own poetry, his concern with a 'Northern' mythology and geography of which England also was a part, was deeply rooted in his heritage and experience, as Peter Salus makes clear in his account of his and Paul Taylor's collaboration with Auden on the translations from the *Edda*. The translations of Erik Lindegren are placed precisely in the context of modern poetics by Göran Printz-Påhlson. Harald Ohlendorf suggests a neglected aspect of Auden's German interests.

Some of Auden's finest translations were those of Gunnar Ekelöf's shorter lyrics, and we are delighted to be able to publish the first translation of Ekelöf's *A Mölna Elegy*, a major modern poem of the order of Eliot's *The Waste Land*, by a poet considered one of the finest lyric poets of Sweden, yet still scarcely known in Britain, despite Auden's translations. The translators of this poem, the well-known American poet Muriel Rukeyser, and Leif Sjöberg, Auden's collaborator in his translations from the Swedish, have received an award from the Anglo-Swedish Literary Foundation, based on George Bernard Shaw's donation of his Nobel Prize for literature.

And as the last shall be first, we are pleased indeed to publish Professor J. P. Stern's Opening Address to the 1977 Conference of the British Comparative Literature Association, in which he continues his complex reassessment of the impact of Nietzsche's thought on the whole of our own period. We shall continue to publish major papers from our conferences.

Thanks are owing to many others who have helped with this volume: let me name only Göran Printz-Påhlson and Michael Hamburger for a great deal of generous advice; Dr Paula Clifford, who undertook the onerous task of collecting the bibliographical material which will form the basis of our knowledge of comparative literary work in Britain, and Professor Ulrich Weisstein for his invaluable counsel in bibliographical matters; Michael Robinson, who has taken time from his post-graduate studies to contribute his extremely efficient editorial assistance; and a considerable number of kindly people at the Cambridge University Press, in particular Peter Burbidge, Judith Butcher, Elizabeth O'Beirne-Ranelagh, and, finally, Michael Black, whose unfailing sympathy and clear-sighted judgement have been indispensable.

The next four volumes of *Comparative Criticism* will address themselves to the following themes: 'Text and Reader'; 'Rhetoric and History'; 'The Languages of the Arts'; 'Biblical and Literary Interpretation'. Translations of poetry and other literary works as well as of scholarly and critical works, past and present, are welcome at all times. We shall continue to publish a selection of the best papers given at the conference of the British Comparative Literature Association. The annual deadline for submission of manuscripts is 1 February; the annual press deadline is 30 June, and the volume should appear in the following spring. Submissions for all the above volumes are now being received. All correspondence should be addressed to the Editor, *Comparative Criticism*, Cambridge University Press, P.O. Box 110, Cambridge CB2 3RL.

E. S. Shaffer

PART I
The literary canon

Living in the metaphor of fiction

OPENING ADDRESS

J. P. STERN

Vielleicht auch siehet Gott an, dass ich das Schwere gesucht und mirs habe sauer werden lassen, vielleicht, vielleicht wird mirs angerechnet und zugute gehalten sein, dass ich mich so befleissigt und alles zähe fertig gemacht...

Perchance, too, God will this descry, that I sought out the hard and laboured with might and main, perchance, perchance it will be counted unto my credit and benefit that I diligently applied myself and strenuously wrought all to its completion.

So hab ich dem ungeachtet mich immerfort befleissigt als ein Werker und nie geruget...noch geschlafen, sondern mirs sauer werden lassen und Schweres vor mich gebracht, nach dem Wort des Apostels: 'Wer schwere Dinge sucht, dem wird es schwer.'

Yet aside from [all my sins] have I busied myself as a labourer does, nor rested nor slept, but toiled and moiled and undertaken all manner of hard things, following the word of the Apostle: 'Whoever seeks hard things, to him it is hard.'

(Thomas Mann, *Doktor Faustus* (1947), chapter 47, translation by the author)

With the appearance of Thomas Mann's *Doktor Faustus* in 1947, a period in the political, social and literary history of Germany comes to its conclusion. The famous lines I have just quoted many of you will have recognized, for they contain the main purport of Adrian Leverkühn's confession at the end of that book, the summing up of his life as he and his creator see it. But beyond that (it seems to me) these lines contain a summing up and motto of a whole epoch, an epoch to which Leverkühn belongs as much as does Thomas Mann himself, and which for Thomas Mann is not historical: by which I mean that he does not stand outside it.

I have tried to show in more than one place that the dominant values of this age – which I see as an age informed by a morality or moral theology of strenuousness – make their appearance in its politics as well as in its literature, and how difficult its greatest writers found it to move

* This paper was given as the opening address to the British Comparative Literature Association Conference, Warwick, December 1977.

3

beyond them, to a different vision of man and of what is of paramount value in him. Their attempts to do so have usually ended in bathos and literary disaster. Stefan George's Maximin, Ernst Jünger's *Der Arbeiter* or Hofmannsthal's 'Kinderkönig' – a sort of glorified head-boy of the Viennese Boys' Choir – are warning examples of what I have in mind.

Thomas Mann made no such awful mistake. Throughout almost his entire work he identifies himself with the ideology of strenuousness. He endorses Adrian Leverkühn's appeal to 'das Schwere'; he nowhere criticizes *this* aspect of his thinking and his work, nowhere renders its validity problematic. He cannot step outside the ideology and view it critically – and yet he, like Rilke at the end of *his* work, is vouchsafed a deliverance of sorts. But perhaps that is putting it too grandly. Perhaps it is better to say that at the end of his time, in *Felix Krull*, his last major work, Thomas Mann is able to cock a snook at the whole business of 'das Schwere' and the value-scheme of the 'dear purchase'. In doing so he is playing a sort of in-joke on Friedrich Nietzsche, the church-father of this theology of strenuousness. But the joke of *this* last joke is that the farewell to the ideology and temper of an age is enacted in *his* – in Nietzsche's – terms. These, I know, are dark words, and the rest of this paper is meant to elucidate them.

It was Nietzsche in whose writings this ideology of strenuousness was formulated for the first time and with a consistency of which he himself was perhaps not fully aware. Nietzsche, we know, meditated on and criticized the Christian commandments and morality, taking it together with certain Socratic injunctions to be a model of all other moral schemes and moralizings. Nietzsche's sustained attacks take as their object not merely this or that rule or law or commandment. He proposes to reject the whole business of making moral judgements and to 'unmask' it as a compensatory activity which is wholly based on feelings of inferiority and grudging resentment, and desire for revenge. All this to him are aspects of what in *Zarathustra* he calls 'der Geist der Schwere', which he identifies with the Second Reich, and with the Germans generally, whom he accuses of eating and drinking too much and of judging the quality of thought by the quantity of sweat it produces. But 'das Schwere' in German means not only heaviness and earnestness and gravity, but also a proud strenuousness and difficulty, and the exacting nature of intellectual and moral effort. In criticizing and repudiating this 'Geist der Schwere', this spirit of gravity, Nietzsche, and after him Thomas Mann, speak from a life-long experience of and belief *in* this spirit; they speak as men who believe that in the attainment of that spirit lies the moral and spiritual validation of their age. Both deeply believe in commitment to strenuousness as a sign of some sort of salvation or validation of modern man. From his earliest writings – that is, the second of his *Thoughts out of Season* of 1874 – to the last notes reprinted posthumously in *The Will to Power*, this is the cardinal theme of Nietzsche's philosophizing.

Thus, in the second of the *Thoughts out of Season* (1874), he exhorts his contemporaries 'to find an exalted and noble *raison d'être* in life: seek out destruction for its own sake! I know of no better purpose in life than to be destroyed by that which is great and impossible!' (II, §9) – as though its impossibility were what makes his 'ideal' great. Again, in the Wagner essay two years later, he commends the cultural and pedagogic function of Bayreuth and offers its tragic masterpieces as lessons to those who are 'preparing for death in the fight for justice and love' (IV, §4), as though only death could validate their cause. Youthful romantic rhetoric? The self-destructive strenuousness of this strange morality never changes. When Nietzsche writes (to Seydlitz, 11 June 1878) that he wishes his life to reflect 'my views about morality and art (the hardest things that my sense of truth has so far wrung from me)'; and again a year later (to Gast, 5 October 1879) referring to the conclusion of *Human, All-too-Human*: '[it is] purchased so dearly and with so much hardship that nobody who had the choice would have written it at that price'; when he proclaims, in the 1886 preface to that book, 'I now took sides *against* myself and *for* everything that would hurt me and would come hard to me'; when he insists (to Gast, August 1883) that the main achievement of *Zarathustra* should be seen as 'a victory over the Spirit of Heaviness, considering *how difficult* it was to represent the problems with which the book is concerned'; when, in the notes to *The Will to Power* (1887–8) he defines 'virtue' as 'the delight we take in opposition', adding that 'I assess the power of [a man's] will by how much resistance, pain and torment it can endure and turn to its advantage' (§382); when again and again he insists on the need to destroy all forms of positive faith and all comforting certitudes, emphasizing the value of scepticism and of despair itself in the battle against the living death of conformity; and when, finally, in *Antichrist* (1888) he roundly condemns every idea of a pre-established harmony between truth and happiness (or even plain utility), claiming that

the experience of all rigorous and profoundly disposed minds teaches the opposite. Every inch of truth has to be wrested from oneself. We have to surrender almost everything that our hearts, our love, our trust in life normally cling to. This requires greatness of soul: the service of truth is the hardest service...*Faith makes blessed*: therefore it lies... (§50) we are left in no doubt that 'the experimental philosophy which I live', unlike the other moral 'experiments', represents Nietzsche's most intimate personal undertaking and purpose, and informs every phase of his creative life. Its fullest expression is to be found in *Thus Spoke Zarathustra*, that disastrous fiction on which he pinned his highest hopes.

This – the ideology of 'the hardest thing', of 'the dear purchase' – is one aspect of the legacy Nietzsche left to the twentieth century. But there is another aspect of this legacy, which is more specifically literary, and which is at odds with the ideology of strenuousness.

From his first book, *The Birth of Tragedy* of 1872, to the end of his conscious life, Nietzsche is attempting to offer what he calls 'an aesthetic justification of the world' (by which, though he shunned the word, he really meant a kind of redemption). Finding life in the world intolerable, he – the great 'Yea-sayer' of the Zarathustrian affirmation – now wishes to present the world as a game or a play (the notorious ambiguity of the German word, 'Spiel', leaves the question open), as a spectacle for the gods; he hopes to fashion an aesthetic philosophy in which 'the World and all being of man' might be presented as free of the curse of moral value-judgements, 'moralinfrei', truly beyond good and evil. Here, from the book of that title, is one of the aphorisms in which this aesthetic 'redemption' is described:

Um den Helden herum wird alles zur Tragödie, um den Halbgott herum alles zum Satyrspiel; und um Gott herum wird alles – wie? vielleicht zur 'Welt'?

Around the hero everything turns into tragedy, around the demi-god everything turns into satyric drama; and around God everything turns into – what? Maybe the 'world'?
(*Jenseits von Gut und Böse* (*Beyond Good and Evil*) §150)

To grasp the full poignancy of this Nietzschean idea of the aesthetic we must bear in mind that it comes from a philosopher who is temperamentally incapable of making any statement, significant or otherwise, without subsuming it by a moral value-judgement of some kind – a philosopher whose countless attacks on Christianity and occasional admiration of Christ derive from the conviction that the religion and its church betrayed its founder, who lived and exemplified a life without judging. The further irony here is that Nietzsche's idea of the aesthetic by definition excludes Nietzsche the thinker and inveterate moralist. And the poignant irony is that he knows it. In what must be one of his most deeply self-revealing reflections he writes: 'How could it be other than obvious that this is the ideal of a heavy, a hundredweight spirit – a spirit of gravity!' (*Der Wille zur Macht* (*The Will to Power*) §1039). Could he not encompass all life in a fiction? Indeed he could. Indeed, he could be bounded in a nutshell and count himself a king of infinite space, were it not that he has bad dreams, dreams of the death of God.

'Only as an aesthetic phenomenon is the world and the being of man eternally justified' – the sentence occurs three times in *The Birth of Tragedy* and he comes back to variations of it in almost every one of his later books. This search for an aesthetic theodicy accompanies the sixteen brief years of Nietzsche's thinking; and just so does the search for the liberation through the genuinely funny fiction accompany the almost sixty very long years of Thomas Mann's métier as a novelist. And an aesthetic redemption – aesthetic in the widest sense of the word – is what, at the end of Thomas Mann's life, Felix Krull is vouchsafed.

But what does 'aesthetic in the widest sense' mean? A very short essay of Nietzsche's of 1873, entitled 'On Truth and Falsehood in an Extra-Moral Sense' (it is the first of his purely philosophical writings) gives us an idea of what Nietzsche means by 'the aesthetic'. Men, he says there, are constitutionally incapable of a true knowledge of the world around them. All their so-called truths about this world or any other are pure tautologies. ('If someone hides a thing behind a bush, looks for it there and finds it, then this seeking and finding isn't much to write home about; but that' – Nietzsche goes on – 'that is what all seeking and finding inside the realm of reason amounts to.')

Well, we may ask, if man is entirely incapable of finding out the truth about the world, how then is it that he survives in this bleak unknown world of alien forms and shapes, to which he remains forever a stranger? To ask this question is to assume what Nietzsche is unwilling to assume, namely that the truth about the world is necessary for our survival in it. Nietzsche says the opposite: what makes life possible is the fact that the true nature of the world is hidden from us, that we are able to fictionalize the world as it really is. We create art in order not to perish of the truth (he will write fifteen years later); the conviction that we create the metaphors of myth in order to be able to bear the reality of the world is the foundation on which his entire theory of tragedy rests; and so the artistic activity becomes the creative, life-giving and life-protecting activity par excellence. Or, to put it in the terminology of that early essay, the way that man manages to negotiate and survive in the world is by forming metaphors about the world, and fictions are the most sustained of the metaphors he creates. Human language especially (Nietzsche continues) is totally incapable of saying anything about the real world (to which, he argues, language does not belong), but the relationship of language with that world is entirely imprecise, approximate, haphazard, almost random – indeed, its relationship is merely metaphorical:

Was ist also Wahrheit? Ein bewegliches Heer von Metaphern, Metonymien, Anthropomorphismen, kurz eine Summe von menschlichen Relationen, die, poetisch und rhetorisch gesteigert, übertragen, geschmückt wurden und die nach langem Gebrauch einem Volke fest, kanonisch und verbindlich dünken: die Wahrheiten sind Illusionen, von denen man vergessen hat, dass sie welche sind.

What then is truth? A mobile army of metaphors, metonymies, anthropomorphisms – in short, a sum of human relations which, poetically and rhetorically intensified, became transposed and adorned, and which after long usage by a people seem fixed, canonical and binding on them. Truths are illusions which one has forgotten *are* illusions.
                              ('Über Wahrheit und Lüge im aussermoralischen Sinn')

I don't propose to inquire whether this is a correct view of language (or, indeed, how a correct or true view of language could possibly be formulated if language is seen as such an arbitrary, shifting structure). But there is no doubt that this view represents consistently Nietzsche's own understanding of language throughout his life as a writer, and that this view says a good deal about his particular use of it – that is, about his predominantly and powerfully metaphorical style. The theoretical structure behind his style goes something like this:

Language is related to reality by nothing more precise than metaphor.

Metaphors are the only access we have to reality.

Metaphors are the creation of artists.

Therefore artists are the least misleading, least imprecise users of language; artistic activity is the paradigm or symbol of all positive human activity.

Art, in this argument of Nietzsche's, is not oblivion or even ecstasy (as it is in *The Birth of Tragedy*), but it is involved in the creation of that spiderweb of metaphors which alone makes life in the world possible: art is a creation, however, which is accompanied by at least an intermittent knowledge which those who merely *use* the metaphorical structure without creating it do not possess – the knowledge that the metaphors are not the real thing, that they are indeed only metaphors. Language, Nietzsche claims, cannot designate true causality. The world contains no truth and no undeflected communication; and there is of course no *real* freedom in the world either. Our only freedom is in the realm of 'as if': it is a metaphorical or aesthetic freedom – aesthetic in that wider sense that I have now described.

Thomas Mann is the principal heir of Nietzsche's bequest to our age: of *both* aspects of that bequest. Not only do the major figures of his fiction – from Thomas Buddenbrook through Tonio Kröger, Gustav von Aschenbach, Prinz Klaus Heinrich, Hans Castorp, the magician Cipolla, to Jacob and Joseph, the old Goethe and Adrian Leverkühn – embody that ideology of strenuousness which I have described; but all his life too, though intermittently, Thomas Mann hoped for a deliverance from that ideology, searching for a way out of this world of existential strain. Throughout his long career he hoped to write, not merely an ironical novel (he had done enough, and we might even think more than enough, of that: irony clearly offered no escape), not even a humorous novel but, speaking up on more than one occasion for the joys of slapstick, what he hoped to write was a funny novel. A novel which would suspend (I am desperately trying to avoid the villainous Hegelian pun: I mean *aufheben*) the weightiness of the spirit of gravity. And in finally achieving *Felix Krull* he had his life-long wish.

Now this is the point where a good many things might be said to characterize Thomas Mann's undertaking in the novel. There is, first and most obviously, its very rich autobiographical background – he began working on it in 1910 and the first volume, which is all we have, was not concluded until 1954. There is Thomas Mann's parodistic exploration of the *Bildungsroman*, its modification by the picaresque tradition, his treatment of that 'art *versus* life' theme to which he had devoted so many earlier works and which has been the standby of every modern language teacher ever since. All these topics have been discussed at length and there is no need to go over them again. Instead, I want to turn to another topic: the strongly anti-mimetic aspect of the work.

Whereas Nietzsche's idea of an aesthetic validation of the world remains a speculative proposal – a proposal to de-pragmatize, aestheticize or fictionalize the world – Thomas Mann turns the proposal into a reality, that is, into an elaborate fiction. Michael Beddow in a recent closely argued essay makes the point: 'The narrative pattern reveals a metaphoric determination of such sustained intensity that the text's ostensible claim to be the autobiography of an adventurer is undercut': or rather, that its credibility is seriously, and deliberately, impaired. Similarly, there is no satirical intention worth mentioning behind the work, and any attempt to see it as a socially conscious critique of Edwardian materialistic morality only shows what extraordinarily modest ideas of satire are entertained by some of our socially conscious friends and colleagues.

I think there is no point in beating about the bush. The hero whom Thomas Mann has created and whose device in life is a delightful ease,

a lightness of touch, a charming grace and an easy, all-too-easy
conscience – that hero is a con man and good-for-nothing who will never
pass the Leavisite test of mature adult responsible behaviour. And the
novel in which he has his being is what Nietzsche said all life was: a
highly immoral or, if you prefer it, *a*moral affair. I do not merely mean
that trickery, lechery, mendacity, theft and deceit are rewarded by
worldly goods and pleasure *and* an easy conscience, but that all these
vices and villainies are metaphorized: presented to us under names and
in forms which are designed to cancel out their viciousness. In other
words, *Felix Krull* is a novel without any sustained or consistently held
moral judgements, a story enacted in Nietzsche's 'moralinfreie Welt'.
This is one of the sources and conditions of its humour: this cancelling-out
of the grounds of moral judgements, the deliberate and consistent
disappointment of our expectations is one of the major sources of fun
in the book.

Similarly, the dominant tendency of the *Bildungsroman* to see the
world in terms of a hero wholly concerned with *using* it, using it for the
sole purpose of enriching his experience at the world's expense – this
tendency is not criticized or discredited but guyed and carried to its
logical conclusion by turning the hero into a confidence trickster and a
thief. Felix Krull, with his magnificent egotism, becomes all the world's
benefactor, for in the very act of exploiting and swindling and stealing
from others he cannot fail to give them the benefit, the blessing almost,
of his charming, easy, generous, uncalculating personality. He is indeed
an artist and a virtuoso, but his instrument is life itself. And the women
he plays along – from servant-maid to prostitute, to a fashionable lady
novelist to, finally, a double affair with the wife and the daughter of a
Portuguese anthropologist – have no complaint. Do we believe, though
he says so himself, that he is a prodigious erotic performer?

Selbstverständlich scheidet hier jede Möglichkeit des Vergleichens aus. Meine private
Überzeugung jedoch, die ich damals gewann und die weder beweisbar noch widerlegbar
ist, geht unerschütterlich dahin, dass bei mir der Liebesgenuss die doppelte Schärfe und
Süssigkeit besass als bei anderen.

Of course, any possibility of comparison is out of the question. But all the same, it is
my private conviction, which can neither be demonstrated nor disproved, that with me
the enjoyment of love was twice as acute and twice as sweet as with others.

                                                            (*Felix Krull*, chapter 8)

Does it matter whether we believe him? The erotic here is the pattern
of Krull's attitude to the world at large: he gives pleasure by taking it,
the giving and the taking are inseparable, even his boasting is not

intended to put others out of countenance but to exhibit his own command of fine words. The words matter, not their truth.

The words – Felix Krull's immense irrepressible grandiloquent flow of words – are not merely descriptive of something that happened in the glorious past (Krull the confidence trickster is writing his memoirs from gaol), they are in and by themselves (the Hegelian manner is catching) a consolation from that past and a continuation of it into the melancholy and grim present. The emphasis, throughout the novel, on Krull's gift of the gab is wholly Wittgensteinian – I mean that it is intended to narrow the traditional distinction between words and world, to show words as active in, and a part of, the world.

The most brilliant example of this process of de-pragmatizing the world by converting it into words, and more specifically into metaphors which stand for other words, and thus for life itself is, of course, the farcical medical examination in the course of which Felix Krull feigns an epileptic attack and is turned down by an army medical board. The scene was written ten years before Jaroslav Hašek in *The Good Soldier Schweik* and forty years before Joseph Heller in *Catch-22* used a similar ploy – the ploy of showing a hero battling against a hostile army bureaucracy and winning the battle by vigorously identifying his own aim with the aim of the enemy. It is by using his own fabulous descriptive powers in order to arouse the army doctor's contradictions that Krull makes him compliant with his desire to be declared unfit for military service, and it is by his constant indignant assurances that he is perfectly well and desperately anxious to become a soldier that Felix Krull eventually works himself into an epileptic fit which is genuine in every sense except the strictly medical one. His fit is the image, the metaphor, of a fit.

Indeed, so perfect is his imitation of it that the category of the 'strictly medical' becomes strictly irrelevant, and so does the idea of dissimulation. The real thing and the pretence or metaphor of the real thing become as one. And this, we now recall, leaving aside the question of intention, happens in several other important scenes in Thomas Mann's novels. How ill is Hans Castorp, the hero of *The Magic Mountain*? How desolate and abandoned by all the world is Joseph when his brothers cast him in the well? How ill is Adrian Leverkühn, and what exactly is the origin and the nature of his disease; how much responsibility does he really bear for the death of his nephew, the little Johann Nepomuk?

All these questions are raised by Thomas Mann and left deliberately open, as though the figurative statement – the intimation of a refusal to

answer the question raised – were all that can be said; as though that
aspect of language which provides us with firm distinctions between
medical and psychic causes, between illness and health, between
pretence and truth (an aspect of language not really provided for by
Nietzsche's scheme) could not be trusted to convey the full meaning of
these scenes; and one had to resort to another kind of language
altogether, which contents itself with presenting events and explanations
as mere images or metaphors of some ineffable and unworded state of
being.

And so it is with Felix Krull's epileptic fit which, as I have said, is
perfectly genuine in every sense except the medical one – genuine
enough, certainly, to take in the medical commission. It is the very image
and metaphor of a fit. When Krull leaves the hall in which he has been
examined and scored his triumphant victory (and, incidentally, even here
Thomas Mann cannot let go without emphasizing the tremendous cost,
in physical and emotional terms, of Krull's victorious deception), a
sergeant whose attention he had attracted earlier says to him, 'Too bad
about you, Krull, or however you spell your name! You're certainly a
promising fellow, you might have got somewhere in the army – anyone
can see that at a glance!' To this the memoirist himself adds:

More mature consideration, however, compelled me to realize that to have entered that
world [of the Army] would have been a gross mistake and error. I had not, after all,
been born under the sign of Mars – at least not in the specific, real sense! [wenigstens
nicht im besonderen und wirklichen Sinne]. For although martial severity, self-discipline
and danger have been the conspicuous characteristics of my strange life, its primary
pre-condition and basis has been freedom – a condition wholly irreconcilable with any
kind of commitment to a grossly factual situation [so beruhte doch (mein Leben) in erster
Linie auf der Vor- und Grundbedingung der Freiheit – einer Bedingung also, welche
mit irgendwelcher Einspannung in ein plump tatsächliches Verhältnis schlechterdings
unvereinbar gewesen wäre]. Accordingly if I lived *like* a soldier, it would have been a
silly misapprehension to believe that I must therefore live *as* a soldier. Indeed, if one
were to define the value of an emotion as precious as freedom, and make that value
available to reason, one might say that to live *like* a soldier but not *as* a soldier, figuratively
but not literally, in short to be allowed to live in the symbol, is the meaning of true
freedom [ja, wenn es gälte, ein so erhabenes Gefühlsgut wie dasjenige der Freiheit für
die Vernunft zu bestimmen und zuzurichten, so liess sich sagen, dass dies eben:
soldatisch, aber nicht als Soldat, figürlich, aber nicht wörtlich, dass im Gleichnis leben
zu dürfen eigentlich Freiheit bedeute].   (*Felix Krull*, chapter 5)

And here the story I have to tell comes full circle. 'How really to live
in freedom?' asks Krull, 'Where is liberation to be found?' And the
answer is, 'To live metaphorically, in the "as if" world of art and of
the imagination', and this of course is the answer, too, of Nietzsche's

aesthetic theodicy (in the essay of 1873): 'Perhaps to live in art – for instance in the art of language, that mobile, unstable army of metaphors, is the only way.'

Nietzsche, as we know, was not greatly interested in the novel as a form of fiction (though he has a good deal to say about a few contemporary French novels as forms of psychological disclosure). What he is concerned with, from *The Birth of Tragedy* onwards, is tragic myth, and the idea of myth as extended metaphor is another aspect of that legacy which was taken up by Thomas Mann's generation.

Nietzsche tells us – in that book for the first time, and repeatedly throughout the entire work – that a healthy national culture needs its life-giving and life-protecting myths, and his early enthusiasm for Richard Wagner derives from his belief – in which he later finds himself to have been mistaken – that Wagner will give Germany those life-enhancing myths which she needs in order to achieve cultural greatness and national health (in the same way as did Aeschylus, Sophocles for Athens). But myth, for Nietzsche, is *instinctive* metaphor, is the creation of those who 'forget themselves as artistically creative subjects'. There is a difficulty in this argument which Nietzsche cannot resolve – or may not even be conscious of: how do you make up a myth? How do you deliberately and purposefully create a cultural situation in which instinctive, non-deliberate, purely inspirational myth-makers will arise and instinctively appeal to the soul of the people? When Bayreuth was created, Valhalla did not become a reality, but a limited company was formed and its shares were traded on the Berlin stock exchange. At this point Nietzsche began to have some doubt about the chthonic and genuinely popular nature of it all. Yet although he then turned his back on Wagner, he still believed that an instinctive inspirational myth is what his world needed, and the complex edifice of *Zarathustra* and of the Superman – a compound of art nouveau emblematic beasts, the syntax and verily-verily tone of the Luther Bible – are the result.

Coming less than half a century later, Thomas Mann wrote no *Zarathustra*. From the late 1920s onwards – from the inception of the biblical Joseph stories – he is drawn toward the idea of building his fiction from the elements of accepted myths, but he is not prepared to sacrifice the articulation of his narrative consciousness or to pretend to a naivety he does not possess. Thus there is nothing in the least naive about the aesthetic validation of the world – the validation through symbol and metaphor – which Krull is describing: the fact *that* he is describing it makes it the opposite of naive, allows him to be conscious of its own artificiality. When the handsome young Felix Krull is in bed with the ageing lady-novelist, Diane Houpflé, her heated poetico-erotic imagination makes him enact the role of the god Hermes, god of thieves, as she invites him to steal her jewelry. He is only too ready to oblige (again: he gives pleasure by taking pleasure). And at this point she discovers that he has never heard of the god – yet of course it is Krull himself, twenty years after, who reports the scene, a scene utterly permeated by self-consciousness and conscious, farcical imitation and re-enactment. Thomas Mann is not only writing a fiction and drawing on a myth, he is also showing the fictionality of the fiction by letting the hero in on the secret, by making him share the author's consciousness of his main narrative devices – by explicitly repudiating the fiction of realism (the single pretence) in favour of the fiction of self-conscious myth (the double pretence). And because the self-consciousness is exploited, is not inadvertent, this Sterneian device comes off.

The difference which arises here between Nietzsche and Thomas Mann is indicative of the generation difference between them. Mann had certainly abundant occasion to experience what Nietzsche did not see – the modern, twentieth-century political uses of the mythopoeic imagination and its products. His consciousness, and indeed his literary self-consciousness, is unabating, and it is his glory. He *says* he is creating myth – both in *Felix Krull* and in the correspondence with Karl Kerényi about the writing of the novel we hear a great deal about Hermes, the god of messengers and travellers and thieves, and about the way Mann hopes to relate certain episodes in his story to the myth. A little irreverently, reading this correspondence, one cannot help being reminded of two giant ants, lugging a huge, mysterious shape along their path with the inscription MYTH on it – they neither wish to abandon it nor do they quite know what to do with it. But one of them, Kerényi, is a good deal more in earnest about it than the other. For in the very act of drawing attention to Hermes and his own mythopoeic undertaking, he – Thomas Mann – is suspending the distinction between consciousness and the mythopoeic imagination and breaking down the phoney isolation of a supposedly unconscious creativeness.

The idea of the aesthetic as we glean it from the works of Thomas Mann's last period is largely what, as far as explicit statement goes, it had been for Nietzsche at the time of *The Birth of Tragedy*: a dream filled with the consciousness of its status as dream, a metaphorical and symbolical freedom which, by being aware of its metaphorical nature, also articulates an awareness of its relative, limited, conditional being – for that, after all, is what all our freedom is: relative, limited, conditional. In the end, the philosophy of Thomas Mann's con man is a thing more modest than the grand aesthetic justification of the world and being which Nietzsche had envisaged. It is, and it is acknowledged to be, an artifact, part of a larger, non-aesthetic world.

I have shown how far Nietzsche's explicit statement goes. But it seems to me that the observations on the metaphorical nature of language in that early essay of Nietzsche's from which I quoted contain an implicit set of stylistic precepts which he was to follow throughout the sixteen brief years of his conscious life: precepts for his remarkable philosophy in a new, metaphorical style, which reveals Nietzsche's unchanging determination not to oppose or critically dissolve the metaphoricity of language, but to develop and exploit it. To put it the other way round: what makes him the dominant influence on German literature in the twentieth century – and a major influence on the English and Scandinavian literature *entre deux guerres* – is of course his incomparably lucid and concrete style, dominated by metaphors and cast precisely in that 'middle mode' (which in that essay he calls 'jene Mittelsphäre und Mittelkraft') halfway between the traditional language of idealist philosophy and figurative narrative prose.

Where does this style find its vocabulary, how is it assembled? The essay of 1873 ends with a description of the creative intellect that has freed itself from all practical considerations and tasks and sets out, disinterestedly, to re-enact the world in images and concepts. So far the young Nietzsche's argument is pure Schopenhauer. But when Nietzsche goes on to show how this creative mind in its freedom takes up the vocabulary of common discourse and the scaffolding of concepts 'in order to dismantle them, break up their order and reconstitute them ironically, bringing together things farthest apart and separating those closest together', for no other purpose than to play with them; and when he concludes that

no regular way leads from such intuitions to the land of ghostly abstractions, it is not for them that the word was created; seeing them, man falls silent or speaks in forbidden metaphors and extravagant combinations of concepts, so that by demolishing and by mocking the old conceptual boundaries (if in no other way) he may show himself equal to the impression with which the mighty intuition seized him

Nietzsche is giving the most accurate description we have of his own future philosophical and literary procedure.

There is a sense in which every forceful, original metaphor is a 'forbidden metaphor'. The very use of metaphor is a challenge – in some languages perhaps the most radical challenge there is – to the conventionality or, as Nietzsche would say, the disheartening commonness of language. The forbidden metaphors work only when they are used sparingly, tactically, when they are allowed to form patterns of contrast with usages which do not challenge the convention, and this of course is how Nietzsche writes at his best. This is not a very surprising conclusion, yet it does not mean that he writes like everybody else. What that image of the artist at work among forbidden metaphors and untoward combinations of concepts suggests is the act of writing as demolition and de-construction: the breaking up of accepted order is manifest in the pointed brevity of each utterance. And with this goes Nietzsche's discovery that his discrete reflections have value and make sense, that discontinuity can be significant, that 'notes for' a philosophy are a philosophy (Bertolt Brecht, Anton von Webern and Jorge Luis Borges made similar discoveries in *their* media). In just this way Nietzsche will 'bring together and separate' the elements of those cardinal metaphors for which his writings are famous: 'amor fati', invoking choice motivated by love where blind fate is sovereign; 'the aesthetic justification', where there is to be no justifying or judging; 'the lie in a supra-moral sense'; 'the eternal recurrence', where 'eternity' is to be merely hideous endlessness; 'the death of God', which does not tell us whether he was ever alive; 'the will to power', which is forever destroying its products and itself – all examples of a metaphysic of which the least confusing thing to say is that it consistently avoids the dangers of dogma and petrifaction at the price of being consistently paradoxical. Here, finally, is the middle ground on which the literary philosopher and the philosophical novelist meet.

For a philosopher, we may say – for a German philosopher at that – Nietzsche is amazingly readable. And for a novelist (we surely feel this again and again) Mann's prose is remarkably (I won't say: unreadable, but) reflective, philosophical, dominated by concepts and the parody of concepts (which Nietzsche had described as ossified metaphors). From opposite sides they both challenge the genre theories and tacit assumptions on which French and English kinds of discourse are founded – each is forever being accused of writing 'neither one thing nor t'other', Nietzsche being attacked for his excessive reliance on metaphor, Thomas Mann for excessive abstractness and reliance on conceptual language. Yet both are concerned with diminishing the difference between the two styles and the two ways of coming to terms with the world. And here, finally, they meet: the one presenting life in the discontinuous metaphors of philosophy, the other presenting life in the sustained metaphor of fiction.

The critical realism of
Francesco De Sanctis

RENÉ WELLEK

Francesco De Sanctis (1817–83) is little known in this country and the United States, though in Italy he is admired not only as the author of the best-known nineteenth-century *History of Italian Literature*, of books on Petrarch and Leopardi and many essays ranging from Dante to Zola, but also as a great figure of the Italian *Risorgimento* who spent almost three years imprisoned in the Castel dell'Ovo in the Bay of Naples, spent years of exile in Zürich (1856–60), became governor of Avellino under Garibaldi in 1860, served as Minister of Public Instruction in the governments of Cavour and his successors, and was a Member of Parliament (and for a time its president) for the first crucial years of the new Kingdom of Italy. In Italy he is a national hero somewhere in the company of Mazzini, Garibaldi and Cavour, and even today the interpretation of De Sanctis excites often violent disagreements, mainly between those who argue that he is a forerunner of Croce and those who argue that he is a forerunner of Gramsci.

This paper was originally prepared for a congress in Naples, which was expressly planned to commemorate the centenary of De Sanctis' retirement from the University of Naples, where he had been Professor of Comparative Literature – the first with that title, not only in Italy, I believe – from 1872 to 1877, and, in particular, his article 'The Principle of Realism', published in 1876. However, I trust that this paper will prove to be of interest even to those who are not acquainted with the writings of De Sanctis, for it raises issues about the whole history of realism in the nineteenth century and its nature in general.

I am, I fear, one of the very few non-Italians to have written about the

* This paper was given at the British Comparative Literature Association Conference, Warwick, December 1977.

17

work of the great critic, Francesco De Sanctis. It is now some twenty years since I wrote a paper on his criticism which I published, in English, in *The Italian Quarterly*,[1] and soon afterwards in an Italian translation by Piero Longanesi in *Convivium*.[2] The paper was conceived from the very beginning as a chapter for the fourth volume of my *History of Modern Criticism* devoted to the later nineteenth century. This appeared in 1965 with the Yale University Press and in 1969 in a different translation by Agostino Lombardo and Rosa Maria Colombo with Il Mulino in Bologna. In writing a general history of criticism I necessarily focussed on the theories of our author and on an exposition and analysis of his chief work, the *History of Italian Literature*. As I am no specialist in Italian literature, I did not pay much attention to De Sanctis' opinions and analyses of individual authors and was rather concerned with his conception of a history of literature and a theory of criticism. One of my early projects was the writing of a history of literary history, at first only in England. My *Rise of English Literature History* (1941) was an attempt to show the slow evolution of the writing of literary history as narrative up to Thomas Warton's *History of English Poetry* (1774–81). Then in the context of the much broader project of a *History of Modern Criticism from 1750 to 1950* on an international scale I discussed all the main literary histories of the nineteenth century from the Schlegels and Sismondi to Taine, Brandes and Scherer. For my Italian chapters I read Emiliani-Giudici, Luigi Settembrini, and, of course, De Sanctis, and came to the conclusion that

his greatness lies in his successful combination of a historical vision and scheme with an intensely searching criticism of the poet's world...He wrote what seems to me the finest history of any literature ever written. It successfully combines a broad historical scheme with close criticism, theory with practice, aesthetic generalization with particular analysis. While a historian, De Sanctis is also a critic, a judge of art.[3]

I am delighted that my paper was noticed, quoted and sometimes criticized in Italy. Natalino Sapegno, Carlo Muscetta, Sergio Landucci, to name only a few outstanding experts on De Sanctis, have commented on it, and several Italian anthologies of criticism have printed excerpts from it.

In a general survey like mine I could not pay proper attention to the different stages of De Sanctis' thinking. I dismissed, too hastily, the writings preceding his imprisonment in the Castel dell'Ovo, and I was content to refer only briefly to the last stage of his career. I alluded to the articles praising Zola's 'realism' and to De Sanctis' effort to re-establish an equilibrium between idealism and realism in his last paper, 'Darwinism in Art'. Among the more than two hundred references to specific passages in the writings of De Sanctis in my chapter, none was drawn from 'The Principle of Realism', though I read it, to judge from the underlinings, question and exclamation marks which disfigure my copy of the Russo edition of *Saggi Critici*.

The invitation to write this paper made me reread the writings of the last decade of De Sanctis' life and examine in particular 'Il Principio del realismo' (1876), which has been singled out as a key document in the history of Italian criticism. I could not assess its significance without having seen the pamphlet on which De Sanctis comments so elaborately, Julius Hermann von Kirchmann's *Über das Prinzip des Realismus*, a lecture published in Leipzig in 1875. Kirchmann seems now completely forgotten as a philosopher, though one comes across his name as the founder of the Philosophische Bibliothek and as an editor and commentator of Kant. Certainly his lecture on the principle of realism is today virtually unknown. Among the United States libraries which are usually well supplied with German philosophy only the University of Illinois at Urbana has a copy I could borrow and xerox, and I suspect that this pamphlet, which Adolph Gaspary brought to De Sanctis,[4] is rare also in Italy. The most fully annotated edition of De Sanctis' paper in volume XIV of the Einaudi set of his *Opere* does not pay any attention to the relation between it and Kirchmann's pamphlet, and in the introductory footnote (XIV, 341) even gives a wrong title to Kirchmann's lecture: 'Über die Prinzipien des Realismus' instead of the correct singular preserved by De Sanctis.

I could go over these two texts and show how skilfully De Sanctis translated, paraphrased, and sometimes abridged Kirchmann's lecture: how he sometimes changed the order of the arguments and how he made substantial cuts at least on two points: he dropped a long, virulent attack on religion, on faith which considers the contradictory to be true, and he skipped almost twenty pages devoted to a sharp criticism of Eduard von Hartmann's *Philosophie des Unbewussten* (1869), surely because De Sanctis could not assume any interest in the subject on the part of his readers, though he kept some allusions to Hartmann and the unconscious.

More interesting might be an examination of De Sanctis' small changes and additions to Kirchmann's text. Thus De Sanctis translates 'There is no such perfect instrument which can define the utmost limits of the corporeal and the molecules of the brain and their vibrations',[5] while Kirchmann states peremptorily that we shall *never* be able to transcend the last limits of the corporeal and the molecules of the brain. We could interpret this change as De Sanctis' clinging to a faith in an ultimate physiological explanation of psychic life. A little later De Sanctis translates a passage on imagination: 'No philosopher or poet has the imagination which could increase, in their respective kinds, the simple determinations of colours, sounds, or simple states of mind, pleasure, pain, desire, moral sense; it is impossible for man to imagine a colour or a feeling other than the one he sees and feels; art can assemble the elements but cannot invent them.'[6] This 'cannot invent them' is De Sanctis' addition which strengthens the rejection of anything that could be called 'creative imagination' and is a reassertion of the common eighteenth-century view voiced, for instance, by Voltaire. It may also be of some significance that De Sanctis, in reproducing the 'forms of relations' enumerated by Kirchmann, gives the list of the twelve complete, but in the further development does not translate Kirchmann's argument about form and content. Possibly he could not accept the view that the same object can be at one time form and at another content. But these are minutiae.

What matters is the nature of Kirchmann's philosophy and De Sanctis' attitude toward it. Kirchmann is so completely forgotten today that it is difficult to find any comment on his philosophy, which he expounded not only in the lecture paraphrased by De Sanctis but in several full-length books preceding and following the date of the lecture. I have seen the first volume of *Philosophie des Wissens* (Berlin, 1864) and the two volumes of an *Ästhetik auf realistischer Grundlage* (Berlin, 1868). There are two near contemporary discussions of Kirchmann: a highly polemical pamphlet by Eduard von Hartmann[7] and a critical but not unfriendly lecture by Adolf Lasson, the editor of Hegel,[8] and there is a fairly recent Bonn dissertation by Herbert Berger.[9] They all point out what seems to me obvious, that Kirchmann gets involved in serious contradictions and hence obscurities and even absurdities. His basic epistemological position is that 'the content of being can be brought to the knowledge of man not through thinking but only through perception and that thinking has only the task to work on this content received through perception' (Kirchmann, p. 5; cf. De Sanctis, XIV, 342). This is clearly a restatement of the position of the so-called Scottish Common Sense philosophy first formulated by Thomas Reid in *An Inquiry into the Human Mind on the Principles of Common Sense* (1764), a view which has been revived in this century by the British neo-realists such as G. E. Moore. Kirchmann actually defends what must be called a dualism of Being and Knowing in which perception is the only bridge between the two: somehow Being mysteriously flows over into Knowing in perception but Being does not *cause* Knowing. The content of Being and Knowing is absolutely identical, while the form remains eternally different. Being thus remains unknowable. While Kirchmann rejects any distinction between perception and representation and even subsumes perception under representation he actually reintroduces a variety of idealism. His view that the perception of reality is a 'sudden, necessary, and pure happening' (pp. 6–7) is refuted by his own theory that the distinction between Knowing and Being is one between content and form as this is a 'relation' which cannot be valid in Being. The thesis of the 'unknowable' Being lands Kirchmann paradoxically in subjective idealism. He introduces 'innate forms of order', kinds of knowing, twelve in number, which look suspiciously like the categories of Kant though they are considered merely 'subjective additions' to the content of Being. The statement that the 'forms of order' which are not valid in Being contain 'truth' seems a blatant contradiction, and so is the view that the criterion of contradiction is derived from 'pure thought' only because it is based on a 'relation of Negation'. The notion that there is a realm of pure Knowing found in the forms of relations questions the whole realistic enterprise. I shall not, however, pursue this criticism of Kirchmann's philosophy any further.

I can only wonder why De Sanctis was taken by it, took the trouble of paraphrasing it very closely and recommending it to the readers of *Nuova Antologia* and the *Nuovi saggi critici*. Actually, at the end of his exposition De Sanctis voices some reservations: he is dissatisfied with Kirchmann's rejection of imagination and sentiment in the pursuit of science and protests that the 'mind cannot be cut into slices' (xiv, 353). He implicitly rejects Kirchmann's central theory when he asserts that perception cannot be divorced from knowing. 'If it is true that without perception there cannot be any knowledge of being, then it is also true that without thought there cannot be perception.'[10] De Sanctis, brushing aside Kirchmann's starting point, thus ends up recommending simply the method of induction: rejecting the empiricism, sensualism, and materialism of Locke and Condillac at the same time, though at the beginning of the article he had praised Kirchmann for having rescued them from oblivion (De Sanctis, xiv, 353, cf. 343). Bacon and Galileo are then singled out as the propounders of the realistic method, though neither Bacon nor Galileo can be simply identified with the inductive approach. Bacon is too full of Platonism, and Galileo was rather the founder of the mathematical method in physics.

De Sanctis at the end of his paper, losing sight completely of

Kirchmann, rejects the idea of an end of metaphysics – as he had rejected Hegel's forecast of an end of poetry. He sees 'metaphysical urges' in 'natural selection, in the principle of heredity and evolution, in the Unconscious, in the internal state of atoms'.[11] De Sanctis concludes with a flourish in favour of serious study, a vague exhortation in that it includes any kind of study, but nevertheless characteristic of De Sanctis' concern for the education of the new Italy, which he served as Minister of Public Instruction in several cabinets.

We thus come to the disconcerting conclusion that 'Il Principio del realismo' does not deserve a high place among De Sanctis' essays: it paraphrases an author finally uncongenial to De Sanctis and recommends a realism in a philosophical sense vaguely identified with the inductive method. It hardly touches literary criticism. Maybe we should *not* celebrate its centenary.

Still, the choice of the article is after all justified if we simply take its title as a slogan. De Sanctis about this time had become interested in literary realism, or rather, as the essays on Zola attest, in literary naturalism. Surprisingly enough, De Sanctis had not shown any particular concern for the French novelists whom we today consider the great realists, nor in the professedly realist movement in France. I cannot find any reference to Stendhal in De Sanctis' writings, except a casual reference to his stay in Milan (XII, 106 (1874)), nor to Flaubert, except in an essay on Zola where Madame Bovary is called 'more interesting than Ghita [apparently Gretchen in Goethe's *Faust*] and above all truer' (XIV, 408). Balzac, however, is referred to several times. In the early review of Lammenais' translation of Dante (1855), De Sanctis contrasts Manzoni and Balzac, very much in favour of Manzoni, who always introduced prose in a just measure 'which in Balzac exceeds every limit and often absorbs poetry'.[12] Shortly afterward De Sanctis defended Balzac's right to represent such 'materialistic persons' as Père Goriot and Triboulet (from Hugo's *Le Roi s'amuse*, the Rigoletto of Verdi's opera) against Saint-Marc Girardin's lofty moralizing. 'I don't know why you need to expel from poetry the materialist men, as you call them, or rather the instinctive men, who are probably the most attractive poetic creations.'[13] But a reference to a similarity between the 'great observers' Pulci and Balzac, who conserve 'something interesting under this aridity',[14] in the Zurich lectures on chivalrous poetry (VII, 72) is very cool, and even in a late lecture (XI, 40 (1872–3)) De Sanctis complains of Balzac's excess in analysis. 'Balzac would, in prosaic form, throw in all the particulars'[15] in contrast to the unrealistic handling of madness in a story by Tomasso Grossi, 'Ulrico e Lida'. Only in the essays on Zola (1877) is there an entirely favourable reference to Balzac as the head of the modern psychological novel (XIV, 395), contrasting it with the novels of intrigue for which De Sanctis quotes *Gil Blas*, *Pamela* and *Clarissa* as examples. They seem badly chosen if one knows Richardson's relentless analysis of human motives and Dr Johnson's saying that 'if you were to read Richardson for the story, your impatience would be so much fretted that you would hang yourself'.[16] Even this passage seems meagre in its praise of 'fineness of observation' in Balzac. I have been unable to discover any reference to the professed realist school in France, the novelists Champfleury and Duranty, who in 1857 proclaimed the slogan 'realism' in art and literature.

The Zola essays are then the only ones in which De Sanctis comes to grips with the new realist or naturalistic fiction. If we examine them we must be struck by De Sanctis' unusual concern for what might be called the background, the social and political material used by Zola. The first two essays describe French corruption under Louis-Philippe and Napoleon III and use the plot of the novels only as illustrations or confirmations. The later essays reject Zola's theory of heredity: De Sanctis believes in the possibility of human freedom and resistance to circumstance. De Sanctis was never a determinist, though one can quote passages that seem to endorse this view. He can say that 'at least recording the connection between spiritual and material fact is the mark of a great historian' (XI, 217). He expressly rejected Hippolyte Taine's theory of *race*, *milieu* and *moment* as 'exaggerated' (XIV, 153 (1875)) and refers to Herbert Spencer as having failed to establish exact laws in the evolution of society (XVI, 155 (1877)). Long before, he had rejected Schopenhauer's view that 'a free man is a *contradictio in adjecto*; because man is a conditioned and determined being' (XIII, 448 (1858)). Then, for the first time in the Zola essays, De Sanctis raises a question of literary criticism. In agreement with his principle of suspicion against mere intention (what we call in America the 'intentional fallacy', a term invented by William K. Wimsatt), De Sanctis rejects the elaborate scheme of the pedigree of the Rougon-Macquart families and their presumed inherited traits. He formulates this objection rather oddly. 'It is his idea and not that of the reader', meaning apparently that we read the novels

novel by novel, take the characters just as they are, and it matters little what happens to be their surname and whose nephews or uncles they may be; it is they who interest us above all; and it is the novel itself that pleases or displeases; we'll leave the derivations, origins, connections and explanations to the author; it is not a matter we can assimilate[17] just as De Sanctis' presumed reader does not bother too much about the theological scheme of the *Divine Comedy*. Zola's scheme belongs to archaeology like the Chain of Being and, even if true, 'What point is there in learning in such a long and intricate manner what we can read in half an hour in the pages of a scientific journal?'[18] De Sanctis admires Zola for his objectivity, his disinterested observation like that of a scientist, a doctor, or a physiologist. He contrasts Zola's method with Manzoni's. Lucia is an ideal construct whom we are to admire; Miette (in *La Fortune des Rougon*) is a real person whom we are to understand (XIV, 410–11). De Sanctis sees this objectivity, the turn to what has been called 'exit author', as an artistic progress in harmony with the trends of nineteenth-century science (XIV, 409), a statement that De Sanctis later had to clarify against the misunderstanding that he thought Zola greater than Manzoni. He asks, 'What has the progress of forms to do with the greatness of artistic genius?[19] The essays defend Zola against the common accusation of immorality and cynicism by pointing to the implied ideals of Zola: the unspoken but nevertheless loud and clear condemnation of baseness and degradation. This theme is then resumed in the later lecture on *L'Assommoir* (1879): 'The ideal is in the things from which the sparks and flashes of human sentiments come.' De Sanctis concludes by quoting Virgil effectively: '*Sunt lacrimae rerum. Give us the tears of things and spare us your own tears.*'[20]

Today I hardly need to dispute De Sanctis' view of Zola. Zola's objectivity seems highly suspect. How could De Sanctis say that Zola 'has no aims...he does not want to demonstrate anything', that 'the illusion is perfect', or even more unconvincingly that 'Zola never growls. He is like marble. There is something Dantesque in that marble'?[21] And how could De Sanctis think that Zola is 'the greatest French stylist since Proudhon'?[22] De Sanctis seems dazzled by Zola's scientific pretensions even though he rejects his theory of heredity and does not see the ultra-romantic, even baroque and comic inflations and exaggerations. A single scene from *L'Assommoir* (translated by A. H. Townsend, Signet Books, 1962), the death and burial of old Madame Coupeau, may serve as an example of macabre fantastic horror. 'Her pallid mask thinned to its final gasp by lust for life' (p. 327); the muffled dribbling of her corpse during the night of the wake makes Lantier say: 'She's draining off' (p. 336). The corpse is put into the coffin: '*Allez-oop*. You couldn't have flipped a pancake more quickly' (p. 340). When the coffin is lowered into the grave, 'the large clods of earth bombard the coffin, banging away like cannon shots that made you think the wood may split' (p. 343). If one remembers the grotesque scenes of the wedding party visiting the Louvre or the brawl between the two washerwomen or the nameday party of Gervaise, one must conclude that we have today a different conception of realism from that of De Sanctis. Zola seems to me a highly melodramatic author, related rather to Hugo than to Flaubert, tendentious, even crassly so, in his declamations against social injustice, corruption, clericalism, militarism, and drunkenness. *L'Assommoir* has rightly been called a temperance tract. *J'accuse*, which De Sanctis did not live to know, is the logical culmination of a life devoted to very concrete attempts at exposing and remedying social and governmental abuses.

Everything depends of course on what we mean by realism. There is today such an enormous, bewilderingly contradictory discussion in West and East on this issue that it seems easy to take the way out of English philosophers of ordinary language by quoting what Humpty Dumpty says to Alice in *Through the Looking Glass*: 'When I use a word it means just what I choose it to mean – neither more nor less.' That is surely what has happened to this word. It may mean almost anything in some relation to reality – and what is not real? But a historian can find out what the term meant in certain contexts and, in particular, what it meant to De Sanctis. I have studied the history of the term in a paper, 'The Concept of Realism in Literary Scholarship'.[23] Here I can only summarize some of my results.

The term, in the modern sense, I believe, cannot be found in any French or British philosopher of the eighteenth century or in any critic such as Diderot, who recommended a faithful imitation of nature. It occurs, as far as I know, for the first time prominently in Kant's *Kritik der reinen Vernunft* (1781), in the Dialectics, when in the discussion of the fourth paralogism of transcendental psychology Kant distinguishes a transcendental from an empirical realism (A 369). 'Realism' then becomes ubiquitous in German philosophy. In Hegel, the one German philosopher De Sanctis studied closely, the term occurs as early as 1801 in the paper 'Differenz des Fichteschen und Schellingschen Systems' (Glockner I, 87). There dogmatic realism is said to 'posit the objective as the real ground of the subjective' whereas 'consistent realism denies consciousness completely as a self-activity of self-positing'. In the *Philosophische Propädeutik*, lectures dating from 1809–10, published by Karl Rosenkranz in 1840, Hegel defines realism as the view that 'things and their properties are by and for themselves outside of the conscious, given to it simply as something foreign and ready-made' (Glockner III,

101–2), and in the *Lectures on the History of Philosophy* Hegel uses the term sparingly. It begins to occur in literary contexts, too. Thus Friedrich Schiller in a letter to Goethe (27 April 1790) asserts that 'realism cannot make a poet', and Friedrich Schlegel in the same year formulates the paradox that 'all philosophy is idealism and there is no true realism except that of poetry'.[24] The term became frequent in German aesthetics but did not then mean either specific writers or a specific period or school but was used simply as the opposite of idealism.

The term appears in France as early as 1826. A writer in the *Mercure Français* even prophesied that 'this doctrine which leads to faithful imitation not of the masterworks of art but of the originals offered by nature' will be 'the literature of the nineteenth century, the century of the true'.[25] Gustave Planche, in his time an influential anti-romantic critic commented on unfavourably by De Sanctis (see IV, 440, and VII, 249ff), used the term 'realism' from about 1833 onward, interchangeably with 'materialism' or 'local colour', particularly for the minute description of costumes and customs in historical novels. Realism, he says, is concerned with 'what escutcheon is placed over the door of a castle, what device is inscribed on a standard, and what colours are borne by a lovesick knight'.[26] Similarly, Hippolyte Fortoul, in 1834, complained of a novel by one A. Thouret that it is written 'with an exaggeration of realism which he borrowed from the manner of M. Hugo'.[27] Realism at that time is thus merely a feature observed in the method of writers whom we would today call 'romantic', in Scott, Hugo and Mérimée. Soon, however, the term was transferred to the description of contemporary manners in Balzac and Murger, but its meaning crystallized only in the debates which arose in the fifties around the paintings of Courbet and through the activity of a mediocre novelist, Champfleury, who in 1857 published a volume of essays with the title *Le Réalisme*, while a friend of his, Duranty, edited a short-lived review entitled *Réalisme* between July 1856 and May 1857. In these writings a definite literary creed is formulated which centres on a very few simple ideas. Art should be a representation of the real world. It should therefore study contemporary life and manners by observing meticulously and analysing carefully. It should do so dispassionately, impersonally, objectively. There is a remarkable, tiresomely monotonous agreement on the main features of realism in the contemporary discussions. Its numerous enemies judged the same traits negatively, complaining about the excessive use of minute external detail, of the neglect of the ideal, and seeing the vaunted impersonality and scientific approach as the cloak for cynicism and immorality. With the trial of Flaubert in 1857 for *Madame Bovary* the term was completely established, at least in France.

It is thus not surprising that De Sanctis uses the term for the first time in 1858 in a lecture on Dante in a context which condemns Goethe's *Tasso* (and *Iphigenia*) as a 'copy of an idea', as an abstraction, as 'the exaggeration of idealism' against which today realism rises up.[28] But both idealism and realism are destined to remain outside of art. 'Thus the idea in itself and the content in itself are not the foundation of poetry; the idea in itself is the foundation of idealism; content in itself, the foundation of realism.'[29] The passage sums up, with the new term, an old idea of De Sanctis, the union of the real and ideal, what Hegelians call the 'concrete universal' and what he calls sometimes 'form' in his special sense, 'the real organic unity'. Two years before, in the deservedly harsh review of Saint-Marc Girardin's *Cours de littérature dramatique*, De Sanctis contrasts the demands of Girardin for ideal types with Diderot's aim of exact reproduction of reality and objects to both doctrines: an abstract ideal faces an abstract real. Poety in Diderot's hand becomes a copy. And De Sanctis asks: what is materialism in art? And answers: 'pure reality, that is, abstract, dead reality' (IV, 287). In the same year, in the 'Address read at the Polytechnic Institute of Zürich', De Sanctis exalted 'the Manzoni type' as 'a harmony of the real and the ideal in such a just proportion that it is called the true'.[30] De Sanctis, to my mind, never changed this basic point of view: the polemical rejection both of idealism in the sense of abstraction, intellectualism, allegory, late neo-classicism, and of realism as mere raw matter, unformed content. Still, the term realism does assume sometimes a meaning oblivious of this synthesis. De Sanctis can use it very loosely for anything genuine, alive, true, authentic, in contrast to the artificial, the false, the contrived, the merely verbal. Thus in the lectures on *La Poesia cavallaresca* (1858–9) the description of Alcina is praised as 'the first trace of realism in poetry'. 'This analysis is a kind of anatomy of material beauty. He describes her from the hair down to the feet. Lessing [in *Laokoon*] censured this description as too material; but here the materiality is the secret of poetry.'[31]

For years the term 'realism' disappears from De Sanctis' usage. It is extremely rare in *Storia della letteratura italiana*. In discussing Beccaria's *Trattato dello stile* his recommendation of the spoken language is considered. 'The principle from which this literary revolution was derived, was the imitation of nature, or, as we might say, realism, in its truth and simplicity, a reaction against declamation and rhetoric'; and at the end of the *History* we are told that 'in the bosom of idealism, realism appears in science, art and historiography'.[32] Realism is thus used simply for the imitation of nature in the eighteenth century and for the whole movement toward secularism, almost identical with materialism, scepticism, and empiricism.

While the term 'realism' is rare, the word 'real' permeates the *History* as an adjective for almost any author who seems to De Sanctis genuine, authentic, true, alive. Thus Guido Cavalcanti is called 'the first Italian poet worthy of this name, because he was the first who had a sense and a feeling for the real',[33] and the word is used in many contexts for Boccaccio, Machiavelli, Parini, Goldoni, Manzoni, Leopardi, who in one way or another succeeded in evoking human life in its concreteness and did not indulge in mere rhetoric, allegory, or musical lyricism. It is sometimes a realism similar to that expounded by Erich Auerbach in *Mimesis*, existential, as we would say today, when De Sanctis approves of the depiction of such powerful limiting situations as those of Francesca, Farinata or Ugolino, or more frequently historical, when it means that an author has depicted a figure accurately, concretely, in its setting. Particularly the praise of Manzoni illustrates this use. In an essay dating from 1873 De Sanctis says, 'What in the time of Manzoni was called the positive, the natural, the historical, is nowadays called realism.'[34] The depiction of Don Abbondio is praised: 'The author gives it a historical finish, gives his character a specific town, his prejudices, his class, everything in brief which is called realism in the modern school',[35] while the somewhat different use of the term I shall call existential seems implied in the praise of Leopardi's scepticism or despair which 'announces the dissolution of this theological-metaphysical world and inaugurates the reign of the arid true, of the real'.[36]

This use of realism and real is, I think, paralleled all over Europe after the 1830 revolution. Heine in Germany proclaimed the end of the *Kunstperiode* and satirized Romanticism; the Left Hegelians such as Arnold Ruge and, we may add, Marx, led this turn to reality as did the Saint-Simonians in France or critics such as Planche. Hippolyte Taine passed through a similar development from Hegelianism to a much more pronounced positivism. Even in Russia, Belinsky, who had started from Romantic assumptions and for a time embraced Hegelianism with conservative political views, turned more and more to the real and propagated what he called the 'natural' school in Russia. But all these writers advocating the real did not impose any specific methods of artistic representation: for Belinsky, for instance, Shakespeare, Scott, and

Cooper were supremely real, as Manzoni and Leopardi were 'real' for De Sanctis.

Only in the essays on Zola does De Sanctis recommend realism as a method or style, or rather the idea of 'objectivity', and the expansion of subject matter to low life and even disease, crime, and all ugliness. All these views were of course defended long before and accepted by him in different contexts when he praised, as the Schlegels had done, the objective poetry of Shakespeare or when he defended the inclusion of the grotesque or ugly as in Hugo and recognized like Karl Rosenkranz in his *Ästhetik des Hässlichen* (1853) that ugliness in its multiformity can be made poetry as well as the beautiful.

While the series of essays on Zola was being published in 1877, De Sanctis felt the necessity of reasserting his belief in the ideal and his old view of the union of the ideal and the real. In opening the second year of lectures in the Circolo filologico in Naples in November 1877, he made a little speech on the ideal as always alive, as the specifically human, but stressed that the ideal is generated by the real. The conviction that 'the history of the ideal is the history of the human spirit' allows De Sanctis to sketch the sequence of ideals from the idea of the infinite expressed in the pyramids to the saying of the Gospel: 'Love one another as brothers.' He then turns to this 'curious time in which everything is realism and in which it is believed that the ideal no longer exists'.[37] He alludes to the descent of man from the ape, to the view that thought is an effect of chemical compositions, that morality is a question of temperament. In art 'the idea becomes instinct; imagination a mechanical manifestation; passion mere appetite'.[38] De Sanctis sees hope in irony and indignation, in the 'cry of pain'[39] of Schiller and Leopardi, a hope that a new ideality will arise out of the laboratory of the second half of the century. 'The ideal is dead, the ideal is resurrected.'[40] A few days later, on 3 December 1877, an essay with the same title, 'L'ideale', appeared in a series of mainly political articles in the Turin *Diritto*. There the same argument is offered with some rather substantial verbal differences. More is made of 'the duty of disinterestedness and sacrifice', of the dependence of the ideal on real conditions. 'But if the real generates the ideal, on the other hand, it is the ideal which, reacting, purifies and exalts the real.' With a slight shift of meaning, 'realism and idealism' are declared to be 'the two exaggerations of every decadence from which comedy hatches in swarms'.[41] Realism and idealism are reconciled in the true. But De Sanctis rejects the new slogan of 'verismo', 'not only a barbarous but also a false term, if it is meant to

signify that only what is real is true. The real and the ideal are both
true.'[42] He had condemned the slogan before in the introductory lecture
to 'Scuola liberale' in 1874 as a 'barbarous catchword'.[43] The second
article in the series, 'Il Realismo moderno', still in December 1877,
reiterates the view that empty idealism leads to a reaction in art expressed
in comedy. 'Comedy is the first form with which realism begins.'[44] The
germ of rebirth (i.e., of realism) is found in every period of decadence.
The Roman Empire prepared the way for Christianity, the Italian
Renaissance (for De Sanctis a period of national decadence) contained
Machiavelli and Galileo, the forerunners of modern times. Modern
realism arises as a protest against the abuse of theological and metaphysical constructions: 'One does not want philosophy and falls into
pure empiricism.' 'If one despises theory, stupid praxis will follow.'
'Everything one takes away from mind, one gives to nature.' 'Man
becomes nature, becomes a beast.'[45] De Sanctis alludes to Zola,
complaining that 'a hereditary, natural and social *fatum* explains
everything and justifies everything.'[46] It leads to moral indifferentism.
But De Sanctis refuses to be a Jeremiah: this phase is only transitory,
a reaction against the fantastic and sentimental. De Sanctis wants a new
synthesis: a realism which would not be 'animal activity' but a scientific
realism.

The third article, 'La Misura dell'ideale' (31 December 1877),
considers the benefit of realism in reducing the ideal to its proper
measure. Belief that the ideal is already real is the error of sentimental
and imaginative men: it produces miracles and revolutions which after
their failure evoke scepticism and pessimism. Sceptics, however, such
as Leopardi, Goethe, Schiller, Byron, Musset and Heine, evoke a new
ideal. 'The torment of this scepticism in tears predicts *l'enfantement* of
the century better than the hymns and poetical speculations of Lamartine
and Hugo.'[47] The morbid stage produces realism, the reign of experience
and science. All the doctrines De Sanctis disapproves of – the view that
the world is merely a fortuitous play of unconscious forces, the struggle
for existence, hereditary and physiological fatalism, the glorification of
brute force, the negation of justice – are only signs of a reaction, a
transition. Realism is the great educator of the ideal. The new investigations into economic, pedagogical and social facts and, above all,
sociology should remake life and restate a new ideal.

The fourth article, 'L'Educazione dell'ideale', develops the same
theme with emphasis on the importance of education. Classical education
is not enough. Man learns to know his origins, his environment, and thus

a sense of the limit is developed. The last of these articles, 'Il Limite', repeats these ideals with some new illustrations. The positive man who looks after the particular alone (De Sanctis alludes to his favourite example, Francesco Guicciardini) belongs only to the first stage of realism. Realism or positivism rightly understood is not negation. As usual De Sanctis complains that in Italy ideas have no limit. They oscillate between the doctrinaire and the empirical. Order makes liberty effective. Socialism is a reaction against an empty and formal concept of liberty.

De Sanctis returned to these problems only in his last article, written in the year of his death: 'Il Darwinismo nell'arte' (1883). It is not really about Darwinism at all: it praises the man but identifies Darwinism simply with positivism, realism, materialism, the inductive, the experimental, the genetic method, the sense of things in their becoming, the sense of the relative. De Sanctis reasserts his old rejection of imitation, convention, artifice in favour of life. He condemns the Nero of Alfieri's *Ottavia* as a frigid construction and seems, jocularly, to prefer the real Nero who burned Rome. 'He was the *verista* of his time.'[48] He confused art and reality as the new 'veristic' writers do. De Sanctis describes then the new taste for operetta, farce, sketch, genre painting, for objective art, for an optimistic approach. He alludes again to Leopardi when he says that nowadays we do not curse nature. We admire force: we prefer Mephistopheles and Iago to Faust and Othello. We prefer the life of the people as the subject of art and do not mind even dialect (such as the Sicilian Giovanni Meli's, on whom De Sanctis lectured in Palermo in 1871). But then De Sanctis draws back. The sense of the real, the living, the popularity of matter, the naturalness of expression is more a promise than a fact. Man today considers himself too much an animal, thinking only of conserving and enjoying life. In phrases identical with the earlier lectures on the ideal, De Sanctis deplores that sentiment becomes sensation, will becomes appetite, intelligence becomes instinct. Genius is considered madness (as in Lombroso's view). We used to have humanism; today we have animalism. There is something base and corrupt in the new atmosphere.

In the Postilla to a new edition of his *Saggio critico sul Petrarca*, written about the same time, De Sanctis formulated his views most clearly, as if he were writing a last will and testament. He had waged a war against the ideal, but now when *verismo*, positivism and realism are victorious, it is rather the ideal which needs defence: 'the ideal can die only with man'.[49] De Sanctis is not averse to enumerating ideals:

beauty, justice, truth, the family, the fatherland, glory, heroism, virtue. True, the greatest artist forgets himself in things, but in finding the accord between things and himself he idealizes the things. But idealization does not mean types. The basis of art is not the beautiful or the true or the just or any other type, but the living, life in its integrity. Allegory, symbol, the type, is a mutilation of life, though cutting out of the individual any trace of the typical, any sign of the group, the class, the genus to which he belongs is also a mutilation. It is all a question of measure: 'this is not the moment to kill either the real or the ideal, which are both, at bottom, that which is living, life. Make living things for me, and call them whatever you want.'[50]

I have summarized the little-known articles in *Diretto* more fully than may be necessary because I want to draw the conclusion that De Sanctis held to the same views, formulated first in the fifties in Turin and Zürich, till the end of his life. Under the impact of *verismo* and the new positivism in Italy De Sanctis expounded Zola with surprising sympathy while rejecting his basic theory. But then, upset by what he considered the excesses of naturalism, he drew back or rather resumed and restated his old position: the unity of the real and the ideal, the limits imposed by the real on the ideal, the ideal growing out of the real. In no way can one speak of De Sanctis ever embracing realism in the sense of the French movement. He remains faithful to a view which allows him to consider Dante, Goethe, Manzoni and Leopardi as fulfilling his ideal of art as a union of the particular and the general, as the concrete universal, the organic unity he called 'life'. The exposition of Kirchmann's pamphlet cannot be interpreted as an acceptance of its confused 'realistic' epistemology, nor does 'Darwinism in art' imply an endorsement of its doctrines. De Sanctis to the last waged a polemical war on two fronts: against the rhetoric of neo-classicism and the fantastic world of Romanticism in favour of the real, the authentic, the living, but also against the determinism, the brutality, and the indifference of the newly emergent generation which we call positivistic. There is a beautiful coherence in all of De Sanctis' work, an *ethos* combined with an aesthetic sense which is rare in the history of criticism, not only in Italy.

NOTES

1 *The Italian Quarterly* (Los Angeles), 1 (1957), 5–43.
2 *Convivium* N.S. 31 (1957), 308–20.
3 René Wellek, *History of Modern Criticism from 1750 to 1950*, 4 vols. (New Haven, 1955 and 1965), IV, 124.

4 See E. and A. Croce, *Francesco De Sanctis* (Turin, 1964), p. 536.

5 'Non ci è istrumento cosí perfetto che possa fissare gli ultimi limiti del corporeo e le molecole del cervello e le loro vibrazioni' (De Sanctis, XIV, 344).

6 'Non c'è fantasia di filosofo o di poeta, che possa aumentare nelle loro specie le determinazioni semplici de' colori, de' suoni, o i semplici stati dell'anima, piacere, dolore, appetito, senso morale; è impossibile all'uomo rappresentarsi un colore o un sentimento altro che ciò che vede e sente; l'arte può collegare gli elementi, non li può inventare' (XIX, 345).

7 Eduard von Hartmann, *Julius Hermann von Kirchmanns erkenntnistheoretischer Realismus* (Berlin, 1875).

8 Adolf Lasson, *Jul. Herm. v. Kirchmann als Philosoph: Vorträge* (Philosophische Gesellschaft zu Berlin, N.F., Heft IX) (Halle, 1885).

9 Herbert Berger, *Begründung des Realismus bei J. H. von Kirchmann und Fr. Ueberweg* (Bonn, 1958), couples Kirchmann with Friedrich Ueberweg, the well-known editor of the *Grundriss der Geschichte der Philosophie*.

10 'Se è vero che senza percezione non ci può essere conoscenza dell'essere è anche vero che senza pensiero non ci può essere percezione' (XIV, 353).

11 Apparently an allusion to Theodor Fechner, who taught a curious theory of spaces filled with ether between the atoms. See *Über die physikalische und philosophische Atomenlehre* (Leipzig, 1855).

12 'Che nel Balzac valiga ogni termine e spesso assorbisce in sé la poesia' (V, 374).

13 'Né so perché dobbiate cacciarmi fuori della poesia gli uomini materialisti, come li chiamate, ovvero istintivi, che sono forse le più attraenti creature poetiche' (IV, 287 (1856)).

14 'Qualche cosa d'interessante di sotto di questa aridità.'

15 'Balzac metterebe qui in modo prosaico tutt'i particolari.'

16 James Boswell, *Life of Samuel Johnson* (Birbeck Hill edn), II, 174–5.

17 'È l'idea sua, ma non è l'idea del lettore' (XIV, 405). 'Romanzo per romanzo, prendiamo i personaggi cosí come sono, e poco ci cale il loro cognome, e di chi sieno o nipoti o zii; sono essi innanzi tutto che c'interessano; è il romanzo in sé stesso che ci piace o ci dispiace; le derivazioni, le origini, le connessioni, le spiegazioni le rendiamo all'autore; non è roba che ci possiamo assimilare' (XIV, 406).

18 'Che gusto c'è ad imparare con sí lungo cammino e intricato quello che si legge in mezz'ora in una pagina scientifica?' (XIV, 406).

19 'Che cosa ha a fare il progresso delle forme con la grandezza dell'ingegno artistico?' (XIV, 452).

20 'L'ideale è nelle cose, dalle quali escono lampi e guizzi di sentimenti umani.' 'Dateci le lacrime delle cose e risparmiateci le lacrime vostre' (XIV, 453).

21 'Non ha fini...non vuol dimonstrare nulla.' 'L'illusione è perfetta' (XIV, 415). 'Zola non ringhia nepurre. E marmoreo. E ci è del dantesco in quel marmoreo' (XIV, 422).

22 'Le più grande stilista francese dopo Proudhon' (XIV, 419).

23 *Neophilologus*, 44 (1960), 1–20, reprinted in *Concepts of Criticism* (New Haven, 1963) and since developed in *The Dictionary of the History of Ideas* (New York, 1973).

24 'Ideen', no. 96, *Kritische Friedrich Schlegel-Ausgabe*, edited by E. Behler, II, 265.

25 Cf. E. B. O. Borgerhoff, '*Réalisme* and kindred words: Their use as a term of literary criticism in the first half of the nineteenth century', *PMLA*, 53 (1938), 838.

26 Gustave Planche, 'Moralité de la poésie', *Revue des Deux Mondes*, 4th series, I (1835), 250.

27 Hippolyte Fortoul, 'Revue littéraire du mois', *Revue des Deux Mondes*, 4th series
    (1 November 1834), 339.
28 'Copia di un'idea.' 'L'esagerazione dell'idealismo' (v, 608–9).
29 'Adunque l'idea in sé e il contenuto in sé non sono una base poetica; l'idea in sé,
    base dell'idealismo; il contenuto in sé, base del realismo' (v, 611–12).
30 'Prolusione letta nell'Istituto politecnico di Zurigo.' 'Il tipo manzoniano.' 'Un
    accordo del reale e dell'ideale, in quella giusta misura che dicesi vero' (VII, 9).
31 'Il primo traccio del realismo in poesia.' 'Quest'analisi è una specie di anatomia
    della bellezza materiale: la descrive dalla chioma a'piedi. Il Lessing ha censurato
    questa descrizione come troppo materiale: ma la materialità è qui il segreto della
    poesia' (VII, 144). The claim for Aristo's priority must be mistaken: such enumerations
    of traits of female beauty were a staple, almost a *topos* in the sense of E. R. Curtius,
    in many earlier medieval texts. In Mathieu de Vendôme, in the twelfth century, we
    find instructions on how to describe beauty by enumerating the excellencies of the
    different parts of the body, always observing the regular order downward from the
    head or the hair to the feet (see Edmond Faral, *Les Sources latines des contes et romans
    courtois* (Paris, 1911), p. 108). Leo Spitzer has commented at length on a Middle
    English poem of the thirteenth century indulging in such a description (see *Essays
    on English and American Literature* (Princeton, 1962), p. 200), and there is a German
    thesis by Anna Köhn, *Das weibliche Schönheitsideal in der ritterlichen Dichtung*
    (Leipzig, 1930), which lists dozens of examples from Gottfried von Strassburg,
    Wolfram von Eschenbach, and many Minnesingers.
32 'Il principio da cui derivava quella rivoluzione letteraria, era l'imitazione della
    natura, o, come si direbbe, il realismo, nella sua verità e sua semplicità, reazione
    alla declamazione e alla rettorica' (IX, 886). 'Del seno dell'idealismo comparisce il
    realismo nella scienza, nell'arte, nella storia' (IX, 973).
33 'Il primo poeta italiano degno di questo nome, perché è il primo che abbia il senso
    e l'affetto del reale' (VIII, 57).
34 'Quello che a' tempi di Manzoni dicevasi vero positivo naturale e storico oggi dicesi
    realismo' (x, 57).
35 'L'autore mette quel finimento storico, dà al suo personaggio il paese, i pregiudizi,
    la sua classe, tutto ciò insomma che nella scuola moderna si chiama il realismo' (x,
    315).
36 'Annunzia la dissoluzione di questo mondo teologico-metafisico, e inaugura il regno
    dell'arido vero, del reale' (IX, 971).
37 'Tempo curioso, in cui tutto è realismo ed in cui si crede che l'ideale non esiste più'
    (XIV, 360–1).
38 'L'idea diviene istinto; la fantasia manifestazione meccanica; la passione appetito'
    (XIV, 360–1).
39 'Grido di dolore' (XIV, 360–1).
40 'Morto è l'ideale, l'ideale è risuscitato' (XIV, 360–1).
41 'Il dovere del disinteresse e del sacrificio.' 'Ma se il reale genera l'ideale, d'altra parte
    è l'ideale che reagendo lo purifica e l'innalza.' 'Realismo e idealismo...le due
    esagerazioni di ogni decadenza dalle quali pullula la commedia' (XVI, 151–3).
42 'Un vocabulo non solo barbaro, ma falso, se si vuole intendere che sia vero quello
    solo che è reale. Reale e ideale sono tutti e due il vero' (XVI, 153).
43 'Barbara frase' (XII, 10).

44 'La commedia è la prima forma nella quale s'inizia il realismo.'

45 'Non si vuole filosofia, e si cade nel puro empirismo.' 'Si disprezza la teoria, e succede la stupida pratica' (XVI, 156). 'Tutto ciò che si toglie alla mente, si dà alla natura.' 'S'innatura, e s'embestia l'uomo' (XI, 156).

46 'Un *fatum* ereditario, naturale e sociale spiega tutto e tutto giustifica.'

47 'Lo strazio di questo scetticismo in lacrime prenunzia *l'enfantement* del secolo, meglio che non gl'inni e le speculazioni poetiche di Lamartine e Hugo' (XI, 164).

48 'Era il verista di quel tempo' (XIV, 464).

49 'L'ideale non può morire se non coll'uomo' (VI, 9).

50 'Non è il caso di ammazare né il reale, né l'ideale, che in fondo sono tutti e due il vivente, la vita. Fatemi cose vive, e battezzatele come volete' (VI, 11).

Tragic ends of lovers: medieval Islam and the Latin West

M. A. MANZALAOUI

The purpose of this paper is to test the notion that it may be useful to make a comparative and contrastive study of the literature produced by parallel cultural circumstances, rather than to point out influence and trace intertraffic. Between the Islamic and Catholic worlds of the Middle Ages, between the aesthetic modes and attitudes of Arabic and of occidental vernacular literatures, there are obvious, easily definable differences. But the resemblances in the cultural make-up and in the literary products are enough to justify an *a priori* decision that such investigations are worth the making. On this, we have words of encouragement from the late Gustave von Grunebaum,[1] supported by Professor Theodore Silverstein.[2]

A specific difficulty in this comparative study arises from the character of one of its three principal components: the Arabic love-treatise, with its embedded poems and *exempla*. It is from these, rather than from the full-scale romances of Arabic literature, that I take certain parallels to my Western examples. They are texts little known to the Western reader, they are often fragmentary in form, and they are found within treatises of which it is not my present intention to discuss the intellectual content or overall design. Without pausing inordinately to situate each example fully, or shelving this study until further background material has become familiar, I shall fall back upon making references to specifics of narrative content in what may seem a regrettably fragmentary and impressionistic manner.

A recent work by Dr Lois Giffen, *Theory of Profane Love among the Arabs*,[3] pinpoints the centre of controversy in the Arabic genre of the

* An earlier version of this paper was read at the Conference on 'Transformations of Twelfth-Century Europe' at the Centre for Medieval Studies, University of Toronto, 14 February 1976. For the opportunity to carry out the necessary research, I am indebted to the Canada Council for a Leave Grant in the years 1974–5.

love-treatise. She finds it is a spurious *Ḥadīth* or 'tradition', that is, an aphorism attributed to the Moslem Prophet, probably invented by the ninth-century Traditionist Suwayd ibn Saʿīd al Ḥadathānī.[4]

The known adages of the Prophet were collected after his death, and transmitted each with a catena of the authorities through whom they had come down. They formed moral guidelines by which, second only to the *Qurʾān*, a good Sunnī, i.e. Orthodox, Moslem could live. In order to lend authority to their own beliefs, various groups among later generations of Moslems attributed false adages to the Prophet in very great number.

The spurious love-*ḥadīth* denotes a desire to lend religious *cachet* to the interest in sentimental and passionate love. It arises from a genuine recognition within Islam of the moral psychomachia as the truest of holy wars: applied to the temptation of a sexual situation, it can be seen to have an ambivalence and a capacity for extension and new interpretation (besides, of course, being open to rebuttal). In its fullest form the tradition reads: 'He who loves, and remains chaste, and conceals his secret, and suffers in patience, and dies, dies a martyr.'[5]

The spurious *ḥadīth* is quoted in several of the love-treatises which form the subject of Dr Giffen's book. In those accounts which treat this tradition sympathetically, the poetic and narrative centre of interest is formed by a lover's predicament, his suffering and death. Thus there is provided a martyrology of victims. These prose treatises range in date from the ninth to the seventeenth centuries A.D., and deal with the phenomenon of love in a descriptive and encyclopaedic manner, illustrating their 'scientific' taxonomy by quoting passages of verse or telling prose *exempla*. Stendhal's *De l'amour* is a conscious latter-day imitation of this genre.

Those *exempla* with which we are concerned form accounts of the sufferings and deaths of lovers: they are embryonic tragic romances, and it is from these quarries of Arabic narrative that, in the pages that are to follow, I adduce examples of 'tragic' forms to parallel the lengthier self-standing romances of the West. (For the most part, I have deliberately eschewed citation from the one Arabic love-treatise well-known in the modern West, that is, Ibn Ḥazm's *Dove's Neck Ring*,[6] and focus attention upon other equally worthwhile representatives of the genre.)

The several variant versions of the love-*ḥadīth* itself, and the phrases appended to it in Ibn Dāwūd's *Kitāb al-zahra* (*The Book of the Flower*),[7] show some manipulation of this aphorism. The inclusion or omission of the injunction to secrecy is not merely part of a code of behaviour towards the loved one, as its function appears to be in the Latin West, but connected with the theological doctrine of *kitmān*, or secrecy, as recommended by the anti-rationalist Ẓāhirite school. This is one of the points brought out in the magisterial study of the Arabic love tradition made by Jean-Claude Vadet in his *L'Esprit courtois en orient*,[8] a work which, because of its very density, is one which we have been all too slow to assimilate, and to which all who are interested in the topic must now, and for a long time to come, turn as their mainstay. The variant versions show some reservations. Thus Ibn Dāwūd's additional phrases declare that if the virtuous lover does not chastely control his passions, it will be wrong of him to stoke up the feelings which his partner has for him.[9] As quoted in one section of the *Rawḍat al-Mushtāqīn* (*The Garden of Yearners*), the treatise by Ibn Qayyim al-Jawziyya, the *ḥadīth* makes God's forgiveness of the lover's passion a necessary stage in his salvation;[10] noting the *ḥadīth* elsewhere in the same treatise, Ibn Qayyim al-Jawziyya adopts a commonsense attitude and takes minor infractions of the sexual ethic to be less injurious than the results of absolute continence: which are sickness, madness, or what he calls total destruction.[11] Without doubt, the *ḥadīth* expresses sympathetic respect for those who are destroyed *by* eros but *for* God; yet a compassion for the sufferings of the sensitive seems at times to draw compilers towards an attitude difficult to distinguish from one of sympathy with those who die *of eros for eros*. This form of compassion, and of wonder at the power of love, more than any other factor, brings the tales in the Arabic treatises close to the romances of North-Western Europe, where surely, though usually less clearly articulated, the same mesh of humane interests can be detected.

As a genre, however, the Arabic tales remain *exempla*, or *vitae* of lover-poets, imbedded in treatises. We are confronted here with one of the instances of the manner in which certain art forms and genres remained short of full efflorescence in the Arabic tradition. For another close analogue to the generic and rhetorical development in occidental romance, we must leave the Arabic tradition for the moment, and turn to the antecedents of the Western compositions, to some of the reading material available in the Latin world of the high Middle Ages.

A word, first, concerning the tragic theme in the medieval romance itself. In the move from the heroic to the romantic, one must agree with Dr A. C. Gibbs[12] that the medieval imagination turned away from the tauter and higher to the more relaxed and lighter, from cultural idealization to entertainment. This move is surely parallel to a similar development in Greek literary history: the move from the profundity of the probings into human nature in Sophoclean tragedy, to the love-affinities and the happy endings in Euripides' tragi-comedies; the further move in Hellenistic times, to the charm and delicate fantasy of the prose romance. In a sense, the twelfth-century vernacular romance takes over where the Greek romance left off. Whether we compare the average romance to Germanic heroic and elegiac works, or to Latin texts of devotional instruction, the sense of relaxation, if not even of truancy, is usually to be felt. The exceptions to this generalization, apart from the romances of the Grail, are the tragic romances: these include the Tristan stories, and those of Marie de France's *Lais* which have sad or fully tragic ends; with them one might class the accounts of the passing of Arthur and the break-up of the Round Table, whether we are concerned with parts of a longer work, as in Geoffrey of Monmouth, Wace, and later in Laȝamon, or later still, with a self-standing chronicle tragedy as in the *Alliterative Morte Arthur*. It was to be the achievement of the French Vulgate cycle and of Malory to fashion tragic romance which combined the courtly love tale with the theme of the collapse of the Round Table (as well as linking with them the story of the achieving of the Grail and the passing of the Grail knights).

In the tragic endings of these romances, and in the scenes of anguished predicament in them, there is a combination of carefully exploited rhetoric with a seemingly true-felt sympathy for the victim of the predicament, a sense, too, of the poignancy of the human situation, as brought about either by destinal forces or by man's folly or malignancy. Nowhere else do the romances come so close to true dramatic tragedy in intensity, poignancy, and depth. Such a combination of literary devices and human sympathy, centring upon the victim of a love-predicament, is also notably to be found in a work by one of the most popular writers whom the medievals had inherited from the classical past. Interestingly, it is a work in which his usually light ironic tones are exchanged for an atypical poignancy. The work is Ovid's *Heroides*. The first fifteen single letters, known to be Ovid's, and the final three pairs of exchanges (of doubtful authorship) can, for the present purpose, be considered as a single literary entity. (When the need for distinction arises, I fall back upon the mercies of adjectival ambiguity and refer to the last six epistles as *Ovidian* ones.)

Those of us who needed the lesson will have learned from Professor Howard Jacobson[13] how to take the *Heroides* as a serious study of situations of pathos. Ovid turns in them from the ironic interest in the social predicaments in which a rake's sexual excesses place him, to a serious-minded sympathy for women placed in extreme anguish by their passion and, in general, by a failure on the part of their beloved. Each situation is a moment of artistically controlled melodrama. Desertion, jealousy, erotic nostalgia, erotic frenzy, imprisonment, infanticide, are among the situations; the types of tragic end include suicide, death at the hands of an irate father, drowning, and the accidental slaying of one's beloved. The monologue itself often constitutes the final words of the heroine: on at least two occasions it is a suicide note,[14] on another the epistle alters direction when the heroine, Dejanira, realizes that her actions are to lead to the death of Hercules.[15] Laodamia's letter contains an ironic twist of fate, since she refers in fear to the prophecy concerning the death of the first Greek to land in the Troad, but has no means of knowing that her husband is in fact to be that man.[16] Other forms of fatality are present: the wrath of Venus, of whom the nervous Cydippe[17] is so afraid; the foolish belief of Paris that Helen's people will never fight;[18] and, to return to Dejanira, her belief that the blood of Nessus was a love-potion and not a poison.

Present also in the *Heroides* in embryo are the paraphernalia of the courtly love tale, encouraging the speculation that if a misunderstanding of Ovid's *Ars amatoria* has been posited as the source of the twelfth-century love-cult, a fairly open-eyed understanding of his *Heroides* might also be posited as an inspiration. Hermione finds herself slipping into using Orestes' name instead of that of her disliked husband;[19] Paris first falls in love with Helen by repute;[20] Canace and Hero both have wise old duennas; Sappho's suicide takes place at a lover's leap;[21] Paris writes of his distaste at Menelaus' dalliances with his own wife, and in a parallel to the miniature realism of the twelfth-century romance he and Helen describe the little social devices he uses in his suppressed anger: he raises his cup so as to hide the husband's love-play from his own sight; he listlessly drops the cup as he watches Helen; he writes her name in the spilled wine on the tabletop.[22] The Ovidian letters between Acontius and Cydippe come particularly close to the medieval romance in tone and detail, with a heroine betrothed to a man she hates, sickness stepping in to prevent her marriage and so preserve her word as well as her honour; with a duenna's advice and a rumour that the lover has used magic potions, and with Acontius offering himself to his lady as a submissive slave:

ante tuos liceat flentem consistere vultus
et liceat lacrimis addere verba sua,
utque solent famuli, cum verbera saeva verentur,
tendere submissas ad tua crura manus!
ignoras tua iura; voca! cur arguor absens?
iamdudum dominae more venire iube...
...servabor firmo vinctus amore tui!...
...ipsa tibi dices, ubi videris omnia ferre:
'tam bene qui servit, serviat iste mihi!'

Let me have leave to stand weeping before your face, and my tears have leave to add
their own speech; and let me, like a slave in fear of bitter stripes, stretch out submissive
hands to touch your feet! You know not your own right; call me! Why am I accused
in absence? Bid me come, forthwith, after the manner of a mistress...I shall be kept
in bonds by unyielding love for you...You will say to yourself, when you have seen
me bearing all: 'He who is a slave so well, let him be a slave to me!'[23]

Though the *Heroides* demonstrate a sensitive analysis of the emotions,
they achieve this through a rhetoric requiring a measure of detachment
for literary enjoyment. One may reasonably compare the epistles with
Fenice's soliloquy in Chrétien de Troyes' *Cligès*, that is, with the 160
lines of ordered perturbation that begin with her recollection of Cligès's
words, which she recalls as

Je sui toz vostres.[24]

Recalling that Chaucer refers to *Book XI* of the *Metamorphoses* as 'a
romance',[25] we might hazard the supposition that in the eyes of the
medieval reader of both, the vernacular tragic love-story and the *Heroides*
belong to the same world of imaginative experience. The bigamy of Jason
and that of Eliduc can be meaningfully juxtaposed: though, by the grace
of God, Guildeluc is a very different spouse from Medea.[26]

The comparatist critic turning from these two genres to examine the
Arab love-treatises will find himself regarding the imbedded narratives
as also belonging to that same world. In now returning to these treatises,
it is not my intention to underrate the differences between them and
occidental romances. The treatises, about twenty in number, form a
single tradition of interrelated texts; they are encyclopaedic in manner,
didactic, and yet sharing a voracious humanistic interest in the variety
of human responses. The catena of authorities cited for each *exemplum*
(similar to those introducing the adages in the great collections of *ḥadīth*)
places the story firmly in its setting in the history of Islamic Arabic
culture. The relevance of each case to the Islamic ethos is clearly the
major issue; there is a very great deal concerning the sainted lovers of

God, heroes closer to St Francis than to Lancelot or even to Galahad. There is a very great deal upon homosexual love; chaste homosexual passion is given sympathy, and some of the compilers identify themselves as suffering those particular pangs. Ushering in the twelfth century, Abū Muḥammad Jaʿfar al-Sarrāj, who died in 1106 at the age of eighty, compiled *Maṣāriʿ al ushshāq* (*The Tragic Ends of Lovers*),[27] written with sympathy for love's sorrows: in the epigraph to *Book XVII*, Sarrāj tells us he has moved from condemning lovers to excusing them.[28] In the second half of the century, Abul Faraj ʿAbd al-Raḥmān ibn al-Jawzī wrote his *Dhamm al-Hawā* (*In Blame of Love*): in spite of the diametrically opposed sentiments implied by the titles, the works are in their detail fairly close to each other. In both, an *exemplum* is sometimes no longer than an aphorism, as with the *ḥadīth* of martyrdom that I have discussed. Sometimes they are anecdotes; more rarely, they are full short tales. (The long self-standing romance of chivalric love, such as the *Sīra* of ʿ*Antar*, seems to have taken its own line of development in Arabic, and lies outside our present view, as do, of course, the whole great lines of Persian and of Turkish romance.) The love-tales in the treatises are divorced to a remarkable degree from battle; many are urban or domestic, in the manner of *Laüstic*, *La Chastelaine de Vergi*, or Jean Renard's *Lai de l'ombre*. But the variety of the tales is such that it is difficult to recognize any one species as more typical than another. One of Sarrāj's finest tales, for example, is the unexpected account, narrated through the friend who assists him, of the lovesick young man who wins an Amazonian young woman whom he first meets in male hunting-attire at a watering hole.[29]

Not all of the tales, by any means, concern tragic ends. But in those which do, the ends are: insanity;[30] a love-sickness ending in the slow wasting away of a lover;[31] the broken hearted dying of one lover;[32] or the double death of the pair as in this tale from Sarrāj:

I learnt from the Prince Abū Muḥammad al-Ḥassan ibn ʿĪsā, grandson of the Caliph al-Muqtadir-billāh, when I studied under him in his quarters in the precincts of the Ṭāhir mosque, in the year 438 A.H. [1046–7 A.D.], that Abul ʿAbbās ibn al-Manṣūr al-Yashkarī says that Abul-Qāsim relates the following, with a chain of authorities deriving from Ibn al-Ashdaq, who says:

I was making my ritual circumambulation of the Kaʿba at Mecca, when I remarked a young man standing under the eaves-trough, his head held down beneath his robe, moaning like a man in fever. I greeted him: he returned my salutation and then said, 'From where do you come?'

'From Basra', I replied.

'Are you returning there?' he asked.

'Yes', I said.

'When you reach al-Nibāj, go forth to the villagers and cry out, "Hilāl, o Hilāl!" A young girl will come forth to you. Recite this verse to her:

> I craved for a doom hurled out of your eyes:
> that you might see in me a man killed by love.'

He died on the spot. When I reached al-Nibāj, I went forth to the villagers and called out, 'Hilāl, o Hilāl!' A girl came forth to me, more beautiful than I had ever seen.

'What have you to say?' she asked.

'A young man at Mecca recited this verse to me...'

'What did he do next?' she asked.

'He died.'

She fell down dead upon the spot.[33]

It is not surprising to find more of 'the loveres maladye of Hereos'[34] here than in the Latin West; the treatises are closer to the medical and psychological interests of the schools than the occidental romances are. I find it strange – though this may be due to an unrepresentative sampling of tales from each of the two cultures – to find that madness is so frequently the *terminal* fate in Arabic tales, while in the occidental ones it occurs (whether in a true or a feigned form) as an *episode* in the life of a lover, rather than as his end.

The sense of fate is one element in the *exempla*. Very early on in his treatise, Sarrāj gives us a directly cerebral statement which is, as it were, a scholastic parallel to such symbolic devices as the love-philtre of *Tristan*; Sarrāj quotes an authority saying: 'If I could do so, I would free lovers of their sufferings, for their transgressions are transgressions through necessity (*iḍṭirār*) and not transgressions through free will (*ikhtiyār*).'[35] Fate, or the preternatural, is not always unfriendly to lovers. The lover 'Urwa, after being courteously treated by the husband of his beloved, 'Afrā', goes out into the wilds and dies. 'Afrā' visits his tomb, dies there, and is buried beside him. This story is told in the very centre of Sarrāj's work.[36] Separately, some fifty pages earlier,[37] Sarrāj cites a conclusion to this tale:

Citing his chain of authorities, Ibn Marzabān says: Isḥāq ibn Muḥammad ibn Abān related to me, saying: Mu'ādh ibn Yaḥyā related to me and said:

I once journeyed to San'ā, and, when we had travelled some distance, someone said to us, 'The tomb of 'Afrā' and 'Urwa is about a mile off the road here'. A party of us, and I amongst them (he continued), made for it. We found two tombs side by side; out of each of the tombs grew the trunk of a tree, and at a man's height from the ground each entwined around its companion.

Isḥāq says: I asked Mu'ādh, 'What manner of tree was this?' 'I do not know,' he replied; 'I asked the neighbouring villagers about it, and they said, "That tree is not known to us in this land of ours".'

There is an added interest in this anecdote for us. This late eleventh-century text is the earliest documentary analogue to the interlacing plants over the graves of Tristan and Iseut: indeed it is the only one which is earlier than Eilhart's text.[38]

More dominant than destiny is the decision-making of the more active and authoritative members of the community, who marry off young women, reject suitors, and decide to move their encampments, so ending the happiness of lovers. Sarrāj's handsome madman of the Monastery of Heraclius suffers through this, though the anecdote itself, which presents a stock situation of earlier Arabic poetry, does not verbally specify the role of the girl's tribal leaders:

I was going past the monastery of Heraclius with a friend of mine, when he asked me, 'Would you care to go in, and see some of the entertaining lunatics in there?'

'As you say,' I replied.

We made our way in, and found a good-looking young man, with neatly-combed hair, eyes attractively shadowed by nature, finely-drawn eyebrows, and eyelashes like the plumes of an eagle's pinions: all graciousness overtopped by beauty, he was chained to the wall by the neck...

...We asked, 'What are you doing in this place? You are fit for a different one.'

He replied,

> 'God knows that I am sick at heart;
> Can I unfold my experience?
> Two spirits I have: one is in one land,
> The second in another:
> The one which lives here gets no help from patience;
> My missing spirit, I surmise, is like the one at hand –
> Where it is found, it goes through the same experience.'

Then he turned to us and said, 'Have I spoken well?'

'Yes', we said, and turned to go.

'My father be your ransom,' he exclaimed, 'but now soon you lose interest! I beg you, lend me your attention and your understandings.'

'Speak,' we said.

He said,

> 'Just before sunrise, they made their pedigree camels kneel for the loading,
> Lifted their saddlebags on,
> And up the camels were rising with my love.
> She glanced back through the howdah curtains,
> Tearbathed eyes toward me:
> She waved farewell, her fingers berry-red with dye,
> And I cried out, 'Camel, oh, if your legs would fail to carry!
> Oh, the separation! What is this that has come upon her and me?
> You who are carrying off these dwelling-tents,
> This is the moment of parting. They are away.

> You who are leading off these fine camels, go lame, so let me take
>   my leave of her.
> You who are leading off these fine camels, linger in your setting out.'
> I have kept my vows, I have not broken with my love.
> Might I know, after so long, what has become of them?'

We did not realize that he was giving an authentic account in what he was describing, and, as a rash jest, we said, 'They are dead'.

'I conjure you to tell the truth! They are dead?'

To see what he would do, we replied, 'Yes, they are dead.' 'By God,' he said, 'I follow them into death.'

He tugged himself forward on his chain, so that his tongue dangled down, his eyes bulged out, and blood spurted from his lips. He fell to the ground, and, in a while, he was dead. I shall not forget our remorse at what we had done.[39]

In these tales, the lover and the beloved, the narrator, the poet of love, and those who can feel sympathy for suffering and admiration for love, are shown acknowledging the value of individual feelings and attachments: institutions and men of authority give them no consideration. We may have here one of the basic impulses behind courtly love literature: the protest of those who see themselves as having refinement of feelings, against those who have the actual power, the cult which satisfies the internal proletariat within the aristocracy, those whose happiness could only be snatched, in the interstices of the political, social, and economic games. The upper-class social framework acted as a hardfaced fate for the Handsome Madman of Heraclea just as it seems to have for Eleanor of Aquitaine's daughter in her real-life marriage, and to Troilus when Priam's council decided to exchange Criseyde for Antenor. Those who could feel pity were those with the *cuor gentil*, the *edele herzen*: the Arabic term was *al-zurafā'* (the plural of *zarīf*), those with polite education, elegance, decency, refinement, and sympathetic response. In the anecdote of the Handsome Madman, the sensibilities of the narrator and his friend go through a process of *éducation sentimentale*: curiosity and irresponsible joking (tinged from the start with awed respect for sensitive beauty) end as compassionate contrition. Ibn Dāwūd, writing of *zurafā'* in the ninth century, had given his own colouring to the concept, when he wrote, 'He who is a *zarīf*, let him be chaste.'[40] The heroes themselves are *zurafā'*, usually lover-poets; many tales consist of prose links binding together snatches of verse which express the lover's feelings at high moments of happiness, or, more commonly, perhaps, of sorrow: often, these verses are dying words and farewell messages. The verbal rhetoric is sometimes paralleled by what may be called a rhetoric of gesture and of small significant actions. The slave-girl loved by a pious youth, in Sarrāj's book, sends him a red rose which he holds strapped to his upper arm as he lies on his sick-bed.[41] The two rival teachers, Abū Bakr and Ibn Samnūn, try to outdo each other in composing epigrammatic warnings, which they cause to be engraved on rings that they then toss to men who look too yearningly at young boys.[42] Abū Nuwās and a woman similarly engrave contradictory epigrams on the stones of each others' rings, and so hold a kind of lapidary flyting.[43] A delight in the wit of these actions is part of the literary pleasure, even if the main interest is a gentle exposition of pain. True, the interest is sometimes so external as to amount to mere curiosity: a *majnūn* (a 'madman', or, here, usually, more specifically a *fou d'amour*) is mentioned as a curious specimen of a special human category. Such was the initial response of the two companions who visit the Handsome Madman: the narrator of the tale of the pious young man who loves a slave-girl, as mentioned already, visits his sick-bed when a friend of his asks him, 'Would you like me to show you a love-sick young man?'[44] The sufferings shown in greatest detail are those of male lovers, but women, as already seen, are not neglected: the girl loved by this same young man is converted by his piety, after having, though she belongs to another master, offered herself to him sexually. When he dies she welcomes the physical ill-treatment to which her owners subject her, and asks the narrator not to interpose himself. Ibn al-Jawzī also tells of a love-crazed girl who pursues a pious youth in Kūfa, is converted by his attitude, and dies after praying that God will unite her to him in heaven. (The young man attends her funeral, and frequents her grave.)

This tale contains an interesting variant on the traditional description of the love sickness. Here a reference to the loved one does not act as a stimulus to the pangs of love, but as an anaesthetic against the physical pains of medical treatment:

She fell seriously ill, and suffered great affliction of her body... At the start of each of his sessions, the medical man who was in attendance upon her would speak to her and say, 'O So-and-so, what is this fear that you feel? Truly I have never seen a man readier and more amenable and more patient in facing any affliction that befalls him, than a young man among my neighbours, called Such-and-such' – and here he would name her beloved. She would fall silent and then she would say, 'Speak to me of him'. During this while, the medical attendant would be cutting at her flesh, but it was as though her content at the mention of the young man so overpowered her feelings that she could sense nothing of what was being done to her. If the doctor stopped speaking of him, she felt the pain and fell into anguish. In this condition she remained until she was dead.[45]

What are the characteristics common to these narrations and the tragic romances of the Latin West, to which we now finally turn? Structurally,

the occidental romances are more fully developed, centred more clearly
upon chivalry and the fighting life. Conceptually, they are less overtly
concerned with religious commitment, and, no doubt because of basic
differences in the organization of court life, they are more frequently
adulterous, but deal hardly at all with homosexual passion. Although,
as noted already, the romance tradition gives one an impression of a
relaxation from the heroic, it should be emphasized that in historical fact,
the first wave of proto-courtly and courtly romances contain as high a
proportion of the tragic as later ones, for to it belong the versions of the
Tristan legend, and the four tragic lays of Marie de France.[46] The
distribution of sympathies and something of the tone and pattern are
close to some of those found in the *Heroides* or in the Arabic treatises.
Fate is perhaps given a more clearly defined instrumentality, such as a
love philtre taken unwittingly, or it is more closely related to narrative
development, in such a form as a chance discovery of the lovers by a
husband or an envious courtier. In this tradition perhaps a distinct
historical evolution may be seen, from elements of what appears to be
folk-magic in the Ur-Tristan, to a deeper sense of a transcendent destiny
in Thomas' version of the ending of the legend. From the pre-courtly
stage, the Western romance took over a willingness to give heroes and
heroines some coarseness of sensibility such as Sarrāj and Ibn al Jawzī
almost totally rule out of order where their protagonists are meant to
be admired. In Ovid it is the two wives of Jason who alone are given
a wild and dramatic cruelty. The extent of love-crazed ferocity which
causes Béroul's Iseut to attempt to kill Braingain, and the lovers' delight
at the killing of their enemies,[47] is echoed in the cavalier way in which
Chrétien's Cligès assaults the unfortunate courtier Bertranz who
discovers his and Fenice's refuge.[48] It is presumably the same
shortcoming of taste which allows the frequent falsehoods, near-
falsehoods, and perjuries of both Tristan and Yseut, and partly accounts
for the often blasphemous assurance with which they assert that God
is on their side. This, however, would have appealed to the courtly
appreciation of wit – especially when the oath is a clever *suggestio falsi*,
falling just short of a lie. We are here in the realm of the European *zarifs*,
appreciating both the sensibility of the lovers and their wit. The use of
what I have called the non-verbal rhetoric of gesture is particularly worth
noting. In this category of action I class Mark's leaving of his gloves over
Yseut's face when he discovers the sleeping lovers,[49] and his final
decision to let the growing vegetation unite the dead pair. Marie de
France's *Chievrefoil* is built up entirely on Tristan's leaving of the

whittled hazel branch as a signal. In *Laüstic*, there is the killing of the nightingale by the angry husband, and the placing of its body in a golden casket by the lover, in that mutedly tragic end which leaves the lovers in separation and living martyrdom. In *Deus amanz*, there is the refusal of the young lover to drink the strengthening potion, even though this leads to his death. The finest example of the rhetoric of gesture is a thirteenth-century one: it is the moment when the lover in Jean Renard's *Lai de l'ombre* (as nameless in that little masterpiece as many of the protagonists are in the Arabic tales) wins his lady by tossing his ring into the well, at her reflection, which he calls the one he loves best next to her. (Let us note that here, as in the Arabic instances already given, the witty play centres upon a ring.) As an example of the way in which narrative structure developed further in the occidental romances, it is to be noted that there are also deceptive or merely ostensible rhetorical gestures, brought about by fate, and not by the wits of the hero: thus, in versions of *Tristan* earlier than Gottfried's, it is not by intent that the sleeping lovers drop the naked sword between their bodies on the day that Mark discovers them.[50]

In the final analysis, in this field of writing, one may say again that the chief intellectual interest is the study of the predicament of sensitive persons pinioned down by social and by moral forces which prevent even those of them who put up a struggle from achieving themselves in any but a tragic way. The study of predicament may produce a fine piece of internal dialogue even in the relatively insensitive verse of Béroul, whose soliloquy of the repentant Tristan, beginning

> Ha! Dex, . . . tant ai traval!
> Trois ans a hui, que rien n'i fal[51]

is an example of this. However much the Islamic treatise-writers differ among themselves as to the value of love, it is seen by all as sensitizing, and by many as ennobling, even when it must destroy. The purpose of Ibn al Jawzī is admonitory, but he remains an admirer of the refined sensibility: there is no gruff dismissal of it. There is little foothold for an orientalist Robertsonian, and the study of the Arabic treatises shows a theistically based humanism with an ambivalent recognition of the role of sensibility. Twenty treatises of six hundred pages each, studying the fine sentiments of lovers with such tenderness, form no onslaught upon concupiscence, but rather a regretfulness concerning it.

Some readers may be disappointed that there is no reference in this paper to the death-wish in oriental religions. The tension in the Arabic tales can be interpreted in terms of the tension between firmness of

Islamic faith and strength of passion: no other metaphysical elements are required – though there *is* no doubt that death *is* seen as the calm end of suffering, that union with the beloved in heaven is prayed for, and that the tombside becomes a place of pilgrimage.

The tradition of martyrs of love carries us, I believe, beyond the formal bounds of the romances, and into a period later than the twelfth century and the Middle Ages as a whole. If we apply conventional generic classifications, the true tragic form of medieval times is not the romance with an unhappy ending, but the latter-day descendants of Seneca, especially, as a derivative, the poems of the 'Fall of Princes' type. Whatever generic aesthetics may inform us, commonsense response, unable to feel roused at the fates of rulers perfunctorily introduced and equally perfunctorily destroyed, surely is right in turning in preference to the tragic romance, with its detailed presentation of genuine human feelings. When the drama of Elizabethan times arises, the 'Fall of Princes' theme contributes to it. So does the revived classical Senecan tradition. In the younger Shakespeare, the former of these two, it is true, produced *Richard III*, an acceptable sign of developing genius. The latter produced *Titus Andronicus*, a skilful but distasteful work, with an inadequacy of sensibility that is little short of stunning. But the tradition of the tragic romance seems to have transmitted itself to the Renaissance novella, and lingered on in the medieval reading of the Elizabethans. And *that*, in the younger Shakespeare, produced the masterpiece which is *Romeo and Juliet*. Which of us reads *Titus* in preference to *Romeo*? With deference to generic criticism, we must acknowledge that *Romeo* is the culmination of our tradition, while Renaissance scholars should recognize that without such lesser works as exemplified by *Deus amanz*, that play would not have taken the shape it took.

NOTES

1 'Avicenna's *Risāla fi 'l-ishq* and Courtly Love', *Journal for Near Eastern Studies*, 11 (1952), 233–8. See also Grunebaum, 'Greek Form Elements in the Arabian Nights', *Journal of African and Oriental Studies*, 62 (1942), 277–92; Grunebaum, 'The Nature of the Arabic Literary Effort', *JNES*, 7 (1948), 116–22; Grunebaum, 'The Aesthetic Foundations of Arabic Literature', *Comparative Literature*, 4 (1952), 323–40.

2 'Andreas, Plato, and the Arabs: Remarks on Some Recent Accounts of Courtly Love', *Modern Philology*, 47 (1949–50), 117–26.

3 *Theory of Profane Love among the Arabs: The Development of the Genre* (New York, 1971).

4 Giffen, p. 112 n. 38 and 'Appendix', p. 149; J. Schacht, *Origins of Mohammedan*

Jurisprudence (Oxford, 1953), part ii, chapter 4; J. Vadet, *L'Esprit courtois en orient* (Paris, 1968), 'Appendice', pp. 459–63.

5 *man 'ashaqa, fa 'affa, fa katama, fa māta, fa-huwa shahīd^{un}.*

6 Abū Muḥammad 'Alī ibn Ḥazm, *Ṭawq al-Ḥamāma fil-Ulfa wal-'Ullāf*, edited by D. K. Petrof (Leiden, 1914); edited by H. K. Ṣīrafī (Cairo, 1950); edited with French translation by L. Bercher as *Le Collier du pigeon* (Algiers, 1949); translated into English by A. R. Nykl as *A Book Containing the Risāla known as the Dove's Neck-Ring* (Paris, 1931), and by A. J. Arberry as *The Ring of the Dove* (London, 1953); also Russian translation by A. Salie, 1933; German by M. Weisweiler, 1944; Italian by F. Gabrieli, 1949; Spanish by E. Garciá Gómez, 1952.

7 Abū Bakr Muḥammad Ibn Dāwūd, *Kitāb al-Zahra* (*the first half*), edited by A. R. Nykl, with I. Ṭūqān (Chicago, 1932), p. 66; 'Abd al-Raḥmān Ibn al-Jawzī, *Dhamm al hawā*, edited by Musṭafā 'Abd al-Wāḥid (Cairo, 1381 A.H./1962 A.D.), p. 326; Shams al-Dīn Abū 'Abd Allāh Muḥammad Ibn Qayyim al-Jawziyya, *Rawḍat-al-Muḥibbīn wa Nuzhat al-Mushtāqīn*, edited by Aḥmad 'Ubayd (Cairo, 1385 A.H./1956 A.D.), pp. 179–80.

8 See note 4 above; pp. 307–13.

9 Ibn Dāwūd, p. 66, ll. 9–12.

10 *Rawḍat al-Mushtāqīn*, pp. 179–80, in the second of three versions of the *ḥadīth* given on that page, includes in it the phrase 'God will *forgive* him'.

11 Ibn Qayyim al-Jawziyya, p. 120.

12 *Middle English Romances*, edited by A. C. Gibbs (London, 1966), introduction, p. 5.

13 H. Jacobson, *Ovid's 'Heroides'* (Princeton, 1974).

14 *Heroides* VII, 'Dido Aeneae' (see ll. 184ff); II, Phyllis Demophoonti', ll. 131ff.

15 IX, 'Deianira Herculi', ll. 143f.

16 XIII, 'Laudamia Protesilao', ll. 93ff.

17 XXI, 'Cydippe Acontio', ll. 5–6: 'Si tibi dura fuissem,/aucta foret saevae forsitan ira deae.' I follow Ovid, *Heroides and Amores*, edited and translated by G. Showerman (Loeb classics) (London, 1914, rptd 1963).

18 XVI, 'Paris Helenae', ll. 341–4.

19   Saepe Neoptolemi pro nomine nomen Orestis
             exist, et errorem vocis ut omen amo.
                              (VIII, 'Hermione Oresti', ll. 115f)

20   Te prius optavi, quam mihi nota fores.
             ante tuos animo vidi quam lumine vultus;
             prima tulit vulnus nuntia fama tui.
                              (XVI, 'Paris Helenae', ll. 36–8)

21   Quoniam non ignibus aequis
             ureris, Ambracia est terra petenda tibi
             ...pete protinus altam
             Leucada nec saxo desiluisse time!
                              (XV, 'Sappho Phaoni', ll. 163f, 171f)

22 XVI, 'Paris Helenae', ll. 225–8, 233–4, 243–8, 253–4; XVII, 'Helene Paridi', ll. 87–8.

23 XX, 'Acontius Cydippae', ll. 75–80, 86, 88–90.

24 Chrétien de Troyes, *Cligès*, ll. 4366–526. Cligès's actual words are, 'Mes droiz est

qu'a vos congié praigne/Com a celi cui ge sui toz'. I follow the edition of A. Micha,
Les romans de Chrétien de Troyes (Paris, 1957), 11.

25 *Boke of the Duchess*, l. 48.

26 Marie de France, *Eliduc*.

27 Abū Muḥammad Jaʿfar ibn Aḥmad al-Sarrāj, *Maṣāriʿal-ʿushshāq*, 2 vols. (Beirut, 1958).

28 *wa-kuntu alūmuhum dāʾiban/fa-ṣirtu lahum aḥada-l-ʿādhirīna*: Sarrāj, I, 9.

29 The story of Abū Mas-har and the daughter of Abū Rabīʿa, Sarrāj, I, 92–8.

30 E.g., the tale of Ghawrak; Sarrāj, I, 125, 324; II, 25.

31 See, e.g., the account of the death of Jamīl as told by Sarrāj, II, 59, and also found elsewhere.

32 E.g., in the tale of the chaste lover whose voice announces from out of his tomb that he has been granted his love's desire after death: Sarrāj, II, 41.

33 Sarrāj, I, 308–9.

34 Chaucer, *Canterbury Tales*, I, 1373–4. For the love-sickness, see J. Livingston Lowes, 'The Loveres Maladye of Hereos', *Modern Philology*, 11 (1914), 491–546.

35 Sarrāj, I, 12.

36 Sarrāj, I, 316–21.

37 Sarrāj, I, 264.

38 Pierre Gallais' view is that the similar Irish tale of Baile and Ailinn was in oral circulation in the tenth century, but that 'C'est avec Tristan qu'apparait dans la *littérature* – du moins à ma connaissance – le motif des arbres entrelacés. Aucun couple d'amants tragiques de l'Antiquité ou de l'orient littéraires ne donne naissance à un couple d'arbres qui enlacent leurs rameaux'. ('Les arbres entrelacés dans les "romans" de Tristan et le mythe de l'arbre androgène primordial', *Mélanges de langue et de littérature medievales offertes à Pierre Le Gentil* (Paris, 1973), pp. 295–310; see esp. pp. 296 and 300. See also the same author's *Genèse du roman occidental: essais sur Tristan et Iseut et son modèle persan* (Paris, 1974); esp. pp. 85 and n. 10, 170 and n. 36, 212 and n. 48. The fact that Sarrāj's anecdote provides a unique, though perhaps wholly unconnected, literary antecedent to the motif in *Tristan* was pointed out to me by Professor Eugène Vinaver (in conversation, 14 February 1976).

39 Sarrāj, I, 19–20.

40 Ibn Dāwūd, p. 66 (chapter heading): *man kāna ḍharīfan fal-yakun ʾafīfan;* see Giffen, p. 99.

41 Sarrāj, I, 16.

42 Sarrāj, II, 5.

43 Sarrāj, II, 5–6.

44 Sarrāj, I, 15.

45 Ibn al-Jawzī, pp. 515–19.

46 *Deus amanz, Chaitivel, Laüstic,* and *Yonec*.

47 Béroul, *Tristan*, edited by A. Ewart, 2 vols. (Oxford, 1939–70), ll. 1729, 1745, 4055–6.

48 Chrétien de Troyes, *Cligès*, ll. 6383–407.

49 Béroul, ll. 2041f.

50 Béroul, ll. 1804f (and 1998f); cf. Gottfried's version, ed. K. Marold, ll. 17416ff.

51 Béroul, ll. 2161ff.

The encyclopaedic tradition, the cosmological epic, and the validation of the medieval romance

PETER W. HURST

I

Two cultures or one? The Snow–Leavis controversy of the 1960s, it is widely supposed, impinged upon medieval studies only to the extent that the Middle Ages were liable to be cited as evidence of a unified culture that fell victim to the scientific revolution and its consequences.[1] In defence of this assumption, the medievalist might point, for example, to a tradition of didactic or scientific poetry, deriving from Hesiod and transmitted by Virgil and Lucretius, which flourishes anew in the 'Chartrian' millieu of the twelfth century.[2] The revitalization of the genre known as the cosmological or philosophical epic by such poets as Bernard Silvester and Alain of Lille apparently affords striking proof of an endeavour to synthesize contemporary scientific and philosophical trends through the medium of poetry.[3] In particular, the literary investigation into the neo-platonic ideal of man as the microcosm of the universe undertaken in Bernard's *Cosmographia* is supported by the ambitious form in which the work is couched: the encyclopaedic survey of the newly created world at once presupposes and advocates the ability of the inspired individual to restore the prelapsarian totality.[4] Furthermore, the coherent programme of instruction offered through the seven liberal arts promoted (we are assured) the realization of the 'microcosmic' ideal on a personal level. In Alain's *Anticlaudianus*,[5] as in the late classical *De Nuptiis Philologiae et Mercurii*[6] of Martianus Capella upon which it draws, the seven liberal arts are represented as personified goddesses, all of whom (in Alain's poem) contribute to the

* This essay is based upon a paper read at the founding conference of the British Comparative Literature Association, Norwich, December 1975. It is a pleasure to acknowledge the encouragement and thoughtful criticism I have received from Professor Roy Wisbey, and from the editor.

53

project that will culminate in the creation of the *novus homo*. Significantly, the seven liberal arts are evoked in some detail through the literary tradition of the *descriptio* or *ecphrasis*,[7] an honour accorded to the 'scientific' subjects of the *quadrivium* no less than to the *trivium*. Nor (it might be added) was the microcosmic ideal, assisted by the scheme of the *artes*, confined to the realm of allusive poetic representation as typified by Alain's poem. It is translated into the tangible and often weighty reality of the scholastic *summae* and a plethora of encyclopaedic works. The fact that several encyclopaedic or longer didactic works of the twelfth century include sections in verse[8] reflects not only the prestige enjoyed by the cosmological epics in the twelfth century (several of the latter being Menippæan satires), but, so it would appear, a deep-seated need to unify the multifarious academic disciplines.

Evidence in favour of a unified medieval culture is therefore easily assembled. But does the medieval ideal necessarily correspond to the reality? Or (to put it another way) is the medievalist still viewing the Middle Ages through Romantic eyes? The notion of a single, unified medieval culture was first advanced in a recognizably modern form by the Romantic historians. One thinks, for instance, of Novalis' *Die Christenheit oder Europa*.[9] Far from dismantling this aspect of late-eighteenth-century medievalism, modern idealists may be charged with having lent a peculiar slant to the Romantic legacy. Even when something approaching modern scientific method is discerned in the scholastic mode of inquiry, the Middle Ages are still commonly thought to be innocent of excessive specialization, and of the attendant problem of the categorization of knowledge. Yet the very proliferation of speculations on the microcosmic theme that characterizes the twelfth century, under the impact partly of Arabic science, partly of a revival of interest in neo-platonic philosophy, could equally well be construed as symptomatic of certain difficulties when it came to putting the ideal of 'microcosmic man' into practice. Several cosmological epics are cast in the form of a dream or vision granted to the narrator,[10] a device which probably cannot be accounted for on the grounds of literary convention alone: it is rather as if the poet would grant less ephemeral expression to an ecstatic vision that partly recaptures Adam's vision in paradise before the Fall,[11] and partly indicates new ways in which that vision may be restored intellectually. Bernard's *Cosmographia*, though it does not take the form of a dream-vision as such, limits itself to a vision of the prelapsarian world, while alluding to the many ills that will beset man once the Fall has taken place.[12] Even the encyclopaedias of the twelfth century prove in some cases to be less than comprehensive upon closer analysis; in some cases, their construction betrays severe organizational difficulties, whilst in other cases the approach is demonstrably selective. Lambert of St Omer's *Liber Floridus*[13] (*c.* 1120), for example, though still firmly grounded in Carolingian tradition, appears to have failed in organizational terms. It can be inferred that Lambert's original intention to epitomize human knowledge by reference to both the historical-typological and the scientific-cosmological axes proved unworkable at an early stage in the process of compilation, notwithstanding the fact that the work is largely untouched by the new science of the twelfth century.[14] The slightly later encyclopaedias of the humanist William of Conches (*fl.* 1120–40), such as the *De Philosophia Mundi*[15] and the *De Substantiis Physicis*,[16] look more coherent; on the other hand, they reveal a clear predilection for the new science, and do not aspire to be encyclopaedic after the manner of Isidore of Seville, Rhabanus Maurus or Lambert of St Omer.

Rightly or wrongly, the twelfth century is still popularly associated with two superficially disparate tendencies: on the one hand, the intellectual renaissance, with its major 'scientific' component; on the other hand, the literary reception of the Arthurian complex of legends (known as the *matière de Bretagne*), coinciding with and possibly stimulating a modification of traditional moral schemes. It might easily be assumed that the two tendencies differ so strongly in their origins and content that any points of contact are purely accidental. (Both the intellectual renaissance and the diffusion of the Arthurian tales pose a challenge to conservative orthodoxy, for example, with the result that a heavy Christian veneer is applied to certain cosmological epics and courtly romances from the late twelfth century on.) This is far from being the case, however. The lack of historical credibility attaching to the *matière de Bretagne* had exposed the Arthurian legends to the charge of 'beautiful, but dangerously misleading lies' from clerical circles.[17] These accusations appear, moreover, to have hit the mark, if the number of source-references and assertions of veracity occurring in some romances provides anything like a reliable guide.[18] One solution was discovered through the adaptation of moral and psychological allegory: the knight's quest thereby signifying man's *peregrinatio* through the world, his opponents various vices and virtues, and so forth.[19] An arguably more ingenious method of verification involved linking the genre of the cosmological epic to that of the romance. Geoffrey of Monmouth experiments along just these lines in the *Vita Merlini*[20] (*c.* 1150). Whether this poem exercised any influence outside Geoffrey's own circle must remain a matter for speculation,[21] although the Latin writer anticipates Chrétien de Troyes in some important respects. Geoffrey intercalates material characteristic of the cosmological epic into the Other World traditions of the *matière de Bretagne*. The poem comprises a loosely organized collection of tales relating to the wild man and prophet Merlin, who withdraws into the forest and, after several unsuccessful attempts to rehabilitate him into society, is finally cured of his madness. While he is living in the forest, Merlin is joined by other, equally clairvoyant wild men, one of whom, Telgesinus (or Talieisin), instructs the hero in cosmology, geography and meteorology. Telgesinus' fulsome account of the creation, the world and its climates, its fishes and its islands, ends with a reference to the island of Avalon, and an account of how the wounded Arthur was transferred there.[22] Telgesinus' reference to Avalon elicits from Merlin a hardly less circumstantial account of the events leading up to Arthur's last battle.[23] Analysed in terms of genres, Merlin's speech points as it were backwards to Geoffrey's earlier work, the *Historia Regum Britanniae*[24] (*c.* 1136). In the latter, Geoffrey had boldly accommodated the Arthurian material in the tradition of the chronicle, synchronizing British history with the events of the Old and New Testament as well as with Graeco-Roman history[25] – thus elaborately but deftly shoring up the fresh but potentially suspect *matière de Bretagne*. This solution to the problem of verification is incorporated in a modified form in Merlin's speech, which exploits the style of the chronicle and, no doubt, the popularity then being enjoyed by the *Historia*. Geoffrey does not content himself with an extended reference to his earlier work, however. The speech of Telgesinus looks across, so to speak, to the encyclopaedic-didactic mode of the cosmological epic, which in the middle of the twelfth century exerted considerable influence in literary quarters. Specifically, the catalogues dealing with aspects of natural history in the *Vita Merlini* recall the first part (*Megacosmos*) of Bernard Silvester's *Cosmographia*,[26] with its survey of the newly created world. It is hardly fortuitous that Merlin's speech takes over from Telgesinus' when it does, the effect being to make the Arthurian story the pivot of cosmology and history alike. Nor is it fortuitous that the Arthurian reference is preceded by a highly derivative[27] account of the creation and the created world: the authority granted to the former is intended to buttress the latter. Geoffrey's organization even suggests that the created world culminates in the paradisal island of Avalon, much as in Bernard's *Cosmographia* the creation of the macrocosm looks forward to the creation of man the microcosm in the paradisal setting of Granusion.[28] At a slightly later point in the narrative of the *Vita*, Geoffrey contrives to insinuate another point of contact between the 'Celtic' and the 'Latin' traditions. After Merlin has uttered his Arthurian prophecy, he drinks of a stream that restores his sanity;[29] whereupon he lauds the Creator in Boethian language,[30] and then provides the cue for another extended exposition on Telgesinus' part by an inquiry about the curative properties of the stream.[31] Telgesinus obliges with an encyclopaedic survey of miraculous springs,[32] whilst the sight of a long flight of cranes causes Merlin himself to launch an ornithological exposition soon afterwards.[33] In redirecting Merlin's expositions into the 'Latin' tradition associated with the cosmological epic and the encyclopaedia, Geoffrey turns the relative literary innocence of the Celtic material to immediate poetic advantage, and suggests the potential coherence of the two traditions in broader terms. At the same time, he outflanks the accusations relating to the veracity of the Arthurian material. It is noteworthy that Geoffrey assigns the exposition of the didactic material not to the standard allegorical goddesses, such as Natura and Philosophia, but to the Celtic wild men who partake of the vision of the cosmos when in a trance-like state.

Geoffrey's *Vita Merlini* thus anticipates the fully fledged vernacular Arthurian romances of the later twelfth century, even though it could not be termed an Arthurian romance in anything more than a partial or embryonic sense. It also anticipates certain developments within the genre of the philosophical epic itself, especially the tendency to turn towards terrestrial locations and themes. This process may be observed in Jean of Hanville's *Architrenius*[34] (*c.* 1184), a poem that also reworks Arthurian material for the purposes of the Latin tradition.[35] Jean's poem also embodies a very particular kind of *peregrinatio* as its theme and structural basis. At about the same time, Walter of Chatillon slants the legends of Alexander towards the genre of the philosophical epic in his *Alexandreis*.[36] It is against this background that Chrétien de Troyes recharts the course of the Arthurian hero in his *Erec et Enide*.[37] Such dramatic motifs as assemblies of deities and cosmic voyages had already been borrowed from Martianus' *De Nuptiis* by Chrétien's Latin contemporaries, who recast them to provide the epic backcloth for an allegorical representation of the manner in which man may be created (or recreated) in the image of God (cf. Genesis 1.26).[38] The motif of the apotheosis (for this is the destiny of Philologia in Martianus' late classical work)[39] is thus partially sacramentalized, but only to the extent that the integumental mould of the philosophical epic permits. In the light of this development, Chrétien perceives that the stereotyped and hitherto frequently trivialized romance motifs of, first, assemblies of knights and kings and, secondly, voyages to exotic lands need not be left to founder on this level. Instead, they may be reframed to invoke their formal counterparts in the philosophical epic. Hence the numinous authority now invested by Chrétien in the courtly assembly suffices for the latter to pass a more absolute form of judgement upon the erring knight. When the latter has been banished from the court that he may renew himself, the process of redefinition will entail far more than the elimination of a purely social stigma. The wayward knight's profound disorientation in the early stages of his quest encapsulates man's disorientation in a cosmological or theological dimension. An allusion to the opening scene in Boethius' *De Consolatione Philosophiae*,[40] for example, or Alain of Lille's *De Planctu Naturae*[41] is facilitated by the vagueness of the historical or geographical location, precisely that aspect which had rendered the Arthurian material vulnerable to clerical censure in the first place. The knight's adventures in one sense externalize the inward, psychomachian[42] struggle he must wage with and within himself; in another sense, they acquire a suprapersonal, even a trans-mundane aspect.[43] His non-courtly opponents, in particular grotesque dwarfs and giants, still betray their origins in Celtic legend, and may occasionally be exploited as figures of fun; but at some ill-defined point they blend with the incorporations of the malign 'powers of the air' and the lesser demons of neo-platonic cosmology.[44] Finally, the restoration of the persevering knight to courtly favour will signal the restoration of the image of God, a particular kind of apotheosis, as the 'new man' emerges.[45] The status of the court that readmits the 'new man' is appreciably enhanced by the analogy with a version of the neo-platonic microcosm, now that it has been transformed from a fallible institution of human making into the source of a system of values and, no less, the aspiration of all who would realize those values.

II

The closing scene in Chrétien's *Erec et Enide* describes at great length the festivities that accompany the coronation of the hero and heroine. An important part in the evocation of the courtly splendour is played by a series of *ecphraseis* devoted to the thrones of Arthur and Erec, Erec's coronation robe, the crowns of the two kings, and the sceptre presented to Erec by Arthur.[46] The *ecphrasis* of Erec's coronation robe manifests an explicit and circumstantial 'cosmological' slant, as does (to a lesser degree perhaps) the account of the sceptre. Chrétien's narrator claims that he derives his description of the coronation robe from the late classical *auctor* Macrobius (*c.* 400), whose commentary on Cicero's *Somnium Scipionis* was a standard textbook in the Middle Ages.[47] Macrobius, the narrator claims, has taught him how to describe the coronation robe:

> Lisant trovomes an l'estoire
> La description de la robe,
> Si an trai a garant Macrobe
> Qui au descrire mist s'antante,
> Que l'an ne die que je mante.
> Macrobes m'ansaingne a descrivre,
> Si con je l'ai trové el livre,
> L'uevre del drap et le portret.   (ll. 6736–43)

As we read in the story, we find the description of the robe, and, in order that no one may say that I lie, I quote as my authority Macrobius, who devoted himself to the description of it. Macrobius instructs me how to describe, according as I have found it in the book, the workmanship and the figures of the cloth.[48]

On the robe, the four sciences of the *quadrivium*, geometry, arithmetic, music and astronomy, had allegedly been represented by four fairies.[49] The fur lining inside the robe is reported to come from some strange multi-coloured beasts living in India and known as *barbioletes*:

> La pane qui i fu cosue
> Fu d'unes contrefeites bestes,
> Qui ont totes blanches les testes
> Et les cos noirs com une more,
> Les dos ont toz vermauz dessore,
> Les vantres vers, et la coe inde.
> Iteus bestes neissent an Inde,
> Si ont barbioletes non;
> Ne manjuent s'especes non,
> Quenele et girofle novel.   (ll. 6794–803)

The fur lining that was sewed within, belonged to some strange beasts whose heads are all white, and whose necks are as black as mulberries, and which have red backs and green bellies, and a dark blue tail. These beasts live in India and they are called 'barbiolets'. They eat nothing but spices, cinnamon, and fresh cloves.

Two questions are prompted by the *ecphrasis* of Erec's coronation robe. First, does it have a more precise meaning than that of a conventionalized panegyric?[50] Secondly, despite the appeal to a late classical *auctor*, does it rather derive from the conjunction of scientific exposition with poetic myth that characterizes the philosophical epics of Chrétien's Latin contemporaries?

The detailed nature of Chrétien's *ecphrasis*, and the emphatic character of his source-reference, do not betoken scientific precision in the modern sense. On the contrary: both the appeal to Macrobius and the reference to the *barbioletes* demonstrably fail to meet such standards. As yet, no wholly satisfactory explanation has been advanced to account for the *barbioletes*. The somewhat bizarre colour scheme, involving white, black, red, green and blue, points to Celtic descriptions of the Other World, particularly in the context of an Arthurian romance.[51] Possibly, Chrétien has slanted his Celtic material towards the expository style of the encyclopaedias, and especially the bestiaries. Geoffrey of Monmouth's account of the 'Arthurian' island of Avalon in the *Vita Merlini* similarly depends for its credibility on the encyclopaedic context, as was indicated above. One important source for the more exotic material in the encyclopaedias and bestiaries is the complex of legends relating to Alexander, with their long accounts of fabulous peoples and strange creatures.[52] Chrétien's assertion that the *barbioletes* live solely on exotic spices points beyond India towards the earthly paradise itself, which Alexander was widely believed to have attempted to storm.[53] Moreover, Alexander had reportedly spent some time inspecting the marvels of India, the land of origin of Chrétien's beasts. It must be asked whether Chrétien is deflecting our attention from his Celtic sources by channelling the still inadequately authorized material into the tradition of Alexander and that of the earlier *romans d'antiquité* (which had taken as their subject-matter the historically verified legends of Aeneas, Troy, Thebes, and so forth). In an earlier *ecphrasis*, portraying the marvellous horse which the sisters of Guivret had presented to Enide, Chrétien had likewise linked an exotic multi-coloured animal with classical tradition as represented by Aeneas – or, more exactly, Eneas as presented in the *romans d'antiquité*.[54] Furthermore, the narrator had claimed a few lines earlier that Arthur's generosity at the coronation festival outstrips the *liberalitas* of Alexander.[55]

Nor is Alexander the only point of reference (and means of validation). The thrones on which Erec and Arthur are seated echo parts of the temple of Solomon. They are made

D'ivoire blanc, bien fez et nués   (l. 6714)

of white ivory, well constructed and new

Furthermore,

> N'i avoit nule rien de fust
> Se d'or non ou d'ivoire fin   (ll. 6724–5)

There was no part of wood, but all of gold and fine ivory.[56]

Solomon was associated in the Middle Ages not only with wise kingship, but, following Jewish speculation, a whole series of exotic legends. The concatenation of Erec and Arthur, Alexander and Solomon furnishes the basis not only for a historical legitimization of the former, following the pattern of synchronization attempted in Geoffrey's *Historia*, but even a quasi-typological relationship between the biblical and modern kings expressed, for example, in terms of a *translatio imperii*.[57] In addition, the stories of Alexander and Solomon cast fresh light upon what happens to Erec. All three come to grief through an outstanding vice: in the case of Erec and Solomon, the vice in question is lust, with the difference that Erec is able to overcome his uxoriousness and advance to higher wisdom, whereas Solomon's career moves in the reverse direction.[58] Alexander's pride and immoderation had induced him to endeavour to conquer the earthly paradise, whereas Erec is able to overcome the pseudo-paradise of his own creation, recapitulated in the adventure of the Joy of the Court,[59] so winning through to true wisdom.

The redirection of Celtic myth towards classical tradition argued above also has a bearing upon Chrétien's reference to Macrobius and the claim that the coronation robe had been made by four fairies. Each of the fairies, it will be recalled, is alleged to have woven the representation of one of the four sciences of the *quadrivium*. The reference to Macrobius might be termed misleading in so far as the late classical commentator nowhere offers an *ecphrasis*. However, he does deal with the neo-platonic hierarchy of creation, and makes reference to powers higher than man in the cosmos.[60] To this extent, there exists a slender justification for Chrétien's reference to the fairies. Secondly, and more significantly, Macrobius expounds the four sciences of the *quadrivium* in some detail. In a far-reaching study on the origins of the Arthurian romance, Claude Luttrell has argued Chrétien's dependence upon the *ecphraseis* of the allegorical goddesses who represent the four sciences of the *quadrivium* in Alain's *Anticlaudianus*.[61] In Luttrell's view, the reference to Macrobius is intended as a smoke-screen to conceal Chrétien's true source, namely, the *Anticlaudianus*, the structure of which provides the key to the organization of the adventures in the Old French poem.[62] As Luttrell points out, the late classical writer who affords a series of *ecphraseis* of the personified sciences is not Macrobius, but Martianus Capella.[63] Martianus introduces each of the seven liberal arts by means of an *ecphrasis* of the respective deity in the encyclopaedic section of his work (*De Nuptiis*, Books III to IX), although *ecphraseis* are by no means lacking in the dramatic part of the work (Books I to II).[64]

The possibility that Chrétien made a slip, referring to Macrobius when he meant Martianus, or that the lines in question were distorted by a scribal error at a very early stage in the transmission of the poem, cannot be disproved absolutely. Both writers were, after all, widely studied and commented on in the medieval schools; and both display a bias towards the *quadrivium*. To analyse Chrétien's debt to Martianus, Macrobius or Alain as if the three Latin writers constituted mutually exclusive sources would, however, be tantamount to reducing medieval source-references to the level of philological footnotes. Even when they turn out to be accurate by modern scientific standards, medieval source-references tend to signal less a precise borrowing than broad guidelines of interpretation. In many cases, no clear distinction is observed between *auctor* and commentary, so that the Bible is identified with Augustine, Plato with Chalcidius, Cicero with Macrobius.[65] In this instance, the reference to Macrobius probably subsumes the *Somnium Scipionis* itself. In Cicero's work, the statesman and general Scipio at once concludes and transcends his earthly career with a vision of the cosmos. In donning the coronation robe, Erec aspires beyond his own career to the divine source of true kingship, and is gently reminded that the king properly derives the reasons of terrestrial governance from their transcendental archetypes. This is the lesson that Erec had earlier ignored, preferring a woman to the tasks of kingship, and coming dangerously close to following Solomon into perdition.

Given the relative imprecision of medieval source-references, how is the modern critic to guard against arbitrary interpretations? How is one to arrange the various authorities who may be conjured up by a single such reference into some kind of coherent order that approximates to the medieval view of the tradition in question? The answer again lies with Macrobius. His commentary on the *Somnium Scipionis* furnishes the Middle Ages with a virtually classic definition of myth and the various categories into which it may be divided.[66] As regards fables about the gods, Macrobius explains, the philosopher is often ill-advised to interpret these stories literally: the Ancients perceived that certain 'higher' matters, such as knowledge about the transcendental powers and the human soul, should not be divulged to the common people, and accordingly wrapped up these mysteries in appropriate coverings.[67] Macrobius thus lays the foundation for the medieval doctrine of the 'integument' (*integumentum* or *involucrum*).[68] In claiming that it was Macrobius who instructed him in the description of Erec's robe, Chrétien's narrator is therefore not loosely associating his own, partly poetic depiction with Macrobius' much more 'scientific' exposition of the *quadrivium*. As we have seen, other authorities, notably Martianus (and possibly Alain), would have served this purpose as well if not better. More specifically, Chrétien insinuates a particular approach to his romance: it must be treated with the same respect that the mythographer would show towards a classical myth. One should, that is to say, beware of a literalistic reading, and not expect the work to yield its deepest meaning immediately. This theoretical vindication of a quasi-classical interpretation of the poem is particularized – but, by definition, not overstated – through the allusions to Alexander. Furthermore, the image of the integument gains additional, but still discreet support from its position in the narrative. Erec is at this stage about to don the coronation-robe, that is, to wrap (cf. *involvere*!) himself in the mantle of regal-philosophical authority.

One major function of the reference to Macrobius is therefore to direct the audience's attention to a tradition of cosmological poetry. Indeed, so insistent is the reference that the narrator effectively reinterprets Macrobius while adducing him as an authority, the very process of reinterpretation underlining Chrétien's conviction that the Arthurian romance itself stands in need of reinterpretation. Where are we to turn for a more telling parallel of situation and literary construction that will vindicate Chrétien's presentation? An answer is implied by the last of the four *ecphraseis*, which is devoted to Erec's sceptre:

> Qui fu plus clers d'une verrine,
> Toz d'une esmeraude anterine,
> Et s'avoit bien plain poing de gros.
> Par verité dire vos os
> Qu'an tot le monde n'a maniere
> De peisson ne de beste fiere
> Ne d'ome ne d'oisel volage,
> Que chascuns lonc sa propre image
> N'i fust ovrez et antailliez.   (ll. 6873–81)

which was clearer than a pane of glass, all of one solid emerald, fully as large as your fist. I dare to tell you in very truth that in all the world there is no manner of fish, or of wild beast, or of man, or of flying bird that was not worked and chiselled upon it with its proper figure.[69]

It would be easy to dismiss the above as yet another reformulation of the totality *topos* that forms an almost indispensable component of the full-scale *ecphrasis*,[70] or as the final part of a protracted, if at times implicit panegyric contrived in Erec's honour through a series of interlocking descriptions. The *ecphrasis* does indeed occupy an important position in a number of late classical panegyrics which extol the recipient in mythological categories, by placing him in the company of the gods, for instance, or by prophesying his apotheosis.[71]

Martianus' *De Nuptiis* shares several features with the standardized panegyric of the Second Sophistic, including rhetorical descriptions and particular dramatic motifs such as assemblies of gods; but it deploys an intricate set of allegorical devices rarely met with in the panegyric. The climax of Book I of Martianus' work coincides with the convocation of the divine assembly where the deities are asked to approve the proposed marriage of Mercury and Philology. First Jupiter, then Juno dons regal attire.[72] In what was to become standard rhetorical fashion, Jupiter's accoutrements are described from top to toe. He sits on a multi-coloured garment woven from peacocks' feathers,[73] recalling Erec's fabulous coronation robe in the Old French romance. Juno is then described in similar terms, though in such a manner as to indicate her inferiority to her husband and brother.[74] Before the royal thrones there is set a heavenly sphere, compacted from all the elements and depicting everything contained in the universe. This sphere, which appears as the *imago...ideaque mundi*, signifies Jupiter's dominance over all creation.[75] The situation is recapitulated at the end of Book II, when the gods gather to witness the marriage of Mercury and Philology after the latter has undergone her apotheosis.[76]

At the end of Chrétien's romance, those kings and knights who owe allegiance to Arthur formally assemble to witness the coronation of Erec and Enide. At a deeper level, however, they also sponsor the reconsecration of a marriage which had been gravely impaired by the one-sided nature of the couple's love for one another. Their affections had to be purified through a particularly testing set of adventures before a more balanced relationship could emerge. The proper subordination of the female to the male principle, unmistakably adumbrated in Martianus' evocation of Juno alongside but slightly below Jupiter, represents the restoration of the cosmic harmony[77] upon which the smooth functioning of the universe hinges. Chrétien's description of the sceptre presented to Erec harmoniously subsumes the various facets of created life (corresponding to the four elements), his sovereignty deriving from the mastery he has established over himself and his spouse; in its own way, it will prove as benign and yet as authoritative as Jupiter's rule, to whom the microcosmic Orphic egg is subordinated in Martianus' work. The catharsis which Enide no less than Erec has experienced proves to be as profound, albeit not as melodramatic as Philology's;[78] but Erec's triumph surpasses that of Martianus' couple to the extent that the Arthurian hero not merely submits to judgement, but himself advances to the throne of judgement (like Solomon). He is deemed worthy to rule alongside Arthur, their equal status signified by the identity of the two thrones on which they sit side-by-side. This affords an illuminating contrast with the hierarchic arrangement of the two thrones in the *De Nuptiis*. Enide too may now advance to the final stage of her earthly career as represented by the divinely sanctioned co-regency. Her career, like Juno's, must nonetheless remain subordinated to that of her husband, however closely she may popularly be associated with him at the moment of triumph, and however closely her sufferings had earlier been interwoven with his. The allusion to the paradisal harmony of the newly created world, in the context of the description of Erec's sceptre, underscores the restoration of the paradisal relationship between man created in the image of God and woman created from the rib of man, and subsumes the allusion to the male and female principles represented by Jupiter (fire/ether) and Juno (air) in Martianus' work. In this way, Chrétien verifies his poetic representation in sacramental as well as mythographic terms, and vindicates the claim of the Arthurian romance to full literary status.[79]

NOTES

1 Cf., however, the moderate position adopted by Aldous Huxley, *Literature and Science* (London, 1963), especially pp. 42–7 on the older tradition of 'scientific' poetry.

2 B. Sowinski, *Lehrhafte Dichtung des Mittelalters* (Stuttgart, 1971).

3 B. Stock, *Myth and Science in the Twelfth Century* (Princeton, 1972); and W. Wetherbee, *Platonism and Poetry in the Twelfth Century* (Princeton, 1972).

4 *Bernardi Silvestris De Mundi Universitate*, edited by C. S. Barach and J. Wrobel (Innsbruck, 1876), 1.3. The work has been translated into English by W. Wetherbee, *The 'Cosmographia' of Bernardus Silvestris* (New York and London, 1973).

5 Edited by R. Bossuat (Paris, 1955), II, l. 235ff; and translated by J. J. Sheridan (Toronto, 1973). Cf. J. J. Sheridan, 'The Seven Liberal Arts in Alan of Lille and Peter of Compostella', *Mediaeval Studies*, 35 (1973), 27–37.

6 Edited by A. Dick, with addenda by J. Préaux (Stuttgart, 1969), Books III to IX; and translated by W. H. Stahl, R. Johnson and E. L. Burge (New York, 1977). Cf.

W. H. Stahl, *et al.*, *Martianus Capella and the Seven Liberal Arts: Volume I, The Quadrivium of Martianus Capella* (New York and London, 1971); and F. LeMoine, *Martianus Capella: A Literary Re-evaluation* (Munich, 1972).

7 E. Faral, *Recherches sur les Sources Latines des Contes et Romans Courtois du Moyen Âge* (Paris, 1913), pp. 307–83; P. Friedländer, *Johannes von Gaza und Paulus Silentarius* (Leipzig and Berlin, 1912); H. J. Hock, *Die Schilderungen von Bildwerken in der deutschsprachigen Epik von 1100 bis 1250* (diss. Heidelberg, 1958); G. Kranz, *Das Bildgedicht in Europa* (Paderborn, 1973); G. Kurman, 'Ecphrasis in Epic Poetry', *Comparative Literature*, 26 (1974), 1–13; and O. Söhring, 'Werke bildender Künste in altfranzösischen Epen', *Romanische Forschungen*, 12 (1900), 491–640.

8 The *Liber Floridus*, for example; facsimile edition by A. Derolez (Gent, 1968).

9 On the background to this work, cf. H. J. Mähl, *Die Idee des goldenen Zeitalters im Werk des Novalis* (Heidelberg, 1965).

10 Thus Adelard of Bath's *De Eodem et Diverso*, edited by H. Willner (Münster, 1903); Peter of Compostella's *De Consolatione Rationis*, edited by P. B. Soto (Münster, 1912); Godfrey of St. Victor's *Fons Philosophiae*, edited by P. Michaud-Quantin (Namur, Louvain and Lille, 1956), and translated by E. A. Synan (Toronto, 1972); and Alain of Lille's *De Planctu Naturae*, cf. n. 41 below.

11 R. A. Wisbey, 'Wunder des Ostens in der *Wiener Genesis* und in Wolframs *Parzival*', in *Studien zur frühmittelhochdeutschen Literatur*, edited by L. P. Johnson, *et al.* (Berlin, 1974), pp. 180–214, especially pp. 180–90. This is a later version of Wisbey, 'Marvels of the East in the *Wiener Genesis* and Wolfram's *Parzifal*', in *Essays in German and Dutch Literature*, edited by W. D. Robson-Scott (Publications of the Institute of Germanic Studies, 15) (London, 1973), pp. 1–41.

12 Thus Saturn prefigures man's future sufferings typologically, II.5, ll. 64–6 (Barach and Wrobel, p. 42).

13 Cf. n. 8 above. See further Y. Lefèvre, 'Le *Liber Floridus* et la littérature encyclopédique au moyen âge', in *Liber Floridus Colloquium*, edited by A. Derolez (Gent, 1973), pp. 1–9.

14 On the principles underlying the arrangement of medieval encyclopaedias, cf. S. Viarre, 'Le commentaire ordonné du monde dans quelques sommes scientifiques des XIIe et XIIIe siècles', in *Classical Influences on European Culture*, edited by R. R. Bolgar (Cambridge, 1971), pp. 203–15. See further the articles by M. de Gandillac and others in *La Pensée Encyclopédique au Moyen Âge* (Neuchâtel, 1966).

15 Edited in J.-P. Migne's *Patrologia Latina*, CLXXII, cols. 39–102A (where, however, the work is wrongly attributed to Honorius of Autun).

16 Edited by W. Gratarolus (Strassburg, 1567).

17 On this problem, cf. E. Köhler, 'Zur Selbstauffassung des höfischen Dichters', in *Der Vergleich...Festschrift f. H. Petriconi zum 1. April 1955* (Hamburg, 1955), pp. 65–79; and Köhler, *Ideal und Wirklichkeit in der höfischen Epik* (2nd edn, Tübingen, 1970), pp. 37–65.

18 U. Pörksen, *Der Erzähler im mittelhochdeutschen Epos* (Berlin, 1971), pp. 60–83.

19 Cf. n. 42 below.

20 *Life of Merlin*, edited and translated by B. Clarke (Cardiff, 1973).

21 Cf. Clarke, *Life of Merlin*, pp. 43–5; M. Manitius, *Geschichte der lateinischen Literatur des Mittelalters*, 3 vols. (Munich, 1911–31), III, 479–81, especially p. 481;

and R. S. Loomis, in *Arthurian Literature in the Middle Ages*, edited by R. S. Loomis (Oxford, 1959), pp. 89–93, especially p. 93.

22 ll. 737–940, especially ll. 906–40.

23 ll. 958–1135, especially ll. 1107–35.

24 Edited by A. Griscom (London, 1929); and translated by L. Thorpe (Harmondsworth, 1966).

25 See the 'Time Chart' in Thorpe's translation, pp. 285–8.

26 1.3: stars and constellations, planets, mountains, animals, rivers, springs, gardens, spices and plants, sea-creatures and birds.

27 Clarke, *Life of Merlin*, pp. 7–11, cf. p. 144ff, notes Geoffrey's dependence on Isidore and Bede. Bernard Silvester is also dependent on Isidore (as well as Pliny and Odo of Meung): see Wetherbee, '*Cosmographia*', pp. 149–52. C. S. Lewis, *The Discarded Image* (Cambridge, 1964), pp. 198ff, inquiries into the reasons behind such catalogues.

28 II.9–14. Cf. Stock, *Myth and Science*, pp. 187–226.

29 ll. 1136–53.

30 ll. 1156–75, especially ll. 1156–60. Cf. such Boethian stanzas as *De Consolatione Philosophiae* I, m. v (*O stelliferi conditor orbis...*), or III, m. IX (*O qui perpetua mundum ratione gubernas...*), edited by L. Bieler (Turnhout, 1957).

31 ll. 1176–8.

32 ll. 1179–242. Cf. Bernard's *Cosmographia*, 1.3, ll. 233–64 (Barach and Wrobel, pp. 22–3).

33 ll. 1292–386. Cf. Bernard's *Cosmographia*, 1.3, ll. 441–80 (Barach and Wrobel, pp. 28–9); although Clarke, *Life of Merlin*, p. 151, identifies Isidore, *Etymologiae*, XII. 7 as Geoffrey's main source.

34 Edited by P. G. Schmidt (Munich, 1974).

35 V.17, VI.1; cf. also Schmidt's discussion of Jean's utilization of Geoffrey's *Historia*, pp. 76–7.

36 *Patrologia Latina*, CCIX, cols. 463A–572D. See especially Book X, cols. 563Aff. Cf. H. Christensen, *Das Alexanderlied Walters von Chatillon* (Halle, 1905); and G. Cary, *The Medieval Alexander* (Cambridge, 1956), pp. 63–4, 173–4, 191–5, and *passim*.

37 Edited by W. Foerster (Halle, 1896). Cf. Wetherbee, *Platonism and Poetry*, pp. 220–41; and C. Luttrell, *The Creation of the First Arthurian Romance* (London, 1974), especially pp. 1–65.

38 Thus Alain's *Anticlaudianus* opens its action with a convocation of the virtues at Nature's behest (Books I to II), who construct a chariot that conveys their petition for the creation of a new man to God (Books IV to VI). On the heavenly journey in Bernard's *Cosmographia*, cf. Stock, *Myth and Science*, pp. 163–87.

39 II.140ff (Dick, pp. 60–1).

40 The narrator's disorientation is expressed through light-metaphors, for example, Book I, m. II, pr. II.6, m. III, pr. III.1.

41 The narrator's disorientation is expressed through the *topos* of 'Nature turned upside down', for example, *Metrum primum*, in *The Anglo-Latin Satirical Poets and Epigrammatists of the Twelfth Century*, edited by T. Wright, 2 vols. (London, 1872, reprinted Wiesbaden, 1964), pp. 429–31 (= *Patrologia Latina*, CCX, cols. 431A–432A).

42 Of considerable importance for the literary reception of Prudentius' *Psychomachia*

in the later Middle Ages is Alain, *Anticlaudianus*, VIII.160–IX.390, cf. Luttrell, *First Arthurian Romance*, pp. 72–9. See further C. S. Lewis, *The Allegory of Love* (Oxford, 1936), pp. 66–73, and *passim*; and H. R. Jauss, 'Form und Auffassung der Allegorie in der Tradition der *Psychomachia*', in *Medium Aevum Vivum: Festschrift für W. Bulst*, edited by H. R. Jauss and D. Schaller (Heidelberg, 1960), pp. 179–206.

43 Cf. J. Stevens, *Medieval Romance* (London, 1973), pp. 119–41; and E. Vinaver, *The Rise of Romance* (Oxford, 1971), pp. 15–32. J. B. Allen, *The Friar As Critic* (Nashville, 1971), studies the interaction of biblical with mythographic exegesis especially in the later Middle Ages. For a rather different approach, however, see P. Haidu, *Lion-Queue-Coupée* (Geneva, 1972).

44 Cf. such biblical passages as Ephesians 6.12, *Biblia Sacra juxta Vulgatam Clementinam* (Rome, Tournai, and Paris, 1956). See Lewis, *Discarded Image*, pp. 2–5, and especially pp. 40–4 (on Apuleius, *De Deo Socratis*). Much relevant material is collected by Wisbey, 'Wunder des Ostens'.

45 Cf. Luttrell, *First Arthurian Romance*, pp. 76–7.

46 ll. 6713–32 (thrones), 6736–809 (coronation robe), 6836–53 (crowns), and 6870–81 (sceptre).

47 Edited by J. Willis (Leipzig, 1970); cf. Lewis, *Discarded Image*, pp. 60–9. On this scene, and especially the reference to Macrobius, see S. Hofer, 'Kristian und Macrobius', *Zeitschrift für romanische Philologie*, 48 (1928), 130–1; and T. Artin, *The Allegory of Adventure* (Lewisburg and London, 1974), pp. 133–40.

48 The translations are taken from *Chrétien de Troyes: Arthurian Romances*, translated by W. W. Comfort (London, 1914, reprinted London, 1975), pp. 87–9; p. 87.

49 ll. 6744–93. Cf. R. R. Bezzola, *Le Sens de l'Aventure et de l'Amour* (Paris, 1947, reprinted Paris, 1968), pp. 235, 237ff, who argues that the *vita activa* represented by Erec's adventures is here complemented by the *vita contemplativa*, the *ecphrasis* signalling the hero's attainment of the full measure of wisdom. Wisbey, 'Wunder des Ostens', deals with orthodox and apocryphal legends relating to the origins of such spirits as those mentioned here, including the children of Cain, who were reputed to be learned in magic and the forbidden arts; cf. also Faral, *Sources*, pp. 345–6, 347. The lore of demons is treated in partly poetic form in several cosmological epics, such as Martianus, *De Nuptiis*, II.150–67, especially 167 (Pans, Fauns, etc.); Bernard, *Cosmographia*, II.7, especially ll. 111–14 (Silvani, etc.); and Alain, *Anticlaudianus*, IV.271–331.

50 F. Bittner, *Studien zum Herrscherlob in der mittellateinischen Dichtung* (diss., Würzburg, 1962); and A. Georgi, *Das lateinische und deutsche Preisgedicht des Mittelalters* (Berlin, 1969).

51 The rich diversity of colours in Celtic descriptions of the Other World clearly emerges from H. R. Patch, *The Other World* (Cambridge, Mass., 1950), pp. 27–59. See in particular 'The Dream of Rhonabwy', in *The Mabinogion*, translated by G. Jones and T. Jones (London and New York, 1949), pp. 137–52.

52 J. Brummach, *Die Darstellung des Orients: in den deutschen Alexandergeschichten des Mittelalters* (Berlin, 1966), pp. 115–48; H. Gregor, *Das Indienbild des Abendlandes* (diss., Vienna, 1964), pp. 47–53; D. J. A. Ross, *Illustrated Medieval Alexander Books in Germany and the Netherlands* (Cambridge, 1971), figs. 390–405, and *passim*; H. Szklenar, *Studien zum Bild des Orients in vorhöfischen deutschen Epen* (Göttingen, 1966), pp. 92–110, 164–9, and *passim*; Wisbey, 'Wunder des Ostens', pp. 202–4;

and R. Wittkower, 'Marvels of the East: a study in the history of monsters', *Journal of the Warburg and Courtauld Institutes*, 5 (1942), 159–97.

53 Cf. Gregor, *Indienbild*, pp. 70–6; Cary, *Medieval Alexander*, pp. 19–21, and *passim*; Ross, *Medieval Alexander Books*, *passim*; and Szklenar, *Bild des Orients*, pp. 81–5. When Phronesis dresses her daughter Philologia in bridal attire in Martianus' *De Nuptiis*, her dress is said to be made of 'illa herbarum felicium lana, qua indusiari perhibent Indicae prudentiae uates accolasque montis umbrati' (II.114 (Dick, p. 48); Stahl translates: 'that fleece from the precious shrub in which, they say, the sages of India and the inhabitants of the mountain of shadow are clothed', p. 39). The complex India/paradise–herbs–wisdom is thus underpinned by a late classical *auctor*.

54 ll. 5316–53, especially ll. 5338–46 for the story of Aeneas. See J. S. Wittig, 'The Aeneas-Dido allusion in Chrétien's *Erec et Enide*', *Comparative Literature*, 22 (1970), 237–53.

55 Cf. Cary, *Medieval Alexander*, pp. 85–91, 154–5, and *passim*, for the background to ll. 6673–6, 6683–5.

56 Cf. III Kings 6, especially 6.18 and 6.22. See further L. Ginzberg, *The Legends of the Jews*, 7 vols. (Philadelphia, 1913–38), IV, 157–60; and F. Ohly, 'Hölzer, die nicht brennen', *Zeitschrift für deutsches Altertum*, 100 (1971), 63–72.

57 The *locus classicus* is Daniel 7 as interpreted above all by Jerome; cf. E. Marsch, *Biblische Prophetie und chronographische Dichtung* (Berlin, 1972). The extent to which the typological schemes that inform medieval historiography (and scriptural exegesis) may recur in secular romances remains controversial. Basically, the establishment of a typological scheme hinges upon the interpreter's ability to elaborate either an intensification ('gradualistic' typology) or a contrast ('antithetical' typology) between two episodes from different ages of Christian *Heilsgeschichte*. In so far as it may legitimately be dubbed 'typological', the relationship between Solomon and Erec would have to be assigned to the 'antithetical' category. On this question, see such essays as 'Synagoge und Ecclesia. Typologisches in mittelalterlicher Dichtung', in *F. Ohly: Schriften zur mittelalterlichen Bedeutungsforschung* (Darmstadt, 1977), pp. 312–37.

58 Cf. III Kings 11; and Ginzberg, *Legends*, VI, 282–3, and *passim*. On Solomon's skill in astrology and magic generally, see Ginzberg, *Legends*, IV, 150, 175, 176; VI, 282, 283, and *passim*. Alexander too was frequently charged with lechery, cf. Cary, *Medieval Alexander*, pp. 99–100, 218–20.

59 l. 5367ff.

60 See, for example, I.11.5–7 (Willis, p. 46) on the location of souls undergoing materialization. For the reception of Macrobius in the twelfth century, especially by William of Conches, cf. P. Dronke, *Fabula* (Leiden and Cologne, 1974), pp. 13–78; and Dronke, 'Eine Theorie über *fabula* und *imago* im 12. Jahrhundert', in *Verbum et Signum*, edited by H. Fromm, *et al.*, 2 vols. (Munich, 1975), II, 161–76.

61 *First Arthurian Romance*, pp. 20–5.

62 *First Arthurian Romance*, pp. 21ff, 66–79.

63 *First Arthurian Romance*, p. 21.

64 Apart from the *ecphraseis* of Jupiter (1.66), Juno (1.67), and the cosmic sphere (1.68), discussed in the text below, see, for example, the account of how Phronesis decks Philologia in her bridal garments (II.114–15).

65 Cf. H. de Lubac, *Exégèse Médiévale*, 4 vols. in 2 (Paris, 1959–64), I, 119–38. On the implications of this attitude for the courtly romance, see Vinaver, *Rise of Romance*, p. 15ff; and C. Lofmark, 'Der höfische Dichter als Übersetzer', in *Probleme mittelhochdeutscher Erzählformen*, edited by P. F. Ganz and W. Schröder (Berlin, 1972), pp. 40–62.

66 1.2.7–21 (Willis, pp. 5–8).

67 1.2.11, 17–18 (Willis, pp. 6, 7).

68 See, for example, H. Brinkmann, 'Verhüllung ("Integumentum") als literarische Darstellungsform im Mittelalter', in *Der Begriff der Repraesentatio im Mittelalter*, edited by A. Zimmermann (Berlin and New York, 1971), pp. 314–39; E. Jeauneau, 'L'usage de la notion d'*integumentum* à travers les gloses de Guillaume de Conches', reprinted in *E. Jeauneau: 'Lectio Philosophorum'* (Amsterdam, 1973), pp. 127–92; Stock, *Myth and Science*, pp. 48–62; and Wetherbee, *Platonism and Poetry*, pp. 36–48.

69 Comfort, *Chrétien de Troyes*, p. 89. Cf. Wetherbee, *Platonism and Poetry*, pp. 238–9.

70 This feature is noted by Hock, *Schilderungen von Bildwerken*; and Kurman, 'Ecphrasis'.

71 Cf. Georgi, *Preisgedicht*, pp. 32–40, on Sidonius Apollinaris' panegyric to Avitus, for example. *Ecphraseis* are to be found in the panegyrics composed by Claudian, edited and translated by M. Platnauer, 2 vols. (Cambridge, Mass. and London, 1963): see the description of Rome's shield in the *Panegyricus dictus Probino et Olybrio Consulibus*, ll. 94–9 (Platnauer, I, 8), or of Eridanus' urn in the panegyric in honour of Honorius' sixth consulship, ll. 167–77 (Platnauer, II, 86).

72 1.66–7 (Dick, pp. 30, 31).

73 1.66 (Dick, p. 31).

74 1.67 (Dick, p. 31): 'nisi quod ille immutabili laetitia renidebat, haec commutationum assiduarum nubilo crebrius turbidatur' (Stahl translates: 'except that he was aglow with an immutable happiness, while frequent changes often troubled her appearance', p. 25). This difference arises from the fact that Jupiter presides over, and signifies, the untroubled superlunary realm, whereas Juno represents the region of the air.

75 1.68 (Dick, pp. 32–3).

76 II.208ff (Dick, p. 77).

77 Cf. n. 74 above on the allegorical signification of Jupiter and Juno; and the statement of theme contained in the opening stanza of the *De Nuptiis*, I.1 (m.), ll. 9–12: 'namque elementa ligas uicibus mundumque maritas/atque auram mentis corporibus socias,/ foedere complacito sub quo natura iugatur,/ sexus concilians et sub amore fidem' (Dick, p. 3; Stahl translates: 'You cause the elements to interact reciprocally, you make the world fertile; through you, Mind is breathed into bodies by a union of concord which rules over Nature, as you bring harmony between the sexes and foster loyalty by love', p. 3). On this theme in other neo-platonic philosophers and poets, especially Boethius, cf. II. R. Patch, '*Consolatio Philosophiae*, IV, m. VI, 20–24', *Speculum*, 8 (1933), 41–51; P. Vossen, 'Über die Elementen-Syzygien', in *Liber Floridus. Mittellateinische Studien. Paul Lehmann zum 65. Geburtstag...gewidmet*, edited by B. Bischoff and S. Brechter (St Ottilien, 1950), pp. 33–46; and P. Dronke, 'L'amor che move il sole e l'altre stelle', *Studi Medievali*, 3rd series, 6 (1965), 389–422.

78 Philology is obliged to vomit the books of earthly knowledge, *De Nuptiis*, II.135ff (Dick, p. 59) before she can drink of the cup of immortality.

79 On the general question of scientific references in medieval literary texts, see further

S. N. Brody, *The Disease of the Soul: Leprosy in Medieval Literature* (Ithaca and London, 1974); W. G. Busse, *Courtly Love oder Paramours* (Düsseldorf, 1975); P. B. R. Doob, *Nebuchadnezzar's Children: Conventions of Madness in Middle English Literature* (New Haven and London, 1974); H.-H. Rausch, *Methoden und Bedeutung naturkundlicher Rezeption und Kompilation im 'Jüngeren Titurel'* (Frankfurt, Bern and Las Vegas, 1977); R. Tuve, *Seasons and Months* (Paris, 1933); S. Viarre, *La Survie d'Ovide dans la Littérature Scientifique des XIIe et XIIIe Siècles* (Poitiers, 1966); and W. Ziltener, *Studien zur bildungsgeschichtlichen Eigenart der höfischen Dichtung* (Bern, 1972).

Of diamonds and dunghills: Voltaire's defence of the French classical canon

A BICENTENNIAL ESSAY

DAVID WILLIAMS

On Saint Louis' Day in 1776, two years before Voltaire's death, a special event took place in the French Academy that was to create something of a stir in literary circles in Paris and London. The event in question was the public reading by the Perpetual Secretary of the Academy and Voltaire's friend, Jean le Rond d'Alembert, of an open letter[1] by Voltaire to the academicians on the subject of the monstrous clown Shakespeare, whose works were currently being translated by Letourneur.[2] The first volume of that 'abominable grimoire' (Besterman D20220)[3] had in fact just appeared in print. As it was a Sunday, the *fête* was celebrated with particular solemnity. Before the transaction of business a Francoeur motet was played, a panegyric by the King's chaplain Copel was pronounced, and Arnaud delivered a learned paper on the study of the Greek language. Chastellux, a leading member of the Letourneur faction, and no mean adapter of Shakespeare's plays himself, was in the chair. The spectators were seated in rows before the immortals' table, and among them was Elizabeth Montagu, whose *Essay upon the Writings and Genius of Shakespeare...with some Remarks upon the Misrepresentations of mr de Voltaire*, published with Elizabeth Carter in 1769, was soon to appear in its French translation.[4] Such was the impact of ensuing editions of her *Essay* that Richard Graves could compare her defiance of Voltaire to Queen Anne's resistance to Louis XIV.[5] The occasion marked a high point in the trial of strength between the theatres of London and Paris that had been a *cause célèbre* ever since Samuel Foote had denounced 'that insolent French panegyrist' in *The Roman and English Comedy Considered and Compared* (1747).[6]

Mrs Montagu had arrived in France on 23 June, and had spent the intervening weeks dining at the tables of Necker, Buffon, Chastellux and other pro-Shakespearian academicians in anticipation of the Saint-Louis

73

Day discourse. On 25 August, like an emissary from a foreign power, she was duly enthroned in the audience, next to Lord Stormont, the British Ambassador, to listen to what Horace Walpole called afterwards 'a silly torrent of ribaldry.'[7] She reported to Smelt that Voltaire's attack on 'our Shakespeare' had been coldly received but she could not suppress her 'profound anguish for a dead friend who can no longer speak for himself'.[8]

The essence of Voltaire's protest was this: Shakespeare had sparks of genius. Indeed, some of his plays contained sublime passages taken directly from nature itself, but Shakespeare had not the slightest conception of art. As an artist, his work was low, barbarous, unbridled and absurd. He had not heard of the unities. In *Julius Caesar*, cobblers and street vendors exchange banter with senators. In *Othello*, which starts off in Venice and ends in Cyprus, the heroine's father is told that his daughter is being mounted by a black bull, that she is being raped by a barbary horse, and that he would soon hear the whinny of his grandsons. In *Macbeth*, at the most solemn moment of the action, when the hero had determined to murder his king and was analysing the full horror of his criminal intent, servants enter and ask each other vulgar riddles. The plot of *Hamlet* was a monstrous farce. The Prince goes mad in the second act, and his mistress in the third. Hamlet kills his mistress's father, pretending to kill a rat, and the heroine then throws herself in the river. Her grave is dug on stage to the accompaniment of scabrous jokes and some stage business with a skull, and Hamlet responds with equally disgusting idiocies.[9] In view of such a hideous galimatias and gross infringements of good taste, Voltaire excoriated the current worship of Shakespeare, and rejected the claim that Shakespeare's plays were superior to those of Corneille and Racine. Letourneur had sacrificed great French artists to his 'god' like pigs to Ceres (Best. D20220), and that was nothing less than an affront to France.

The day after the Academy meeting, Mme Du Deffand sent a copy of Voltaire's manifesto to her lover Horace Walpole, who in turn wrote to Mason, author of the medieval tragedy *Elfrida*, asking him to lash the old scorpion a little and to teach him awe of English poets.[10] In the event, the lashings were to go on long after the old scorpion's death, and the echo of Voltaire's academy address and the response to it in the form of essays, books, lampoons and ditties on both sides of the channel was to be clearly heard for the next two decades and beyond.[11] All this is of interest to literary historians if only because it marks the climactic moment of Voltaire's defence of French classicism in the face of aesthetic philosophies that in his view threatened to engulf it. Ironically, Voltaire himself had contributed considerably to the spirit of experimentation and deviation from classical precept that marked mid-eighteenth-century theatrical life, and that he came to deplore in later years. In 1732 in *Eriphyle* he had introduced a ghost on the French stage in the form of the shade of Amphiaraüs, a direct borrowing from *Hamlet*. *Eriphyle* failed miserably and deservedly in Paris, and Voltaire picked up the debris, including the ghost, and reworked it in the shape of the much more successful *Sémiramis*. *Othello* came in useful as a model for *Zaïre*, and was indeed played back to the English as *Zara* – prompting the adapter/translator, Aaron Hill, to remark that he was only handing back to the English what belonged to them anyway: 'From racked Othello's rage [Voltaire] raised his style/and snatched the brand that lights his tragic pile'.[12]

Such was the English imprint on such plays as *Zaïre* and *Brutus* that both could be safely played at Westminster before the royal family, and the English were flattered to hear what they considered to be the echo of their own national taste in *La Mort de César*, *Alzire*, *Oreste*, *Mérope*, *Mahomet*, *Sémiramis*, *Amélie ou le duc de Foix*, *L'Orphelin de la Chine* and the less successful plays of the later period – particularly *Tancrède* and *Les Scythes*. Voltaire's success as a dramatist on the London stage grew considerably throughout the century, particularly after 1744 (the year of *Mérope*), and flourished even during the years of anathema resulting from his public war on English taste. As an innovative writer, responsible for the introduction of greater movement and spectacle, new rhyming practices, philosophical propaganda, blood, music and gothic scenery into the cool serenity of French classical repertoire, Voltaire's reputation in France was just as buoyant as in England, and his influence over dramatic theory profound and long-lasting. He was indisputably the most imposing figure in eighteenth-century French theatrical life, and it is not coincidental that critics like La Harpe, Diderot, Condorcet, Marmontel and Mercier preferred Racine to Corneille, and Voltaire occasionally to both.

As a creative writer for the theatre Voltaire casts a very long shadow. As a writer *on* the theatre, he was a committed polemicist in the forefront of the conflicts generated by the advent of a new aesthetic, and his shadow is rather more controversial. His public position did not change one iota from the moment of writing Letter 18 of the *Lettres philosophiques* (1734) to the public reading of the 1776 letter to the Academy referred to earlier. France was in a state of profound decline – in art, as in world affairs.

In Voltaire's view, the Sun King's reign had brought France, and Europe, out of the barbaric twilight. Under the stimulus of a powerful royal patron, the arts had prospered, and France had become the leading cultural and political force in the civilized world. Sublime greatness had emerged with the triumph of *Le Cid*, crested with Racine and Boileau, and waned with the closing years of Louis XIV's reign. In his own time, Voltaire saw only the symptoms of cultural exhaustion. France was left merely with the dregs of seventeenth-century greatness, and these did not even make passable vinegar. The age of Enlightenment was in artistic matters at least merely the excrement of the age of Louis XIV.[13] The supreme cultural-historical moment in French affairs had passed; the autumn of good taste had set in, and the winter of decadence was advancing. With a flourish of alarmist metaphors, Voltaire accepted with unfailing zeal responsibility for the protection of the established canons of taste, reminding his contemporaries of the greatness of their classical heritage, of their debt to France's greatest men of the theatre, and of their duty to defend and enhance that heritage, and so recover pride in their nation and confidence in the cultural values for which it stood. In literary matters, those values drew their breath of life from the seventeenth-century theatre as it had flowered at the time of Richelieu, and perfected itself with Racine. This ideological commitment to the dream of classical perfection, whilst it was less myopic and nostalgic in practice, remained in theory for Voltaire unshakeable and absolute. In addressing himself to the aesthetic issues of his own time, he was thus obliged during the course of a long career as a literary critic constantly to re-evaluate the seventeenth-century theatre, and in particular the works of Corneille and Racine. As he contemplated the rising star of Shakespeare's fortunes, the process of re-evaluation became correspondingly more urgent.

It is notoriously difficult to look at the details of Voltaire's position with regard to the French classical theatre in terms of a single, cohesive block of thought from which one can extract statements and say that this or that represents Voltaire's interpretation of Aristotelian time or catharsis, or of the historical significance of *Le Cid*, or of the meaning of Racinian passion. He does have very definite views on all these things, and they are central to his long, and at times convoluted, defence of the classical achievement. However, no doubt as a result of Voltaire's dislike for monolithic systems, they are scattered in a surprisingly random way throughout his voluminous works and correspondence – in the notes for a tragedy, in articles for the *Dictionnaire philosophique*, in literary chapters forming part of historical studies, in the interstices of a dedicatory epistle, in poems and odd stanzas, in miscellaneous polemical tracts, in letters to friends, enemies and publishers, in prefaces, *avertissements*, fragments and even in *contes*. It is partly because of the diffuse, fragmentary and often contradictory nature of his aesthetic statements that Voltaire is not best known today for his achievement as a literary critic.

There is, however, one work which by its scope and length, as well as by the circumstances in which it was composed, occupies a position of unique interest and importance in the otherwise confusing lexicon of Voltairean writings on the classical theatre. This work was published originally in twelve volumes in 1764, and is now known in a more compressed form as the *Commentaires sur Corneille*. The *Commentaires* is the longest piece of Voltairean literary criticism in existence, and concerns itself not only with Corneille, but also with Racine, Thomas Corneille, Calderón and Shakespeare. It thus draws a number of important threads together, and was specifically conceived as a key device in Voltaire's campaign to ensure the survival of French classical values. In this context, it illustrates some of the philosophical tensions between literary criticism and literary politics that characterize so much of Voltaire's writing on art and the theatre. Moreover, the work links issues that had been smouldering since *Sémiramis* with the 1776 confrontation with Mrs Montagu.

The *Commentaires sur Corneille*, the composition of which dates back to 1761, originated as a project undertaken on behalf of the French Academy to publish a magnificent edition of Corneille's plays financed by public subscription. It would serve as a timely reminder to Europe of the greatness of Corneille, and at the same time would provide a handsome dowry for young Marie Corneille, the granddaughter of a cousin of Pierre Corneille.

The *Corneille*, which emerged from Cramer's press in March 1764 after three years of gruelling work, contained twenty-five plays by Corneille with their accompanying prefaces, a play by Racine, and two plays by Thomas Corneille, together with Corneille's three discourses on tragedy, Fontenelle's biography of Corneille, and sundry other texts, including a translation 'pour vous faire rire' of the first three acts of *Julius Caesar* – juxtaposed with *Cinna*, much to Mrs Montagu's disgust – and the translation of three *jornadas* of a Calderón play *En Esta Vida todo es verdad y todo mentira*, another example of the uncivilized grotesquery of foreign theatre to be juxtaposed with *Héraclius*. All of these edited and translated texts, with the exception of some half dozen of Corneille's comedies, carried with them a substantial commentary, and are frequently prefaced by long essays. The critical apparatus was further expanded in 1774 by Voltaire with a new revised edition of the work, a telling testimony to the prolonged controversy and interest that had been aroused.[14] At the start of the project to edit Corneille, and to promote Cornelian theatre as a glittering diamond in the crown of French genius, Voltaire had blazed with enthusiasm. Nowhere is this enthusiasm more vividly reflected than in the extraordinary series of letters written by Voltaire in 1761 and 1762 to potential subscribers to the *Corneille*:[15] 'Nous travaillons donc pour le nom de Corneille, pour l'Académie, pour la France. C'est par là que je veux finir ma carrière' (Best. D9852). His work on Corneille, he intimated to many subscribers, was to be the crowning achievement of his life (Best. D9794, D9851, D9854, D9855).

The promotion of Corneille on what might be called the political level encompassed in fact a number of rather disparate elements, none of which was entirely new, but all of which were to dominate Voltaire's critical philosophy in the post-1764 period.

The edition coincided first of all with the opening of a major offensive against English 'insolence', which since 1758 had come to mean the decadent influence of the English sentimental novel and the subversive example of Shakespearean theatre. Secondly, by 1761 Voltaire had become acutely concerned with the protection at all costs of the integrity of the French language. As a literary critic, Voltaire had always conceived his primary role as being that of a guardian of language, and the *Corneille* is more than anything else a linguistic commentary for the practical guidance of young poets. 'Ce n'est pas pour les neuf lettres qui composent le nom de Corneille que je travaille, c'est pour ceux qui veulent s'instruire' (Best. D10320). It was his taut sensitivity to the use of language that first alerted him to the flaws in Cornelian theatre soon to merit the term 'dunghill' ('fumier': Best. D10037) when rediscovered on a larger scale in such tragedies as *Pertharite*, *Agésilas*, *Othon* and *Suréna*. Thirdly, there was the problem of taste. Voltaire had a cyclical theory of historical processes that profoundly affected his view of the dynamics of art and culture, and bears the stamp of his classical formation. His feeling for the historical moment in the evolution of a nation's genius, and its manifestation within a barbarism–perfection–decadence pattern, is central to his critical perspective. The *Corneille* was conceived with a view to analysing the nature of Corneille's contribution to such a moment – when French genius flowered with an epoch-making play, *Le Cid*, before which no theatre of any nation had produced a work capable of speaking directly to the heart.[16] Finally, of course, there was the question of Corneille himself. In Voltaire's view Corneille had died neglected after a life-long struggle against the blighting circumstances of an autocratic system of patronage, a victim of the petty persecutions of a powerful cardinal during his formative years, and a shamefully forgotten figure in his later life.[17] The father of French tragedy, the inventive genius who had established the basis of France's theatrical pre-eminence in Europe, had received little in the way of public encouragement during his lifetime, or public recognition after his death. Moreover, the persistent lack of national recognition of Corneille's achievements was a further sign of France's deplorable treatment of her artists, and a source of continuing national dishonour. The *Corneille*, sponsored by the Academy, the very body that had dared to pronounce judgement at Richelieu's behest on *Le Cid*, would now become a focus of national homage, and serve as the monument that was so conspicuously lacking in the squares of Rouen. All of these congruent issues and motivating factors behind Voltaire's great edition relate, however, to matters of literary politics, and are in a sense divorced from any objective defence of the classical canons of taste and from the more vexing issues of Cornelian art *per se*.

When Voltaire confronted the technicalities of Corneille's theatre in his commentary, he found that the political dimension to his perception of Corneille became increasingly difficult to sustain, if his insights as a critic, his instincts as a dramatist, his concern for language, and his notion of good taste were not to be all hopelessly betrayed. To begin with, however, the diamonds would receive priority, and his scrutiny would be positive and selective. Thus Voltaire's letters at the outset of the enterprise are full of delight and admiration at the rediscovery of the fountainhead of France's classical greatness. 'J'ay relu le Cid – Pierre je vous adore' (Best. D9790). On reading *Cinna* again, 'il me semble que j'ouvre une porte d'or pour sortir du labyrinthe des colifichets où la foule se promène...C'est un créateur, il n'y a de gloire que pour ces gens là... Il me semble que je commence à connaître l'art en étudiant mon maître à fond' (Best. D9852, D9854, D9883). Indeed, Voltaire did not find it difficult to reconcile the burning of incense to Corneille with the 'truth' as far as Corneille's masterpieces were concerned: *Le Cid*, *Horace*, *Cinna*, *Polyeucte*, *Pompée* and *Rodogune*. It was with these plays in mind that Voltaire had always referred to Corneille's theatre as being the 'Temple of Corneille', to be defended against all sacrilege. It was to these plays that Voltaire devoted the most substantial amount of research and critical attention, and it was from work on these plays that he derived the greatest pleasure. He was to turn to them again when he wished to select for Horace Walpole the finest moments in Corneille's theatre (Best. D14179). However, by mid-October 1761 Voltaire's attitude was hardening, and he began to feel that the temple was turning into a mausoleum. As the commentary grew, he became increasingly impatient with the blemishes in Corneille's style, with the faults of dramatic structure, and above all with the lapses in language. It became clear to him that all he really liked of Corneille's thirty-two plays were parts of five or six tragedies: most of *Cinna*, the best scenes of *Horace*, of *Le Cid*, of *Pompée*, of *Polyeucte*, the last few scenes of *Rodogune*. He told d'Alembert, to whom he reported regularly on the progress of his commentary, that sometimes he was treating Corneille as a god, sometimes as a carriage horse (Best. D9979). In the case of *Polyeucte* he had even taken up a pig's bladder instead of a thurible (Best. D10013): 'Je donne quelquefois des coups de pied dans le ventre à Corneille, l'encensoir à la main' (Best. D10024). Thus, within a few months of embarking on his most ambitious defence of the French classical theatre, the commentary on Corneille had undergone a fundamental change of direction. Voltaire took pains to define his critical position carefully, only too aware of the likely consequences of his decision not to criticize Corneille 'à la Dacier'.[18] 'J'ai dit ce que tout homme de goût se dit lui-même quand il lit Corneille' (Best. D11891).

Even the masterpieces did not escape entirely intact. The versification of *Le Cid* was naive, the play was less 'exact' than Pradon's *Pyrame*, and the scene sequence was inconsequential.[19] *Horace* grossly infringed unity of action with a plot that moved in three unrelated directions – Horace's victory, the death of the heroine and Horace's trial. Camille's death-scene was not successful from a technical standpoint as it alienated the audience from Horace, whose main characteristic was now transformed from heroic grandeur into petty vanity.[20] Camille's death created, moreover, a disruptive subsidiary action that necessitated the unfortunate fifth act which was merely 'un plaidoyer hors d'oeuvre'.[21] On balance, *Cinna*, not one of the most popular of Corneille's plays in the middle years of the eighteenth century,[22] was the tragedy that Voltaire had always preferred, 'le chef d'oeuvre de l'esprit humain' (Best. D10117). The play contained good verse; the theme was absorbing, the structure impeccable and the moral impact edifying.[23] Once more, however, Voltaire's admiration was reserved for specific 'morceaux sublimes' rather than for the play as a whole, and his criticism becomes markedly more severe after the examination of Act II. The play was a masterpiece, but it did not reach the sublime heights of tragic emotion (Best. D10213). Voltaire found that his interest in Cinna as a tragic hero soon began to wane, and the dramatic focus of the play changed as a consequence of the flawed portrayal of the hero,[24] a criticism that led to an interesting little debate with d'Alembert on the real nature of the play's dramatic strength. In this context, Voltaire was very unhappy about the presentation and timing of Cinna's remorse,[25] and he refused to accept the view, defended by the Academy, that unity of interest was preserved through the actions and characterization of Auguste. His strictures with regard to *Cinna* were reinforced with the revisions made to the *Corneille* in 1774.

Polyeucte could arouse strong emotions in an audience,[26] but Voltaire found Corneille's handling of rhyme and imagery in the play to be negligent, and that the impact of Corneille's poetry in the play depended on maxims rather than tragic emotion. Pauline's dream was unnecessarily absurd, and the portrayal of Félix, the inherent improbabilities in the action, and the use of 'galanterie' in the treatment of the love theme were all sharply criticized.[27] The latter factor was in Voltaire's view the main weakness not only of *Polyeucte*, but of the French theatre generally – with the exception of Racine. In *Rodogune* Voltaire found sublimity, but only fleetingly – in the last half of the last act; and indeed this half act, together with the climactic scene in *Horace* (III.iv), was one of the few examples of originality in Corneille's theatre that Voltaire was prepared to acknowledge consistently. His long-standing view, as exemplified best perhaps in the article 'Anciens et modernes' in the *Dictionnaire philosophique*,[28] was that the final sublime scene was preceded by four and a half acts that abounded in faults. In the 1774 revisions, however, his enthusiasm even for this fragment faded, and by the end of 1776 his condemnation of *Rodogune* was almost total. He felt that there was not a grain of common sense in the whole action, and that the public, and presumably he himself, had been seduced into thinking that the play was a masterpiece. Even the much praised last act did not survive his change of heart: 'Pour moi, je n'ai jamais vu quatre plus mauvais actes, et la moitié du cinquième, préparer plus détestablement une dernière scène admirable…La dernière scène même qui semble demander grâce pour le reste n'est nullement vraisemblable, mais il y a tant d'illusion théâtrale d'un bout à l'autre, que le public a été séduit' (Best. D19298, D19323, cf. *Lettre de m. de La Visclède*).

Pompée too had moments of tragic grandeur although Voltaire had criticized it as early as 1734 in the *Lettres philosophiques* (Letter 18), where he compared it unfavourably with Addison's *Cato*. The play produced the requisite amount of the tears and fears that every neo-classical audience expected, but it was not a coherent work of art. The love theme was insipid.[29] Cornélie was 'une diseuse de galimatias et une faiseuse de rodomontades' (Best. D11971). Her first great scene with César was a failure (III.iv), her cries for vengeance irrelevant to the plot, and even her apostrophe to the urn containing Pompée's ashes (V.i) – a *coup de théâtre* in many ways – was an unnecessary diversion. Cornélie had serious weaknesses of characterization, and the language used in her speeches was singularly cold, inflated and lacking in propriety, but she was ultimately redeemable, being responsible for moments of powerful tragic beauty in the play. Photin, however, was irredeemable, the worst of Corneille's characters, a mere formulator of 'execrable maxims': 'maximes cent fois plus dangereuses quand elles sont récitées devant les princes avec toute la pompe et toute l'illusion du théâtre, que lorsqu'une lecture froide laisse à l'esprit la liberté d'en sentir l'atrocité' (Best. D9959).

The commentary goes on to encompass sixteen further Cornelian tragedies or tragi-comedies. Voltaire, although he devotes considerable space to some of these, notably *Sertorius* and *Héraclius*, found them all to be quite worthless as theatre and barely readable as texts. The last few plays stand conspicuously denuded of any critical comment at all. 'C'est un cruel employ de lire Attila, Agésilas, Pulchérie, Othon, don Sanche d'Arragon, Andromède, la Toison d'or, Pertharite, Théodore, Tite et Bérénice...Comment peut-on tomber ainsi de la nue dans la fange?' (Best. D10617). The detailed features of Voltaire's critical reaction to Corneille have been analysed at length by modern critics. His negative comments are often balanced by 'adoucissements', but this fragmentary sampling of the tone as well as the substance of his strictures will, it is hoped, suffice to demonstrate the degree to which Voltaire's mood darkened as the *Corneille* made its laborious way through the composition and proofing stages, and his disapproval of Corneille's dunghills became correspondingly more severe. Pradon was Sophocles and Danchet Euripides compared with Corneille's later performances: 'Quel exécrable fatras que quinze ou seize pièces de ce grand homme ...Comment a-t-on pu préférer à un homme tel que Racine, un rabâcheur d'un si mauvais goût, qui jusque dans ses plus beaux morceaux, qui ne sont, après tout, que des déclamations, pèche continuellement contre la langue et est toujours trivial ou hors de la nature?' (Best. DI1021). If Corneille was the father of the French theatre, he was also the father of galimatias.

Voltaire had never been enthusiastic about Corneille's later plays, of course, and his antipathy towards these lesser productions certainly did not develop solely as a consequence of having to deal with them in the *Corneille*. It will be remembered that in the *Temple du goût* he had even obliged Corneille to throw *Pulchérie* and *Suréna* on the fire, and in *Le Siècle de Louis XIV* at least twenty of Corneille's plays were declared to be among the worst in the French repertoire. Basically, therefore, his position on Corneille was fairly consistent, although in the context of the 1764 *Corneille* 'telling the truth' about Corneille's lesser achievements proved to be a delicate matter, which, in the hostile aftermath of the work's publication, was to cause Voltaire many problems.[30] Voltaire was quite aware of the risks involved in offering an unglazed appraisal of Corneille's works in an edition that was, after all, intended to be an authoritative testimony to the achievement of a great French genius, subscribed to by the royal family and sponsored by the Academy. D'Alembert and d'Olivet had warned him of the Academy's likely objections to controversial frankness, and he anticipated that he would be judged 'fort insolent' (Best. DI0495). However, he had told the truth about Louis XIV, and he was not going to flinch from telling the truth boldly but modestly about Corneille (Best. DI0074). Professions of objectivity and impartiality were futile. From 1764 until his death Voltaire was accused of destroying Corneille for reasons of self-interest. Outside his immediate circle of friends and supporters, he was seen quite simply as a jealous rival who in the cause of his own self-aggrandizement had wielded with brutal cruelty and injustice what Sabatier called rather graphically 'le scalpel de la malignité'.[31]

Voltaire's *Corneille*, written ostensibly in defence of a great exponent of French classical theatre, was to provoke more controversy in French literary circles than any other piece of theatrical criticism to appear in France for a century. It matched the furore in English critical circles caused by his declaration of war on Shakespeare. Never, before or since the publication of what Collé called 'ce détestable ouvrage, à tous égards et en tous sens',[32] has Corneille found so many critics ready to enlist so vigorously in his cause. The adverse effects on Voltaire's reputation and honesty are still being recorded and perpetuated. As late as 1972 a critic could still accept Fréron's vilifications, and state bluntly that what may have prevented Voltaire from moderating his commentary was his

secret envy of a man whose work, flawed though it was, he suspected
he could not surpass.[33] Force of historical circumstance had obliged
Voltaire to locate the centre of gravity for his defence of French
classicism in Corneille's theatre. The conflicts between his official
mission and his inner convictions meant that his twin roles as a public
defender of the French classical canon before the tribune of Europe and
as an honest critic of Corneille could never happily coincide, given his
view of a literary critic's responsibilities.

He would have preferred to write a commentary on Racine's plays,
and said so frequently.

Je veux que Pierre ait cent fois plus de génie que Jean. Pierre n'en est que plus
condamnable d'avoir fait un si détestable usage de son génie dans la force de son
âge...mais encore une fois, vive Jean! Plus on le lit et plus on lui découvre un talent
unique, soutenu part toutes les finesses de l'art. En un mot, s'il y a quelque chose sur
la terre qui approche de la perfection, c'est Jean.   (Best. D11125)

His well-known preference for Racine could scarcely be concealed in the
Corneille. It was in the dunghill of Corneille's work that Racine
discovered and polished the diamonds of his art, and in the process of
dealing with Corneille in the commentaries Voltaire had in effect
rediscovered his love for Racine: 'Je vous confie qu'en commentant
Corneille, je deviens idolâtre de Racine' (Best. D11041). The diamond–
dunghill metaphor was resorted to continuously in the correspondence
of 1762. Certainly, after 1764 Voltaire's enthusiasm for Racine's divine
perfection became accentuated and much more explicit, developing in
proportion to his distaste for the imperfect Corneille. A diamond was
a diamond; it mattered little in which mine it was found: 'je regarde
à son poids, à sa grosseur, à son brillant, à ses taches. Enfin, je ne puis
ni sentir qu'avec mon goût, ni juger qu'avec mon jugement. Racine
m'enchante, et Corneille m'ennuie' (Best. D11971). Racine was the poet
of the heart, the only tragic poet of his century whose genius was
disciplined by taste: 'le premier homme du siècle de Louis XIV dans
les beaux arts, et la gloire éternelle de la France'. Even with Racine,
however, there are nuances in Voltaire's idolatry and his praise did not
extend to all of Racine's theatre. As with Corneille, it was selective,
although not as radically so. It encompassed *Iphigénie* and *Athalie*, the
roles of Phèdre, Acomat, Roxane and Monime, the first act of *Britannicus*
and most of *Andromaque*, with the exception of one scene of pure
coquetry.[34] With 'l'admirable Racine, non assez admiré', however,
Voltaire contemplated a more reliable model for imitation, or as – his
enemies would put it later – a model corresponding far more closely to

his own dramatic talents. Be that as it may, Voltaire could not resign himself to keeping Racine's work out of his edition of Corneille's theatre, and Racinian art is represented by *Bérénice*, and its presence justified by its comparative function in relation to Corneille's *Tite et Bérénice*.[35]

Of course, Voltaire's reservations about Corneille and his preference for Racine had been a familiar feature of his literary criticism for many years before he came to write the commentary on Corneille, and there is nothing essentially new in what he had to say after 1764. Nevertheless, as in other issues, editing Corneille and defending his theatre against Shakespeare and his legion of imitators and adapters was a cataclysmic experience after which Voltaire's attitudes hardened considerably. Corneille and Racine, previously balanced in Voltaire's criticism – one the 'inventeur' and discoverer of the diamonds of genius, the other the polisher and refiner of those rough minerals – now became polarized. In the *Corneille*, the commentary on *Bérénice* is severe at times, *Bérénice* being in Voltaire's view the weakest of Racine's tragedies and described in the 1731 letter to the *Nouvelliste du Parnasse* as 'une élégie bien écrite' (Best. D415). However, even a weak Racinian tragedy provided ample evidence of that aspect of Racine's genius upon which Voltaire placed crucial importance: noble elegance of style in the poetic manipulation of the language of tragic emotion. This was precisely the area in Corneille's theatre that drew Voltaire's most corrosive criticism. Even in *Bérénice* Voltaire found that indefinable charm and purity, the *je ne sais quoi* that Corneille never knew, and that post-Racinian dramatists were never able quite to reproduce. More importantly, the core of Voltaire's admiration for Racinian art was to be found in his association of Racine's genius with the French language at its climactic moment of perfection. Only Racine had succeeded in overcoming the severe technical problems imposed on French poets by the nature of their language and poetic traditions – a triumph that illuminated for Voltaire the reality of that austere guarantor of high art, 'le mérite de la difficulté vaincue'.

Between 1760 and the 1776 letter to the Academy, Voltaire's concern with the threat to the French language was at its most extreme, and this is possibly the most important single factor in the polarization of Racine and Corneille in his thought during those years. Corneille failed miserably precisely where Racine succeeded so brilliantly: 'Je sais bien que Racine est rarement assez tragique: mais il est si intéressant, si droit, si pur, si élégant, si harmonieux, il a tant adouci et embelli notre langue rendue barbare par Corneille, que notre passion pour lui est bien excusable' (Best. D14054). With Racine a palace had been built on the débris of the French language. By 1764 the distance between Racine and Corneille in Voltaire's writings on the classical theatre had widened into an unbridgeable gulf. Between 1760 and 1776, a period of decline in Racine's popularity among theatre audiences,[36] we see Voltaire becoming almost fanatically Racinian. In a real sense his aesthetic prejudices demanded the demise of Corneille, in spite of his continuing respect for him as the father of the French theatre. In asserting what Corneille stood for, Corneille had to be deified and then immolated in the greater cause of Racine's theatre, and the need to defend this theatre against the Shakespearean party in France. In the event, of course, Corneille, rather like the gentle Shakespeare in the Thomas Holcroft poem, 'safely smiled and slumbered on'.[37] By 1776, Corneille's fortunes at the box-office had started to pick up again in preparation for the nova-like brilliance with which they would shine during the Revolution. Already anti-Voltairians, when they were not applauding Shakespeare, were rallying round Corneille in reaction to Voltaire's 'basses vilénies sur le grand Corneille'.[38] As it turned out, the father of the French theatre was as safe from marauding English savages from Stratford-upon-Avon as he was from the strains and stresses of being a figurehead in Voltaire's championship of the French classical aesthetic. History has shown that the defence of the seventeenth-century French theatre was not the life or death issue that Voltaire had perceived it to be. The challenge of Shakespeare proved to be the challenge of coexistence, not of survival. In the last decade of his life, when Voltaire's campaign was reaching for new heights of aggressive rhetoric, there is extraordinary irony in the fact that for many of Voltaire's contemporaries, Corneille and the classical theatre lived on *in spite* of Voltaire, not because of him. The *Corneille* had ensured that Voltaire would be widely viewed not only as the arch-enemy of English taste, but also as a traitor to the classical canons of taste. Bachaumont, Collé, Dorat, Sabatier, Clément, Fréron, Gilbert, La Serre, and even Mme du Deffand, all joined in the expressions of outrage.[39]

Voltaire himself, of course, never accepted the accusations that were hurled against him. In devoting three years of his life to the *Corneille*, his aim, he always insisted, was to be 'useful', by which he meant the wise guidance of young artists still serving their apprenticeships. Nothing could be of service to them, if it distorted the truth. 'Quoy; Mélier en mourant aura dit ce qu'il pense de Jésus! et je ne dirai pas la vérité sur vingt détestables pièces de Pierre! et sur les défauts sensibles des bonnes! Oh par dieu je parlerai' (Best. D10342). The preservation of good taste was paramount. But then, as Mercier pointed out, men of taste are not always the best judges of men of genuis.[40] Some believed in the integrity of Voltaire's criticism of Corneille; many more did not, and it was largely the judgement of Voltaire's enemies and detractors that carried the day. It is their judgement that has been echoed by posterity. It is perhaps all the more remarkable that so many of Voltaire's comments on Corneille have been incorporated nevertheless into thirty-five complete or partial editions of Corneille's works between 1801 and 1870. A long, scholarly tradition in the editing of Cornelian texts in the nineteenth and twentieth centuries, encompassing the Pléiade edition, has ensured the survival and to some extent the status of what Voltaire had to say about Corneille and French classical values.

Voltaire's edition of Corneille's theatre, with its glittering subscription list purporting to demonstrate that Corneille, unlike Shakespeare, found international approval, was originally conceived as a propagandist mechanism for the re-establishment of the apparently dwindling prestige of the French classical theatre in the face of the triumph of English taste. It contains prophetic signals of Voltaire's later, more strident, warnings against the fanaticism of the pro-Shakespeare party in France. Paradoxically, however, the actual composition of the commentary obliged Voltaire to confront the ambivalence of his feelings towards Corneille's art, and to acknowledge finally the distance between the greater part of Corneille's theatre and his own vision of what constituted the essence of classical sublimity. In the end, Corneille, the revered founder of the French classical canon, was found wanting by the very standards of that canon as Voltaire understood them.[41] In his work as a theorist of the theatre, and as a practising dramatist, Voltaire never sought refuge in literary dogma or aesthetic systems. His relationship with the French seventeenth-century theatre, and beyond that with the ancient Greek theatre, remained an open and dynamic one. In times of shifting standards and uncertain taste, exacerbated in France by the tantalizing enigma of a natural foreign genius in the form of Shakespeare, blissfully unaware of the rules of art, Voltaire sought solid, time-tested bases for dramatic judgement and practice. He never sought to re-establish classicism *per se*; his concern was with the re-discovery of its spirit and *envergure*, and hence with the revival of a lost greatness in French art.

Behind all this, and behind the *Corneille*, lay always the challenge of Shakespeare, for whose presence in the French literary scene in the mid eighteenth century Voltaire held himself – with only partial justification

– to be primarily responsible.[42] The genius, content and polemical shape of the *Corneille*, and the frustrations that Voltaire encountered in dealing with the constituent elements of Corneille's theatre, stem ultimately from the pressures of the Shakespearean war in which, by 1761, he was heavily engaged. The exigencies of the campaign against Shakespeare and his French imitators and admirers are thus central to an understanding of the issues at stake in the Corneille edition. Indeed, such exigencies govern much of what Voltaire had to say about the theatre subsequently. It remains therefore one of the more piquant ironies of literary history that in his attempts to find in Corneille the sources of French aesthetic superiority over the crude talents of Shakespeare, Voltaire discovered only faults and disillusionment. Coincidentally, moreover, as his attack on the Shakespearean 'chaos' mounted in intensity, he remained only too aware of the 'cent traits de lumière' (Best. D15140) that illuminated persistently the monstrous clown's barbaric genius. As a result of such irreconcilable tensions between Voltaire's public intentions as a literary politician and his basic intuition as a literary critic and dramatist, one of the main roles for which the *Corneille* was designed – namely, to serve as the nucleus of a defence of the French classical canon – was gravely compromised.

It is true to say that since the work's publication Voltaire's criticism has caused more embarrassment and anger than admiration. The surgical precision with which he exposed the minutiae of Cornelian language and technique has, it would seem, taxed beyond endurance the patience of all but a handful of contemporary supporters. Among Voltaire's modern readers, even those normally prepared to give him a sympathetic hearing still tend to pass over the *Corneille* in relative silence. After two centuries of mostly hostile comment, it takes an effort of imagination to recall that for the last thirty years of the eighteenth century, and for most of the nineteenth, Voltaire's spectacular edition of Corneille's theatre provided, in spite of everything, the point of departure, and sometimes of arrival, for a substantial corpus of opinion and criticism.

NOTES

1 This letter had already been read at a private *séance* on 3 August. It had been sent to d'Alembert on 26 July, and was being printed in Geneva at the time of the public reading on 25 August.

2 P. P. F. Letourneur, *Shakespeare traduit de l'anglois*, 20 vols. (Paris, 1776–82). Catuélan and Fontaine-Malherbe collaborated on the first two volumes.

3 All references to Voltaire's letters are to the definitive edition of the *Correspondence and Related Documents*, edited by Theodore Besterman (The Voltaire Foundation, 1968–76).

4 *Apologie de Shakespeart [sic], en réponse à la critique de m. de Voltaire* (London etc., 1777).

5 *Euphrosyne, or Amusements on the Road of Life. By the Author of the Spiritual Quixote*, 2 vols. (1780), II, 67–8.

6 See A. M. Rousseau, *L'Angleterre et Voltaire*, in *Studies on Voltaire and the Eighteenth Century*, 145–7 (1976), 458.

7 *The Yale Edition of Horace Walpole's Correspondence*, edited by W. S. Lewis (Oxford, 1937–), XXVIII, 278.

8 Rousseau, p. 486.

9 Voltaire recast the letter to the Academy in two parts for purposes of publication. The complete text is to be found in the *Oeuvres complètes de Voltaire*, edited by L. Moland (Paris, 1883–5), XXX, 350–70.

10 *Walpole's Correspondence*, XXVIII, 276.

11 Rousseau, pp. 489–508.

12 From the prologue to *Zara*.

13 Best. D15500, cf. Best. D12100, D15876. See also *Oeuvres complètes de Voltaire/The Complete Works of Voltaire* (The Voltaire Foundation, 1969–), LIII, 196, n. 259. References to this work will be given as *Voltaire*.

14 See E. P. Kostoroski, *The Eagle and the Dove: Corneille and Racine in the Literary Criticism of Eighteenth-Century France* in *Studies on Voltaire and the Eighteenth Century*, 95 (1972), 122–42, and *Voltaire*, LIII, 338–61.

15 *Voltaire*, LIII, 64–88.

16 See the 'Préface historique de l'éditeur sur Le Cid', *Voltaire*, LIV, 39.

17 Corneille's experience with Richelieu illuminated for Voltaire the whole problem of patronage in France. It will be remembered that Corneille ranked fifth in a 'school' of writers favoured by Richelieu, the other four being Rotrou, Colletet, L'Estoile, and Boisrobert.

18 Dacier was one of the 'compilateurs' castigated in the *Temple du Goût*.

19 See the commentary to Act I, Scene 3.

20 See the commentary on Act IV, Scene 5.

21 See the commentary to Act V, Scene 3. Cf. preface to *Le Triumvirat*.

22 There were only five performances between 1751 and 1761.

23 See Best. D9959, D10229, D10126.

24 See the commentary on Act II, Scene 2, and Best. D9959.

25 See the commentary to Act III, Scene 1, Best. D10024, D10029. Cf. *Réponse à un académicien*.

26 Best. D415, *Notebooks* (*Voltaire*, LXXXII, 455).

27 See the commentary on Act I, Scene 4, Act II, Scene 1, Act III, Scene 3, Act IV, Scene 3, Act V, Scene 1 and Act V, Scene 5.

28 See also Best. D9910, D9470, D11891. In the *Discours sur la tragédie* (the preface to *Brutus*) Voltaire's appraisal of the fifth act was more cautious.

29 In this context the role of Cornélie was the primary target. Cf. 'Goût', *Dictionnaire philosophique*, Best. D9933.

30 See *Voltaire*, LIII, 338–61.

31 *Les Trois Siècles de la littérature française, ou Tableau de l'esprit de nos écrivains, depuis François Ier jusqu'en 1781* (The Hague, 1781), II, 45–6.

32 *Journal et mémoires sur les hommes de lettres, les ouvrages dramatiques et les événements les plus mémorables du règne de Louis XV (1748–1772)*, edited by H. Bonhomme (Paris, 1868), II, 371.

33 Kostoroski, p. 137.

34 The final scene of Act II of *Andromaque* was the one Voltaire was not prepared to endorse.

35 See *Voltaire*, LIII, 213, 308–9.

36 Between 1761 and 1771 a total of 153 plays by Racine were performed at the Comédie française, as compared with 331 performances between 1721 and 1730.

37 *Memoirs of the Late Thomas Holcroft, written by himself and continued till the Time of his Death, from his Diary, Notes and Other Papers*, edited by W. Hazlitt (1816), I, 41–3. The whole of this amusing stanza can be found in Rousseau, p. 483, n. 51.

38 The words are those of Charles de Brosses, see Best. D15431.

39 See Kostoroski, pp. 126–40.

40 *Mon Bonnet de nuit* (Lausanne, 1788), II, 133.

41 For a detailed discussion of this very broad topic, see my *Voltaire: Literary Critic*, in *Studies on Voltaire and the Eighteenth Century*, 48 (1966), 142–93, 334–52.

42 See the *Lettres philosophiques* of 1734: 'J'ay été malheureusement le premier qui ait fait connaître en France la poésie anglaise. J'en ay dit du bien comme on loue un enfant maussade devant un enfant qu'on aime et à qui on veut donner de l'émulation; on m'a trop pris à mon mot' (Best. D9753). In fact, there had been several informative allusions to Shakespeare by Frenchmen which went beyond a mere name reference long before Voltaire. See J. A. A. J. Jusserand, *Shakespeare en France sous l'ancien régime* (Paris, 1898), pp. 144–54; J. G. Robertson, 'The Knowledge of Shakespeare on the Continent at the beginning of the Eighteenth Century', *Modern Language Review*, I (1906), 313–21.

The German *Bildungsroman* and 'The Great Tradition'

MARTIN SWALES

Let me begin with a few truisms: it is generally held that the *Bildungsroman*, the novel of personal growth and development, is the principal German contribution to the novel genre. It is also generally held that the *Bildungsroman* genre displays all the usual debilitating features of German literature as a whole: it tends to be long and tedious, it is desperately learned, it shows a thoroughgoing concern for the play of values and ideas, but has precious little time or narrative energy for the social world, for the institutions, the economic and moral sanctions that play so vital a role in the shaping of an individual's existence in practical reality. Because of this lack of realism, it has been maintained, the *Bildungsroman* is a peripheral (i.e. merely German) phenomenon within the context of the nineteenth-century European novel. And this is essentially because of the backwardness of Germany in the nineteenth century compared with, say, England or France, a backwardness that derives from the half-heartedness of the bourgeois revolution, from the much-analysed 'deutsche Misere'.

Now these truisms – like all truisms – are misleading in that they blur a number of vital issues. Let me then try very briefly to establish a somewhat more differentiated (and, I trust, more accurate) model of the *Bildungsroman* as a genre before going on to explore some of the implications that the genre can have for the poetics of the novel as a whole.

First, a theoretical issue: why bother with genres anyway? Now obviously there is no reason why any critic should not establish a theoretical – or, as I should prefer to put it, taxonomic – genre for the purposes of comparison and contrast. One could, presumably, envisage

* This paper was given at the British Comparative Literature Association conference, Warwick, December 1977.

the novel of adultery, the novel of business, the novel of bankruptcy, and so on. Such a model of a genre would have no pretensions to historical status: it would simply be a heuristic tool, a grid which allows the critic to select a number of novels for analytical and comparative purposes. But this notion of the taxonomic genre should not prevent us from realizing that there are such things as historical genres, and that they have to do with that interlocking of tradition and the individual talent which informs the process by which the work of art is made. I want to suggest, then, that the historical genre partakes of that 'horizon of expectation'[1] with reference to which an individual work is both created by the writer and received by its contemporary – or subsequent – audience. Of course, no genre remains a constant: it is always modified in the process of its transmission. Indeed, that modification *is* the transmission as reader expectations are activated, explored, challenged, transgressed – perhaps even parodied. In this process we find both the historicity and the individuality of each specific work; in it we find the newness within the continuity of which Todorov speaks[2] when he distinguishes between the relative stability of the scientific species and the relative volatility of the species, the genre, when it has to do with products of the human mind. Moreover, it should be stressed that the historical genre is not an extra-literary construct: rather, it is embedded in the specific texts which are written with a view to that genre. The activation of the genre-bound expectation is the life-blood of the genre: whether those expectations are or are not fulfilled is not the criterion for genre-ascription. Even parody can represent the reinstatement of a genre in and through its immanent critique.

So what is the *Bildungsroman* as a historical genre? It is a novel form vitally concerned with the whole man, with the totality of human selfhood. It is born in precise historical circumstances, marked by the publication of Wieland's *Agathon* in 1767 and of Blanckenburg's *Versuch über den Roman* of 1774, the latter being the theoretical response to the former. For Blanckenburg, Wieland had managed to confer distinction on the novel by endowing the traditional, episodic, adventure-story plot with real human significance. He had contrived to re-shape it, to make it articulate the diffuse growth, the *Werden* of an individual in all his complexity. Blanckenburg's comments on *Agathon* are indeed pertinent: two features of Wieland's novel should be highlighted here. First, *Agathon* is a novel which explicitly challenges traditional novel convention, that convention which entails characters who are known quantities throughout, which entails an epistemologically stable, that is, unreflective relationship between narrator, reader, and character. Second, Agathon's essential personality emerges as more elusive and complex than can ever be realized (in both senses of the word) at any given stage of the experiences chronicled. To review the sequence of Agathon's life is to perceive the *Nacheinander* (the one-after-another) of linear time, of plot, of story. But the true self is a complex clustering of potentialities of which only a small proportion can be expressed outwardly. That clustering is a coexistence, a *Nebeneinander* (one-alongside-another). This tension between *Nacheinander* and *Nebeneinander*, of course, makes it particularly difficult for Wieland to find an ending. His solution is irony: he purveys the traditional happy ending of novel convention while undercutting it with the constant intimation of the sheer inauthenticity and inappropriateness of such a premature foreclosing of the hero's *Werden*.

Let me make one general point here about what I take to be the starting point of the *Bildungsroman*. In many ways, of course, *Agathon* and the genre which it inaugurates are recognizably permeated by the *Humanitätsideal* of late-eighteenth-century Germany. One thinks of the concern for the whole man articulated by Humboldt, Goethe, Schiller and many others. The implications of the German reverence for *Bildung* have been explored in a number of recent publications.[3] But I want to insist as forcefully as I can on the difference between the novel genre of the *Bildungsroman* on the one hand, and the theoretical tract about *Bildung* on the other. For where the discursive statement can offer the espousal of an unequivocal value, the novel genre has to embed that value in some kind of lived context. Hence the all-important tension between the *Nebeneinander* of the hero's inwardness and the *Nacheinander* as the ineradicable ontological dimension of the individual biography, of a life lived. The *Bildungsroman* is, in my view, animated by a complex irony – a quality often missing from the discursive statements about *Bildung*. And precisely that irony, that dialectic of the *Nebeneinander* and the *Nacheinander* will become a recurring feature not only of the *Bildungsroman* but also of novel theory in Germany throughout the nineteenth century. What Hegel perceives as the central issue of the novel – the conflict 'between the *poetry* of the heart and the resisting *prose* of circumstances'[4] – will be repeated with remarkable unanimity by subsequent novel theoreticians. In my view, the concepts of poetry and prose in the novel are precisely to do with that narrative tension which I have highlighted in *Agathon*.

A comparable irony pervades Goethe's *Wilhelm Meisters Lehrjahre* (1795–6). Our eager young hero turns his back on his bourgeois background in order to join a theatrical company. Both in social and psychological terms the theatre promises (and in part delivers) a fuller extension of the essential personality than the career of a merchant could offer. But in the second part of the novel, Wilhelm progresses beyond the theatre. In what seems to be the climax of the novel, and the culminating point of Wilhelm's *Werden*, he is admitted to the Society of the Tower, a secret society dedicated to human growth, self-knowledge, to the totality that is man. The ceremony of Wilhelm's admittance is suitably grandiose, and the Abbé who presides over the Society pronounces the hero's apprenticeship over. And yet Wilhelm feels none the wiser; moreover, as subsequent events show, he *is* none the wiser. Human wholeness is glimpsed – but only in a set of admirable principles and wise sayings. The law of linear experience, the *Nacheinander*, refuses to be gainsaid. Not that the novel ends on a note of Flaubertian disillusionment. There is a happy ending, but it is so abrupt, so much produced by a beneficently stage-managed chain of good fortune, that we feel an implicit irony at work: an irony reminiscent of Wieland's ending to *Agathon*, an irony mounted against traditional novel expectations. (Goethe clearly activates these, one feels, both in his title, which refers to a 'master's apprenticeship', and in his employment of the motif of the secret society which was particularly popular in novel fictions of the late eighteenth century).[5] What, then, do we make of Wilhelm? He seems (as Schiller so finely perceived) to be both an individuated character who has certain practical decisions to make and a reservoir of human potential which can never fully exhaust itself in the achievement of certain finite, knowable goals. His over-endowment makes him, as it were, both master and eternal apprentice.

Of all the novels that I shall be discussing in this paper, one, Stifter's *Der Nachsommer* (1857), resolves the dialectic of which I have spoken. It evokes a world that is utterly resistant to the common norms of human (and narrative) interest. For within the confines of Risach's 'Rosenhaus' there is no discrepancy between values and actions, between, in Hegel's terms, the poetry of the heart and the prose of circumstances. The modest activities of the estate are underwritten by a detailed narrative assent that leaves one with the impression of a kind of sacramental pedantry. In other words, the attempt to solve the dilemma of the *Bildungsroman* genre can only be undertaken by converting the novel into a monolithic litany. The contrast with the other great nineteenth-century German *Bildungsroman*, Keller's *Der grüne Heinrich* (1879–80), could scarcely be more striking. For in this work there is a total disjunction between the hero's inwardness and the social world around him, with the result that his imaginative life becomes dissociated and unfocussed, while outward reality is by definition reduced to the banal. With an astringency that is rare (many commentators would say all too rare) in the *Bildungsroman* tradition, Keller's narrative insists on the moral irreversibility of Heinrich's failures: the life lived is a journey into aridity which is alleviated only by glimpses of the fuller human self that might have been.

I want to conclude this sketch of the *Bildungsroman* genre with brief comments on two twentieth-century texts. Thomas Mann's *Der Zauberberg* (1924) chronicles the experiences undergone by a young man from North Germany during a seven year stay at a sanatorium in Davos. In the thin and heady air of the Magic Mountain, Hans Castorp undergoes a number of challenging experiences that the practical world of the 'flatlands' would never have vouchsafed him. The climactic point of his journey seems to come in the chapter 'Snow' when he has a dream vision of human wholeness and goodness. But, as was the case with *Wilhelm Meister*, the goal is not so much attained as by-passed, for the young man who blunders back through the snow forgets everything that he has seen and learnt. The totality, the *Nebeneinander*, can be glimpsed briefly, it can be discursively formulated, but it cannot be achieved as an abiding possession. Castorp's story does not stop at the 'Snow' chapter: his history continues until he is overtaken by that other kind of history which seems to make such little impact in the rarefied world of the 'Berghof' sanatorium – political and social history. For at the end of the novel the hero is plunged into World War I. Hans Castorp, like Wilhelm Meister before him, is both a cipher for human potentiality and a definite individual who has but one history, a life that is his and nobody else's. He is often referred to as 'mittelmässig': mediocre. And in that epithet both strands of his function in the novel interlock: he is the 'Mittel-mass', the middle way in which all values, ideologies, attitudes seem to be potentially present; he is also an ordinary young man whose life runs its wayward, largely uncertain course.

Thomas Mann's deeply affectionate, yet also profoundly critical, employment of the *Bildungsroman* model is part of his urgent attempt to review the intellectual and cultural traditions of Germany in response to the experience of the 1914–18 war. Hesse's *Das Glasperlenspiel* (1943) involves a similarly critical examination of the genre, one necessitated by the turmoil of the 1930s in Germany and the outbreak of World War II. Its title gives primacy to a cultural institution, the Glass Bead Game, as the highest expression of the aspirations of the Castalian province, aspirations which are to do with spiritual wholeness and universality. The novel is narrated by a Castalian who expresses his dislike of the bourgeois convention of the biography or life history, because for him (and for the province) it implies an overvaluing of the personal. But, in trying to celebrate the significance of the supreme Master of the Bead Game, Josef Knecht (the name is clearly a contrastive echo of Goethe's Meister), the narrator has to tell of a man who comes to repudiate Castalia and all it stands for. To put it another way, the narrator finds himself, in spite of the Castalian ideology, telling a story, recounting the biography of a man. Moreover, one of Knecht's decisive experiences is his discovery of history as an ontological dimension. When he turns his back on the ahistorical values of Castalia, he vindicates the lesson he has learnt in the most immediate of terms: he asserts his own history, the fact that his life is undeniably a *Nacheinander* in answer to that espousal of a synchronic *Nebeneinander* which is Castalia.

The foregoing has been a somewhat breathless package tour through the theory and praxis of the *Bildungsroman*.[6] I hope I may be forgiven for the indecent haste, but my purpose is to inquire into the implications that this novel tradition has for the European novel as a whole. I have already made the point that the German *Bildungsroman* has tended to be relegated to the periphery of the European novel tradition from the eighteenth century on. In answer to such summary pigeon-holing, it should be said that many of the features of the *Bildungsroman* tradition which I have highlighted – the concern for the flux of human character, the sceptical yet never sundered narrative relationship to plot in the novel, the discursiveness and (for want of a better term) 'essayism' – strike us now not as pathological departures from the authentic novel form, but as commonplace experiences for readers of the twentieth-century novel. Moreover, the birth of the *Bildungsroman* tradition, in chronological terms, runs parallel with that change in European sensibility that makes possible the 'rise of the novel': and this, too, should make us pause before allocating the *Bildungsroman* purely provincial (i.e. marginal) status.

It is an obvious feature of the bourgeois novel that it articulates the conflicting values of the society from which it derives. In that conflict there resides – in Raymond Williams' phrase – a 'creative disturbance'[7] which often manifests itself as irony. The place of irony – of a thoroughgoing self-consciousness – in the novel has been asserted with unparalleled force by German theoreticians of the novel from Friedrich

Schlegel and Hegel (think, for example, of the latter's appropriation of *Le Neveu de Rameau* in the *Phänomenologie des Geistes*), to the Lukács of the *Theorie des Romans*. In this context it is, I think, appropriate to recall a comment made by Ian Watt in his *Rise of the Novel*. In discussing *Moll Flanders* he asks after the status of the informing irony: is it a structurally integrated and reflected mode, or is it immanent in the conflicting norms which the novel enacts (without scrutinizing)? He concludes that the latter is the case, that in consequence *Moll Flanders* is an 'ironic object', whereas the former situation would produce the 'work of irony'.[8] I want to borrow Watt's distinction here and to suggest that those novels which display what J. P. Stern has called the 'epistemological naivety'[9] of realism tend, by definition, to be 'ironic objects'. But the German *Bildungsroman*, although it may be prone to a good many naiveties, is not *epistemologically* naive: its concern to articulate and to reflect upon the conflict of values which it uncovers makes it, then, a 'work of irony'. This is another way of putting the standard reproach to the *Bildungsroman* tradition: that it is peculiarly deficient in its relationship to literary realism. Clearly, I accept this charge: but I would go on to ask whether novels have to be realistic in order to qualify for more than a peripheral place in the European tradition. In my view they don't, for many reasons. First, a number of recent theoretical investigations[10] into the workings of prose narrative have suggested to us that fictions are sustained not simply by their referentiality, by their ability to invoke the shared world of economic pressures, of institutions, of social experience, but also by the codes inherent in the collusion between narrator and reader. Second, I want to argue that the *Bildungsroman* is most appropriately viewed within the context of the self-conscious novel, and that, as Robert Alter has shown,[11] such a novel, far from being peripheral, constitutes a large tradition which both precedes and succeeds the achievements of literary realism in the novel mode. Third, I would suggest that we do not have to mount the barricades in defence of *either* the realistic *or* the self-conscious novel. If it would be accepted that the realistic novel is frequently concerned with the conflict between individual aspirations and the resistant presence of practical circumstances, then the *Bildungsroman* is another voice articulating this same theme. But with a difference, of course. Within the framework of literary realism, this clash of values is seen in essentially moral terms – human growth and development is plotted on a graph of moral understanding; whereas in the German novel tradition the questions raised are epistemological rather than moral, are embedded in the hero's the narrator's – and, ultimately, the reader's – capacity for reflectivity.

Let me try now to use the *Bildungsroman* model as a framework within which to comment on a number of English novels. I should stress that I am not seeking to use one novel tradition to belabour another. And it should also be said that I am concerned to register not only differences but also similarities. For we should not forget that, as a number of commentators have shown,[12] both the theory and the practice of English novel writing from about 1870 on turns away from the commitment to realism and espouses a greater concern for what Arnold called the 'application of ideas to life'. The vindication of the romance form, say in the philosophical romance, is not, historically speaking, an unheard-of departure from native traditions: it is, rather, a re-discovery of fictive possibilities that existed before the middle of the eighteenth century, before the famous repudiations of the romance expressed by Dr Johnson and Fielding.

One observation by way of introduction: it is intriguing that the term *Bildungsroman* seems to be gaining increasing critical currency in Anglo-Saxon literary criticism. Often the term is employed simply to mean a novel of personal development through adolescence to early manhood. Such a rudimentary definition does not tell us much, I think, about the German tradition which I have outlined. But it does allow us to compare the treatment of the growing-up process in a number of very different novels. If one looks at some of the best-known English novels about adolescence, the differences become immediately apparent.

A great number of English novels concerned with adolescence operate with a precise articulation of those palpable pressures – economic and moral sanctions, tyrannical parents, poverty, blighted educational opportunities – which militate against the young man's quest for self-realization. The *Bildungsroman* has infinitely less to tell us about these factors (about, for example, such fathers as Thomas Gradgrind or Sir Austin Feverel) than does the English novel tradition.[13] Yet this should not, I think, lead us to assume that the *Bildungsroman* is purely a scenario of the inner life, with outward reality being employed simply as a cipher for the hero's growing self-awareness. For there *are* resistances in the German *Bildungsroman*: but they are founded less in the specifics of a given society than in the ontological limitation which the linear chronology of practical living entails. The growth in which the protagonist of the German *Bildungsroman* is engaged is, then, not essentially a process of moral growth, of development to the point where he can, as it were, realize himself in the right marriage, in the right career. It is precisely that concern which, for example, distinguishes *David Copperfield* from the *Bildungsroman*. Dickens' novel opens with the words: 'Whether I shall turn out to be the hero of my own life, or whether that station will be held by anybody else, these pages must show.' The problem raised – about being 'the hero of my own life' – is not to do with the epistemological elusiveness of the self that is so central to the *Bildungsroman*. What is involved is, rather, the problem of ethical clear-sightedness, of the ability to take a hand in the sensible and morally right shaping of one's life. David is a young man of artistic sensibility who ultimately becomes a writer. But the role and place of art is not explored as a philosophical problem: rather, we are concerned with the psychological and practical question as to whether or not the hero can recognize his gifts, can find a way of putting them into practice. In the *Bildungsroman* – one thinks, for example, of that radically parodistic validation of the genre that is Thomas Mann's *Felix Krull* – the artistic sensibility is used to focus certain epistemological concerns which can be extended to include a reflective collusion between narrator and reader about the artistic object, the novel, which is being narrated and read. (Incidentally, the distinction I have in mind even holds true, in my view, for two later works where the overlap in narrative concern is much greater: I am thinking of Robert Musil's *Törless* and James Joyce's *Portrait of the Artist as a Young Man*. Musil's novel has a good deal to tell us about the philosophical and perceptual issues involved in the artistic sensibility: Joyce's novel is much more immediate in rendering the psychological result of a clash between the imaginative self and the world of family and school.) But let me return briefly to *David Copperfield*. The fact that David spends much of his life infatuated with the diminutive figure of Dora, the 'child wife', is symptomatic of emotional immaturity: it does not have those philosophical and aesthetic implications which inform Heinrich Lee's love for Anna in Keller's *Der grüne Heinrich*. Nor indeed does the narrative perspective in Dickens' novel (like Keller's novel, it is in the first person) raise the kinds of thematic issue (about the relationship of art to practical reality) that are characteristic of Keller's text.

The comparison with the *Bildungsroman*, then, serves to highlight the 'epistemological naivety' (by which no pejorative implication is intended) of *David Copperfield*. The same also holds true of that other Dickens novel whose material recalls the *Bildungsroman*: *Great Expectations*. Here we sense what is a recurring pattern in the Victorian novel: the hero desires, like his *Bildungsroman* counterpart, more than his actual experience can vouchsafe him. As a result, he tends to erect false gods for himself, images of behaviour and experience which he will shed in the course of his moral growth. Psychological growth is, then, synonymous with moral growth: and the goal to which the hero attains is a validly constituted mode of community (and commerce) with his fellow man. In the course of his experience, Pip learns to see through the great expectations which take him away from Joe Gargery and all he stands for. The novel closes with what is a circumscribed and intelligible definition of the vital needs of the human self. The obliqueness and discursiveness with which the *Bildungsroman* worries at the problem of personality are just not part of the imaginative world of the realistic novel.

Many of these observations also apply to a much later English novel of adolescence, *The Way of All Flesh*. What makes Samuel Butler's narrative so unforgettable is its portrayal of the embattled self in the toils of the repressive Victorian family. The liberated Ernest Pontifex at the closing sections of the novel is, I think, somewhat of a disappointment. He comes into money, he can afford to live the life of a leisured writer of critical pamphlets. The narrator, Overton, assures us that Ernest is a decent fellow. Philosophical issues are raised about the self and its relationship to the social facts that surround it – but they are immediately dismissed with a certain heartiness: 'sensible people will get through life by rule of thumb as they may interpret it most conveniently without asking too many questions for conscience sake'.[14] The key terms here are 'sensible', 'get through', 'rule of thumb', 'conveniently'. The stress falls on pragmatic accommodations: in themselves not objectionable, perhaps, but in the context of this narrative they feel like the very apotheosis of the unreflective. One is here reminded of Edmund Gosse's autobiographical memoir *Father and Son* where the pressure of the father's authority is superbly conveyed, but where the emancipated self of the son can do little more than articulate a vague sense of how-nice-it-is-to-be-normal. The contrast with the *Bildungsroman* could hardly be more striking. For in the latter the fiercely resistant world is replaced by a much more beneficent one, and this allows the protagonist a freedom unknown to his English counterpart. All of which, however, serves to compound and complicate the problem of how to define and know the liberated, whole self. And ultimately, of course, the *Bildungsroman* suggests that even if the particular reality confronting the hero does not provide outward obstacles, yet it is inescapably there as an ontological dimension, and within that dimension there are limits set to human cognition and being.

I want, in conclusion, to offer some brief observations about the English novel towards the end of the nineteenth century and in the early years of the twentieth, and to suggest that it is here that we come much closer to the concerns of the *Bildungsroman*. I am thinking of the, on the face of it, unlikely trinity of Meredith, James, and D. H. Lawrence. For Meredith egoism was a cardinal sin which he never tired of pillorying: and it is important to recognize that Meredith was concerned not simply with a moral flaw, but with a particular form of existential impoverishment. As one recent critic has put it, 'the danger of egoism, as Meredith realized, is that it reduces the individual to a personality. To develop, one needs a supple mind: Willoughby's limitation of mind necessarily leads to a limitation of his own freedom.'[15] This concern for freedom, for an adequate realization (in both senses of the word) of the self is central to that novel of Meredith's which stands closest to the *Bildungsroman* tradition – *Harry Richmond*. Harry is torn between the solid practical world of Squire Beltham and the claims of grandiosely imaginative existence as embodied in the figure of his father, Richmond Roy. The conflict is not a simple one between stable quantities: limitation is pitted against fantasy, but fantasy is seen, in its turn, to imply an impoverishment and, hence, limitation of the self. Harry's growth is, of course, directed towards moral maturity, and in that process, the contrasting figures of Janet and Ottilia play a shaping – and evolving – role. We are concerned not simply with a process by which Harry sheds or grows out of infatuations, unworthy attachments. Because even that which is left behind has its continuing part to play in the changing patterns of the emerging personality. As Gillian Beer so acutely reminds us, Meredith 'was able to experiment far more radically than his contemporaries with...the flux as distinct from development of character'.[16] And Margaret Taggart comments on the importance of the mediocre hero, his 'somewhat shapeless personality', expressing the 'non-partisan element in human nature'.[17] Moreover, it should be stressed that *Harry Richmond* is concerned not only with the conscience of the hero but also with his consciousness, with the complex clash of values, principles, ideas, and intimations that make Henry's inwardness part of the highly discursive and symbolic texture of the novel. All of which, I think, reminds us in a number of ways of Henry James. For with his novels, the progression along the difficult axis of human growth is essentially registered not in ethical crises and decisions but in the complex clusterings of consciousness within the evolving sensibility. The Henry James novel is the aesthetic validation of this extension and enrichment of the sensibility. One knows what is meant (both in terms of Henry James *and* in terms of the *Bildungsroman* tradition) when Barbara Hardy describes *The Ambassadors* as a *Bildungsroman*, a novel which uses the point of view of a spectator 'convincing by his sensibility rather than his actions'.[18] No other novelist in the English tradition has so richly affirmed the endangeredness and the glory of the complex sensibility. And in James the tension between the *Nebeneinander* of that consciousness, compounding the reflectivity to the point of paralysis in practical affairs, and the *Nacheinander* of objective demands, decisions, relationships becomes a key factor in the overall narrative intimation of the novel.

D. H. Lawrence would seem a strange figure with whom to bring this discussion to a close. But I think that there are, for our purposes, a number of suggestive pointers in his work. Raymond Williams has commented[19] on the fact that the later novels – and particularly *Women in Love* – have forfeited that sense of a given community which is so strong in the early Lawrence. And hence the later fiction embarks on the re-discovery and re-creation of that sense of community through the relationships of a small group of characters. Throughout *Women in Love* one senses the quest for ontological wholeness and integrity in and through the complex chemistry of affection that unites Ursula and Gudrun, Rupert and Gerald. Constantly one feels the characters' need to shatter the discreteness of individuated identity in order to find a totality that is the pure re-discovery of the regenerate self. What emerges is both the urgency of this need and the ineradicable fact that the actuality of the specific relationship, of specific selfhood, always asserts its claims, that the gritty otherness of the partner militates against the mythical otherness that is sought for. In other words, there is a *Nacheinander*, a chain of experience, peopled by individuals who cannot shed their selfhood. When, in *Der Zauberberg*, Hans Castorp returns from the snow-covered landscape, he returns to that *Nacheinander* which relativizes his vision of human totality. When Gerald goes off into the snow at the end of *Women in Love*, it is precisely in order not to return to that *Nacheinander* which has so persistently refused to be gainsaid.

Mention of *Der Zauberberg* leads me to stress a point of contrast: with D. H. Lawrence we have, narratively, a hectoring concern with one area of experience, sex, which promises access to human totality. It is unthinkable that the Lawrentian protagonist could find this totality also intimated in a medical text book, in his differentiated relationship to a work of art (the 'Lindenbaum') – in the way that Hans Castorp does. For Lawrence it is only love that allows a glimpse of the roots of being. This gives a passion and intensity that the *Bildungsroman* rarely generates. But what is missing is the differentiated ability to handle the consciousness, the reflectivity of the protagonist (and of the reader), and to make that reflectivity part of the novel's own reflectivity – in the way that Mann and the other *Bildungsroman* novelists do so superbly. Let me try to illustrate the point very briefly. In *Aaron's Rod*, a novel that is almost exactly contemporary with *The Magic Mountain*, we have frequent and passionate passages of general reflections on the complex interplay of love and the individuated self. At one point, the narrator breaks off and writes: 'Don't grumble at me, then, gentle reader, and swear at me that this damned fellow wasn't half clever enough to think all these smart things, and realize all these fine-drawn-out subtleties. You are quite right, he wasn't, yet it all resolved itself in him as I say, and it is for you to prove that it didn't.'[20]

This is an extraordinary passage: clearly ironic (but not with the force of a sustained and integrated irony) in its address to the 'gentle reader'. And the irony betrays, I think, a damaging (because unreflected) uncertainty of tone. Indeed, it is unreflected in the precise sense that it seeks to countermand the reflectivity of the reader by an onslaught of bluff, no-nonsense assertions. The comparison with *The Magic Mountain* would make it clear just how impoverished Lawrence is here: and the impoverishment derives in part from his standing heir to a novel tradition in which such epistemological debate between reader and narrator is rarely taken up or explored.

Let me sum up. Goethe speaks at one point of his intention (in the novel *Die Wahlverwandtschaften*) to convey social circumstances and their conflicts in terms of symbolic comprehension: 'soziale Verhältnisse und die Konflikte derselben symbolisch gefasst darzustellen'.[21] The implications of this remark extend also to the *Bildungsroman* tradition with its concern to articulate the values and assumptions on which human experience rests, rather than to document those specific experiences and the palpable demands they make on the self. It is from this undertaking that the *Bildungsroman* emerges as a tradition which engages its reader in a narratively mediated debate about sentiments and ideas, a debate in which the conflicting positions are not only stated but also reflected upon. To view the *Bildungsroman* with the expectations of literary realism is to condemn it to insignificance. To view it within the notion of the self-conscious novel is, I think, to see it as a potent voice within the European novel tradition. Michel Zéraffa has suggested that all great fictions betray the world from which they emerge.[22] And he uses the verb 'betray' in two senses: fictions betray (i.e. they bear the imprint of) the world in which they are conceived, but they also betray that world in that they transcend (and transgress) its specific epistemological limitations. The *Bildungsroman* has, I would suggest, a knowingness about this act of betrayal. And the knowingness is the source of our insight. Marxist critics are often fond of suggesting that in hindsight we can perceive the conflicts at work in a given literary text: perhaps one could re-formulate and suggest that the hindsight is not simply something perceptually extrinsic to the text: rather, we possess that hindsight precisely because these works of literature have made it available to us. The works *are* what we know. And this is as much (or arguably even more) true of the self-conscious genre of the *Bildungsroman* as it is of the realistic novel.

NOTES

1 H. R. Jauss, *Literaturgeschichte als Provokation* (Frankfurt am Main, 1970), p. 177.

2 Tzvetan Todorov, *The Fantastic: A Structural Approach to a Literary Genre* (Cleveland and London, 1973), pp. 5ff. See also the discussion of Todorov's theory of genre in *New Literary History*, 8 (1976), pp. 145–70.

3 See W. H. Bruford, *The German Tradition of Self-Cultivation: 'Bildung' from Humboldt to Thomas Mann* (Cambridge, 1975), and R. H. Thomas, 'The Uses of "Bildung"', *German Life and Letters*, 30 (1977), pp. 177–86.

4 Hegel, *Vorlesungen über die Asthetik*, edited by F. Bassenge (Berlin, 1955), p. 983.

5 See M. Beaujean, *Der Trivialroman in der zweiten Hälfte des 18. Jahrhunderts* (Bonn, 1964) and H. Emmel, *Was Goethe vom Roman der Zeitgenossen nahm* (Bern, 1972).

6 For a more detailed discussion of these and related issues see my study, *The German 'Bildungsroman' from Wieland to Hesse* (Princeton, 1978).

7 Raymond Williams, *The English Novel from Dickens to Lawrence* (St Albans, 1974), p. 70.

8 Ian Watt, *The Rise of the Novel* (Harmondsworth, 1968), p. 135.

9 J. P. Stern, *On Realism* (London, 1973), p. 54.

10 G. von Graevenitz, *Die Setzung des Subjekts: Untersuchungen zur Romantheorie* (Tübingen, 1973); Wolfgang Iser, *Der implizite Leser* (Munich, 1972) and *Der Akt des Lesens* (Munich, 1976); R. Barthes, *S/Z* (Paris, 1970).

11 Robert Alter, *Partial Magic: The Novel as a Self-Conscious Genre* (Berkeley and London, 1975).

12 Richard Stang, *The Theory of the Novel in England 1850–1870* (London, 1959); Kenneth Graham, *English Criticism of the Novel 1865–1900* (Oxford, 1965).

13 The one German novel that offers precise documentation of the repressive family

is K. P. Moritz's *Anton Reiser* (first published in parts 1785–90). Its astringency and urgency make it a cautionary tale about a blighted childhood rather than a *Bildungsroman*. For the English novel, see Jerome H. Buckley, *Season of Youth: The Bildungsroman from Dickens to Golding* (Cambridge, Mass., 1974).

14 *The Way of All Flesh*, chapter 69.

15 Donald D. Stone, *Novelists in a Changing World* (Cambridge, Mass., 1972), p. 126.

16 Gillian Beer, *Meredith: A Change of Masks* (London, 1970), p. 189.

17 Margaret Tarratt, '*The Adventures of Harry Richmond*: "Bildungsroman" and Historical Novel', in *Meredith Now*, edited by Ian Fletcher (London, 1971), p. 181.

18 Barbara Hardy, *The Appropriate Form: An Essay on the Novel* (London, 1971), p. 44.

19 Williams, *The English Novel*, p. 144.

20 *Aaron's Rod* (London, 1954), p. 161.

21 Letter from Goethe to F. W. Riemer, *Werke, Briefe und Gespräche*, edited by Ernst Beutler (Zürich and Stuttgart, 1949–), XX, 500.

22 Michel Zéraffa, *Fictions: The Novel and Social Reality* (Harmondsworth, 1976), p. 43.

French and American sources of
Victorian realism

CHRISTOPHER HEYWOOD

Studies of the Victorian conflict over realism and naturalism[1] were for long dominated by the Zola controversy of the 1880s. The historical patterns and polemical positions of academic and critical writers inherited the influential arguments put forward in studies by Ferdinand Brunetière and D. C. Murray,[2] claiming that a native English tradition of realism, *naturalisme anglais*, was threatened by the imported tradition from France. This historical thesis was dramatized in opposite ways but without alteration to its outlines in numerous essays and investigations. One side supported the imported influence, the other opposed it. Dean Inge warned his Cambridge audience against surrender and pointed to the 'palmy days' of the mid-Victorian decades: 'Our nation has a great tradition in fiction, and we shall be wise to stick to it, instead of preferring a corrupt following of the French.'[3] Ford Madox Ford exhorted his readers to turn their eyes towards a school headed by Flaubert, Stendhal, and to a lesser extent Balzac, with George Moore 'in a class quite apart as a serious and conscious artist', Hardy a grade lower, 'a writer whose works are not technically very interesting', and Conrad, W. H. Hudson and Henry James 'by themselves quite above all others'.[4] This article[5] will support a number of more recent writers who have pointed to the mixed origins of Victorian literary thought and expression;[6] among early essays contemporaneous with those of Brunetière and Murray, a more secure, albeit biased, starting guide to the complexities of Victorian realism can be found in Ruskin's essay of 1880, 'Fiction, Fair and Foul'.[7]

Ruskin's distaste for the forensic elements in the fiction of the preceding half-century, its preoccupation with the affairs of the clinic, the divorce and police court, the asylum, the cemetery and the morgue, and the general Victorian dislike of clinical objectivity, were warnings of a storm which had already broken over the novels of Zola by the time

Ruskin's essay appeared. Contrary to the assumptions of most studies which placed a too heavy reliance on the claims of George Moore to have introduced naturalism, the Victorian controversy over naturalism began five years before the appearance of *A Mummer's Wife* (1885), and was taken a stage further by Moore's novel. The climax was reached with the publication of *The Soil* (1888), Vizetelly's translation of *La Terre* (1885). The imprisonment and untimely death of Vizetelly was an early climax in a protracted debate which ended, for the time being at least, with the appearance in 1960 of D. H. Lawrence's *Lady Chatterley's Lover* (1928). 'I know I shall be accused of rank Zola-ism in putting forward this plea', William Archer wrote in defence of *Drink* (1879), Charles Reade's adaptation of *L'Assommoir* (1879), and went on: 'So be it. If it be Zola-ism to demand that the stage shall "hold as 'twere the mirror up to nature", then Hamlet and I are Zola-ists.'[8] Archer's defence against criticisms in *The Times* and elsewhere of the production which took London by storm in June 1879, and provoked numerous imitations and echoes, undoubtedly lent impetus to Moore's choice of themes and methods for his second novel.[9] Besides managing the production of Reade's play at the Princess Theatre, John Hollingshead was manager of the Gaiety Theatre, the source of the literary contacts which led Moore to journey to Hanley in search of background material for *A Mummer's Wife*.[10] Reade's dramatized version fell back on a device which had for long served the purposes of 'sensation' novelists when faced with the problem of adapting French sources to English taste, that is, the free relationship of Gervaise, Lantier and Coupeau is set out as a bigamous marriage relationship. Despite this intrusion from the tradition of *Lady Audley's Secret* and *East Lynne*, the originality and forcefulness of Zola's art is well represented through the bold simplification of the *dramatis personae*, the strong enactment of a burning social issue,[11] and the loose articulation of symbolic scenes with a pictorial rather than a narrative bias, a 'succession of tableaux' rather than 'a well-knit story', as Joseph Knight observed.[12]

Zola's considerable late-Victorian influence is taken in some studies to be the first of a succession of external influences, French, Russian and American, on a stable national tradition.[13] The tradition had, however, already undergone a radical transformation through the persistent pressure of numerous precursors of Zola, Turgenev and Hemingway: among these, the dominant influences were Balzac, Hawthorne, Flaubert, and, as Patricia Thomson has shown in a commanding study, George Sand.[14]

By the late 1870s the Victorian tradition was an amalgam of themes and methods borrowed from a multiplicity of sources. The long association between the English 'gothic' and the American 'frontier' novels, and the work of Poe and Balzac, stood at the head of a well-established mid-Victorian habit of borrowing from French and American fictional sources. Victorian criticism adopted many of its modes from French examples, and by mid-century London no longer lagged behind Boston in its enthusiasm for Balzac and George Sand.[15] Less well studied than the parallel interests of Balzac, Zola's exposure to the fiction of England and New England was considerable as a result of his period of work as publicity manager to Hachette, who issued numerous translations in the 1850s and 1860s.[16] This fertile source of contact contributed substantially to the social commitment and stratification of naturalism. A close association between 'realism' and the 'literature of sensation', including the English novels known as 'sensation novels', emerged in the 1850s and 1860s. All the writers in this phase of Victorian realism were involved in a debate about the value of 'sensation' as a source of knowledge and moral control. The article by Henry Longueville Mansel, which gave direction to the debate after its appearance in 1863,[17] recognized both the social and the intellectual implications of 'sensation', and placed Miss Braddon at the centre of the storm which eventually merged into the controversy over naturalism. 'All art...appeals primarily to the senses', Conrad wrote in his preface to *The Nigger of the Narcissus*: 'the artistic aim when expressing itself in written words must also make its appeal through the senses, if its high desire is to reach the secret spring of the responsive emotions'.[18] Fidelity to sensuous experience provides the writer with an entry to the reader's response; Jean Richard's *Littérature et sensation* (Paris, 1974), and studies of individual authors such as Pierre Danger's *Sensations et objets dans le roman de Flaubert* (Paris, 1973), have explored this question with fruitful results. But the counter-current, of which Mansel's article 'Sensation Novels' and Ruskin's 'Fiction, Fair and Foul' are typical examples, together with the review of Flaubert by J. J. Weiss, 'La Littérature brutale',[19] brought recoil as well as insight. 'The nineteenth-century dislike of realism is the rage of Caliban seeing his face in the glass', Wilde suggested in his preface to *The Picture of Dorian Gray*; yet the impulse towards realism is irresistible: 'The nineteenth-century dislike of romanticism is the rage of Caliban not seeing his face in the glass.'

Zola's repudiation of the *Revue des deux mondes* and his knowledge of its objectives were stimulated by his work as advertising editor for Hachette. In essays on Dickens, Mrs Gaskell, Hawthorne, Poe, and many others, Émile Forgues and Émile Montégut sought to influence the taste of the age towards a liberal optimism, not unlike that of Brunetière, but retaining a firmer control than his over the links between the traditions of France, England and America. Of *The Scarlet Letter*, a potent source for Victorian writers for themes of domestic tragedy, Forgues observed:

L'immense popularité de ce livre par-delà l'Atlantique et chez nos voisins d'outre-Manche est un véritable phénomène littéraire, un signe du temps. Les anathèmes lancés naguère contre *Lélia* par le choeur des *Revues* et *Magazines* britanniques ne nous avaient pas absolument préparés à comprendre par quel miracle un roman tout aussi hardi, et plus franchement hardi que celui de George Sand, a pu recevoir un acceuil si différent, conquérir tant de suffrages, rencontrer si peu de détracteurs.[20]

In his essay on the 'sensation novel' question, partly an echo but predominantly a sensitive riposte to Mansel's article in the *Quarterly*, Forgues gave excellent insights into the strengths and weaknesses of Miss Braddon and Wilkie Collins, and paved the way for the translations which passed through the hands of Zola as Hachette's publicity manager. The praise, in terms taken from Hugo's funeral oration on Balzac – 'enfin et surtout ce je ne sais quoi d'encore innomé qui permet de créer un type et de lui donner la consistance, le mouvement, l'animation, la physionomie, l'accent d'un être humain' – for 'Miss Braddon, une *authoress* qui se proclame fort expérimentée (quoque jeune)',[21] proved too much for Zola, who made his reply two years later. In an 'aside' appended to a review of G. W. M. Reynolds's *Fernanda*, he objected to 'Miss Braddon, une *authoress* qu'on a tenté vainement de transplanter chez nous', revealed the burden imposed on him by Hachette, 'J'ai été forcé à lire toutes les traductions françaises de ses romans', and added: 'J'ai manqué en faire une maladie.'[22] His objection in this review against the narrative methods of the English tradition, 'd'indigestes auteurs qui ont besoin de six cents pages pour vous réciter la moindre anecdote', echoed Forgues' complaint that 'sensation' novels were 'des histoires à commencer par la fin'. In the substantive debate about the role of sensation in social and individual experience, Zola nevertheless adopted a position which tallied at many points with that of the principal sensation novel, *Lady Audley's Secret* (1862).

Lady Audley's numerous secrets, as Forgues pointed out, converge in a single revelation. Miss Braddon's boldly constructed portrayal of a woman's extinction within the mechanisms of a brutal society, partly through her moral weakness but principally through her exposure to an inescapable economic and hereditary determinism, foreshadows Zola's treatment of similar themes in the novel which made its first appearance towards the end of the year in which his note on Miss Braddon appeared. Poverty, a hastily executed and instantly repented marriage made under deceptive parental pressure, the ensuing imposition of childbirth on a weak temperament with nervous disabilities inherited from her insane mother, and the rigours of economic recession, drive the distracted heroine to clandestine criminal actions. A bigamous second marriage, recognized at once by Forgues as a Victorian euphemism for adultery, but one which remains, like those of Hester Prynne and Honoria Dedlock, unconsummated, leads to a chain of failed crimes starting with the attempted murder (in self-defence, however) of her first husband, the father of her child, on his unexpected return from Australia. Blackmailed by the bull-necked ('cou de taureau', in *Le Secret de Lady Audley*, Hachette, 1863) landlord of the local inn, whose marriage to her maid gives him possession of her guilty secret, persecuted to distraction in three admirably dramatized scenes by her ageing husband's barrister nephew, who for a while falls in love with his young aunt by marriage, and thus precipitated into nervous collapse and confession, the heroine embarks at last on her final journey to an asylum in Belgium. Though taken almost universally among literary historians as a mere tale of suspense and crime, *Lady Audley's Secret* prepared the ground for the dark treatment of nervous disintegration and near-crime in novels such as *Thérèse Raquin* (1867), *Daniel Deronda*, *Tess*, and *The Secret Agent*. Miss Braddon's novels were well known in Eastwood, where the Mechanics' Institute library had twenty-three titles by 1895, in a collection notable for its strength in the fiction section,[23] and many of their themes re-appear, tinged still with the heritage of criminality and nervous despondency which was her particular signature, in novels with Eastwood settings such as *Women in Love* and *Lady Chatterley's Lover*.

Zola's conception of his characters as 'des personnages souverainement dominés par leurs nerfs et leur sang, dépourvus de libre arbitre' (preface to the second edition of *Thérèse Raquin*), echoes Miss Braddon's treatment of her heroine within the context of a neglected, yet central, area of the physiological debate about 'sensation'. This topic owed much to the work of the English physiologist, Marshall Hall (1790–1857), whose explanation of the 'reflex arc' mechanism of the spinal cord, in a paper given to the Royal Society in 1833,[24] represented the start of a new age for the experimental and philosophical discussion of involuntary nervous activity. Hall's work led to his campaigns for sanitation, against slavery, flogging and blood-letting, and attained a particular distinction in the invention of the modern method of artificial respiration which for long bore his name. His interest in convulsive diseases and loss of responsibility had many followers, of whom one appears to have been Henry Maudsley, whose definition of nervous functioning rests on the controversial 'reflex' principle which Hall had first explored. 'Probably the modern sensation novel', Maudsley suggested in a penetrating footnote, 'with its murders, bigamies, and other crimes, was an achievement of the epileptic imagination'[25] – that is, of an area of nervous activity which particularly interested Hall. The suggestion made by Robert Niess that Zola's source for *Thérèse Raquin* may have been *The Scarlet Letter* (*La Lettre rouge*, translated by E. D. Forgues, Hachette, 1861)[26] bears investigation, since *Lady Audley's Secret* owed its abrasive treatment of society and its injured heroine both to *Bleak House* and to Dickens's principal literary source, *The Scarlet Letter*,[27] a novel which Miss Braddon described as 'Hawthorne's beautiful story' in a later work.[28] The praise for *Lady Audley's Secret* which Arnold Bennett offered in purely literary terms, 'slowly raise the curtain and raise it, till the full history of this beautiful creature stands beautifully clear...it has the genuine vital impulse – the impulse which created *The Duchess of Malfi, Wuthering Heights*...',[29] can be extended into a large literary, social and intellectual context. Of Miss Braddon's poignant personal history as the companion of a man long debarred from marriage to her by reason of his wife's confinement in an asylum, Michael Sadleir notes: 'It is impossible that she should have acquired her...power to depict feminine nature in contact with a world both dangerous and indifferent, without having herself lived a fuller and more hazardous life than has been (or is ever likely to be) recorded.'[30]

The central physiological action in *Lady Audley's Secret* hinges not so much on the evocation of sensory excitement, a feature to which Margaret Oliphant took exception – 'flesh and muscles...strong arms that seize her, and warm breath that thrills her through, and a host of other physical attractions...this eagerness for physical sensation'[31] – as, paradoxically, on the exclusion of sensation from the arena of reflex action which had been argued by Hall. In a lengthy attack, George Henry Lewes objected to the 'reflex arc' theory and sought to replace it by his doctrine of a 'stream of Consciousness'[32] affecting equally all parts of the nervous system through the 'neurility' or 'sensibility' which he saw as inherent in nervous activity. Hall's explanation of involuntary nervous action as a function performed without sensation within the spinal cord was modified in later explanations of involuntary processes, notably those of Claude Bernard (1813–78) and Walter Holbrook Gaskell (1847–1914), whose work led to the modern picture of an interlocking system based on common functions and structures.[33] Hall's theory, and with it the whole question of sensation as an aspect of mental life, played a role in the controversy over 'sensation' novels. Zola owed to an intermediary, *Le Secret de Lady Audley*, the theme of nervous degeneration which dominated *Thérèse Raquin*. Retribution through nervous disintegration, strikingly described as 'metaphysical dry rot' by Miss Braddon (*Lady Audley*, chapter 34), and the cry '"My brain is on fire"' (Chapter 36) which brings the heroine to confession, prefigure the 'étouffements continus, des sourires pâles et navrants, des silences écrasants de vide et de désesperance' which spring from the heroine's murder of her husband in *Thérèse Raquin* (Chapter 19). Zola's immediate literary source, *La Vénus de Gordes* (1885), by Alphonse Belot and Ernest Daudet,[34] a tale of adultery, murder, police detection and routine judiciary retribution without remorse of conscience or nerves, lacks the spontaneous self-destruction which overtakes the heroines of Zola and Miss Braddon. Zola was at this time not yet immersed in the ideas of Claude Bernard which dominated his later writing,[35] but through Miss Braddon's text he had access to physiological thinking based on that of Hall. The figure of 'Dr Alwyn Mosgrave' to whom Lady Audley makes her confession, the 'specialist in nervous diseases' from Saville Row, is, it may be reasonably supposed, a muffled portrayal of Marshall Hall ('Al–, M–s–ra––'), not unlike Miss Braddon's other portrayals of known persons. Miss Braddon here echoes the picture of Hall which appeared in *The Caxtons* (1849), a novel by her admired mentor, Bulwer-Lytton, which she had read and which is acknowledged in the biography of Hall by his widow, Charlotte Hall.[36]

The 'sensation' novel, the most realistic and potent of the forms of *le naturalisme anglais*, had its roots in the complex tradition stemming from Balzac, 'notre père à tous', as Zola called him in *Les Romanciers naturalistes* (1881). With some justification, Ruskin pointed to Victor Hugo as the origin of a sensationalism which, as he saw it, infected the whole of literature in the age following the death of Scott:

The effectual head of the whole cretinous school is the renowned novel in which the hunchbacked lover watches the execution of his mistress from the tower of Notre-Dame, and its strength passes gradually into the anatomical preparations for the general market, or novels like [Wilkie Collins's] *Poor Miss Finch*, in which the heroine is blind, the hero epileptic, and the obnoxious brother is found with his hand dropped off, in the arctic regions.[37]

The rival view prevailed among Thackeray, Lewes, the Stephens, Wilkie Collins, and eventually Dickens; they found in Hugo and Balzac the mastery of social and psychological processes towards which the novel inevitably gravitated. In his reply to the founding article of the tradition followed by Ruskin, Croker's essay 'French Novels' in the *Quarterly Review*,[38] G. W. M. Reynolds wrote:

The literature of France, previous to the Revolution of 1830, resembled that of England at the present day; in as much as moral lessons were taught through the medium of impossible fictions. Now the French author paints the truth in all its nudity; and the development of the secrets of Nature shocks the English reader, because he is not just yet accustomed to so novel as style.[39]

Among various influences shaping the practice of Victorian novel writing, those of Balzac's *Eugénie Grandet*, Hawthorne's *The Scarlet Letter* and Flaubert's *Madame Bovary* share the palm for their penetration of the central works in the Victorian tradition. The analysis of processes shaping social, domestic and nervous life, the bold use of large social and psychological planes of action, the gradual atrophy of the author's intervention and its replacement by the personality of a discernibly limited narrator, and the uses of 'rendering' which Ruskin, Pater, and James projected as the key to a convincing art of fictional or pictorial portrayal, were the dominant impulses of the transforming process.

Literary adaptation in this process of change emerges through chance hints, parallels of structure and theme, and contrasted intellectual purposes, rather than through literal plagiarism of the type explored by Louis James in the popular fiction of the 1830s and 1840s.[40] Miss Braddon's portrayal of a 'sensation' author, Sigismund Smith, the heroine's companion in *The Doctor's Wife* (1864), gives a satirical version of a widespread practice: '"Don't empty one man's pocket"', he explains to the admiring heroine, '"but take a little off all round. The combination novel enables a young author to present his public with all the brightest flowers of fiction all neatly arranged into every variety of garland"' (Chapter 4). Generations of novelists found in *The Doctor's Wife* the best available model for introducing in combination the vexed, problematic but haunting ideas of *Madame Bovary*, *The Scarlet Letter* and *Eugénie Grandet* before a reading public which was appalled and fascinated by their themes. The heroine's yearning temperament, her blighted marriage, domestic despairs and exposure to the possibility of an adulterous relationship, reappeared as the stock configuration in subsequent novels by George Eliot, Hardy, Henry James, George Moore, Somerset Maugham, Galsworthy, and (in a late flowering of the tradition) Joyce Cary. *The Saturday Review* praised *The Doctor's Wife* for its author's 'real excellence in the highest and purest walks of art' and her powers of 'dazzling us by the unlooked-for versatility of her powers'. The 'perfect truth and high moral perception in making the doctor's wife simply triumphant of the world and the flesh', the review went on, was acceptable, but 'what is false to nature lies in making her unconscious of any temptation of the kind'.[41] The detailed evocation of the Stoneleigh and Coventry region of Warwickshire, the exact portrayal of persons and scenes known to George Eliot, the concentration on a single phase of action in the development of a romantic temperament, and its importance, like that of an obscure market town given legendary proportions by the presence of a school or railway junction, gave to *The Doctor's Wife* a position not inconsistent with the neglected praise of *The Saturday Review*.

Miss Braddon's procedures for importing the themes of *Madame Bovary* into the central Victorian literary arena were more complex than might appear from the slighting observation of Henry James in his review: 'If another of her heroines is tempted, she resists.'[42] Across a scheme of action borrowed from Flaubert's great original, the heroine's blighted marriage, her reliance on the companionship of a sympathetic but emotionally distant friend, and her resistance to the approach of a would-be seducer, she drew a veil skilfully borrowed from *The Scarlet Letter* and *Eugénie Grandet*. The meetings of the lovers in the fields and woods, the vengeful jealousy which ensues upon the rupture and the heroine's leaning towards a spiritual clergyman, the death of the hypocritical, will-less lover, the heroine's devotion to good works after the lapse of her emotional life, and the frustrations of a marriage somewhat awkwardly patterned on the *mariage blanc* of *Eugénie Grandet*, stem from Miss Braddon's declared admiration for the two rival masterpieces. 'There was no scarlet letter with which these people could brand her as the guilty creature they believed her to be', Miss Braddon assured her readers (chapter 26), at the height of her heroine's yearning towards the spirituality of the Rev. Austin Colborne in 'Hurstonleigh' (Stoneleigh) church. The result, as Eneas Dallas suggested in his review, clearly replying to *The Saturday Review* and written for the paper edited by Miss Braddon's cousin, John Delane, was the compromise which vexed and challenged her successors: 'It would be impossible to make the story of *Madame Bovary* agreeable to English tastes, and Miss Braddon has made out of it a story that need offend no-one'; furthermore, 'women do at times cherish a sort of spiritual life which is independent of mundane relationships'.[43] Like most reviewers, Henry James exploited the criminal interests of Miss Braddon's early work for purposes of ridicule, but in passing he made a penetrating remark on the essentially *balzacien* fusion of heightened action, searching analysis, and detailed, sensuous observation which lent strength to these works:

Of course, the nearer the criminal and the detective are brought home to the reader, the more lively his 'sensation'. They are brought home... by a happy choice of probable circumstance, and it is through their skill in the choice of these circumstances – their thorough-going realism – that Mr Collins and Miss Braddon have become famous.[44]

Attending more to thematic than to technical problems, Margaret Oliphant pointed to the debt of the 'sensation' novelists to Hawthorne: 'Mr Wilkie Collins is not the first man who has produced a sensation novel... the higher class of American fiction, as represented by Hawthorne, attempts little else'.[45] Despite the insistence that *The Doctor's Wife* was '*not* a sensation novel' (chapter 34), it offered many elements from the *genre* which specialized in criminality, pursuit, and buried mysteries. The naming and setting of its characters, however, an Isabel who sees herself as 'a simple Dorothea', the more perceptive Gwendolen, the romantic Roland and the dull Dr Gilbert whom she marries, form the paradigm explored again and critically re-handled in *Middlemarch*, *The Portrait of a Lady*,[46] and *The Return of the Native*.

The explosive power of *Madame Bovary* was well-known to George Eliot, who read of Meredith's struggle with the text in his review for the *Westminster Review* in 1857: 'We flung the book to the four corners of the room; but we took it up again, and we finished it.'[47] In *Middlemarch*, the double challenge of Flaubert's theme and of Miss Braddon's travesty of its central action were taken up. Here again, a story taken from Flaubert's plot, with greater expansiveness in its physiological aspects, was protected within a veil borrowed from *The Scarlet Letter*. The first sketches of the tale of a doctor and his worldly wife included the dangerous figure of Will Ladislaw.[48] Development of his obvious attractions would have yielded an unprintable text; their suppression (as in *The Doctor's Wife*, where Léon Dupuis becomes the charming Sigismund Smith, who reappears in *The Portrait of a Lady* as the doomed Ralph Touchett) would have exposed the story to ridicule from *The Saturday Review*. George Eliot's remedy lay once again in the sexless arena of spiritual struggle, to which *The Scarlet Letter* was the abiding monument. The sensitive orchestration of Will's union with a second heroine patterned on Hester Prynne rather than Emma Bovary, the 'crack and roll' of the thunder, the 'great swoop of the wind' and the 'intense consciousness of many things' at the end of *Middlemarch* (chapter 83), has not exempted George Eliot from criticism brought by readers at home in the wider tradition of literary experience.[49] The rough jointing which brought the two stories together and the evidently improvised death of the aged scholar who persecutes the successful lover, can be read as evidence of Victorian hypocrisy, as in most early studies of the problem, but should rather be seen as the effort of an artificer to admit chinks of light into the literary gloom. The formula perfected by Miss Braddon underwent further strain in the hands of Thomas Hardy, whose interest in *The Scarlet Letter* is less widely documented than George Eliot's.[50] His revisions of *The Return of the Native* for Miss Braddon's periodical, *Belgravia*, included the notorious happy ending, but in a less readily discernible development of the process of revision, his use of *The Scarlet Letter* as a veil for the themes of *Madame Bovary* produced the obvious problem inherent in the texts: the harsh realities in Hawthorne's text reappeared, provoking widespread suppositions about the carnality of Wildeve's early relations with Eustacia Vye.[51]

The quest for clarity in the portrayal of emotional and social relationships, that is, the painful achievement of George Moore's ambition that 'the nineteenth century should possess a literature characteristic of its nervous, passionate life',[52] produced, in the case of *A Mummer's Wife*, a text at once bold in its frank development of a theme borrowed from *Thérèse Raquin*[53] and conservative in its retention of themes from the Victorian tradition.[54] The tradition had been transformed already, in successive waves, by George Sand, Balzac, Hawthorne and Flaubert. The powerful impression made by Hawthorne began in 1851 with Dickens' reading of *The Scarlet Letter* and his embarking on a wholesale adaptation of its themes and methods in the following year, when he began writing *Bleak House*. He wrote to Forster in 1851:

I finished reading The Scarlet Letter yesterday. It falls off sadly after that fine opening scene. The psychological part of the story is very much overdone, and not truly done I think. Their suddenness of meeting and agreeing to go away together after all these years, is very poor. Mr Chillingworth ditto. The child out of nature altogether. And Mr Dimmisdale [*sic*] certainly never could have begotten her.[55]

The development of Victorian realism under the guidance of the dramatic, analytical and pictorial art of Balzac in the half-century following the 1830s obeyed a more complex law than that offered by T. S. Eliot in his assessment of the process: 'Hawthorne in America and

Balzac in France invented dramatic form separately, and passed it on to Henry James.'[56] No less than close, sensuous observation of texture and surface, the dramatic rendering of plausible actions was a principal component of the movement, as Symons suggested in his evaluation of the importance of Balzac: 'Pose before him a purely mental problem, and he will resolve it by a scene in which the problem literally works itself out.'[57] Dickens' handling of Hawthorne's theme brought the resources of the Victorian novelist to an unprecedented height. From Balzac, Thackeray had already learned the use of a large social canvas as the background to domestic and economic rises and falls.[58] Hawthorne's art was not, as Eliot suggested (drawing on James) the provincial improvisation of isolated genius, but rather a skill redevelopment of literary themes from Balzac and others within the context provided by Melville, Emerson, and the sinewy literary life of Boston.[59] In *Ferragus*, Hawthorne would have found a model for his tale of a lover's jealous watch over the suspected affair of a heroine, but his emphasis is constantly on the mental aspect of a drama long since buried in the past. 'The man is placed upon the rack, but our compassion is aroused, not by feeling our own nerves and sinews twitching in sympathy, but by remarking the strange confusion of ideas produced in his mind', Leslie Stephen argued in his definition of the strength of Hawthorne's treatment of Dimmesdale.[60] Dickens' use of Hawthorne's theme proved in practice to be less bold, and more fraught with the kind of lurid detail which offended Ruskin and which the austerer art of Hawthorne had avoided, than his first response might have promised. Lady Dedlock's transgression proves to be a forgivable lapse in youth, the lovers die without reunion, and (as in *The House of the Seven Gables*, which Dickens read in 1851) the evils of the past are briskly redeemed by a marriage founded on the social value of a technical skill. Despite these evasions, Dickens' handling of Hawthorne's theme compares favourably with the play of 1888 by the Hon. Stephen Coleridge, *The Scarlet Letter*, which outraged a lively (and largely American) audience at its first night by its lurid travesty of Hawthorne's tragic ending: a ring-trick proves that Chillingworth is the father of Pearl, and he is hanged for his hypocrisy by a lynching party assembled from the Election Sermon congregation, thus leaving the clandestine lovers free to embark upon a legalized romance.[61]

Hawthorne's boldness, and his kinship with the romantic realism of the 1830s, were seen by Forgues:

Les anathèmes lancés naguère contre Lélia par le chœur des *Revues* et *Magazines* britanniques ne nous avaient pas absolument préparés à comprendre par quel miracle un roman tout aussi hardi, et plus franchement hardi que celui de George Sand, a pu recevoir un accueil si différent, conquérir tant de suffrages, rencontrer si peu de détracteurs.[62]

Dramatic clarity was included in the principle of 'rendering', a key idea developed by Ruskin in the prefaces to *Modern Painters* (1843–60) and upheld by Pater, Henry James, Symons, Conrad, and Ford Madox Ford as the creative principle of communication underlying realism. Symons' use of the term in its complex sense of dramatic projection, portrayal through sensuous experience, and ambiguous moral effect, provides a *locus* for the idea in relation to *The Scarlet Letter*: 'And note, also, with how perfect a sympathy he can render the sensation itself, what is exultant, liberating in a strong sin...For guilt has its rapture too. The foremost result of a broken law is ever an ecstatic sense of freedom.'[63] In the performance of this function, the mind of the mediating protagonist played a central role, as Fitzjames Stephen observed against the background of his unreserved admiration for Balzac:

There is a large class of novels in which all the incidents are arranged so as to give prominence to one particular view of life, and to present it, as it might be supposed to present itself to the eyes of one person, who (with some modifications) acts as hero in a whole series of novels...it is like looking at the world through coloured spectacles.[64]

The same point is elaborated as a mark of the excellence of Dostoevski in a penetrating review by T. S. Eliot. Dostoevski's 'point of departure', Eliot argued, was 'a human brain in a human environment and the "aura" is simply the continuation of quotidian experience of the brain into seldom explored extremities of torture'.[65] Victorian and Edwardian novelists worked in an unbroken line, selectively re-interpreting lessons learned in the volatile social conditions of Europe and America. In expressing his admiration for *Eugénie Grandet* and working its themes into his first published novel, *The White Peacock* (1911), Lawrence spoke within a settled idiom:

I consider the book *Eugénie Grandet* as perfect a novel as I have ever read. It is wonderfully concentrated; there is nothing superfluous, nothing out of place. The book has that wonderful feeling of inevitableness which is characteristic of the best French novels. It is rather astonishing that we, the cold English, should have to go to the fleshy French for level-headed, fair unrelenting realism. Can you find a grain of sentimentality in Eugénie? Can you find a grain of melodrama, or caricature, or flippancy? It is all in tremendous earnestness, more serious than all the profundities of the German thinkers, more affecting than all English bathos. It makes me droop my head and be silent. Balzac can lay bare the living body of the great life better than anybody in the world.[66]

Miss Braddon's novels were developed similarly against the background of her admiration for 'Balzac's matchless Eugénie Grandet', as she expressed it, and of a conception of fiction near to Lawrence's. A novel, she argued, should be 'a picture representing, with more or less truth and faithfulness, the manners and customs of society. A work of fiction delineating dramatic or humorous characters. A web in which are skilfully wrought the passions, emotions, or feelings, supposed to fill the human breast, as well as the incidents which bring them into play.'[67]

The source of a long Victorian tradition of admiration for, and adaptation of, *Eugénie Grandet*, was undoubtedly the review by Croker which inaugurated the tradition of antagonism to the French novel in Victorian times. Balzac's social and psychological themes were, Croker argued, acceptable to Wilhelmine taste: 'The story of Eugénie Grandet *...* has the almost singular merit, that it may be read by a man without indignation, and by a woman without a blush. It is... *a Dutch picture of an interior...*'[68] The heroine's choice of a mercenary marriage and her betrayal in a passionate attachment to a worthless object reappears in *Aurora Floyd* (1863), the novel in which Miss Braddon confirmed the celebrity attained in *Lady Audley's Secret*, where a comparable mechanism rules the action. The complexities attending the study of French, German and mythological sources for the Brontës' novels enjoin caution in any approach to this field.[69] In *Wuthering Heights*, however, Emily Brontë made strong use of the themes of *Eugénie Grandet*, with alterations not more trenchant than those in better authenticated cases of borrowing, for example Bennett's *Anna of the Five Towns* and James's *Washington Square*. The *Quarterly* for the period (and thus Croker's encouragement to read this work) was available in the Keighley Mechanics' Institute Library.[70] The heroine's scarcely controllable passion, its lapse, the degeneration and avarice of its object, the choice of mercenary marriage partners and the power of families to destroy their weaker members, that is, the central themes of Balzac's novel, emerge subtly transformed by Emily Brontë's psychological and folkloric approach to her subject.

Mastery of a tradition greater than any suspected by Inge fell to James, Hardy, Conrad and Lawrence, and to the uncompromising strength of Joyce. The sensuous and dramatic pursuit of 'rendering' involved purifying a flawed language: 'fiction... strives for resolutions based upon maximum fulfilment, rather than the illusory kind achieved by denying or slighting certain claims; it seeks resolutions which, to use a happy word of Robert Penn Warren's, are "earned" rather than forced'.[71] No single rule could fit all cases. In his preface to *The Nigger of the Narcissus*, Conrad outlined the progress of the artist's pilgrimage: 'Realism, Romanticism, Naturalism, even the unofficial sentimentalism (which like the poor, is exceedingly difficult to get rid of), all these gods must, after a short period of fellowship, abandon him.' The climax of nervous energy which brings the action of *The Secret Agent* (1907) to its resolution parallels the destruction of the nerves in *Lady Audley's Secret* and *Thérèse Raquin*, but ranges further than these into the obscure political environment and into the inner conscience of the tortured Stevie. His destruction is 'remembered...pictorially (chapter 11) by Winnie and her 'whole being was rocked by that inconclusive and maddening thought. It was in her veins, in her bones, in the roots of her hair.' Her personality is destroyed and she becomes a creature 'torn into two pieces, whose mental operations did not adjust themselves very well to each other'. In the murder scene she re-enacts, with greater precision, the drama of Lady Audley and Thérèse. Her *milieu intérieur* is in ruins, 'her heart, hardened and chilled into a lump of ice, kept her body in an inward shudder' (chapter 11), and she re-lives the anarchy of a hectic *milieu extérieur*: 'her immemorial and obscure descent, the simple ferocity of the age of caverns, and the unbalanced fury of the age of bar-rooms' (chapter 11).

In its Victorian setting, 'realism' developed in a succession of waves or 'terraces', in sympathy with the literature of France, New England, and, later, of Russia. Though the Zola crisis was probably the largest step in the process, the shock of recognition which followed the appearance of *Madame Bovary*, and the strong Victorian sympathy for *The Scarlet Letter*, formed important preliminary stages. 'The old blandishing graces of Dumas, Sand, and De Balzac, are quite excluded from the story', Meredith observed in his review; 'all is severe matter of fact painfully elaborated.'[72] The special development in the nineteenth century of the great tradition traced by Auerbach in *Mimesis* reflected the local influences and pressures which modern theory has only recently sought to decipher.[73] In tracing 'the hidden roads that lead from poem to poem',[74] the student of Victorian realism emerges with a picture of simplicity behind the chaos of impressions, like Pater who saw behind Shakespeare's histories a 'unity of effect, as if a song or ballad were still lying at the root'.[75]

NOTES

1 C. R. Decker, *The Victorian Conscience* (New York, 1952); W. C. Frierson, *L'influence du naturalisme français sur les romanciers anglais de 1885 à 1900* (Paris, 1925); Ian Gregor and Brian Nicholas, *The Moral and the Story* (London, 1962); Donald D. Stone, *Novelists in a Changing World* (Cambridge, Mass., 1972).

2 Ferdinand Brunetière, *Le roman naturaliste* (Paris, 1883); D. C. Murray, *My Contemporaries in Fiction* (London, 1894).

3 W. R. Inge, *The Victorian Age* (Cambridge, 1922), p. 48.

4 Ford Madox Ford, *Henry James. A Critical Study* (London, 1918), p. 79.

5 I thank the Research Fund Committee of Sheffield University for grants enabling me to consult material noted in this study.

6 See especially: Christophe Campos, *The Vision from France. From Arnold to Bloomsbury* (London, 1965); Louis James, *Fiction for the Working Man* (London, 1963); Ruth Zabriskie Temple, *The Critic's Alchemy* (New York, 1953).

7 John Ruskin, 'Fiction, Fair and Foul', in John Ruskin, *Works*, edited by E. T. Cook and Alexander Wedderburn, XXXIV (London, 1908), pp. 265–302.

8 William Archer, *English Dramatists of Today* (London, 1882), p. 38. Also J. Pascoe, *The Dramatic List* (London, 1879), p. 371; Charles Reade, *Drink* (British Library Add. MS. 53218, LCO Papers 1879, no. 94); *Pernicious Literature. Debate in the House of Commons. Trial and Conviction for sale of Zola's novels* (National Vigilance Association, 1888); G. J. Becker (ed.), *Documents of Literary Realism* (Princeton, New Jersey, 1963).

9 Imitations include the following British Library Add. MSS. (LCO Papers): Anon., 'Another Drink' (1879, no. 129); Anon., 'The Worship of Bacchus' (1879, no. 132); F. K. Hazleton, 'Intemperance, or, a Drunkard's Sin' (1879, no. 133); Alfred George, 'Man's Folly or Drink' (1879, no. 137); E. Romaine Callender, 'D.T., or Lost Through Drink' (1879, no. 140); Anon., 'A Free Adaptation of the Curse of Drink' (1879, no. 192); Anon., 'L'Assommoir, or the Demon of Drink' (1879, no. 193); Buller Stanhope, 'L'Assommoir (1879, no. 195); George Roberts, 'Gin' (1880, no. 63). Reade's play and two of the above are noted in M. Elwin, *Charles Reade* (London, 1931), pp. 341–5; and in Eileen Pryme, 'Zola's Plays in England, 1870–1900', *French Studies*, 13 (1959), 25–38.

10 John Hollingshead, *Gaiety Chronicles* (London, 1898), p. 134; Joseph Hone, *The Life of George Moore* (London, 1936), pp. 92, 98.

11 Brian Harrison, *Drink and the Victorians. The Temperance Question in England, 1815–1872* (London, 1971).

12 Joseph Knight, *Theatrical Notes* (London, 1893), p. 260.

13 F. W. J. Hemmings, *Zola* (Oxford, 1953); Angus Wilson, *Émile Zola. An Introductory Study of his Novels* (London, 1952); also David Baguley, 'Les Oeuvres de Zola traduits en anglais', *Cahiers Naturalistes*, 16: 40 (1970), 195–209; David Baguley, 'Zola devant la critique anglaise', *Cahiers Naturalistes*, 18: 43 (1972), 105–23; William F. Colburn, 'The Vizetelly Extracts', *Princeton University Library Quarterly*, 23 (1962), 54–9; F. W. J. Hemmings, 'Zola par delà la Manche et l'Atlantique', *Cahiers Naturalistes*, 9: 23 (1963), 299–312.

14 Patricia Thomson, *George Sand and the Victorians* (London, 1977).

15 Albert L. Rabinowitz, 'Criticism of French Novels in Boston Magazines, 1830–1860', *New England Quarterly*, 10 (1941), 488–504; René Wellek, 'The Concept of Realism in Literary Scholarship', in René Wellek, *Concepts of Criticism*, edited by Stephen J. Nichols, Jr (New Haven, 1965), pp. 222–55; J. P. Stern, *On Realism* (London, 1973); Damian Grant, *Realism* (London, 1972); Roland N. Stromberg, *Realism, Naturalism and Symbolism* (New York, 1968). For Victorian criticism, see R. Stang, *Theory of the Novel in England, 1850–1870* (London, 1959); Kenneth Graham, *English Criticism of the Novel 1865–1900* (Oxford, 1965).

16 M. G. Devonshire, *The English Novel in France, 1830–1870* (London, 1929). Also L. Rives, *Charles Reade: sa vie, ses romans* (Toulouse, 1940); Lewis F. Haines, 'Reade, Mill, and Zola', *Studies in Philology*, 40 (1943), 463–80.

17 Henry Longueville Mansel, 'Sensation Novels', *Quarterly Review*, 113 (1863), 481–514, reprinted in H. L. Mansel, *Letters, Lectures and Reviews*, edited by H. W. Chandler (London, 1973), pp. 215–47; W. C. Phillips, *Dickens, Reade, and Collins, Sensation Novelists* (New York, 1919); Jean Ruer, 'Plaidoyer pour la littérature à sensation', *Bulletin de la faculté de lettres à Strasbourg* (1969), 233–47; P. D. Edwards, *Some Mid-Victorian Thrillers. The Sensation Novel, its Friends and Foes* (St Lucia, 1970).

18 Joseph Conrad, preface to *The Nigger of the Narcissus* (Everyman's Library, 980) (London, 1945), p. 4. The preface was first published in *The New Review* (December 1897).

19 J. J. Weiss, 'La Littérature brutale', *Revue contemporaine* (15 January 1858), 144–85 ('vous croirez percevoir la sensation immédiate du paysage', p. 157); also Bernard Weinberg, *French Realism. The Critical Reaction. 1830–1870* (London, 1937).

20 E. D. Forgues, 'Le Roman anglais contemporain. Miss Braddon et le roman à sensation', *Revue des deux mondes*, 45 (1863), 953–77.

21 Forgues, 'Le Roman anglais'.

22 Emile Zola, 'Livres d'aujourd'hui et de demain', *L'Evènement* (15 February 1865), p. 5. In Martin Kanes, *L'Atelier de Zola* (Geneva, 1963), p. 37, *Fernanda*, a novel by Reynolds which formed the subject of Zola's review and to which he appended his observations on the Victorian literary tradition, is mistakenly attributed to Miss Braddon.

23 *Catalogue of the library of the Eastwood and Greasley Mechanics' and Artizans' Institute* (Eastwood, 1865), pp. 26–7, items 698–723; L. Paulin, 'Old Libraries of Nottinghamshire' (typescript, Nottinghamshire Country Library, 1950). I thank the Nottinghamshire Country Librarian for assistance.

24 Marshall Hall, 'On the Reflex Functions of the *Medulla Oblongata* and *Medulla Spinalis*', *Philosophical Transactions*, 26 (1833), 635–65.

25 Henry Maudsley, *Responsibility in Mental Disease* (4th edn, London, 1881), p. 243.

26 R. J. Niess, 'Hawthorne and Zola: an Influence?', *Revue de littérature comparée*, 27 (1953), 446–52.

27 E. Stokes, 'Hawthorne and *Bleak House*', *Proceedings of the Australian Universities Modern Language Association (AUMLA)*, 32 (1969), 177–89.

28 Mary Elizabeth Braddon, *Dead Love Has Chains* (London, 1907), chapter 1.

29 Enoch Arnold Bennett, *Fame and Fiction* (London, 1901), pp. 26–9.

30 Michael Sadleir, *Things Past* (London, 1944), p. 79.

31 Margaret Oliphant, 'Novels', *Blackwood's Magazine*, 102 (1867), 257–80.

32 George Henry Lewes, *The Physiology of Common Life*, 2 vols. (London, 1859–60), II, 280. See also William James, *The Principles of Psychology*, 2 vols. (London, 1890), I, 224–90, chapter 9, 'The Stream of Thought'; Henri F. Ellenberger, *The Discovery of the Unconscious. The History and Evolution of Dynamic Psychiatry* (New York and London, 1970); Edwin C. Boring, *Sensation and Perception* (New York, 1942). I thank Dr Adrian Bower for assistance.

33 Lewes's position can be evaluated through the following: Anon., 'Dr Marshall Hall's Discoveries of the Nervous System', *The Lancet* (8, 15, 29 August 1846), reprinted in Charlotte Hall, *Memoirs of Marshall Hall, F.R.S.* (London, 1861), pp. 465–99; Max Neuburger, *Die historische Entwicklung der experimentellen Gehirn- und Rückenmarksphysiologie vor Flourens* (Stuttgart, 1897); D. Shehan, 'Discovery of the Autonomic Nervous System', *Archives of Neurology and Psychiatry*, 35 (1936), 1081–113; Sir Geoffrey Jefferson, 'Marshall Hall, the Grasp Reflex and the Diastaltic Spinal Cord', in *Science, Medicine and History. Essays...in Honour of Charles Singer*, edited by E. Ashmole Underwood (London, 1953), pp. 303–20; Richard Hunter and Ida MacAlpine, *Three Hundred Years of Psychiatry, 1535–1869* (London, 1963); Edwin Clark and C. D. O'Malley, *The Human Brain and Spinal Cord* (Berkeley, 1968), pp. 347–51.

34 Denise Le Blond-Zola, *Émile Zola. Raconté par sa fille* (Paris, 1931), p. 39.

35 Reino Virtanen, *Claude Bernard and his Place in the History of Ideas* (Lincoln, Nebraska, 1960), chapter 6, pp. 117–28, 'Claude Bernard and Literature'.

36 Robert Lee Wolff, 'Devoted Disciple: the Letters of Mary Elizabeth Braddon to Sir Edward Bulwer-Lytton, 1862–1873', *Harvard Library Bulletin*, 22 (1974), 5–35, 129–61; Charlotte Hall, *Memoirs of Marshall Hall*, p. 135.

37 John Ruskin, 'Fiction, Fair and Foul', in John Ruskin, *Works*, edited by E. T. Cook and Alexander Wedderburn, XXXIV (London, 1908), pp. 265–302 (p. 272).

38 John Wilson Croker, 'French Novels', *Quarterly Review*, 56 (1836), 65–131.

39 G. W. M. Reynolds, *Modern Literature in France* (London, 1839), p. xvii.

40 Louis James, *Fiction for the Working Man*, pp. 131–69 (chapter 8).

41 Anon., 'The Doctor's Wife', *The Saturday Review*, 5 (1864), 571–2.

42 Henry James, 'Miss Braddon', *The Nation*, 1 (1865), 593–4; reprinted in Henry James, *Notes and Reviews*, edited by Pierre Chaignon de la Rose (Cambridge, Mass., 1911), pp. 108–16.

43 Eneas Dallas, 'The Doctor's Wife', *The Times* (30 December 1864), p. 8. Authorship kindly identified by Gordon Phillips, Esq.

44 Henry James, 'Miss Braddon'.

45 Margaret Oliphant, 'Sensation Novels', *Blackwood's Magazine*, 91 (1862), 564–84.

46 George Levine, 'Isabel, Gwendolen and Dorothea', *ELH*, 30 (1963), 244–57.

47 George Meredith, 'Belles-Lettres', *Westminster Review*, 12 (1857), 594–604; Gordon S. Haight, 'George Meredith and the *Westminster Review*', *Modern Language Review*, 53 (1958), 1–16.

48 George Eliot, 'Quarry', Harvard College Library MS. Lowell 13. I thank Dr W. H. Bond for assistance. For an alternative reading of the disposition of characters in the MS., see Jerome Beaty, *Middlemarch from Notebook to Novel* (Urbana, Illinois, 1969), p. 109. Also, Anna Theresa Kitchel, *Quarry for Middlemarch* (Berkeley, 1950); C. Heywood, 'A Source for *Middlemarch*: Miss Braddon's *The Doctor's Wife* and *Madam Bovary*', *Revue de littérature comparée*, 44 (1970), 89–94. The possibility of

literary borrowing is not considered in Barbara Smalley, *George Eliot and Flaubert* (Athens, Ohio, 1974).

49 George Steiner, 'A Preface to Middlemarch', *Nineteenth-Century Fiction*, 9 (1955), 262–79; Florence Maly-Schlatter, *The Puritan Element in Victorian Fiction* (Zurich, 1940), p. 99.

50 Thomas Hardy, *Literary Notebooks*, edited by Lennart Björk (Gothenburg, 1974), I, 130. Also William F. Hall, 'Hawthorne, Shakespeare and Tess', *English Studies*, 52 (1971), 533–42.

51 J. Paterson, *The Making of 'The Return of the Native'* (Berkeley, 1960); also C. Heywood, 'Miss Braddon's *The Doctor's Wife*. An Intermediary between *Madame Bovary* and *The Return of the Native*', *Revue de littérature comparée*, 38 (1964), 255–61; C. Heywood, 'Somerset Maugham's Debt to *Madame Bovary* and Miss Braddon's *The Doctor's Wife*', *Études Anglaises*, 19 (1966), 64–9. For a modern rendering, see Brian Moore, *The Doctor's Wife* (London, 1976). For the critical reception, see Annie Rouxeville, 'The Reception of Flaubert in Victorian England', *Comparative Literature Studies*, 14 (1977), 174–84.

52 George Moore, *Literature at Nurse* (London, 1885), p. 22.

53 Milton Chaikin, 'George Moore's *A Mummer's Wife* and Zola', *Revue de littérature comparée*, 31 (1957), 85–8.

54 Lilian R. Furst, 'George Moore et Zola. Une réévaluation', *Cahiers Naturalistes*, 17 (1971), 42–57; W. C. Frierson, 'George Moore Compromised with the Victorians', *Trollopian* (*Nineteenth-Century Fiction*), 1 (1947), 37–44; C. Heywood, 'Olive Schreiner's Influence on George Moore and D. H. Lawrence', in *Aspects of South African Literature*, edited by C. Heywood (London and New York, 1976), pp. 42–53; C. Heywood, 'Flaubert, Miss Braddon and George Moore', *Comparative Literature*, 12 (1960), 151–8.

55 John Forster, *The Life of Charles Dickens*, 2 vols. (London, 1876), II, 76. Cited in E. Stokes, 'Hawthorne and *Bleak House*'.

56 T. S. Eliot, 'Introduction' to Wilkie Collins, *The Moonstone* (London, 1928), pp. i–ix (p. vii). Also, T. S. Eliot, 'Wilkie Collins and Dickens', in T. S. Eliot, *Selected Essays* (London, 1951), pp. 460–70.

57 Arthur Symons, 'Balzac', *Fortnightly Review*, 65 (1899), 747–57; also, Sylvère Monod, 'La Fortune de Balzac en Angleterre', *Revue de littérature comparée*, 24 (1950), 181–210.

58 Anon., 'The Style of Balzac and Thackeray', *Dublin University Magazine*, 61 (1863), 437–42: W. C. D. Pacey, 'Balzac and Thackeray', *Modern Language Review*, 36 (1941), 213–24: E. Mâitre, 'Balzac, Thackeray, and Charles de Bernard', *Revue de littérature comparée*, 24 (1950), 279–93: A. C. Taylor, 'Balzac, and Thackeray', *Revue de littérature comparée*, 35 (1960), 354–69; also, Stephen Wall, 'Trollope, Balzac, and the Reappearing Character', *Essays in Criticism* (1975), 123–44.

59 Jane Lundblad, *Nathaniel Hawthorne and European Literary Tradition* (Cambridge, Mass. and Upsala, 1947), p. 167.

60 Leslie Stephen, 'Nathaniel Hawthorne', *Cornhill Magazine*, 26 (1872), 717–34; reprinted in Leslie Stephen, *Hours in a Library* (London, 1876), pp. 169–98.

61 Stephen Coleridge, *The Scarlet Letter*, British Library Add. MS. 53403; *The Times* (5 June 1888), p. 8. See also Donald Crowley, *Hawthorne. The Critical Heritage* (London, 1970); Bertha Faust, *Hawthorne's Contemporaneous Reputation* (Philadel-

phia, 1939); Clarence Gohdes, *American Literature in Nineteenth-Century England* (New York, 1944), pp. 165–6.

62 E. D. Forgues, 'Poètes et romanciers américains. Nathaniel Hawthorne', *Revue des deux mondes* (15 April 1852), 337–65.

63 Arthur Symons, 'Nathaniel Hawthorne', *Studies in Prose and Verse* (London, 1904), pp. 52–62.

64 James Fitzjames Stephen, 'On the Relation of Novels to Life', in *Cambridge Essays* (London, 1855), pp. 148–67 (p. 163).

65 T. S. Eliot, 'Beyle and Balzac', *The Athenaeum* (20 May 1919), 382–3.

66 D. H. Lawrence, *Collected Letters*, edited by Harry T. Moore (London, 1962), p. 35.

67 [Mary Elizabeth Braddon], 'French novels', *Belgravia*, 3 (1867), 78–82.

68 John Wilson Croker, 'French Novels', *Quarterly Review*, 56 (1836), p. 91. See also Jeanne Delbaere-Garant, *Henry James. The Vision of France* (Paris, 1970), pp. 99–114.

69 Enid L. Duthie, *The Foreign Vision of Charlotte Brontë* (London, 1975); John Hewish, *Emily Brontë. A Critical and Biographical Study* (London, 1969), pp. 118–35; Q. D. Leavis, 'A Fresh Approach to *Wuthering Heights*', in F. R. Leavis and Q. D. Leavis, *Lectures in America* (London, 1969), pp. 83–152; Patricia Thomson, '*Wuthering Heights* and *Mauprat*', *Review of English Studies*, 24 (1973), 26–37; Tom Winnifrith, *The Brontës and their Background. Romance and Reality* (London, 1973), pp. 84–109.

70 Anon., 'Where the Brontës Borrowed their Books', *Brontë Society Transactions*, 60 (1950), 344–58 (p. 354, item 211).

71 Simon O. Lesser, *Fiction and the Unconscious* (Chicago and London, 1957, Midway reprint, 1975), p. 79.

72 George Meredith, 'Belles-Lettres', *Westminster Review*, 12 (1857), 594–604.

73 Modern studies with a bearing on these problems include D. Howard, J. Lucas and J. Goode, *Tradition and Tolerance in Nineteenth-Century England* (London, 1966); Richard K. Cross, *Flaubert and Joyce. The Rite of Fiction* (Princeton, 1971); D. W. Fokkema and Elrud Kunne-Ibsch, *Theories of Literature in the Twentieth Century* (London, 1977); Robert Weimann, *Literaturgeschichte und Mythologie* (Berlin and Weimar, 1971), pp. 47–128, 'Tradition als literaturgeschichtliche Kategorie'.

74 Harold Bloom, *The Anxiety of Influence* (New York, 1973), p. 61.

75 Walter Horatio Pater, *Appreciations* (London, 1904), p. 203. See also Alan Friedman, *The Turn of the Novel* (New York, 1963), *passim*.

PART II

Translation in the canon of
W. H. Auden

A translation of 'The Sun Song'

W. H. AUDEN

Grim Greppur brought grief to many,   1
   Robbed them of riches and life:
No man escaped unscathed who dared
   To walk the roads he watched.

Very often he ate alone,   2
   Never shared his meat with men,
Till one day a weary stranger
   Sought shelter in his house.

Weak from hunger, weak from thirst,   3
   That weary traveller was,
But his heart misgave him, for Greppur, he knew
   Had done many evil deeds.

Yet meat and wine to his weary guest   4
   Greppur willingly gave,
Granted him shelter as God willed,
   Repenting his wicked past.

The thoughts of the other, though, were wicked,   5
   He rewarded help with harm:
When he rose in the morning he murdered the sleeping
   Good and merciful man.

Greppur cried 'God save me!'   6
   When he felt the fatal stroke,
And so his sins descended on the man
   Who had killed him without a cause.

Holy angels from Heaven came   7
  To bear his soul above:
A life of joy he shall live for ever,
  Beholding the Father's face.

          *   *   *

No man is ruler of his riches or his health,   8
  Though often he may be happy:
Ill-luck may befall when least foreseen;
  No man may command his peace.

Never did Unnar, nor Saevaldi,   9
  Believe that their luck could turn:
Naked they became, nothing was left them,
  They fled as wolves to the woods.

          *   *   *

The power of pleasure had brought pain to many: 10
  Women often cause harm:
They grow evil, though God the Almighty
  Created them pure-in-heart.

Svafodur and Skarthedin were sworn friends,   11
  Lived their lives for each other;
But the same maiden maddened them both,
  Caused a quarrel between them.

Compared with her beauty no pleasure they took   12
  In games or the glad daylight:
No other thing could they think about
  Than that bright body of hers.

The dark night became drear to them,   13
  No longer could they soundly sleep:
Out of such grief there grew a feud
  Between the closest of comrades.

The unpredictable often may   14
  Have sad and cruel results:
They went to the island for that woman's sake,
  And death was the doom of both.

          *   *   *

Hringvor and Listvor sit in Herdir's doorway, 76
　　Astride Organ's stool:
Drops of iron drip from their nostrils,
　　Stirring men to strife.

On the earth-ship rows Odin's wife, 77
　　Inflamed by fleshly lust:
Impure winds puff her sails
　　Which are rigged on ropes of passion.

I alone, heir of my father, 78
　　I and Solkotlu's sons
Have read the horn of the hart that wise
　　Vigdvalin bore from the barrow.

Read its runes that were roughly scratched 79
　　By the nine daughters of Njord,
Scored by Krepvor, scored by Bodveig,
　　And their other seven sisters.

Svafr and Svafrlogi sucked marrow 80
　　And shed blameless blood:
They dealt in witchcraft and did evil,
　　Ever eager to destroy.

*   *   *

Let no man walk in the ways of pride: 15
　　I can truly testify,
Those who follow them in folly forsake
　　The wise ways of God.

Radny and Vebodi were rich and strong, 16
　　Thought none as good as they:
Now in torment they sit, turning their scorched
　　Flesh towards the fire.

They trusted in their might, imagined themselves 17
　　All-powerful over others,
But their state presented itself to God
　　In a less glorious light.

Many their pleasures, many their delights,
   Gold they enjoyed and girls:
Now they are punished, for in pain they walk
   Between the frost and the flame.

*   *   *

Never put faith in foe's word,   19
   Though he speak fair before you:
It is good, I say, good to be warned
   By the fate that befalls others.

Sorrow for himself did Sorli get   20
   When he fell into Vigulf's hands,
And took for truth the treacherous lies
   Of the base who had slain his brother.

He forgave them all from his good heart,   21
   And they promised to give him gold:
Peace and good-will they pledged together,
   But evil came out of that.

For the next day, the next morning,   22
   After riding to Rygjardal,
With swords they hewed the innocent one,
   And let his life go forth.

They hauled the corpse by a hidden path,   23
   And heaved it into a well:
They wished to hide it, but Holy God
   Saw all from His heaven.

The Just God enjoined his soul   24
   To abide with Him in bliss:
But his foes are in torment, and the time, I think,
   Will be long before their release.

*   *   *

Ask the disir who do Him service   25
   To pray that God give you grace:
For a week after all will go
   As well as you could wish.

Do not add to the evil you know 26
 A deed done in anger,
But comfort grief with good works:
 You will benefit thereby.

Pray to God for good things, 27
 To Him who made all men:
Great reward shall wise men have
 Who honour the Heavenly Father.

A man should pray with especial care 28
 When he lacks something he longs for:
Nothing asked, nothing given;
 Few notice the needs of the silent.

He called me early, I came late 29
 To the door of the Wielder-of-doom:
But when He named me, I willed to obey,
 So He won the soul He sought.

Sins rule it so that sadly we journey 30
 Out of this wonderful world:
None need fear who refrain from evil;
 It is good to be free from guilt.

All faithless hearts to the Eye of the Lord 31
 Are fell as wicked wolves:
After death for ever they shall
 Plod Hell's burning paths.

There are bright virtues that bring wisdom, 32
 Seven to number and name:
Let your soul love them and forsake them never,
 For in these is health and hope.

* * *

First let me say how I felt happy 33
 In the abode of bliss:
Second let me say that the sons of men
 Are in dread when they have to die.

Lust and pride and love of riches 34
 Have turned many men from the truth:

Greed for gold brings grief in the end,
  Money makes apes of many.

I seemed happy to men in many ways,   35
  Being so blind to evil:
The Lord created the earth we dwell on
  Full of lovely delights.

Long I leaned, long I bent over,   36
  Much I longed to live:
But God the Almighty was more powerful:
  Unfree are the paths of the fated.

I was hard bound in Hell's ropes,   37
  Sinews about my sides:
Tough they were when I tried to cut them;
  Lucky is he who can loose them.

I found how in all ways affliction swells   38
  Within my troubled heart:
Much I trembled when Hell's Maidens
  Asked me home every night.

I saw the sun, saw how it lightened   39
  The din-world at dawn:
But heard elsewhere Hell's gates
  Shut with a shuddering clang.

I saw the sun, setting in blood,   40
  My breath was nigh out of my body:
Mightier it seemed in many ways
  Than it ever had before.

I saw the sun and it seemed to me   41
  That I looked on the Living God:
I bowed low to it for the last time
  On this middle-earth of mortals.

I saw the sun, such was its radiance   42
  That I seemed to myself in a trance:
But elsewhere ocean roared,
  Mingled with the blood of men.

I saw the sun; at the sight I trembled, 43
    I was downcast and in dread:
My heart was grieved and greatly troubled:
    My soul was torn asunder.

I saw the sun, so saddened was I 44
    That my breath was nigh out of my body:
My tongue felt hard as timber and the world
    About me was bitter cold.

I never saw the sun again 45
    After that downcast day:
The underground waters closed over me then,
    And I turned, cold, from my torments.

Hope fled, so afraid I was, 46
    Like a bird out of my breast:
High it flew but found nowhere
    A place where it might repose.

Longer than all was that long night 47
    When I lay stiff on straw:
I grasped then what God had said –
    'Man is made from the dust.'

Know and wonder at the works of God 48
    Who made heaven and earth:
To many their paths are pleasureless,
    Although they forsake sin.

All believe their own works good; 49
    Rewarded is he who does well.
After wealth what I wish for most
    Is a tomb covered with turf.

                      *   *   *

The lusts of the flesh allure men, 50
    Many a soul is enslaved:
Holy water was one of the things
    Which I had hated most.

For nine days in the Norns' chair 51
    I sat, then was set on a horse:

Misshapen suns shone grimly
   Out of the clouds of the air.

Through the victory-worlds I wished to travel,   52
   Through all the seven spheres:
Above and below I looked for a path,
   A way that would be open.

Now I shall say what I saw first   53
   When I entered the realm of Hell:
Souls changed into singed birds
   Flew in a mass like midges.

Dragons-of-hope flew out of the West   54
   And plunged into Glaevald's path,
So wildly they flapped their wings I thought
   They would split heaven and earth.

Then from the South came the Hart-Sun,   55
   Two kept him tame with reins:
On Middle-earth his hooves stood,
   But his horns reached to heaven.

Wonderful from the North came the waning moon's   56
   Sons – there were seven together:
From brimming horns pure ale they drank
   At Baugregin's sacred spring.

The wind dropped, the waters calmed,   57
   But then there came a great cry
From false women who for foolish men
   Were milling dust as meat.

Gory stones did those grey women   58
   Drearily drag along:
Their breasts were torn; their bloody hearts
   Hung out, heavy with sorrow.

Many maimed men I saw,   59
   Plodding Hell's burning paths:
All reddened were their wretched faces,
   As if bathed in women's blood.

Men trod the dust who had died without   60
    Receiving the sacrament:
Heathen stars, stained with runes,
    Hung evil over their heads.

Then I saw there those who had envied   61
    The fair fortune of others:
Their breasts were scored with bloody runes,
    Punishing sin with pain.

Then I saw there those who in life   62
    Had turned from the paths of truth:
In the after-world the wages for that
    Are to ape the errors of this.

Then I saw there those who had cheated   63
    Others out of their rights:
They trudged in gangs to Greed City,
    Bearing burdens of lead.

Then I saw there those who had robbed   64
    Many of money and goods:
Through their breasts, threading their wounds,
    Darted poison-dragons.

Then I looked on those who had least wished   65
    To observe the Sacred Days,
Beheld that their hands into hot stone
    Were painfully impaled.

Then I saw there those who from pride   66
    Looked down with disdain on others:
The garments they wore were woven cunningly
    From fierce undying fire.

Then I saw there those who on earth   67
    Had been false and faithless in speech:
Out of their heads Hell's ravens
    Without pity pecked their eyes.

There is no end to all the torments   68
    Sinners suffer in Hell:

For sweet sins sore is the penance,
  Lust is repaid with pain.

*   *   *

Then I saw there those who had offered   69
  Gifts to the glory of God:
Holy over their heads stood pure
  Candles burning brightly.

Then I saw there those who had taken   70
  Pity on the sick and poor:
Over their heads the angels read them
  Gospels and sacred Psalms.

Then I saw there those who had tended   71
  And fed their father and mother:
Their beds were bathed in the beams of heaven,
  Their couches neatly kept.

Then I saw there those who had often   72
  Subdued their flesh by fasting:
The angels of the Lord bowed low to them,
  Showing them highest honour.

Then I saw there those who had often   73
  Laid the scourge to their skin:
Holy maidens had made them clean,
  Washed away their faults.

High in the heavens horses I saw,   74
  Pacing on paths to God:
The men who rode them had been murdered on earth
  For no crime or cause.

God the Father! God the Son!   75
  God the Holy Ghost!
Creator of men, I ask you now
  To keep us all from evil.

*   *   *

You shall recite my song to the living,   76
  This tale I have told in your ears,

My Sun Song, a song which I think
  Has lied the least to the most.

Part we must now, but shall meet again 77
  On the final Day of Doom:
May the God of righteousness give rest to the dead,
  Show mercy to men that live.

Englishing the *Edda*

PETER H. SALUS

In his article for the 'Auden Double Number' of *New Verse* (November 1937), Isherwood wrote:

> If I were told to introduce a reader to the poetry of W. H. Auden, I should begin by asking him to remember three things:
> ...that Auden is a Scandinavian. The Auden family came originally from Iceland. Auden himself was brought up on the sagas, and their influence upon his work has been profound...
> The saga world is a schoolboy world, with its feuds, its practical jokes, its dark threats conveyed in puns and riddles and understatements...I once remarked to Auden that the atmosphere of *Gisli the Outlaw* very much reminded me of our schooldays. He was pleased with the idea...

Iceland, Fuller remarks, is 'Auden's ethnic homeland (his family is of Icelandic descent), his favourite saga world and a place of "natural marvels"'.[1] Auden tells us (referring to his father): 'some of the most vivid recollections of my childhood are hearing him read to me Icelandic folk-tales and sagas, and I know more about Northern mythology than Greek'.[2] And in the immediately preceding section of the 'Letter to Lord Byron', Auden writes:

> With northern myths my little brain was laden,
>   With deeds of Thor and Loki and such scenes;
> My favourite tale was Andersen's *Ice Maiden*;
>   But better far than any kings and queens
>   I liked to see and know about machines:
> And from my sixth until my sixteenth year
> I thought myself a mining engineer.[3]

But Auden also had a less romantic view of the culture: 'I love the sagas, but what a rotten society they describe, a society with only the gangster virtues.'[4] However, the saga fantasies of his boyhood were of prime

141

importance and 'the journey to Iceland would not have taken place' without them.[5] More precisely, the Auden–MacNeice–Yates trip was 'a quest for some private image of the North, which is tested against reality'.[6] Yates' piece in the Spender volume makes quite clear just how trying Auden found that reality to be.[7] Yet decades later, he looked back on his Icelandic heritage with pride. He repeatedly referred to himself as having a 'Northern' rather than a 'Southern' temperament; and he was inordinately proud of his (alleged) ancestor's appearance as the protagonist of the greatest of the medieval Icelandic short stories (þáttr): 'Auðunn and the Bear'.

> My passport says I'm five feet and eleven
>   With hazel eyes and fair (it's tow-like) hair,
> That I was born in York in 1907,
>   With no distinctive markings anywhere.
>   Which isn't quite correct. Conspicuous there
> On my right cheek appears a large brown mole,
> I think I don't dislike it on the whole.
>
> My name occurs in several of the sagas,
>   Is common over Iceland still. Down under
> Where Das Volk order sausages and lagers
>   I ought to be the prize, the living wonder,
>   The really pure from any Rassenschander,
> In fact I am the great big white barbarian,
> The Nordic type, the too too truly Aryan.[8]

I met Wystan Auden in the autumn of 1963. I had returned to New York from a Fulbright year in Iceland, where I had met Basil Boothby (then Her Majesty's Ambassador to Reykjavík), who had met Wystan in Hankow in 1938. Wystan was full of questions about Iceland – which he had not visited for nearly thirty years – and I was awed by the Great Poet. As Boothby points out in his contribution to the Spender volume,[9] I was instrumental in getting Wystan to make his visit to Iceland in 1964.

The plans of the Weird Sisters being what they are, Paul Taylor was the Fulbright Professor in Iceland at that time, and I returned to Iceland in the summer of 1964 (courtesy of the American Philosophical Society) to succeed Wystan as a guest of the Boothbys and to meet (in August) Paul Taylor. Thus set down, it appears to be a trick of the Norns: Auden and MacNeice in Iceland in 1936; Auden, Isherwood and Boothby in China in 1938; Boothby and Salus in Iceland in 1962–3; Auden and Salus in New York in 1963–4; Auden, Boothby and Taylor in Iceland in spring 1964; Boothby, Salus and Taylor in Iceland in summer 1964.

Following our meeting, Paul Taylor and I corresponded a good deal

on Old English and Old Icelandic matters and, when the Ford
Foundation benevolently established the National Translation Center
with W. H. Auden on its Board, I spoke with Wystan about Paul's
long-standing interest in translating the *Poetic Edda* into English verse,
and conveyed Wystan's enthusiasm to Paul. Paul applied for a grant from
the N.T.C. in 1965 and received one, but Wystan was not satisfied with
the first fruits from a poetic point of view (he remarked that Paul was
a 'wretched metricist') and so our tri-partite, trans-Atlantic collaboration
emerged.

After his second trip (in 1964), from which the haiku-like stanzas of
'Iceland Revisited' emerged, Wystan seems to have given up entirely
his 'gangster society' image of the saga world. In his brilliant second
T. S. Eliot Memorial Lecture,[10] he discusses the settlement of Iceland,
the structure of Icelandic society, and the reflections of this structure
in the family sagas: 'The combination of these factors [the aristocratic
settlement of Iceland, the lack of an indigenous race to subject, the
paucity of slaves, the small total population] created, for the first and
last time in civilized history, a rural democracy' and 'The primary world
contemporary with the writers of the saga [the *Laxdæla saga*] is not the
world they describe. By their time the attempt to create a rural
democracy had failed. The family-blood feuds over matters of personal
honour had degenerated into ruthless power-politics...'

This is quite different from the 'gangster virtues' of 1936 or the
'schoolboy world' of 1937, though one can trace both of these in the
sagas themselves. The good impression that Iceland (and the Icelanders)
made can be seen in 1936 in his note. 'I must say at once that I enjoyed
my visit enormously; that...I met with unvarying kindness and
hospitality; and that as far as the people themselves are concerned, I can
think of none among whom I should prefer to be exiled.'[11] It can also
be seen in a comparison of: 'I saw...few whose wealth made them
arrogant, ostentatious and vulgar' (1936)[12] with

> Fortunate island,
> Where all men are equal
> But not vulgar – not yet.

which closes 'Iceland Revisited', written twenty-eight years later.[13]

One of the things about the sagas and the Eddaic poetry which
fascinated Wystan was its naturalism. The Homeric world, as he pointed
out, was full of heroes who acted and spoke like heroes; the sagas were
full of people who talked and acted like people: heroic men who cringe
before their harridan wives; men who are valorous in battle, but fearful

before it; men who talk a better battle than they fight; women who
store up slights and insults and jealousies for use at crucial times (the
instances of Kari and Bjorn and of Gunnar and Hallgerd in the *Njáls
saga* are two examples Wystan used in 'The World of Sagas'). But what
became Wystan's favourite example never appeared in *Secondary
Worlds*, for he felt its tone was inappropriate to the occasion.

In the winter of 1966–7, while working on the Eliot lectures, Wystan
pillaged my library. He made off with every saga translation I owned
(the ones that come to mind are *Njáls saga*, the *Laxdæla saga*, *Grettis
saga*, *Eriks saga*, *Hrafnkells saga*, the *Völsung saga*, *Heidreks saga*, and
the *Heimskringla*) and returned about half of them. Early one morning
he telephoned me to say that there was 'something missing' from *Grettis
saga*. He went on to tell me that there was a line of asterisks in the
Everyman translation and that something had obviously been left out.
I promised to look at the Icelandic text and to stop by St Mark's Place
at 'cocktail time' with an answer. At lunchtime I looked at the text and
found that Wystan was right: a few paragraphs and some verse had been
deleted, doubtless by a prudish editor. Wystan was delighted when I
provided him with a scrawled translation later in the afternoon.

Briefly, Grettir and some companions are in exile on an island. One
of the group (Glaum) lets the fire go out and Grettir says he will swim
to the mainland and fetch fire from a friendly farm. He makes Reykjaness
by sunset, walks to the farm at Reykir and, wet and cold, takes a hot
bath, soaking in the hot pool for a goodly time. He then goes to the hall
and falls asleep on a bench. A maidservant and the farmer's daughter
discover him – asleep – in the morning and recognize him.

The maidservant said: 'What do you know, that's Grettir, lying there. He's big enough
around the chest, but strangely small lower down. That part's not of heroic size at all.'

The farmer's daughter said: 'Silly, don't talk like that. Be still!'

The maid said: 'I can't keep still, dearie. I never would have believed it, even if I'd
been told.'

She kept on running over to Grettir and running back to the farmer's daughter,
giggling. Grettir heard her remarks and when she ran over, grabbed her and said these
verses:

> 'You're taking a risk, hussy.
> Rarely do you get
> A good look
> At a hair-ringed sword.
> I'll bet no man's balls
> Are bigger than mine,
> Though their pricks
> May be larger.'

He then tumbled her on to the bench. The farmer's daughter ran out of the room. Then Grettir said these verses.

> 'The bitch complained
> That my prick's too small,
> And the boastful slut
> May be right.
> But small things grow
> And I'm still young,
> And big enough
> To serve you, girl.'

The serving girl cried out, but before they parted she had long stopped taunting him.

(chapter 75; my translation)

Wystan loved the passage. It could never have occurred, he felt, in the classical literatures, nor in the courtly romances – such naturalism was a purely Icelandic phenomenon.

While several critics have noted Auden's literary debt to Old English, little has been noted (save the sort of general remark cited above) of the debt to Old Icelandic. Fuller, for example, says that Book I, Part 3, 'Statement', of *The Orators* (1932) is heavily indebted to the *Exeter Book*, though the immediate source is apparently R. K. Gordon's *Anglo-Saxon Poetry* (1926). To the best of my knowledge, however, no commentator has pointed out that 'The Airman's Alphabet' in Book II of *The Orators* is derived from the Old Icelandic runic poem (or that its immediate source is the translation of Bruce Dickins).[14]

When I visited Wystan in Kirchstetten in the summer of 1965, he was already talking of the possibility of the *Edda* translation. By the time he returned to New York that autumn, he had already hit upon an operating procedure. Early the next year, when the translation was actully begun, Wystan gave me his copies of Kershaw's *Anglo-Saxon and Norse Poems* and the Dickins volume. This was a habit of Wystan's: he would 'borrow' books and rarely return them – mainly because he had in turn lent (or given) them to someone else. This was not intended to be cruel or malevolent, it was just that once a book was read, it could be passed on – for Wystan it had served its purpose. Relatively few items remained statically on the shelves, on the bureau, or under the bed at St Mark's Place. Occasionally remorseful, Wystan would recognize that he had absconded with something, and would 'return' something else (in addition to the sagas, I lost some Tolkien and some Peake to Wystan in the mid 1960s; but I received some books on Iceland, some murder mysteries, and a number of critical books in recompense). I recall glancing at Kershaw and Dickins cursorily, but they had been left relatively untouched on my shelves until I began this essay early in 1978. Looking at them more carefully, along with Phillpotts' *The ElderEdda* (1920), which Wystan had given me in 1964, I realized that they were 'marked up' in Wystan's hand. The great find was the Dickins, where Wystan had not only marked passages in the Norwegian and Icelandic runic poems, the Old High German 'Lay of Hildebrand', and the Old English 'Deor', but had also written what appears to be the first draft of 'The Airman's Alphabet' on the rear flyleaf and the inside rear cover. The Kershaw volume contains pencil marks on 'The Wanderer', 'The Ruin', 'The Battle of Brunanburh', and 'The Lay of Erik'. In the Phillpotts, Wystan marked a passage from 'The Lay of Skirnir' and two from 'The Song of the Grinders'.

The pencillings on the Old Icelandic runic poem and the draft of the 'Alphabet' make their relationship quite clear: Wystan's poem is a direct imitation of the Icelandic one. The markings on the various Old English poems make one much less certain that Gordon (1926) was the source of the *Exeter Book* material in *The Orators*, rather than Dickins and Kershaw. The draft of the 'Alphabet' shows most vividly the early influence of Old Icelandic verse on Wystan's poetry (he was twenty-four in 1931 when it appears to have been written). Of further interest is Wystan's brief (two-paragraph) review of Phillpotts' *Edda and Saga* where he expresses his hopes that future editions

will be able to include some original quotations from the Edda...The poems are not easy to procure..., and even the plainest reader would like to know what Old Norse looked and sounded like...

This book cannot fail to stimulate a greater interest in the sagas, and we can only hope that, as a result, we shall soon have new translations of all of them, less Wardour-Street in style than those of Morris and Dasent, and cheaper to buy.[15]

Antonio tells us that 'what's past is prologue' (*The Tempest*, II, 1), and all of the preceding – Auden's reminiscence about his Scandinavian ancestry and about the Norse legends heard from his father, his study of Old English and Old Icelandic, his use of this material in *The Orators*, the trip to Iceland in 1936, the second visit in 1964 – all these served as prologue to the venture of 1966 through 1970: the translation of all of the *Poetic Edda* as well as a number of Eddaic poems from manuscripts other than the *Codex Regius*. The basic translation of the poems was done between the spring of 1966 and that of 1969. The last poem was done in December 1969, when Paul Taylor visited Wystan in New York, bringing with him the draft translation of 'The Sun Song'. Paul wanted Wystan's approval to include this poem, which is a late imitation of the traditional forms, on the grounds of its poetic quality. Paul returned to St Mark's Place the next afternoon for tea to find Wystan finishing off his rendering of the poem: apparently he, too, had been caught up by it, and had spent much of the night working on it. He insisted on reading it aloud to Paul, and told him (and me) that only 'Song of the Sybil' (the *Völuspá*, the first poem of the *Edda* published) had given him as much pleasure working over. (It receives its first publication here.)

Our collaboration was a strange one: until 1967 I lived in New York and our procedure that first year or so was for Paul to send me his verse translations of the poems from Geneva, together with textual notes, questions and comments. I added notes and comments to these and went over the texts with Wystan (usually in his flat on St Mark's Place; occasionally in mine). Wystan would then rework the poems and summon me for a reading. Frequently, I would judge that he had gone too far astray from the original and he would (often with complaints that I was too 'literal minded') rework the verses.[16]

In fact, Auden had what I would consider a 'fair' reading knowledge of Icelandic. As a student he had worked his way through Gordon and Taylor (the standard O.U.P. textbook) and he was capable of reading with the aid of a dictionary or glossary. More important, though, was his ability to 'hear' the metrics as a result of this slight familiarity.

The reworked versions were sent to Geneva, where Paul, occasionally, rejected what I had approved, and a number of verses went through four or five stages before all of us were happy with them. When I moved to Massachusetts in 1967, I began transmitting poems to Wystan by mail, but as I was in New York several times each month, the 'conferences' continued. Wystan visited us in Massachusetts once, and several times flew to Toronto after our move there in 1969. Strangely, Paul Taylor and Wystan met only four times to discuss general matters and there was little correspondence between them, so that I became the negotiator as well as the midwife. I am not certain that ours was the strangest collaboration in literary history; I do know that my wife still tells of our 'honeymoon' in Geneva where Paul and I read proof on 'Song of the Sybil'.

I mentioned earlier that Wystan had marked three passages in Phillpotts' *The Elder Edda* and one in Kershaw which we later Englished. I give some here, so that the differences between the older renderings and ours will be apparent.[17]

The Eiríksmál

1 What dream is this? said Othin, a little before daylight I thought I was preparing Valholl for a slain host. I was awakening the Einherjar, and bidding them rise up and cover the benches and cleanse the beakers – I was bidding the Valkyries bring wine as if a prince was coming. I have hope of some noble heroes from the world; so my heart is glad.

2 'What uproar is that, Bragi, as if thousands were in motion – an exceeding great host approaching?'

'All the timbers of the benches are creaking as if Balder were coming back to Othin's abode.'

3 'Surely thou art talking folly, thou wise Bragi,' replied Othin, 'although thou knowest everything well. The noise betokens the approach of the hero Eric, who must be coming here into Othin's abode.'

4 'Sigmundr and Sinfjotli! Arise quickly and go to meet the prince. If it be Eric, invite him in! I have now confident hope that it is he.'   (Kershaw, p. 97)

The Lay of Erik

Odin Before dawn in a dream I saw
     Valhalla preparing to honour the dead;
     Busy at my bidding was the band of warriors
     Benches they strewed and beer-jugs washed,
     And the Valkyrie brought out the best wine.
     I expect men from Middle-Earth,
     Great warriors such as gladden my heart.
     Bragi, it thunders like a thousand fighters,
     A mighty host is on the march.
Bragi The benches tremble as though Baldur were coming
     Back to Odin's Hall.
Odin Foolish are your words, wise Bragi,
     Erik it is, as you know,
     For whom all echoes: he will enter soon,
     The boar, into Odin's Hall
     Sigmund! Sinfjötli! swiftly now
     Go to greet the prince
     And bid him welcome, if he be Erik,
     The hero I am expecting.   (Auden)

From 'Gröttasöngur'

And rocks we rolled   o'er giants' dwellings
so that the earth   thereat went trembling.
Fame we earned   for feats in battle.
With sharpened spears   we sheared asunder
bleeding wounds   while brands we reddened.   (Phillpotts, p. 60)

We yanked rocks from the yard of the giant,
So that the ground began to shake.

[So we acted for half a year]
And won fame among fighting men;
We reddened blades, we bit flesh
With sharp swords, we shed blood.   (Auden)

From '*Skírnismál*'

Dark 'tis without,   'tis time for us to fare
   over the reeking fells
   over the goblin folk;
Together we'll win through   or together he shall take us,
   that mighty giant.   (Phillpotts, p. 13)

Night has fallen: now we must ride
   Over the misty mountains,
The fells of the troll-folk;
We shall both arrive or both fall into
   The hands of the horrible giant.   (Auden)

The translations we executed involve forty-three poems and prose fragments, together with a number of prose links. Of the poems, two remain in 'poetic prose': 'Gripir's Prophecy' and the 'Short Lay of Sigurd'. Wystan felt that both of these were just not amenable to a verse rendering, and so they remained 'unversed'. Sixteen of the poems – most of them 'mythological' (rather than 'Viking' or 'heroic') – were published by Faber and Faber (in London) and Random House (in New York) in 1969. We had hoped for a small volume containing the heroic poems (those of the 'Niflung' or 'Sigurd' cycle, familiar to Wagnerites all over the world), but after lengthy negotiations, this hope never materialized. One further poem, 'The Song of Rig', appeared in the *Atlantica and Iceland Review* in 1970. The remainder are still unpublished, but the Pontifical Institute for Mediaeval Studies (Toronto) will publish a volume containing the translations in full.

A word about 'The Sun Song', the translation we have chosen for inclusion here. Unlike many of the religious-didactic poems of twelfth- to fourteenth-century Iceland, 'The Sun Song', the greatest of the Icelandic Catholic monuments, is anonymous. 'The Sun Song' is a visionary poem, somewhat like the Eddaic 'Words of the High One' and 'Song of the Sybil', but combined with medieval Christian literary notions of *exempla*, *visio*, and *allegoria*.[18] The unknown author was undoubtedly a *skáld*, or court poet, skilled at imitating the traditional Eddaic forms. The adaptation of the older forms to a distinctively Christian subject matter, while common in Anglo-Saxon England, was rare elsewhere in the Germanic north.

In 'Song of the Sybil' and in 'Waking of Angantyr' we have the pagan revelations of a dead person who has been conjured up; in 'The Sun Song' we have the words of a father, returned from the grave, directed toward his son.

When the *Völuspá* (the 'Song of the Sybil') was translated in 1967, Wystan felt that the poem made better sense if some of the strophes were re-ordered. Later, be felt the same was true of the *Hávamál* ('Words of the High One') and a few of the other poems, including 'The Sun Song'. As the parchment manuscript of 'The Sung Song' is incomplete, and can be filled out only from relatively late paper manuscripts, neither Paul Taylor nor I felt there was any strong scholarly objection to accepting the version Wystan felt made better 'poetic sense'.

The poem begins with a series of *exempla*, designed to illustrate the ways of evil men and their fates. The father follows this with an admonition to pray, and then a review of his own pleasant but wayward life. At the point of death, the father has a vision (the strophes beginning with 'I saw the sun...'). This sun is Christ in allegorical form: its blood-stained rays and the ocean into which it sinks are reminders of the *Dies Irae*. When the sun has sunk, death comes and the soul flies off (as a star of hope). On its way through the seven heavens, the soul is waylaid by Lucifer (the dragon) and his minions, but is aided by the hart of the sun (Christ) and the seven star-angels led by St Michael. The soul then sketches two worlds, 'the world of pain' and that of 'the blessed', and the reader is left with little doubt as to which is the desirable one. The section ends with an invocation to the Trinity. The final section contains a number of more-or-less obscure allegories, and ends with an impressive echo of *Requiem aeternam dona eis, Domine*.

All in all, 'The Sun Song' is a magnificent work, moving and effective, more subdued in tone than its insular and continental counterparts, its visions subordinated to the theme of the whole work.

NOTES

1 J. Fuller, *A Reader's Guide to W. H. Auden* (London, 1970), p. 113.

2 W. H. Auden, *Letters from Iceland* (London, 1937), p. 214.

3 *Letters from Iceland*, p. 205.

4 *Letters from Iceland*, p. 119; cf. Isherwood's comment in *New Verse* quoted above.

5 G. T. Wright, *W. H. Auden* (New York, 1969), p. 76.

6 B. Everett, *Auden* (Edinburgh, 1964), p. 61.

7 Michael Yates, 'Iceland 1936', in *W. H. Auden: A Tribute*, edited by Stephen Spender (London and New York, 1975), pp. 59–68.

8 *Letters from Iceland*, p. 201. The second of these stanzas – and a number of others in this section – was deleted from the 'Letter to Lord Byron' in Auden's revisions. The comment on his name thus occurs in the 1937 edition and in *The English Auden*, edited by Edward Mendelson (London and New York, 1978), but not in the *Collected Poems*, edited by Edward Mendelson (London and New York, 1976).

9 Basil Boothby, 'An Unofficial Visitor', in *W. H. Auden: A Tribute*, pp. 93–7.

10 'The World of Sagas', *Secondary Worlds* (London, 1968); the citations are from pp. 63 and 82.

11 'Letter to Kristinn Andrésson, Esq.', *Letters from Iceland*, pp. 214f.

12 *Letters from Iceland*, p. 216.

13 'Iceland Revisited' (April 1964).

14 *Runic and Heroic Poems*, edited by Bruce Dickins (Cambridge, 1915).

15 *The Criterion*, 11 (1932), 368.

16 Soon after Wystan's death, I donated all the correspondence and all drafts of the manuscripts in my possession (save only the ultimate and penultimate drafts) to The Berg Collection of The New York Public Library. As these manuscripts are inaccessible to me at this time, no citations illustrative of the earlier stages of translation are offered here.

17 I am grateful to Edward Mendelson and the Estate of W. H. Auden for permission to quote from the various works cited.

18 The poem exists in several seventeenth-century paper copies. The text used is from *Den Norsk-Isländska Skaldediktningen*, edited by Ernst A. Kock (Lund, 1946). There is little available in English about 'The Sun Song', but there is some discussion in Stefán Einarsson's *History of Icelandic Literature* (Baltimore, 1957), and several pages are devoted to it in P. Hallberg's *Old Icelandic Poetry* (Lincoln, Nebraska, 1975). Further afield, W. Lange's *Studien zur christlichen Dichtung der Nordgermanen 1000–1200* (*Palaestra* 222) (Göttingen, 1958) is of interest.

A translation of
three poems by Erik Lindegren

W. H. AUDEN AND LEIF SJÖBERG

OLD RED INDIAN

Yes, I remember my youth: a flame amid much smoke.
I remember it narrow from fear: how it ascended and singed
its own heart: in an all-embracing desire to climb; to become wings
and soar straight up towards the blue crystal of space.

Now I see life becoming broader
for I know the cruelty of life.
The nest of the vanished hawk in the fire of the sunset
is burned to blessed ashes,
and I know that wings
are for climbing no higher than the eye can see
in grand recapitulation in the clear light of pitilessness,
the hunting grounds and landscape of our youth.

From this hill
you then see your own death,

your end,

as your quarry.

SNOW FLUTE

Time snows down from the tree
the valley soars into the depth
the path beside the well entices
the wound wears garlands of snow

the voices are asleep in the valley
the seconds are resting so far away

153

so remotely distant from one another
as if they were dancing off with somebody else

the paws of hares are dipped into the well
the minutes breathe so far away
years like the sails of snow-flakes
fluttering by without ships

my wolf-run races over garlands
the well drinks its snow
the tree is without sky
the wound without wound

ZERO POINT

What is it that steps out of me
and leaves me
like smoke

       in this street with unknown numbers
       and houses that seem to stand on a grey plain
       where stone upon stone is all that remains

What is it that is left of me
and sinks like a stone

       like a stone through stone after stone
       as if the horizons had disappeared
       or lost their power of attraction

and here:
once I led someone
by the hand like a child
in the belief that it was my life

       and now:
       a sinking stone
       a drifting smoke
       and a child taller than a mountain.

The canon of literary modernism:
A note on abstraction in the poetry of
Erik Lindegren

GÖRAN PRINTZ-PÅHLSON

I

In 1943 the Swedish poet Erik Lindegren – at that time still comparatively unknown – published a long essay, in the Swedish journal *Ord
och Bild*, on the poetry of W. H. Auden.[1] It is important not only in
that it adds to the bibliography of early Auden criticism and gives an
ingenious and sometimes striking interpretation of Auden's poetry and
character, mainly based on 'Paid on both Sides' and 'Journal of an
Airman' from *The Orators* (1932), but also in view of the light it sheds
on Lindegren's own poetics and poetic practice, then in a period of fertile
development.

It is known that Auden himself was not very satisfied with 'Journal
of an airman'. In his illuminating preface to *The English Auden*,[2]
Edward Mendelson quotes several letters from Auden, who deplores its
'obscurity' and in particular the equivocal nature of its political
'message'. 'It is meant to be a critique of the fascist outlook, but from
its reception among some of my contemporaries, and on rereading it
myself, I see that it can, most of it, be interpreted as a favourable
exposition.'[3]

Not so Lindegren, who is admirably clear on its political implications
and who in addition recognizes the paramount importance of Lawrence
for the psychotherapeutic element running through this work. Auden
corroborates this in a letter to a friend: 'In a sense the work is my
memorial to Lawrence; i.e., the theme is the failure of the romantic
conception of personality.'[4]

What particularly fascinated Lindegren was what he refers to as
Auden's specific 'perspective', the bird's-eye view:

> Consider this and in our time
> As the hawk sees it or the helmeted airman.   (*Poems*, XXIX (1930))

It is true that the 'vertical' is Auden's favoured dimension and that
there are many bird images in his poetry; but the Auden who admits,
in the 'Letter to Byron', that his overriding desire as a child had been
to become a mining engineer, is always more likely to let the vertical
get its proper extension in some gloomy subterranean world. Even when
he assumes the persona of a bird, as the seagull in the humourously
auto-analytical 'The Month was April',[5] it is not the soaring so much
as the ultimate bringing down of the bird that interests him.

When Lindegren writes: 'The hawk and the airman are among the
constant symbols with Auden, the concentrated, detailed observation of
the quarry and the extended, always varying panorama regularly recur',[6]
it may be partially true as description of Auden but is even more a
description of an ever present theme in Lindegren's own poetry, at
this time mostly still to be written. 'Old Red Indian' and 'Zero Point'
are two splendid instances.[7] An even more apt illustration is found in
'Icarus' (Auden's Icarus poem, 'Museé des Beaux Arts', had previously
been translated by Ekelöf, as Leif Sjöberg notes[8]):

> His memories of the labyrinth go numb with sleep.
> The single memory: how the calls and the confusion rose
> until at last they swung him up from the earth.
>
> And how all cleavings which have cried out always
> for their bridges in his breast
> slowly shut like eyelids,
> and how the birds swept past like shuttles, like arrows,
> and finally the last lark brushing his hand,
> falling like song.
>
> Then: the winds' labyrinth, with its blind bulls,
> cacophonous lights and inclines,
> with its dizzying breath which he through arduous
> struggle learned how to parry,
> until it rose again, his vision and his flight.
>
> Now he is rising alone, in a sky without clouds,
> in a space empty of birds in the din of the aircraft...
> rising toward a clearer and clearer sun,
> turning gradually cooler, turning cold,
> and upward towards the spring of his blood, soul's cataract:
> a prisoner in a whistling lift,
> a seabubble's journey toward the looming magnetic air:
> the bursting of the foetal membrane, transparently near,

and the vortex of signs, born of the springtide, raging of azure,
crumbling walls, and drunkenly the call of the other side:
Reality fallen
> Without reality born!
>> (translation by John Matthias and Göran Printz-Påhlson)

The poem is in many ways a reversal of Auden's Icarus poem (or any conventional treatment of the Icarus theme). While Auden is content to follow the Brueghel painting in noticing the surroundings of the fall more than the fall itself, and in particular the indifference of the surroundings, Lindegren boldly concentrates on the protagonist. Auden's language is resolutely discursive and expository:

> . . . some untidy spot
> Where the dogs go on with their doggy life and the torturer's horse
> Scratches its innocent behind on a tree.

Although 'the aged' were 'passionately waiting for the miraculous birth' the fall is for the busy ploughman 'not an important failure'. Life goes on, Auden seems to be saying; even when tragedy occurs 'someone else is eating or opening a window or just walking dully along'.

This sapient moralizing is not for Lindegren. The indifference in his poem is not a property of the surroundings but the exalted ataraxia of the protagonist himself. The very fall is in defiance of the law of gravity: it is a *fall upwards*, toward empty space, leaving the contingent things of this world almost contemptuously behind. 'The miraculous birth', tentatively dismissed by Auden, here becomes a reality, a bursting of the foetal membrane of the sky, even if the reality born is, although triumphantly proclaimed, syntactically ambiguous.[9] The heroic identification of protagonist and poet is never in doubt in the Lindegren poem.

In the aforementioned essay, Lindegren says about the airman: 'It is not unimportant to remember that his genealogy goes back to Icarus, the symbol of the tragedy of setting one's goal too high, or that the mythical aura surrounding him may derive ultimately from popular ideas of the nature of epilepsy.'[10] Epilepsy is, of course, the 'falling disease' (in Swedish, *fallandesjuka*) and altogether this seems to be more a prophetic gloss on the future poem of his own than on Auden's text. One has no difficulty in recognizing this protagonist as the true hero of modernism; Walter Benjamin presented him admirably in relation to the grandeur and squalor of Paris in the Second Empire and called him Baudelaire. 'The hero is the true subject of modernism. In other words it takes a heroic constitution to live modernism.'[11]

The hero is dandy, *flâneur*, suicide, sufferer, social outcast, diseased, in his pursuit of the absolute. Like Baudelaire's Icarus he has broken his arms in trying to embrace the clouds.[12] This is indeed a far cry from Auden's innocent Icarus, let alone from his crafty airman.

It seems probable that Auden's poem exerted some influence on the rhythm and organization of Lindegren's 'Icarus'. But the real sources of inspiration for the poem have to be sought in other quarters, in a tradition of modernist exemplars which are by and large alien to Anglo-American poetry.

When Icarus-the-Poet soars to greater and greater heights, shedding gradually the encumbrances of things, his flight or fall may be meant to illustrate the pursuit of a pure language or an absolute diction. Clearly, the poem lends itself willingly to an allegorical interpretation on even a merely personal and mundane level. There is the distinct possibility that it can be read as a description of Lindegren's own poetic development.

II

There is perhaps a sense in which it is altogether useless to talk about *the* 'canon of modernism' or even about 'canons of modernism'. 'Modernism' or its *etymon* 'modernity' is clearly, historically and logically, opposed to the formation of the models or measuring rods that infuse the classical mode with rigour and stability. 'Canon formation in literature must always proceed to a selection of classics', says E. R. Curtius, quoted with approval by Harold Bloom, who writes on canon-formation in relation to his own theory of revisionism: '"Canon" as a word goes back to a Greek word for a measuring rule, which in Latin acquired the additional meaning of "model"...Canon-formation or canonization is a richly suggestive word for a process of classic formation in poetic tradition, because it associates notions of music and of standards.'[13] Bloom goes on to consider the relationship between religious and secular canon-formation with the hardly surprising result that secular canon-formation is more amenable to 'intruders of genius', and thus to revisionism. Bloom's now well-known essay, 'The Primal Scene of Instruction' in *A Map of Misreading*, does not, however, seem particularly useful in dealing with either the classical or the modernist mode, owing to his dependence on the Freudian model of nuclear family relations. This may be obscured by his customary brilliance of analysis in writing on some 'modern' poets, but for the Anglo-American poetry

he is confining himself to almost exclusively, the romantic and historicist
mode reigns supreme. 'Modernism' is as militantly anti-historical as it
is anti-classical: what is 'modern' is dependent on what models offer
themselves for emulation *today*, not at any past or future *illud tempus*.[14]

The dilemma of the modernist is that he will invariably find that this
has always been the case. 'When they assert their own modernity, they
are bound to discover their dependence on similar assertions made by
their literary predecessors; their claim to being a new beginning turns
out to be the repetition of a claim that has always already been made.'[15]
So the only course open to the modernists is to set out on a quest for
their lost traditions, their forgotten ancestors. In modernism it is not the
oedipal Primal Scene of Instruction sketched by Bloom which is
invoked; the modernist is not a parricide because he is already an orphan:
the mythic figure of his choice must rather be Telemachos, looking for
a lost father. Joyce was, of course, very much aware of this when he had
his hero of modernism, his Icarus-figure, address the old craftsman and
inventor in the well-known lines from the end of *A Portrait*: 'Old father,
old artificer, stand me now and ever in good stead.' He could then send
Stephen Dedalus on a quest for a paternal substitute, donning the
disguise of Telemachos, in *Ulysses*.

If the modernist *chef-d'oeuvre* tends in this way to include an
allegorical account of the conditions of its own creation, it will also more
and more be inviting readings of a flat and abstract character. Lindegren's
poem has been read as an allegory of the poetic development of its
author.[16]

Erik Lindegren did not leave a voluminous poetic *oeuvre* behind him.
After a conventional first book of poetry, *Postum ungdom* (Posthumous
youth, 1935), he produced his first major opus, *mannen utan väg* (The
man without a way), a rigidly formalized collection of forty 'broken
sonnets', in a highly personal surrealist style, which has been one of the
most influential and normative works in Scandinavian modernism. It was
privately printed, in the austere publishing climate of the war years, in
1942. In 1945 it was re-issued commercially and had subsequently an
enormous impact in Sweden on the then prevalent 'style of the Forties'
and the concomitant critical debate on modernism in which Lindegren
took part as an eloquent defender of modernism of the more traditional
kind. In 1947 he published *Sviter* (Suites) in a more lavish and sensuous
surrealist manner, which book proved to be, if possible, even more
seductive than the previous austerity. A third major collection, *Vinteroffer*
(Winter sacrifice, 1954) exhibited a more subdued and reflective mood

developing alongside a growing desperation. Both these volumes are, in true modernist fashion, strewn with analogies and parallels with music and the fine arts. For the remainder of his life he wrote some highly praised opera libretti, mainly in collaboration with the composer Karl Birger Blomdahl. He died in 1968. His influence and reputation, although to some extent eclipsed by his friend and near contemporary Gunnar Ekelöf's uncommonly fertile poetic flowering in the late fifties and the sixties, remains strong in Sweden. Lindegren was also a proficient translator, from several languages, of Faulkner, Rilke, St John Perse, and of modern French poetry in general.

It is tempting to read 'Icarus' – which is the introductory poem to the last volume – as a poetic summary of his momentous and short career. The labyrinth can be read as referring to the labyrinthine labours of *mannen utan väg*, the contortionist encompassing of experience in maze-like patterns. 'The winds' labyrinth' is then clearly related to *Suites* with 'its dizzying breath', the transports of sensuous experience, gradually shedding its objects. And the remaining flight towards a cooling sun associates with the wintry landscapes of the last volume a voice like icicles faintly dripping under a bleak sky. No more poetry can be conceived after the rebirth, which represents the final silence towards which all poetry strives. The poem is thus read as a history of its own language, fugitive of its content.

This represents a paradigm familiar from at least one mainstream of continental modernism (French and German) which can be associated with a line from Hölderlin to Baudelaire, to Mallarmé, to Rilke, to Celan. These are indeed the ancestors claimed by Lindegren in translations and essays (which also led him, mistakenly, to make the same claims for Auden's 'true ancestors').

III

In 1942, the same year as *mannen utan väg* and one year before the Auden essay, Lindegren claimed another, somewhat more surprising ancestor in an essay on Ibsen's *Brand*.[17] This is indeed another 'vertical' hero, but Lindegren is not interested in psychological analysis. Instead he praises its 'classical' virtues of 'abstract clarity' and, following a hint from Ibsen, 'syllogistic structure', and says, very characteristically: 'The Idea is put forward in such an objective way that it becomes form rather than content, that it is chilled through by the elevated meaninglessness which for many seems to be immanent in the great shaping energies of history.' The wording is perhaps more revealing of

Lindegren's own method than of Ibsen's. He further enlarges on the same theme: 'Central to the nature of objectivity is also the fact that it conceals the truth about the individual. In any case, it transposes truth to an esoteric level. Truth is not to be seen, as little as the works of a watch.'

Abstract, objective: the qualities referred to are more easily assimilated in a classicist poetic than in a modernist one. The amphibological structure of modernism is such, however, that it most readily tends to direct its canon-formation towards models of the classicist mould. The destruction of the past that is a commonplace strategy in modernism since Nietzsche makes it necessary to create a canon outside history: the precursors in time are not so much instructors or mentors as problems of assimilation. For that purpose they have to be deprived of all contingent qualities, to be reduced to abstract formulae applicable to all times and all places. This is in sharp contrast to romanticism which sees history as an organic succession, a handing down of skills through generations. One could be tempted to say, reductively, that modernism equals romanticism minus its historicism, classicism minus its primitivism.

To put a hasty end to this farrago of -isms, let us be reminded by Walter Benjamin, sometimes so surprisingly down to earth, that this attitude of the modernist is to a large extent created by the 'polemical situation'.[18] This is certainly applicable to Lindegren who attained his status as modernist hero in a harsh polemical climate. It is, in such a situation, of paramount importance to select your right team-mates. And that is what canon-formation in modernist practice ultimately comes down to.

The question of abstraction, of objectivity, is no doubt, as almost everything else, in the last analysis a question of language. Hegel asked himself 'Wer denkt abstrakt?' and came up with an answer which discredited abstract thinking outside the sciences for a long time to come. Modern poetry of the romantic persuasion has been involved in a drawn-out campaign against abstraction, taking its arsenal from various modern, not always correctly understood, philosophies of language. It is good to be reminded, in the recent book by Robert Pinsky, that words are not to be confused with things and that a word is always an abstraction in relation to its referent.[19] Perhaps somewhat misleadingly, he relates the common mistake of thinking otherwise to the conflict between realism and nominalism which he sees as a crucial area of dispute in most recent poetry.

Even leaving aside the old question of the arbitrariness of the relation of words to things, familiar from a long tradition of contention, from *Cratylus* to Saussure, we may notice that any possible realist theory of language has been severely undercut by the largely nominalist, positivist and pragmatic accounts of language acquisition of the last hundred years. In their insistence on making usage and naming the basics of linguistic understanding and in their neglect of formal principles, these also favour the position that language is in essence a system of designation of things rather than ideas, of individuals rather than universals, and that the abstractions of language are somehow secondary and supererogatory to its real core of concrete semantics. The reductive and primitivist notions of this kind have been seriously challenged from various most dissimilar positions in more recent years.

Even the simplest first order-logic operations involve a great deal of abstraction, and as Bruno Shell very convincingly pointed out in relation to the formation of the Greek mind, even the naming of primitive objects requires some degree of comparison and classification.[20]

Attacks launched against 'vapid generalities' or 'empty abstractions', whether these occur in poetry or in any other context, are, of course, always valuable,[21] but they are essentially a concern of a legitimate demand for specified information and in no way linked to abstraction as a principle of language. It is not possible to say that a dog is a more abstract animal than, say, an Irish setter, nor is the word 'dog' in any significant way either 'abstract' or 'concrete' (one can regard it as either a token or a type).

In the case of poetry this whole matter has been obscured by the general confusion about what a poem refers to. Can it possibly be linked to 'reality' in some way that insures it against drifting to some misty land of generalities? T. E. Hulme and the imagists believed that this could and should be done through some undefined property of language that constituted an 'Image' as 'an intellectual and emotional complex in an instant of time'.[22]

'Imagism' is perhaps only an extension of the *Pictura ut poesis* doctrine in modern terms (it is to be noted that the famous *Imagines* of Philostratos may have given rise to the nineteenth-century prose poem, through Goethe's admirable translations, but, far from being imagist 'instants of time', they are just descriptions of pictures, real or imaginary, and not to be mistaken for substitutes of these pictures).

Representations, whether in words or in pictures, whether of concrete objects or of abstract concepts, always involve abstractions, and in order to be representational a work of art has to be selective. The crucial question comes when a work of art is representational of a representation, when it is two steps removed from what was originally represented. This one can call, in accordance with the usage of Walter Benjamin in particular, *allegory*.[23] Representation as abstraction, in its turn, involves interchangeability.[24]

Lindegren shows himself to be very well aware of the nature of these principles when he stresses the *timelessness* of the representative work of art, in his essay on *Brand*. The warning against historical contingencies should be taken seriously. In particular as regards *mannen utan väg* it has been very tempting to offer specific interpretations or critical translations of its surrealist imagery (here following hints given by Lindegren himself).[25] The critic Bengt Holmqvist ingeniously specified the meaning of a famous line of the poem (from Sonnet xxvi):[26]

> and the dismal flight of fate in the feathered garb of somersault

This line, according to Holmqvist, could be 'translated' as referring to the flight of von Ribbentrop, then foreign secretary for Germany, to Moscow in August 1939. No doubt many of the lines of the poem could be translated in a similarly reckless way into the world events of these dramatic years. This does not make the poem a history of World War II.

Paul de Man has in an unusually subtle piece of argumentation attacked the view expressed by Hans Robert Jauss and his colleagues and pupils that 'modernism' can be regarded as a 'movement' in history, with a beginning and a (possible) end.[27] He is particularly concerned with an interpretation of Mallarmé's 'Tombeau de Verlaine' by the German critic, Karlheinz Stierle. He quotes from this: 'For Mallarmé the concrete image no longer leads to a clearer vision.' If one considers what makes the object of the poem unreal, one is bound to realize that it is 'a poem of allegorical reification [*Vergegenständlichung*]. This is in contrast to traditional allegory, the function of which was 'to make the meaning stand out more vividly'.

Although agreeing with Stierle about the importance of allegory (here taken in the sense championed by Walter Benjamin), as opposed to the merely representational, de Man maintains quite convincingly that there is no fixed point where representation ends and allegory takes over: 'Up to a very advanced point, not reached in this poem and perhaps never reached at all, Mallarmé remains a representational poet as he remains in fact a poet of the self, however impersonal...'[28] From what was said above about representation one can draw the conclusion that all the possible readings of the poem exist simultaneously. The allegorical reading does not follow on the representational, or on any other reading. They are interchangeable, but not in an ordered sequence as in the solution of a riddle.

The French critic Georges Périlleux has in a recent article, bravely and successfully written in Swedish, given a detailed analysis of the rhetorical tropes used in *mannen utan väg*.[29] The highly intricate and artificial rhetorical patterns revealed (Périlleux adapts the methods of analysis of *Rhétorique générale* by the 'groupe μ') point to the rigidly formal organization of the work. But rhetoric in this sense – as a set of linguistic or paralinguistic rules – is, as Harold Bloom has recently reminded us, defiantly anti-historical.[30] This is rhetoric which has renounced all pedagogical intent, thus keeping company with an allegory which has renounced all representational intent.

Lindegren is clearly realizing this in his frequently invited parallels between his poetry and music or mathematics. 'Poetry as higher calculus' is the formula given in his polemical apologia.[31] Twenty years ago I suggested – following a hint from William Empson's treatment of George Herbert[32] – that the mathematical analogy could be more than vaguely useful for this kind of poetry, as the elements seem to be freely interchangeable while the structure remains the same.[33] From his point of view, and from the fact that, in contrast to traditional allegory, the readings or transformations are unordered, it follows that no reading can be regarded as in any way privileged. Is there any sense in calling the reading of the political content in the Lindegren poem representational and the personal reading allegorical, and not vice versa? The significance of the allegory is ultimately that it signifies nothing.

How is this dilemma to be resolved? Lindegren seems to be going even further in some poems in *Vinteroffer* where no hints of representation or allegory remain, and the rhetorical devices seem to provide merely a mechanical inspiration:

Meditation

Feel the throb of spring in the glade of simple hearts
(in aliens' oblivion we live and we die)
Mark our shadow there beneath the arch of night
(for what we never uttered we remember best)

See the desert tracks which evanesce like roses
(the wild is not astray, but it is fugitive)
Remember trees like dogs leashed tight in dreams
(domesticity's not home, but it is ill)

Cover with your glance the dying mayfly's gleam
(like scythes the grass is waving on our grave)
Contain the arch of spring, and touch the desert trees
(and yet we all are like the grass)
(translated by John Matthias and Göran Printz-Påhlson)

This poem seems to be moving its symbols at random within a confined space where no references to public or personal experiences are possible. It could evidently go on forever. Maybe it is just the anticipated exhaustion of the poet, in realizing that it *could* go on forever, that makes him put an end to it at this early stage.

IV

The canon-formation of literary modernism is in quite a profound sense an act of recognition, not of affinities but of identity of content. If Harold Bloom has for our time given a romantic interpretation of a literary theory of succession in saying that the meaning of a poem is always another poem, one is perhaps justified in offering a rival modernist theory of discontinuity in saying that all modernist poems have the same meaning which the poets try to approximate in stating its essential inaccessibility. As this inaccessibility *is* the meaning of the modernist poem, they have, in the vein of classical paradox, quite literally managed both to express the meaning and fail to do so. The only possible remaining step must be silence.

There is no evidence that when translating Lindegren's poetry Auden approached it with anything but suspicion and misgiving.[34] The vatic stance, the orphic mysticism, the rhetoric of paradox: this is a tradition of modernism he could not make his own. Only in the attraction to the renunciation of poetry could these two poets meet. Auden's revolt against poetry as a high vocation was clear already in his early acceptance of a tradition of light verse, of Carroll, Lear, Chesterton, Belloc, Kipling, as his true ancestry. Perhaps it could be said that he had renounced serious poetry for verse by the time of, say, *The Age of Anxiety*. For Lindegren, adhering to a more exacting canon, there was only one way to go, to silence. The moving last lines of *Winter Sacrifice* give his version of the modernist question:

Why blow on the candle of life
with all this talk
of life or death...

NOTES

1 Reprinted in Erik Lindegren, *Tangenter* (Stockholm, 1974).
2 *The English Auden: Poems, Essays and Dramatic Writings 1927–1939* (London, 1977).
3 *The English Auden*, p. xv.
4 *The English Auden*, p. xv.
5 *The English Auden*, pp. 130–5. First publication of the poem.
6 Lindegren, p. 123.
7 From *Sviter* and *Vinteroffer* respectively. Translations above by Auden and Sjöberg.
8 See 'Translating with W. H. Auden', below.
9 The last line in Swedish contains an untranslatable syntactic ambiguity.
10 Lindegren, p. 125.
11 Walter Benjamin, *Charles Baudelaire: A Lyric Poet in the Era of High Capitalism* (London, 1973), p. 74.
12 'Les plaintes d'un Icare' in *Les Fleurs du mal*.
13 *Poetry and Repression: Revisionism from Blake to Stevens* (New Haven and London, 1976), p. 29.
14 Cf. Trotsky's penetrating critique of *futurism* in *Literature and Revolution* (Ann Arbor, Mich., 1960).
15 Paul de Man, *Blindness and Insight: Essays in the Rhetoric of Contemporary Criticism* (New York, 1971), p. 161.
16 Göran Printz-Påhlson, *Solen i spegeln* (Stockholm, 1958), p. 155.
17 Lindegren, pp. 102–5.
18 Benjamin, p. 82.
19 Robert Pinsky, *The Situation of Poetry* (Princeton, New Jersey, 1976), p. 5.
20 Bruno Snell, *The Discovery of the Mind* (New York, 1960), pp. 191ff.
21 'Go in fear of abstractions.' Ezra Pound, *Make it New* (London, 1934), p. 337.
22 Pound, p. 336.
23 Walter Benjamin, *Ursprung des deutschen Trauerspiels* (Frankfurt, 1972); translated by Hans J. Osborne as *The Origin of German Tragic Drama*, with an introduction by George Steiner (London, 1977).
24 Cf. Sigurd Burckhardt, *The Drama of Language* (Baltimore, 1970), esp. chapter 1.
25 *Bonniers Nyheter*, no. 2 (Stockholm, 1946).
26 *40-talsförfattare*, edited by Lars-Olof Franzén (Stockholm, 1965), p. 38.
27 Paul de Man, 'Lyric and Modernity', in *Blindness and Insight*.
28 *Blindness and Insight*, p. 182.
29 In *Literature and Reality: Creatio versus Mimesis*, edited by Alex Bolckmans (Ghent, 1977), pp. 291–309.
30 Harold Bloom, *Wallace Stevens: The Poems of our Climate* (Ithaca, 1976), chapter 14.
31 'Tal i egen sak', reprinted *Tangenter*.
32 William Empson, *Seven Types of Ambiguity* (2nd edn, London, 1947), pp. 118–19.
33 *Solen i spegeln*, p. 162.
34 Translations from Lindegren are my own where not otherwise indicated. A useful French translation exists by Jean-Clarence Lambert, *L'Homme sans voie* (Paris, 1952).

W. H. Auden:
'In Memory of Ernst Toller'

HARALD H. OHLENDORF

Auden's elegy to Toller is a minor work, rarely discussed in the Auden literature,[1] yet a close examination of the poem brings to light a broad, multi-faceted background which is rarely or only vaguely evoked in Auden studies.

Auden's *oeuvre* is seen by his more recent critics to be marked by a gradual and continuous process of integration: of technical experimentation towards unexcelled mastery, of diverse utterances into one voice, of psychologically and politically perspicacious poetic criticism into encompassing love for man, God and nature. Wholeness, integration and continuity of the work emerge from a biographical background of discontinuities, of relocations, of new beginnings.

The private printing of Auden's first volume of poetry was in 1928, a year which saw the young Oxonian break with the provincialism of the academy and break the confines of Mortmere. *Paid on Both Sides* (1930), the poetic fruit of this break, is 'uncompromisingly "modern"'.[2] Although a first draft existed before he went abroad, Auden rewrote the play extensively in Berlin.[3] Whether the changes and emendations were influenced by the experiments and new departures he may have observed on the stages of Berlin is, of course, beyond proof.[4] What is certain is that the Berlin experience brought about an enlivening of Auden's psychological awareness. And in the rise of Nazism, Auden encountered at first hand a political and social phenomenon for which Marxism seemed to offer the only coherent ideological antidote. *Paid on Both Sides* shows the influences of psychoanalytic and Marxist thought, both of which Auden explored further during the following decade. The increasing political turmoil of the thirties undoubtedly provided ample

* Quoted material is by permission of Professor Edward Mendelson and the Estate of W. H. Auden, and the Humanities Research Center, University of Texas at Austin.

provocation to test and examine these complementary world views as bases for poetic utterances and for his own public role.

Auden's decision on the return from his travels to China in late 1938 to leave Europe for the United States marks the second major break in his life.

Auden emigrated to America, self-consciously choosing the role of the literary exile and leaving behind a disgruntled English literary group. That breaking off old literary ties was a principal reason for Auden's move is indicated by a comment of Cyril Connolly's. 'He reverts always to the same argument, that a writer needs complete anonymity, he must break way from the European literary happy family.'[5]

Buell and Connolly, I believe, are taking Auden's remark too literally. One cannot wholly disregard the lines in *New Year Letter* (1940):

> Twelve months ago in Brussels, I
> Heard the same wishful-thinking sigh
> As round me, trembling on their beds
> Or taut with apprehensive dreads,
> The sleepless guests of Europe lay,
> Wishing the centuries away;
> . . .
> There crouched the presence of The Thing:
>
> (*New Year Letter*, lines 12–21)

But whatever one's speculation as to the reasons for the decision, what it did accomplish was a distancing from the pressures to combine the poet's avocation with political involvement. Confronted with the black and white of the Continental struggle soon to explode into chaos, Auden chose the either/or of Kierkegaardian theology and the relative political calm of the United States. His was a poet's choice in favour of continuing moral and aesthetic creativity. If he left behind a 'literary happy family', he certainly continued to be immersed deeply in a European philosophical and poetic tradition. The portrait poems and the elegies in *Another Time*, if nothing else, testify to this.

If *New Year Letter* is seen as the first great poem of a new Auden, *Another Time*[6] can be regarded as his poetic account of the turmoil out of which *New Year Letter* grew. All the poems in this volume were written, with perhaps one or two exceptions, between the spring of 1937 and the winter of 1939. The book has three sections: 'People and Places', 'Lighter Poems', and 'Occasional Poems'. The first section ranges across a broad spectrum of moods, styles, forms and voices, while the second section, the 'Lighter Poems', serves as a counterweight. The 'Occasional Poems' of the third section, individually and as a group, portray a stark encounter between historical reality and poetic temperament. Although few in number, these concluding poems shed a melancholy light over the entire volume. Two deal with war ('Spain 1937' and 'September 1, 1939') and three are elegies ('In Memory of W. B. Yeats', 'In Memory of Ernst Toller', and 'In Memory of Sigmund Freud'). The ostensibly reconciliatory final poem 'Epithalamion' does not dispel the shade.

The sequence of the poems in this last section is strictly chronological, in contrast to the preceding sections, where Auden organized the poems according to a purposeful, if at times loose, rhetorical argument. The observation of a temporal sequence of occasions in the third section seems to surrender the principle of poetic organization to the arbitrary chronology of historical events. But the 'random' arrangement does not disassemble. Rather poetic language and mood resolve the events in a final melancholy chord.

The Faber edition of *Another Time* went through several unrevised reprintings.[7] There is one noteworthy fact, however, as regards the poems of the final section. Of the six poems, Auden rejected three from further publication after they appeared in *Collected Shorter Poems* (1950).[8] The poems he retained are the elegies. This is not the place to comment on the merits of the author's decision, but reflection on his decision with regard to the last section of *Another Time* is appropriate. This final rearrangement by exclusion creates a uniformity of mood, since the broader spectrum of events is reduced to poems on the occasions of the deaths of three personalities. Of these, the poems on Yeats and Freud have received much critical attention. The importance of the works and ideas of these two men for Auden and for us is only too apparent. The elegy on Ernst Toller has been neglected. In large measure, I am sure, this is because Toller has become relatively unknown to us. Yet I believe that the elegiac triad in *Another Time* is not properly understood as a final chord in the volume unless the Toller poem is considered.

Ernst Toller (1893–1939)[9] was a poet and a playwright, a writer of short stories and travelogues. His plays were widely performed in Germany between 1919 and the spring of 1933. A volunteer at the beginning of World War I, he received a medical discharge in 1916, a disenchanted man who fervently embraced pacifism. At the end of the war, within a timespan of little more than a year, he was catapulted into the forefront of the German revolution in 1919, becoming, for a few days, the leader of the short-lived revolutionary government in Bavaria. For his revolutionary activities he was condemned to five years' imprisonment for high treason. As a prominent member of the Left (though never a communist) and as a Jew, he was among the first writers whose books were burned and whose citizenship was revoked by the Nazis. He found himself exiled in 1933 and committed suicide in New York on 22 May 1939.

Toller tried to live with two commitments: a private literary one and a public political obligation. He was torn between the two. During his imprisonment and after his release in 1924 he devoted most of his time to writing; public speeches and political activity came second. After 1933, however, he travelled widely throughout Europe, Russia and the U.S., speaking to Writers' Congresses, testifying against the Nazis before British and American government bodies, and organizing aid for the victims of fascism. His most ambitious campaign was undertaken in 1938. After a two months' journey through Republican Spain in the fall of 1938, Toller began to work on a large-scale relief plan for the civilian population in war-torn Spain. The first food shipments were underway when the civil war ended in the defeat of the Republicans. Toller was completely downcast at this miscarriage. Around that time his latest play, *Pastor Hall*, was about to be published, and Toller experienced a creative let-down which was intensified by doubt as to whether the play would be staged. The combination of the failure of the relief campaign and his self-doubt about the play threw him into a deep depression. As a close friend later wrote:

His fate was as manic depressive as he was himself... An intuitive writer, who only wrote in intervals, he believed during every creative pause that he was done as a writer. He knew that he owed his reputation not only to his literary accomplishments but also to his political fate, and he suffered from this interfusion. He tried to withdraw from the loud world and to live in quiet, and he suffered in the deadly solitude, which envelops everyone who does not constantly want to beat the great drum of daily public exposure. So he plunged back into the noise of the day, beat the drum and suffered, when he drew more recognition than his work. He was jealous of himself though never of others.[10]

We do not know how well Auden knew Toller. Aside from the elegy there is no thematic treatment of Toller or his work in Auden's writing. However, Auden translated and adapted the songs for the English version of Toller's play *No More Peace*.[11] The play itself was first produced in London at the Gate Theatre, on 11 June 1936. One of the lyrics, 'Noah's Song', was published in the *New Statesman and Nation* (13 June 1936), with three others ('Socrates' Song', 'Rachel's Song', and 'Duet') published in October of the same year in the *London*

Mercury.[12] Toller's play was never published in German. The German typescript in the Toller Collection at Yale does not contain German texts for all of the songs that appeared in the English translation, so some of Auden's 'adaptations' may, in fact, be original songs. It is also possible, of course, that the translations were prepared from a different German version, now lost.[13] Conclusive evidence is not yet available. A monologue by Toller and Auden entitled 'The Demagogue' was performed as part of the revue *Pepper Mill*, produced by Erika Mann at the Chanin Auditorium (New York) on 5 January 1937. This was actually 'The Dictator's Song' from *No More Peace*. Finally, Auden translated the 'Song of the Moor Soldiers' for Spender's translation of *Pastor Hall*.[14] It has also been suggested that there are parallels between *No More Peace* and Auden and Isherwood's *On the Frontier*.

Auden may have seen performances of Toller's plays while he was in Berlin in 1928 and 1929.[15] He may also have read Toller's poetry at that time.[16] It is certain that the two men met, in Sintra, Portugal in March or April of 1936, while Auden and Isherwood were at work on *Ascent of F6*.[17] By that time most of Toller's works had appeared in English, and were being widely discussed.[18]

There is nothing in Auden's writing which would even allow conjecture about Auden's opinion of Toller, the man or the writer, if we disregard the elegy for a moment. The indirect evidence is anecdotal. Stephen Spender has described one social meeting with him in 1938.[19] Spender, it seems, had mixed feelings with respect to Toller, to judge from the tone of his account of the meeting. This is further brought out in remarks he made to Breon Mitchell.[20] Christopher Isherwood wrote a portrait of Toller which appeared under the title 'The Head of a Leader' in *Encounter* in 1953.[21] His attitude towards Toller was considerably more positive than Spender's. There is also a relevant casual remark by Gabriel Carrit in his memories of Auden: 'In two ways Wystan initiated interests that greatly influenced my life. Talking about Homer Lane, he made me want to study adolescent deviance and later I went to New York and enrolled as a student at the School of Social Research. Secondly he introduced me to Brecht and Toller and set me on the road to study Marxism...'[22] Auden himself spoke to Breon Mitchell concerning possible German influences on his work and is said to have expressed dislike of the works of Georg Kaiser and Toller.[23]

This material hardly amounts to a background for a possible personal relationship, whatever its nature, between Auden and Toller. For the interpretation of the poem the anecdotes yield very little.

Let us, then, look at the evidence of the poem itself:

In Memory of Ernst Toller
(d. May 1939)

The shining neutral summer has no voice
To judge America or ask how a man dies;
And the friends who are sad and the enemies who rejoice

Are chased by their shadows lightly away from the grave
Of one who was egotistical and brave,
Lest they think they can learn without suffering how to forgive.

What was it, Ernst, that your shadow unwittingly said?
O did the child see something horrid in the woodshed
Long ago? Or had the Europe which took refuge in your head

Already been too injured to get well?   10
O for how long, like the swallows in that other cell,
Had the bright little longings been flying in to tell

About the big and friendly death outside
Where people do not occupy or hide;
No towns like Munich; no need to write?

Dear Ernst, lie shadowless at last among
The other war-horses who existed till they'd done
Something that was an example to the young.

We are lived by powers we pretend to understand:
They arrange our loves; it is they who direct at the end   20
The enemy bullet, the sickness, or even our hand.

It is their to-morrow hangs over the earth of the living
And all that we wish for our friends: but existence is believing
We know for whom we mourn, and who is grieving.

Auden first published the elegy on Ernst Toller on 17 June 1939 in *The New Yorker*. There is an undated typescript of the poem in the library of the Humanities Research Center of the University of Texas at Austin containing some emendations in text and punctuation in Auden's hand, not all of which found their way into the first printed version. The most important variant is in lines 9 and 10:

> O did the child see something horrid in the woodshed
> Long ago; and the Europe which took refuge in your head,
> Had it been too hurt already to get well?

The poem was reprinted in *New Writing* (N.S. 3, Christmas 1939) preceded by 'Song' ('Say this city has ten million souls...' written in March 1939) and followed by 'Underneath the Leaves of Life' (June

1939). There are two changes in punctuation: line 2 now ends with a semicolon and the comma at the end of line 13 has been deleted. The text contains two changes: in line 17 'campaigners' is replaced by 'war-horses' and in line 23 'that' is inserted: 'And all *that* we wish. . .'

The elegy next appeared in *Another Time* (1940). The original title 'In Memoriam: Ernst Toller' is changed to: 'In Memory of Ernst Toller (d. May 1939)'. The text has been altered further: in line 2 'why' has been changed to 'how'; in line 14 'travel' has been deleted, along with the comma after 'occupy'; and in line 21 the wording has been inverted to read: 'The enemy bullet, the sickness, or even our hand.'

The version in *Penguin New Writing* (no. 14, July–September 1942), where the poem appeared preceded by 'Palais des Beaux Arts', is identical to the text in *New Writing* (not that of *Another Time*).

The poem was included in *Collected Poetry* (1945), and in *Collected Shorter Poems 1930–1944* (1950), with the text identical to that in *Another Time*. The last changes were done for the *Collected Shorter Poems 1927–1957* (published in England 1966; U.S. 1967): The 'O' at the beginning of lines 8 and 11 was deleted, and to preserve the metre words were added: line 8 now reads: 'Did the *small* child see something horrid in the woodshed'; and line 11 reads: 'For *just* how long, like the swallows in that other cell'. I shall base my discussion of the poem on the version first printed in *Another Time*. The changes in *Collected Shorter Poems 1927–1957* are minor and reflect, I believe, Auden's later discontent with an earlier metrical device rather than an actual reworking of the text.

The elegy consists of eight stanzas each of three rhymed lines. Though the lines are of moderate length, they vary in syllable count from nine to sixteen, and do not submit to a clear metric pattern. The speech-rhythm produces three to five stresses per line, although not in any discernible pattern either. Nor do the stanzas cohere syntactically. Their rhyme frame is frequently broken by enjambement. It quickly becomes apparent that the structure of the poem is based on rhetorical grouping. There are four segments. The first two stanzas state the general nature of the occasion, thus establishing the genre, and they introduce enough references and reflections to be specific without naming the dead person. The following three stanzas consist of four rhetorical questions addressed to the dead man, each more comprehensive than the preceding, each probing into the cause of the death which, it becomes clear, was suicide. In so doing, each question presents aspects of Toller's life and personality. This segment is followed by the farewell to the dead man in the sixth stanza. The poem ends with general reflections on life and death, which, though provoked by the specific occasion, transcend it to a level of reflection which encompasses both speaker and reader. The structure, then, is surprisingly conventional.

What is intriguing about the elegy is the tension created by the interplay between the poem's various formal features and Auden's ability to integrate into this form a poetic voice which is soft and intimate when compared with the more public voice of the elegies on Yeats and Freud.[24]

The first sentence compactly introduces a multiple setting of time and place. Toller died at the end of May, the beginning of summer, a man in the prime of life and, at least to the public eye in Europe, at the height of his career as a writer and political figure. Yet the metaphoric meaning of the first phrase is scaled down to the concrete and temporal. Summer is neutral as a season and this neutrality characterizes the place, America, politically also.[25] At the same time this striking neutrality is to be questioned, perhaps judged. The absence of a public voice to inquire allows, then, for a private voice to probe, not into the immediate circumstances of this death, but rather into the life which led to it. The question of 'how a man dies' is also 'how a man lived'. The seemingly minor textual change Auden introduced for the text in *Another Time* ('how' instead of 'why') becomes quite significant for the entire thread of argument.

This apparent neutrality with its public ubiquity is contrasted sharply to the shadows cast by friends and enemies. Both stand outside of it, because both have taken sides in the political battle in which Toller was involved, but beyond that, there is a neutrality which transcends that of public posture, the neutrality of death which Toller has chosen following

> The Immanent Imperative
> By which the Lost and Injured live
> In mechanized societies
> Where natural intuition dies
>
> (*New Year Letter*, lines 1026–30)

Shadow, then, is also a sign of life, or aliveness, dark, furtive and friendly, encompassing the entire range of human emotions. It accompanies as a distinct yet also impenetrable form all survivors. Auden sustains the multiple ambivalence of light and dark in these opening lines with such ease that the pun in line four goes practically unnoticed, it is so integrated. By contrast, the characterization of Toller as 'egotistical and brave' is stark and unambiguous. Yet this change from multi-faceted language to unequivocal utterance conveys a sense of the largeness and strength of the man whose death invokes an understanding of the humanity of his life and challenges the living to the painful experience of one of the greatest virtues: forgiveness. The Jewish Toller appears almost Christ-like.

The high poetic rhetoric of the opening lines is scaled down in the next three stanzas. The grave site is deserted, the speaker turns to the dead man himself. The tone of the questions is quiet and intimate at first, only slowly climbing toward a more public level, as if the speaker were becoming gradually aware that this personal death has meaning on the public level alone. The address 'Ernst' intimates personal familiarity between the speaker and the deceased. The first question is brief and obliquely searches for the immediate reason for the death. The reference to 'shadow' – the word occurs once in each of the first three sections – ties Toller to the sphere of the friends and enemies who are alive and still governed by their shadows. The crucial word, though, is 'unwittingly', which characterizes (if ever so briefly) the non-rational nature of this shadow side of life. As an adverb it suggests an accidentality of the act, a misunderstanding, being out of touch while in touch. To jump ahead for a moment, it connects structurally with the opening sentence of the final section (line 19), where the 'shadows' are raised to 'powers we pretend to understand'.

The questions to the dead man become increasingly analytical. In fact, the second one is brashly orthodox-Freudian, its tone almost mockingly paternalistic, in contrast to the tone reached earlier. It is rhetorical and not a reference to some occurrence in Toller's life. There is no traumatic childhood experience mentioned in Toller's autobiography, for instance,[26] and I doubt that Auden is referring to unpublished bits of biography. I prefer to see this as a lead in to the third question, containing (as it were) one of the elements which make for Toller's 'shadow'. Toller did hold a utopian notion of Europe, of the world in fact, which grew out of profound personal experiences. There was his initial pacifism, a result of his experiences in World War I. There was, further, a view of political organization conceptually rooted in a socialism based on Marxist and more conservative German idealist notions, a view closer to that of Gustav Landauer than of Luxemburg or Liebknecht, and one which failed disastrously in its reach for power in Munich in 1919. Lastly, there was a fervent, unmitigated antifascism which threatened Toller's own pacifism. The various elements of this rather personal ideology were never fully reconciled. In fact, the continuous

questions posed by the political developments of the thirties – especially
the rise of fascism and emerging Stalinism – eroded the idealistic
wholeness of Toller's vision of a continuous European culture borne by
a revolutionary political structure. It is this 'Europe' which is undoubtedly referred to in lines 9 and 10, since it was the basis of the
countless speeches, appearances, and involvements of Toller. In the
sequence of the questions there is added, then, an ideological trauma
to one of childhood.

The final, longest and most comprehensive question sharpens the
focus. It pointedly raises the problem of the reconcilability of the roles
of political activist and poet. The simile of the swallows in line 10 is a
direct reference to Toller's lyrical cycle *The Swallow Book*,[27] which here
becomes an image of the tension between the two roles, incorporating
at the same time a large and significant portion of Toller's life. Auden's
choice of this work is rather significant. Toller was known primarily for
his plays, most of which are at times full of only thinly veiled reflections
on his own life and problems. *The Swallow Book* shares a number of
the features of the plays. It differs in that its language is simple and highly
lyrical. If many of Toller's plays are marred by too strenuous an attempt
at sustaining a dialectic, he is content in this cycle to work with the
polarity that is given to him by the nesting swallows. He exploits the
metaphoric potential to the fullest, to be sure, but he doesn't force it.
This may have been one of the reasons it appealed to Auden. The other
may have been that Toller developed a 'found' occasion, linking acute
and loving observation with metaphoric reflection.

The occasion was this: Toller was incarcerated in 1919 for high
treason as a result of his involvement in the Munich uprising. During
a few months in 1922, a pair of swallows built their nest in his cell. They
became for him a sign of hope, of life, and of suffering, the latter because
the prison guards, acting under orders, destroyed the nest several times,
till the birds finally gave up and disappeared.

The reference to *The Swallow Book* in the elegy accomplishes a
multiplicity of things. It clearly establishes Toller as a poet. It concretely
establishes Toller as a political figure. It further refers to the period in
his life which was the most poignant and in its daily bleakness the most
traumatic. It was a time of enforced passivity and of great artistic activity,
and it was seminal for his reputation as a writer. The irony is rather
blatant: without the enforced abstention from political activity,[28] Toller
would never have acquired the prominence as a writer, which (especially
after 1933) made so many of his political activities possible. There is one

other feature, though, to *The Swallow Book*, which ties it rather closely as a metaphor to the preceding lines in Auden's poem and their questions. Toller's cycle opens with deeply melancholic verses culminating in a welcoming of death just before the poet hears the first twitter of the birds.

> Ich friere.
> Die Welt gerinnt.
> Es muss schön sein einzuschlafen jetzt
> Kristall zu werden im zeitlosen Eismeer des Schweigens.
> Genosse Tod.
> Genosse, Genosse...
>
> Zirizi Zirizi Zirizi
> Zirizi
> Urr
>
> Dass man nahe der dunklen Schwelle,
> Solche Melodie vernimmt, so irdischen Jubels, so irdischer Klage trunken...
> Träume, meine Seele, träume,
> Lerne träumen den Traum der Ewigkeit.
>
> (Ernst Toller, *Das Schwalbenbuch* (1924), p. 8)

> I freeze.
> The world congeals.
> It must be beautiful to fall asleep
> A crystal in the agelong floes of silence.
> Comrade Death.
> Comrade, Comrade...
>
> Zirizi Zirizi Zirizi
> Zirizi
> Urrr
>
> That one should hear such melodies
> So drunk with earthly joy and melancholy
> Upon the very threshold of the darkness...
> Dream, my spirit,
> And learn to dream the dream eternity.
>
> (translated by Ashley Dukes (London, 1924), p. 8)

Here then, if anywhere, is also the source for Auden's 'bright little longings' (line 12), those dreams of eternity which throughout Toller's life strove to gain transformation into reality.[29] Line 15, the concluding line of this section in the elegy, sums up the central dilemma of Toller's life with its simple and effective cryptic parallelism. Death knows 'no towns like Munich' where Toller failed as a revolutionary; it allows 'no need to write', that irrepressible urge of the literary man which throughout refused to be reconciled to the political circumstances and their call on the social man Toller. The elimination of 'to travel' from line 14 in the first revision is further evidence of Auden's view that this period in Toller's life is the most crucial. Toller obviously could not travel then. He did that almost frantically during the years after his release. The textual change, furthermore, makes for a parallelism between the verbs in the second half of line 14 and all of line 15, which, enforced by the rhyme, closes this portion of the poem skilfully with a tight weave of cross references.

The questions follow a clearly graspable pattern. They are carried by sympathy and informed understanding. They are low key in tone. They unveil something of the tormented complexity of the public man, yet stop short at becoming too intimate. Rather than unfolding the causes of death, they illuminate the forces which made for what was significant in that life. What remains for the speaker is to take leave.

The tone of the farewell is the same as that of the queries. What jars at first is the word 'war-horses'. An emendation of the earlier and flatter 'campaigners', its incongruity makes for a mildly mocking accent of unease on the part of the speaker. It sketches the asserted exemplarity of Toller's existence as both monumental and dated, and adds a touch of affectionate irony to the low-key farewell.

Turning away from the grave, the speaker involves his readers in an assertive 'We'. The apodictic nature of the first sentence, 'We are lived by powers we pretend to understand:', evokes bewilderment in the reader. The startlingly passive mode of the first phrase relativizes the analytical lucidity of the earlier questions. It dismisses the usefulness of rationality in coming to grips with this death, with death as such, and insists on our being subject to precisely those 'powers' which previously appeared as almost daemonic 'shadows'. But though their force was earlier seen as haunting friends and enemies of the dead man (and him as well), they now appear as informing life with its most valuable asset: love. And yet these powers are also imbued with the ominous archaic features of classical Fates. They, not we, determine the mode of death, and in so doing remove the taint of inappropriateness or even sinfulness which we place upon it through our lack of ultimate understanding and our desire to judge. The words here illuminate in retrospect the remark in line 6: 'Lest they think they can learn without suffering how to forgive.' The all-encompassing pervasiveness of these powers is affirmed once more in lines 22 and 23. The poem concludes with marvellous ambiguity. The end caesura in line 23 contains the words 'but existence is believing' at first, letting the positive strength of the redefinition grow before the syntax forces the enjambement into the last line, expanding and rephrasing the definition and undercutting the intensely apodictic quality of the antithesis of existential passivity and active faith. The poem ends with a declarative sentence, restating the emotion which informs the elegy, drawing the reader into it and yet suspending clarity of involvement with what amounts to a riddle. 'We know for whom we mourn, and who is grieving.'

I implied at the outset that the three elegies at the end of *Another Time* form a concluding triptych, not only to this volume, but in a way also to the post-Berlin, pre-New York phase of Auden's life, an impression, moreover, which the later rejection of the other three poems in the final section of *Another Time* seems to strengthen. In a very obvious sense, the Yeats and Freud elegies represent Auden's poetic account of the impact these two personalities had on his life: Yeats as a dominant poet in the English language, Freud as a humanist and philosopher. The question that remained was to determine the role of the Toller poem. I hope that the preceding interpretation has helped to answer that question in some measure.

Toller was a socialist humanist. Auden certainly was a humanist and he drew in great measure, if unorthodoxly, on proto-Marxist social theories to come to grips with the political situation at that time. The difference obviously was that Toller was an activist and revolutionary. Both were writers and whatever the differences were as regards the body of their writing and its quality, both attempted to incorporate into their work the acute social topics the times presented. Auden, moreover, by referring to Toller's lyrical work in the elegy, seems to stress an even greater artistic kinship than the prevailing view, then and now, may allow, a view which characterizes Auden as a major poet and Toller as a dramatist. And lastly, both shared the common fate of being exiles. To be sure, Auden chose to emigrate, Toller was expelled by the Nazis. Auden continued to live in a linguistic environment that was his own, Toller needed to have his work translated. But whatever the differences, the experience of exile was a common ground.

A last observation may help to strengthen my view that the nexus of the Toller elegy is the question of the writer's role in society. Auden frequently published poems individually or in small groups in papers and journals. This is no startling fact. What has not been looked at, though, to my knowledge, is the way in which he organized these groups of poems so that they appeared not just as a series of unrelated poetic items but formed a larger if loosely structured whole, rather similar to sections of an essay. This purposeful aleatory practice establishes contexts for the individual poems created by the author, which the reader ought to include in his reading of a poem. They provide the only clue as to authorial interpretation.

Prior to the publication in *Another Time*, the elegy to Toller was published together with 'Refugee Blues' and 'Underneath the Leaves of Life'.[30] The bitter levity of the song deals with the bleak and depressing fate of the German Jewish refugees in New York. It is furiously accusatory and full of deep sympathy. It precedes the Toller poem, establishing a specific background of place, time and shared experience for the informed reader. With respect to the 'Blues' the elegy provides a climax in as much as Toller did in fact commit the suicide alluded to as a way out in the 'Blues'. And yet he also was among those who tried hard to help ease the fate of the victims of fascism. The connection is all the closer in that both poems are made up of three-line stanzas. Within this group, 'Underneath the Leaves of Life' seems to sum up, restating motifs of the preceding two poems and transcending them in an avowal of the powers of love. The echoes of both poems in 'Underneath...' are unmistakable:

> In a trance of grief
> Stand the fallen man and wife...
>
> And the birds fly in and out
> Of the world of man...
>
> So the giant who storms the sky
> In an angry wish to die
> Wakes the hero in us all...
>
> All our terrors burned away
> We can learn at last to say:
> All our knowledge comes to this,
> That existence is enough.
>
> (*Collected Shorter Poems 1927–1957* (1966), pp. 149–51)

As regards the structure of *Another Time*, it should be noted that 'Underneath...' is the last poem in the first section and 'Refugee Blues' the last in the second section. To be sure, I do not claim that the three poems were written together or as a unit. Each one easily stands on its own. But I do claim that Auden, in grouping them for this separate publication, must have been very conscious of a larger statement in poetic form of which these poems are the constituent elements. One can read them as a synoptic private announcement and an interpretive guide to *Another Time*, which was about to appear.

Against the background of these two contexts the figure of Toller as victim and maker exemplifies a tragic dilemma less of a poet but more of a unique and modern social man. Auden's response as a writer is the attempt to develop an idiom which is adequate to this dilemma, which is modern, analytical and mythopoetic.

NOTES

1 John Fuller, *A Reader's Guide to W. H. Auden* (New York, 1970) could be regarded as an exception among more recent Anglo-American criticism. Relying on W. Willibrand's *Ernst Toller and his Ideology* (Iowa City, 1945), Fuller weaves some biographical comments on Toller into his interpretive remarks (p. 168).

2 Samuel Hynes, *The Auden Generation. Literature and Politics in the 1930s* (London, 1976), p. 47.

3 *The English Auden. Poems, Essays, and Dramatic Writings, 1927–1939*, edited by Edward Mendelson (New York, 1977), pp. xiii–xiv and 409–16.

4 For two opposing views on possible German influence on Auden see Breon Mitchell, 'W. H. Auden and Christopher Isherwood: The "German Influence"', *Oxford German Studies*, 1 (1966), 163–71, and Sigurd Dzenitis, *Die Rezeption deutscher Literatur in England durch Wystan Hugh Auden, Stephen Spender und Christopher Isherwood* (Geistes- und Sozialwissenschaftliche Dissertationen 21) (Hamburg, 1972).

5 Cyril Connolly as cited by Frederick Buell, *Auden as a Social Poet* (Ithaca, 1973), p. 187; from Richard Hoggart, *Auden, an Introductory Essay* (New Haven, 1951), p. 136.

6 *Another Time, Poems by W. H. Auden* (New York and London, 1940).

7 *W. H. Auden. A Bibliography 1924–1969*, 2nd edn edited by B. C. Bloomfield and Edward Mendelson (Virginia, 1972), p. 45.

8 They are 'Spain 1937', 'September 1, 1939', and 'Epithalamion'. Auden states the reasons for rejecting 'Spain' in the 'Foreword' to *Collected Shorter Poems 1927–1957* (London, 1966), pp. 15–16, and for rejecting 'September 1, 1939', in the 'Foreword', to *W. H. Auden. A Bibliography. The Early Years through 1955*, edited by B. C. Bloomfield with a foreword by W. H. Auden (Virginia, 1964), p. viii. In both instances the reason given for the rejection is 'dishonesty'. (In the case of *Collected Poems 1927–1957*, some poems were rejected 'because they were dishonest, or bad-mannered, or boring'.) I have not found any statements by Auden with regard specifically to 'Epithalamion'.

9 There is as yet no comprehensive biography of Toller in print. My sketch is based on a variety of materials. Very useful were John M. Spalek, 'Ernst Tollers Vortragstätigkeit und seine Hilfsaktionen im Exil', in *Exil und Innere Emigration II. Internationale Tagung in St Louis*, edited by Peter Uwe Hohendahl and Egon Schwarz (Frankfurt, 1973), pp. 85–100, and Wolfgang Frühwald, 'Exil als Aus-

bruchsversuch. Ernst Tollers Autobiographie', in *Die deutsche Exilliteratur 1933–45*, edited by Manfred Durzak (Stuttgart, 1973), pp. 489–98. See John M. Spalek, *Ernst Toller and his Critics. A Bibliography* (Charlotteville, 1968) for a comprehensive listing of primary material and criticism.

10 Hermann Kesten, 'Ernst Toller', *Neue Zürcher Zeitung*, 328 (29 Nov. 1938), 12, quoted in John M. Spalek, 'Ernst Tollers Vortragstätigkeit', p. 88. The translation is by Harald Ohlendorf.

11 Ernst Toller, *No More Peace*, translated by Edward Crankshaw, lyrics transated and adapted by W. H. Auden, music by Herbert Murrill (New York, 1937). The reviews of the various performances were mixed. For a summary see Spalek, *Ernst Toller and his Critics*, pp. 775ff.

12 *W. H. Auden. A Bibliography*, p. 128.

13 Dzenitis, *Die Rezeption*, pp. 59–67. Spalek, *Ernst Toller and his Critics*, pp. 53–4, 97–8.

14 Ernst Toller, *Pastor Hall*, translated by Stephen Spender and Hugh Hunt. Ernst Toller and Dennis Johnston, *Blind Man's Buff* (New York, 1939), p. 60. The original song is not by Ernst Toller. S. Dzenitis, *Die Rezeption*, p. 68, quotes from a German typescript of Toller's play: 'Es ist das "Moorsoldatenlied", das "ein unbekannter Gefangener im Konzentrationslager geschrieben, ein anderer unbekannter Gefangener in Töne gesetzt hat".'

15 Auden may have seen *Hinkemann* produced at the Piscator Bühne im Lessingtheater beginning March 1928, though the number of performances is uncertain, and *Bourgeois bleibt Bourgeois* at the Lessingtheater, which ran for about eight performances beginning 2 February 1929. Beginning 1 October 1934, the Gate Theatre (London) gave eighteen performances of *Miracle in America*.

16 By 1928 two volumes of poetry by Toller had appeared in Germany: *Gedichte der Gefangenen. Ein Sonettenkreis* (1st edn, Munich 1921; 3rd edn, Potsdam, 1924), and *Das Schwalbenbuch* (1st edn, Potsdam, 1924; 3rd edn, 1927).

17 Christopher Isherwood, *Christopher and His Kind* (New York, 1976), p. 240. My thanks to Prof. Edward Mendelson and Prof. Gerd Hillen for this reference.

18 Prior to the meeting in Sintra these works by Toller had been translated and published in England: *Masses and Man* (1923), *The Machine Wreckers* (1923), *The Swallow Book* (1924), *Brokenbrow* (1926), *Hoppla!* (1928), *Which World – Which Way. Travel Pictures from America and Russia* (1931), *The Blind Goddess* (1934), *I was a German. An Autobiography* (1934), *Draw the Fires!* (1935), *Seven Plays* (1935), *Letters from Prison* (1936).

19 Stephen Spender, *World within World* (London, 1951), pp. 258–9.

20 Mitchell, 'The German Influence', pp. 165–6.

21 Reprinted in Christopher Isherwood, *Exhumations* (London, 1966), pp. 125–32. See also Isherwood, *Christopher*, p. 240.

22 Gabriel Carritt with Rex Warner, 'A Friend of the Family', in *W. H. Auden. A Tribute*, edited by Stephen Spender (New York, 1975), pp. 57–8.

23 Mitchell, 'The German Influence', p. 165. Unfortunately, Mr Mitchell quotes very little indeed from his conversations and correspondence with Auden.

24 Fuller, *A Reader's Guide*, p. 168.

25 See 'September 1, 1939', line 34, for a similar use of 'neutral'.

26 Ernst Toller, *Eine Jugend in Deutschland* (Amsterdam, 1934); translated by Edward Crankshaw as *I was a German* (London, 1934).

27 Ernst Toller, *The Swallow Book*, translated by Ashley Dukes (London, 1924).

28 During his imprisonment Toller wrote four plays, *Masse Mensch* (1920), *Die Maschinenstürmer* (1922), *Der deutsche Hinkemann* (1922), *Der entfesselte Wotan* (1923), one puppet play, *Die Rache des verhöhnten Liebhabers* (1920), two volumes of poetry, *Gedichte der Gefangenen* (1921) and *Das Schwalbenbuch* (1924), and contributed to journals and newspapers.

29 Ludwig Marcuse, *Mein zwanzigstes Jahrhundert* (Munich, 1960), pp. 253–4. See also L. Marcuse's letter to Hermann Kesten in *Deutsche Literatur im Exil. Briefe europäischer Autoren 1933–1949*, edited by Hermann Kesten (Munich, 1964), pp. 106–7.

30 *New Writing*, N.S. 3 (Christmas 1939), pp. 37–40. 'In Memory of Ernst Toller' appeared subsequently, preceded by 'Palais des Beaux Arts', in *Penguin New Writing*, 14 (September, 1942), pp. 70–1. I have ignored this context, since, according to Prof. Edward Mendelson, Auden did not resubmit individual poems to journals once they had been published or collected.

* My thanks are due to Professor Edward Mendelson and the Estate of W. H. Auden for permission to quote published and unpublished material.

Translating with W. H. Auden:
Gunnar Ekelöf's last poems

LEIF SJÖBERG

'Why? Do you have a contract?' replied W. H. Auden the first time I earnestly posed the question: would he consider translating Ekelöf's poetry into English? I had to pause, slightly embarrassed because I had no contract, and Auden offered a bit of advice: 'One should never translate on spec. It's bad for everybody's morale!' I politely suggested that not much poetry would have been translated into English had it not been for initiatives of poetry lovers labouring on speculation. The (legitimate or illegitimate) concern for profit among major British and American publishers creates a kind of 'gold curtain' that tends to insulate English readers from the rest of the world's poetry.

To illustrate how difficult it was to get poetry from 'neglected' (minor) languages published in English, I mentioned that in the early 1960s Ekelöf's poetry had been translated 'on spec' by no less a poet than Muriel Rukeyser – in collaboration with me – and that a publisher (after several months) returned the book-length manuscript – unopened! The accompanying rejection letter, composed of select phrases from a variety of form letters, amounted to both a 'yes' and a 'no'! How could this happen? Later, when pressed for an explanation, the editor excused himself by saying, 'Sending Swedish poetry to us [i.e., a reputable university press], in whatever translation, is like sending us Outer Mongolian poetry: it does not stand much of a chance, because we have no market for it'.

This story may have made a certain impact on Auden. He gradually became convinced that the competition to get good foreign poetry published in English was fierce, perhaps unfair, and might even, under unfortunate circumstances, act like a form of censorship against his colleague poets in 'critical' languages. But what could *he* do to alleviate the situation? Even if he were to care enough about certain poetry to donate his time and translate it, what difference would it make? The basic problems would remain the same.

In this, of course, Auden was right. His reluctance to get involved was, I suspect, due to his great workload, his wish not to appear one-sided in his interest in things Swedish, and his realization of the many problems to be faced. What I intend to discuss in this essay is merely a few of these problems, primarily with reference to unidentified quotations, with or without quotation marks – i.e., 'borrowed' lines – and what they do, or fail to do, for a translation.

The collaboration between Auden and myself did not begin with Ekelöf. I was teaching Swedish and Scandinavian literature at Columbia University when I first submitted samples of literal translations, as well as copies of Ekelöf's originals in Swedish, to Mr Auden. Nothing was heard from his quarter for several months, so I began to expect I would never hear from him, but in the autumn of 1963 he called me and asked if I had read Dag Hammarskjöld's secret diary, *Vägmärken*; he wondered whether I would like to work with him on an English translation of that book. Naturally, I was delighted. We met in his apartment on the Lower East Side, usually for tea. He was always very pleasant to work with and strict about keeping appointments.

It turned out that Dag Hammarskjöld was quite sympathetic to Ekelöf's poetry, and even quoted three lines in *Vägmärken* as the fifth item under the heading '1953':

> Kommer den, kommer den ej,
> dagen då glädjen blir stor,
> dagen då sorgen blir liten?
>
> Will it come, or will it not,
> The day when the joy becomes great,
> The day when the grief becomes small?[1]

In *Markings* Auden added underneath this unidentified quotation: '(Gunnar Ekelöf)'. These were the first lines of Ekelöf's poetry that Auden rendered into English – but not the last. He also found time to translate several poems or prose poems by Werner Aspenström (b. 1918), Johannes Edfelt (b. 1904), Erik Lindegren (1910–68), Artur Lundkvist (b. 1906), Harry Martinson (1904–78), and Karl Vennberg (b. 1910). There was also one major translation, consisting of fifty-one out of the sixty-two poems of Pär Lagerkvist's book *Aftonland*, which Auden had completed but not revised, and which appeared in a bilingual edition as *Evening Land/Aftonland*.[2] *Evening Land* was, in fact, Lagerkvist's

ninth collection of poetry, and it remains the first and only book of his
poetry in English. It is to Auden's everlasting credit that he performed
this service, which no other poet had found it possible to do. At one time,
though, when faced with a particularly 'gloomy' poem by Lagerkvist,
Auden confessed in a note, perhaps tongue in cheek: 'My decorous
Anglican piety is rather shocked.'

Whatever Dag Hammarskjöld may or may not have had in common
with the modernists in poetry, the English poet had a high opinion of
him, as expressed in the *Encounter* article[3] and in the foreword of
Markings.[4] Auden never found any entirely *new* image in *Markings*, but
an abundance of intriguing and personal statements. The technique
Hammarskjöld sometimes employed in quoting without quotation marks
or accompanying (explanatory) notes posed no problems for Auden who
(with my assistance) located the many biblical references in *Vägmärken*.
I think he liked the idea that he was the first to do so. (The Swedish
edition had identified neither Hammarskjöld's quotations nor any of the
allusions or references. As far as I know, such notes appeared in the
Swedish, German, and other versions only *after* Auden's groundwork
had been published – and with no credit given to Auden.)[5] In the limited
time available for the translation and research, the difficulties were such
that, in instances, even Auden's enormous reading proved inadequate
to solve the problems. This was one reason why Auden (for the first time,
I believe) went to Sweden in the spring of 1964. With the eager assistance
of diplomat friends of Dag Hammarskjöld's, but above all of the poet
Erik Lindegren, most of the still unresolved attributions, including
references to Thomas Browne's *Religio Medici* (29 July–16 August 1956,
in *Markings*),[6] were taken care of.

When Hammarskjöld in a 'marking' dated 25 November 1956 quoted
in Norwegian:

> Hvis alt Du gaf foruden Lifvet,
> saa ved at Du har intet gifvet.
>
> If you give all, but life retain
> Your gift is nothing and in vain.[7]

Auden simply added: '(Ibsen: *Brand*)', and, since he was even able to
keep the rhyme, it caused him no problem as a translator. In a 'marking'
dated 13 February–13 March 1961, Hammarskjöld wrote:

> O Du som förde oss till detta själens nakna liv, öde
> som svävar över vattnen, skall Du en jordisk kväll berätta
> vems handen är som iför oss en sagas brinnande tunika –[8]

Quotation marks and source were left out. The word *tunika*, tunic, almost ruled out a Swedish author – indeed, the author was St John Perse.

In 'Letter to Lord Byron' Auden had written (August 1936),[9] 'at any language other than my own, I'm no great shakes...'. But since that time his German, at least, had advanced considerably, and as a result German was sometimes used for expressions and sentences in my literal translation of *Vägmärken*, when English equivalents were unavailable or stilted. Although Auden never studied Swedish and therefore needed linguistic expertise, he had a remarkable grasp of what Swedish texts were all about – presumably largely due to his knowledge of German, but also due to his being a genius with words. This was apparent when it was necessary to locate specific words – he frequently knew at least the general area in which to search for a word. Sometimes he found the particular word or sentence, even before I could point it out to him.

One of Auden's strong points was his logic. He could rearrange the order of clauses when logic demanded that one clause precede the other, or when the meaning would be clearer that way in English. Since the English is so much richer in vocabulary than the Swedish, he now and then found fault with the original. Having considered the most obvious alternatives for a word and, repeatedly, being reminded of the literal translation, he might still say, 'logic demands that *this* word be used', rattling off a number of arguments. Usually those were hard to refute, if not irrefutable. When I persisted and said, 'Let us see what the text says!' and read straight from the original in front of us, playing over again the literal translation with possible variations, he might shake his big head and say 'No, my dear, that won't do! It can't be said like that in English!' or 'That's not English!'

The many long, compound words in Swedish and the multiple 's-genitives' (i.e., genitives ending in 's') naturally caused some trouble, but Auden never despaired while working at the translation. He always started 'full steam ahead' and with great enthusiasm. What was gained in vividness and geniality through this method was partially offset by occasional infelicitous interpretations, due primarily to lack of time for research. One such example for which I was responsible comes to mind. In one of the 'markings' from 1952, Hammarskjöld writes:

Give me something to die for –!

Die Mauern stehen
sprachlos und kalt, die Fahnen
klirren im Winde.

What makes loneliness an anguish
Is not that I have no one to share my burden,
But this:
I have only my own burden to bear.[10]

Hammarskjöld had naturally not identified the German quotation from Hölderlin, which Auden translated as follows:

The walls stand
speechless and cold, the banners
faffle in the wind.

The trouble was that 'klirren' (rattle) seemed to us an odd verb to apply to 'Fahnen' (flag, banner); in the translation Auden used 'faffle'. What we failed to realize was that 'Fahne', flag in German, had developed from Old High German *fano*, akin to Old English *fana*, banner; this in turn was related to *vane*, weather vane. The correct literal translation would therefore have been 'vanes rattle', rather than 'banners faffle'.

Occasionally Auden would exclude a word or two if they were repetitious or superfluous; he found a contracted sentence more effective. This happened in the translation of Ekelöf's *Selected Poems* where, in one poem, four to five lines were condensed into one, which Ekelöf authorized, with some consternation. On occasion Auden would say: 'I think we had better abandon that one; it's getting to be too complicated, and too far from the original.' (This applied only to the rhymed poems by Lagerkvist, published as *Evening Land/Aftonland*.)

I made sure that on his visit to Stockholm (via Iceland) Auden would meet Ekelöf, who lived at Sigtuna, a town on the Lake Mälar, forty-five minutes from the capital. Both Georg Svensson, of Bonniers (Auden's Swedish publisher), and Lindegren had previous commitments and could not go to Sigtuna, but the poet Östen Sjöstrand (b. 1925) who had translated the Auden–Kallman libretto of Stravinsky's *The Rake's Progress*[11] accompanied Auden to the Ekelöf home.[12]

Ekelöf, 'a modern mystic',[13] as his friend Lindegren called him, was decidedly non-Christian, non-dogmatic, and an introvert, 'an outsider', while, of course, Auden was a believer, an extrovert and an insider; nonetheless they could be expected to have lots of things to discuss: both were deeply appreciative of music and modern poetry, after all. In leafing through my copy of Ekelöf's *Valfrändskaper* (Elective affinities)[14] in New York, Auden had found Ekelöf's translations of Petronius, Villon, Baudelaire, Rimbaud, Whitman, Butler, Joyce, Leon-Paul Fargue, D. H. Lawrence (which seemed to surprise Auden), Jalálu'd-din-Rúmi, the Sufi mystic who was so central to the Swedish poet – but also a substantial presentation of Apollinaire and another of Ekelöf's favourites, Desnos. Among the 'elective affinities' Auden was himself represented by a Swedish version of 'Musée des Beaux Arts' (which Auden promptly asked me to translate – or some lines of it – back into English, *prima vista*, while he waited, so to speak, and since Ekelöf's translation was felicitous and my knowledge of the original was reasonably good, I think Ekelöf came out rather well). Auden mentioned that he had been spending Christmas in Brussels when he wrote the poem. It seemed like such an excellent idea to get these two together.

Auden, perhaps comparing his own shabby apartment on New York's St Mark's Place, thought Ekelöf's house 'rather extravagant' for a poet – the furniture being 'expensive looking' antiques. (Most of them, actually, were inherited, but he admitted that the setting was idyllic.) He found Ekelöf 'severely depressed', perhaps 'due to a drinking problem'. On the other hand, Ekelöf found Auden 'diplomatic, with Hammarskjöld in the foreground, the conversation diplomatic but cordial'.[15] A few days later Ekelöf commented on how 'amiable' (*angenämt*: very pleasant) and how 'nicely shrivelled' (*trevligt skrumpen*) Auden had appeared – and how 'ignorant of languages'.[16] This, no doubt, referred to Auden's disinclination towards the French language, which surprised some of the people he met in Stockholm, and his limited familiarity with Italian, Latin, and Greek, and perhaps also Near Eastern languages. (Ekelöf had studied Hindustani for a few months at the London School of Oriental Studies in 1926 and had taken one semester of Persian at Uppsala University, 1926–7. In 1958, the same year as he became a member of the Swedish Academy, he was given a Ph.D. *honoris causa* at Uppsala.) The tea-drinking was, apparently, pleasant enough – but, as Ekelöf put it, there was 'noll contact'[17] (*sic!*), zero contact.

The caution with which these very considerable poets approached each other precluded real friendship beyond superficial cordiality. It was only much later that Auden took such an interest in Ekelöf that he asked me for 'some stuff' to translate. He got Ekelöf first. It proved to be to Auden's liking. The cooperation from Gunnar Ekelöf was remarkable, for Ekelöf was then fatally ill – his wife, Ingrid Ekelöf, read and commented on the translations as they progressed. Auden was very pleased with the results: 'We've got the best', he said, broadly smiling.

Ekelöf had thirteen collections of poetry to his credit – including *Sent på jorden* (Late on earth, 1932); *Färjesång* (Ferry song, 1941); *Non Serviam* (1945); *Strountes* (Triflings, 1955); *Opus incertum* (1959); and

En Mölna-elegi (A Mölna elegy, 1960), 'a major translation by a major poet', according to Göran Printz-Påhlson, and published here for the first time in English; as well as an assortment of selected poems (1949, 1956 and 1965) plus volumes of his essays and translations from many languages but above all from the French – when in 1965 he commenced what was to be perhaps his most remarkable achievement: a trilogy, consisting of *Dīwān över Fursten av Emgión* (Dīwān over the Prince of Emgión, 1965), *Sagan om Fatumeh* (The tale of Fatumeh, 1966) and *Vägvisare till underjorden* (Guide to the underworld, 1967).

Almost all of the poems of *Dīwān* and *Fatumeh* were translated by Auden and authorized by Ekelöf, with the exception of those few poems that did not work in English, and those that Auden considered redundant or repetitive. Occasionally Auden was so pleased with a poem that he read it aloud for comments, although I was his entire audience. One of those poems was 'ayíasma':

> In the calm water I saw mirrored
> Myself, my soul:
> Many wrinkles
> The beginnings of a turkey-cock neck
> Two sad eyes
> Insatiable curiosity
> Incorrigible pride
> Unrepentant humility
> A harsh voice
> A belly slit open
> And sewn up again
> A face scarred by torturers
> A maimed foot
> A palate for fish and wine
> One who longs to die
> Who has lain with some
> In casual beds – but for few
> Has felt love – a for him
> Necessary love
> One who longs to die
> With someone's hand in his
> Thus I see myself in the water
> With my soiled linen left behind me when I am gone
> A Kurdic Prince called a dog
> By both Rumaians and Seldjuks
> In the water my bald forehead:
> All the mangled tongues
> Which have convinced me
> That I am mute

> And those stains on my shirt
> Which water will never wash out –
> Indelible like blood, like poison
> The stains of the heretic
> Shall strike them like the plague
> With still blacker stains.[19]

The note appended to the poem reads: 'Ayíasma (Hagíasma): purifying well. The water cult is still alive in Greece and the Near East. A glass of cold water is the holy welcoming drink among the people.' Another 'ayíasma', beginning

> The black image
> Framed in silver worn to shreds by kisses[17]

Auden cared for particularly. He also read the last poem of *Fatumeh* with admiration:

> Moon! Moon! so might a poor farmer's wife see you
> When, having driven one furrow with her wooden plough
> She raises her face
> And wipes the sweat from her forehead
> Before starting upon the next one
>
> – Are you an egg in space
> A hen's egg with a wrinkled shell
> Or are you a wind egg that dimly mirrors
> Our fields and mountains?
>
> But the angel grips her arm
> and points to where
> A Star has just fallen
> Leaving an empty space
> Inside the Moon's sickle.[20]

In this poem elements from music and art fused into a unity of their own. The original poem begins with 'Avgó! Avgó!', and has here been translated 'Moon! Moon!' (if I remember correctly, at the suggestion of Nikos Stangos, the British poet and translator). Ekelöf was a great fan of Boris Christoff's interpretations of Moussorgsky's song cycles, and played some of his recordings over and over again. On the day when I had an appointment with Ekelöf at his home at Sigtuna, he was tired and tense. Almost the only subject he could converse on with any flair at all was music, and whichever way the conversation turned, it always seemed to come back to Moussorgsky; when the topic was exhausted, the conversation started over again with the marvellous bass, Boris Christoff (I believe Ekelöf had seen Chaliapin in Paris in the early thirties). The session ended with Ekelöf playing LP records of children's songs by Moussorgsky. He hummed and gesticulated, he lay back on his bed, his face became peaceful, and he fell asleep, while the music of Moussorgsky continued. One of his favourites was a lullaby with a recurring phrase, 'Bajú! Bajú!', (Lull! Lull!), which Ekelöf, according to Ingrid Ekelöf, heard as 'Avgó! Avgó!', thus associating it with the Greek word for 'egg'. In his imagination Ekelöf identified this song 'Avgó! Avgó!' with a reproduction of a fresco from a Serbian church, in which an angel standing before an old shepherd points up towards the sky, his arm around the shepherd's shoulders. The old man looks up with pious awe. In the picture there is neither egg nor moon! But the poet made the Russian 'Bajú!' into the Greek 'Avgó!', then made his egg into a moon: moved by the shepherd's simple piety, and his own profound experience before the sublimity of the scene, Ekelöf sang 'Avgó! Avgó!' Later he went on to make the old shepherd into an old woman, thereby further underscoring the female dominance – the almost frenzied devotion to women – in *The Tale of Fatumeh*. Auden was pleased and amused by these transformations.

About his *Dīwān* poems Ekelöf wrote to me, in English, in the spring of 1965 this revealing, previously unpublished note. It should be remembered that he was in a hospital at the time and had no access to a copy-editor, even if he had wanted one:

In four weeks, beginning in Constantinople, I have written a mystical ode of some fifty or sixty poems, translated from the idiom of my forefather, the Prince of Emghión, or Jemdján, an Akritical Prince, that is a Border protector on the Arab frontier, who was blinded in Constantinople, in the Vlacherne Caverns, under the reign of Nikifóros Votaniátes. It is my greatest poem of love and Passion. I cannot touch it nor see it because I grow ill, when seeing this blind and tortured man. (I must have somebody else to copy it for me, maybe Ekner, maybe you.) Nobody else could have done it in Europe but me. And this is not boasting. As you said on a postcard, (the reverse of which I knew well, a protecting Canopy Goddess), vain glory has no good position with me. I absolutely cannot comprehend but that someone has written with me as a medium [*skrivit genom mig*]. I'd like to send it to you and have it published in English first but do not dare to touch it nor see it for a couple of months. Not vain, but proud. Still perfectly normal and without a headache.

Really, I have never had such an experience, or, not one so complete.

I am between East and West, a self-made Prince. And one who has it as a heritage or Fate. I am what's really noble – what is it? I'm half a noble, half a man, half an artist, etc., and the opposites of all those, *almost* whoever you may choose, almost, because I do not want to out-bishop Bishops nor to out-whore whores, for instance. Not even to out-Middle the Golden Medium. There is another scale of temperature, [illegible], and Measure. I'm anti-Goethe as well as anti-Nietzsche but pro-Mozart.[21]

Auden never seemed to have any difficulties understanding what Ekelöf had in mind with his rather ecstatic poems. As Ekelöf wrote to me in a letter, explaining why he had become interested in the Byzantine, the Greek life: 'Byzantine life, traditionally and according to deep-rooted custom, is like the political life in *our* cities and states. I am intensely interested in it because I hate it. I hate what is Greek. I hate what is Byzantine...'[22] Auden's comment was: 'I understand him (Ekelöf) very well when he speaks of Byzantine life, both loving and hating it.'

Not until the work was done, and the translations were neatly typed up, did Auden raise the question of a publisher. How right he was when he warned against working 'on spec', because when I offered the manuscript to major publishers the answers were disappointing, stating that 'we here after careful consideration have come to the conclusion that we are not the right publisher for this verse'. This time the difficulties were not insurmountable, to be sure, but when Ekelöf's *Selected Poems*[23] appeared (Penguin, 1971 and Pantheon, 1972), Ekelöf had already numbered among the dead for several years. He died on 16 March 1968. If there was any British review of the book, we never heard of it; however, there was a sprinkling of encouraging, favourable, reviews in professional American journals – and without fanfare the beautiful volume was soon remaindered in New York at Marboro bookstores for $1 – where, I hope, some poetry lovers finally may have picked it up and enjoyed it. In London the Penguin edition of Ekelöf is still in stock, fortunately. The commercial success of Hammarskjöld – staying on the National Bestseller List for almost a year, selling half a million copies in hardcover in the U.S.A. and thousands in hardcover and paper in Britain and still selling, – and the relative commercial failure of Ekelöf's poetry in the English-speaking world, could hardly have formed a greater contrast.

Since Auden had given his readers the benefit of more than 1,700 lines on the insights which his quotes, etc., were supposed to communicate, was I correct in assuming that Auden's *New Year Letter*[24] (1 January 1940) contained the most extensive notes of explanations given by any poet in the English language? 'No', he said, 'that honor belongs to David Jones', referring to *The Anathemata*,[25] approximately one third of which is devoted to the notes, i.e., roughly eighty pages of the book. Eliot, as we know, commented on some of the lines in *The Waste Land*, and later he expressed himself on the effect of his footnotes and explanatory notes: 'But authors' notes [as is illustrated by *The Waste Land*] are no prophylactic against interpretation and dissection: they merely provide the serious researcher with more material to interpret and dissect.'[26] Nevertheless, certain poets, including Empson,[27] Richards,[28] and others, have felt compelled to footnote their poems.

But why had Auden more or less given up on providing notes for his readers? 'I realized that the poet's task is great enough, *without* footnotes and explications.' For this reason the notes were completely excluded from the latest editions of his collected poems.

Reasonably familiar quotations of wit or insight are likely to add to the pleasure of the reader, whether or not this was the author's intention. The reader with strong scholarly inclinations will look up the source and make observations, preferably after having considered the full context of the quotation. But if it is time-consuming enough to look up 'familiar', i.e. half-remembered, quotations, it will be so much more demanding to locate totally obscure quotations, especially if they are 'hidden'. When the 'hidden' quotations are in English, French, German, Italian and/or Spanish, somebody educated in a traditional manner might enjoy the challenge of trying to identify them. If the suspect 'hidden' quotations have an Eastern (Japanese, Chinese, or Indian) source – such as in Ezra Pound's *Cantos* – they are complicating factors indeed, and there is an obvious need for an authoritative commentary. If the writer in an Eastern language were to employ 'hidden' quotations, Eastern and Western readers alike would require a commentary, and the Western reader – so unknowing about the treasures of Eastern literature – would need a translation as well, if such were to be found! From a purely practical, translator's point of view, if a text with 'hidden' quotations is to be accurately translated into other languages, it is of paramount importance that all the details about the quotes be found.

It would be presumptuous to try to predict the shape of things to come, but it seems probable that there will be an increase in the use of quotations of all kinds. Since the tasks ahead for the humanities are multiplying at a rapid speed – while public support is being reduced – it would not be unreasonable to insist that authorized explanatory notes accompany any 'learned' poem or prose poem, so that in future we do not with increasing frequency find ourselves bogged down in an unmanageable mass of unidentified quotations. Our Western ignorance of the literatures of the world is such that we need a great deal of help in orienting ourselves towards more global horizons. What is, or should be, more than an intellectual amusement, could conceivably deteriorate into drudgery if readers were overwhelmed by too many unfamiliar quotations – a sad prospect, since there is no longer any accepted canon of works or any 'orthodoxy' of literatary conventions. Johnson's claim that 'every quotation contributes something to the stability or enlargement of the language' might be more to the point if it were rephrased to read: not every quotation contributes to the stability of the language – confusion might also be the result! The poet's own notes might save us all in the end.

NOTES

1 *Vägmärken* (Stockholm, 1963), p. 73; *Markings* (London/New York, 1964), p. 90.
2 *Evening Land/Aftonland* (London, 1977).
3 *Encounter*, 17:5 (November 1961), pp. 3–4.
4 *Markings*. On p. xxii, Auden calls Hammarskjöld 'a great, good, and lovable man'.
5 When *Vägmärken* (1963) appeared as a Delfinbok (Stockholm, 1966), a substantial notes section had been added (pp. 181–8).
6 16 August 1956; *Vägmärken*, p. 108; *Markings*, p. 136.
7 *Vägmärken*, p. 112; *Markings*, p. 141.
8 *Vägmärken*, p. 164; *Markings*, p. 203.
9 *The English Auden. Poems, Essays and Dramatic Writings 1927–1939*, edited by Edward Mendelson (New York, 1977), p. 170.
10 *Vägmärken*, p. 70; *Markings*, p. 85.
11 Bonniers Operabibliotek (Stockholm, 1961). Cf. Staffan Bergsten, *Östen Sjöstrand* (Twayne's World Authors Series 309) (New York, 1974), pp. 69–70.
12 Letter from Gunnar Ekelöf, 17 April 1964.
13 *Kritiskt 40-tal*, edited by Karl Vennberg and Werner Aspenström (Stockholm, 1948), pp. 282–304, and 'Gunnar Ekelöf – A Contemporary Mystic', translated by Robert Bly, *Odyssey Review* (New York), 2 (1962), 238–56; excerpts in *I Do Best Alone at Night, Poems by Gunnar Ekelöf*, translated by Robert Bly (Washington, DC, 1968), pp. 44–50, and in *Friends, You Drank Some Darkness: Three Swedish Poets, Harry Martinson, Gunnar Ekelöf and Tomas Tranströmer*, chosen and translated by Robert Bly (Boston, 1975), pp. 158–63.
14 (Stockholm, 1960). Auden, p. 51.
15 Letter, 17 April 1964.
16 Letter, 21 April 1964.
17 Letter, 21 April 1964.
18 Gunnar Ekelöf, *Selected Poems*, edited by A. Alvarez and N. Stangos (Penguin Modern European Poets) (London, 1971), pp. 38–40.
19 *Selected Poems*, p. 42.
20 *Selected Poems*, pp. 140–1.
21 Undated annotation in pencil on the front and back of a reprint from *Germanic Review* (March 1965). The English is that of Ekelöf, except for a few words supplied by me.
22 *Selected Poems*, p. 10.
23 As Robert Bly has pointed out, the book is somewhat mistitled, 'since it includes

poems only from two very late books of the Byzantium trilogy' (*Friends, You Drank Some Darkness*, p. 71). The choice of title was made by the editors.

24 (London, 1941 and 1965).

25 (London, 1952).

26 T. S. Eliot, a note of introduction in David Jones, *In Parenthesis* (1937) (New York, 1961), p. vii.

27 *Collected Poems* (New York, 1948), in which pp. 87–113 contain the author's notes.

28 In *The Screen and Other Poems* (New York, 1960), pp. 88–101 contain the notes.

Gunnar Ekelöf's *A Mölna Elegy:*
The attempted reconstruction of a moment

LEIF SJÖBERG

Muriel Rukeyser's translation marks the first English publication of Gunnar Ekelöf's *En Mölna-elegi* (Stockholm, 1960). Classified as 'work in progress' for more than twenty years prior to its publication, the *Elegy* demanded nearly a decade for the location and identification of its learned allusions and borrowings and nearly two decades for its publication in entirety in the English language.

Ekelöf's poem 'concerns itself with the relativity of time and time-experience, perhaps also with a kind of *Lebensstimmung*. It is not a description of a time lapse but (theoretically) is supposed to occur in one moment. In other words: it is a cross-section of time instead of a section lengthwise', wrote Ekelöf in a note in *BLM* in 1946.[1] Later he warned against attempts to overemphasize the 'one moment'. He added:

Time and time, What is it? It is supposed to occur not in a lapse of time but outside [of] time, in a mood of passivity and receptivity towards one's self, when everything and anything is possible and nearby. *The ideal psychoanalytical moment* [my italics]. What matter if the hand of your watch has moved one minute or ten from the point when you started summarizing (or memorizing) your situation, your dreams, etc.? It is a moment all the same.[2]

> I sit on a bench of the past;
> I write on a page of the past.   (lines 1–2)

The place is the jetty at Mölna, consisting of a few strange-looking old buildings on the island of Lidingö, close to Stockholm, which, a couple of years earlier, had functioned as a summer camp for crippled children. (Ekelöf used to walk to Mölna in the early 1930s). 'Mölna is a symbol of something *cut off*, something posthumous', he commented, adding, 'but the past is alive in you'.[3] The year is that of the beginning of World

* Muriel Rukeyser and Leif Sjöberg are grateful to the Anglo-Swedish Literary Foundation for a grant in recognition of the translation of *En Mölna-elegi*.

War II, presumably 1939–40, and the season is the autumn. It should
be noticed that the 'I' is not set in a social context: on the contrary,
it is relegated to itself, isolated independent and unattached. It functions
as a passive, experiencing medium.

There are many 'personalities' which live in that which I call me. The 'I' functions
as a practical spokesperson, however, and each 'personality' must speak in turn. But
what the spokesperson, the 'I', ought to say is not: I want it to be this way. He or she
ought to summarize and make distinctly audible what is said in me – so 'distinct' that
even the obscure uncertainty experienced may remain mysterious, uncertain as it is, as
long as it remains that way.[4]

It is obvious from this that Ekelöf's central concern is the problem of
identity, even in this initial scene. A problem Ekelöf touches on is thus
the lack of constancy, on the one hand, and the abundance of change
in reality, on the other. His view of identity is evident in one manuscript
of *A Mölna Elegy*: 'Each person's contents of people and worlds. He
who has experienced experiences and re-experiences; this is one, not one,
but many in one. He calls himself I; *that* is merely a psychical-
geographical attribute.'[5]

While most people prefer not to discuss their sudden and abrupt shifts
in identity, for fear that they may be considered unsteady or lacking in
character – as Strindberg points out – Ekelöf more than once expressed
the opinion that he himself (or humans in general) had the ability to
change identity, that he virtually could *be* the person he was not. The
transformations begin early in the *Elegy*:

> Windrush and wavespray
> waverush and windspray
> spray of the roller's blow
> cool upon cheeks and brow –
> isolation and I:
> the selfsame or another
> I or not I?
> The future – now – the past
> time running wild
> years last for minutes
> with a tail of yellow leaves
> or time held
> stockstill in the elms'
> wetblack branches held –
> Clotho cuts off the button...
> Proud city –   (lines 62–77)

A Mölna Elegy has a subtitle, *Metamorphoses*, which links it to a certain
kind of literature. It is the task of the reader to attempt to sense where

and how the changes occur. Promptly, in the stanza following the one just quoted, the protagonist appears as the 'Old actor' who speaks of his 'appointment with the past'. He is waiting for his Victoria, thus suggesting Strindberg's Officer in *A Dream Play*, written in Stockholm in 1901.

> That was another season, when the legless sprang
> and the fingerless played their guitars till they rang...   (lines 8–9)

are lines from the 'absurd' ditty, perhaps suggesting the times of war as well as absurdity in general. The section ends with the structurally important line, 'A flying moment...', which is re-intoned just before the '1809' episode and echoed in the 'Marche funèbre' section, and which was given *in extenso* in the opening scene:

> A flying moment robbed me of my future...

The proper interpretation of this central line (*Ett flyktigt/nyckfullt ögonblick*: a flying/flighty moment) is open to question. Suffice it to say that it is taken – in slightly modified form – from one of Ekelöf's favourites, the Finnish–Swedish poet, Edith Södergran (1892–1923). Her poem, 'Min framtid'[6] ('My Future') reads as follows:

> A capricious moment
> stole from me my future,
> the casually constructed.
>
> I shall build it up much more handsomely
> as I had intended it from the beginning.
> I shall build it upon the firm ground
> that is called my will.
> . . .
> I shall build it with a high tower
> called solitude.

It is worth pursuing the theme of time, if only for 'a moment'. *A Mölna Elegy* begins with the greeting *Ave viator!* ('Hail to thee, wanderer!') and, appropriately, it ends with *Vale viator!* ('Farewell, wanderer!'). Such inscriptions are traditional greetings to be found on gravestones along the Appian Way, the famous Roman highway from Rome to Greece and the East, built in 312 B.C. There is something symbolic in this: the 'wanderings' in *A Mölna Elegy* may originate in Ekelöf's beloved and hated Stockholm, and its surroundings, such as Mölna, and they end there, too, via a reference to the mystic, Emanuel Swedenborg, taken from *Drömboken* (*Journal of Dreams*, written in 1743–5 but not published until the middle of the nineteenth century):

- I left Oehlreick
and there was deep water in the road...[7]

There are numerous allusions to the past, especially to Ekelöf's favourite
period and place, eighteenth-century Sweden, and references to the
poet's own ancestors (the sections marked '1809', the year of revolution
in Sweden, and '1786'); but the main 'action' in the *Elegy* is set in the
Mediterranean area and some of it even in the East. The reader, in the
person of a wanderer examining the *Ave!* and the *Vale!* is greeted by
the dead, almost literally in the moment between putting one foot down
and putting the other down. If the completion of the wanderer's step
takes but a moment, it is in this compressed – or extended – moment
that the *Elegy* is in imagination contained. This idea of a *frame* – some
kind of 'moment' – was not merely a casual whim of the poet's, as is
shown in 'The Return Journey' (at the beginning of the *Elegy*):

> The sun setting
> glows through fading
> greens...clucking of jetties   (lines 44–6)

and towards the end just before the 'March funèbre' section:

> The sun in perpetual sunset
> Fire-clouds shifting flaunting
> Beyond reach burning images
> O holy clouds! –   (lines 605–8)

from which it is evident that, while Ekelöf's 'moment' passes, the sun
proceeds to set.

   When the 'Old actor' drops off – that is, *in the very moment* he drops
off to sleep for a while – we hear a version of Shakespeare in reverse:
the trees of Mölna speak about his ageing since last they saw him. A
blind window at the gable of Mölna remembers him as Prospero,
the magician, the genius loci, from *The Tempest*. A drop of water and
an apple, falling, remind us of the 'momentary' aspect of 'time'. While
the mill-gnome is from an old tale, the elf in the snowberry bush,
representing one kind of woman, appears to be Ekelöf's invention. She
wishes to prevail over him by degrading him, since she refers to him
as 'the punk', literally 'the ugly one', thereby meaning Caliban. In
mockingly humourous language, referring us to Joyce and Desnos, the
Biedermeier sofa and the front gable clock comment on some kind of
transgression, while the blind window contemplatively wonders: 'But
how can Prospero be alive? And here?' The drop falling into the barrel
indicates that the 'moment' is still going on. That is why it is emphasized

(in line 174) that the 'same' apple thuds dully, bumps, lies dumb. The 'same' wind in the trees sighs, in a longing, romantic fashion: 'Away! Away!'[8]

Then starts a round of recollections of the past in which the poet's ancestors appear: in the '1809' section, Anna Catharina Hedenberg (Madame Mont-Gentil), peripherally involved in a revolutionary episode in Sweden in the year 1809; and in the '1786' section, her brother (Gustaf Lewin), a naval officer who in that year experienced a cosmic occurrence near the equator, while on a slave trade mission.

> So I feel
> in the depth of my midriff these dead:
> The air I breathe is clogged with all the dead,
> the thirst I drink is mixed with all the dead   (lines 262–5)

The recollection of these dead relatives, and their bad and good deeds in times gone by, can be seen as an effort at synthesis on the part of the poet: all things – people, objects, concepts – interact, and all of them have series of complex relations with their neighbours or surroundings.[9] None of them can be fully understood until they have been placed in their proper context, i.e., in relation to their past.

If everyone and everything is dependent on everything else, the past lives of the dead are part of the present life of the poet and are relived by him. This idea was expressed in Ekelöf's 'A Dream (Real)' (1951)[10] and in his poem 'A World Is Everyone' (1941).[11] Like other poets, such as Yeats, Eliot, Robert Lowell, or James Wright, Ekelöf had a strong sense of family tradition, of what has been handed down and entrusted to the next generation. But the poet also rebels against tradition when it grows stale. The very fact that his *persona* is a complete outsider in *A Mölna Elegy* can be seen as an act of rebellion.

From an experience of being near death when as a child he is in bed with fever, in acute pain and distressed for want of breath, an episode which exemplifies two aspects of psychological 'time': 'in one moment/of intolerable speed and in the next unendurably slow' (lines 276–7), there is a neat transition to pleasant memories of country excursions and 'rewards' for diligent learning at school.

> And then I remember the hours clocked, the long hours clocked,
> the ticked minutes, minute minutes tocked,
> slowly lockstepping, slowly
> shoulder-borne –
> I remember the seconds, the dropped moments
> or the held, riveted ones. I remember

> Time,
> I carry it in me
> I bear it in me like a rock, a child of stone,
> complete and unborn – (lines 311–20)

Moments that have dropped out of memory because of some repressive mechanism, but also those almost intolerable moments, 'the riveted ones', obsessive thoughts that recur incessantly – all is remembered, but by whom? By the one who carries time, literally, like a stone-child, 'like a rock, a child of stone, / complete and unborn – '. The concept 'stone-child' is a clinical reality, although rare. *Lithopedion*[12] is a dead fetus that has become petrified. In a note to Muriel Rukeyser on 'stone-child', Ekelöf stated: 'Taken out of an Elzevier *De renum et vesicae* in my father's bookcase.'

If it is not too far-fetched to look for a mythological carrier of the 'stone-child', perhaps Chronos himself, or more correctly, Cronus, would fit. Cronus is 'primarily a harvest-god'[13] and just before the quoted passage, 'harvest-times' appears. Cronus, being afraid of an oracle's prediction that his sceptre would be struck out of his hand by his own offspring, swallowed his children, until Rhea out-witted him and gave him a 'black stone wrapped in swaddling clothes, and he swallowed the stone',[14] after which Poseidon was born. Marianne Moore refers to this at the end of 'Four Quartz Crystal Clocks':

> hearing Jupiter or jour pater, the day god –
> the salvaged son of Father Time –
> telling the cannibal Chronos
> (eater of his proxime
> newborn progeny) that punctuality
> is not a crime.[15]

Whatever the correct interpretation is, it is striking that the Mediterranean material, especially the use of myth, increases from now on, i.e., in the latter part of the *Elegy*, which is introduced by a graffito from Pompeii, actually from the coition chamber of the Villa dei Misteri. The text is very difficult to decipher, but a scholar claims she has identified five or six words, 'sufficient for her to divine the character of the text', Ekelöf noted,[16] and thus the graffito has more than a decorative, or even 'timely' purpose.

Almost all these Latin inscriptions are documented in Diehl's anthology of inscriptions, *Pompeianische Wandinschriften* (1910).[17] Readers with no more than school Latin are likely to find it strenuous work to decipher the vulgar wall inscriptions that Ekelöf – perhaps as an antidote to the many 'respectable' quotations and references – found worthy of inclusion in his *Elegy* (all on the left-hand pages). What is the general content of these inscriptions from Pompeii? Some are friendly or hostile greetings, others deal with business matters, but by far the greatest number are concerned with love or lovemaking of one kind or another.

The incantation beginning with 'Atracatetracatigallara', allegedly spoken by the witch, the Saga, actually consists of three authentic *defixiones*, nailings, which Jan Stolpe[18] located in Audollent's *Defixionum tabellae* (1904). We can easily recognize the phrase in the second nailing:

> dii iferi
> vobis comedo
> si quicqua sanctitates habetes
>
> (You gods of the underworld!
> I commend you,
> if you have something holy.)

This *defixio* is from Latium. The third *defixio* is from Nomentum, north of Rome: 'On this leaden tablet I rivet Malchio, Nico's son's eyes, hands, fingers, arms, nails, hair, head, feet, thighs, stomach, buttocks, navel, chest, nipples, neck, mouth, cheeks, teeth, lips, chin, eyes, forehead, eyebrows, shoulderblades, shoulders, muscles, bones, marrow, stomach, phallus, shins, his proceeds [?] and profit.' The *defixio* continues: 'Rufa, Pulica's daughter, her hands, teeth, eyes, arms, stomach, breasts, chest, bones, marrow, stomach, shins, legs, feet, forehead, nails, fingers, stomach, navel, womb, vulva, abdomen, Rufa, Pulica's daughter, I rivet on this tablet.' Finally the magical incantation from the beginning is repeated.

The *Carmen faeculare*, 'Excrement song', alludes to Horace's *Carmen saeculare*. Ekelöf has arranged the graffiti into an alternating song, 'a dramatically composed dialogue between [heterosexual] boys, girls, and homosexual adults, as well as the old industrious couple Philemon and Baucis'.[19] Ekelöf has occasionally made small changes. A case in point is Baucis ('recocta vino / trementibus labellis'), which is to be found in Petronius's *Fragmenta 21 v.*[20] What Baucis (old wino, lips shaking) says is, roughly, 'An experienced woman is better than a girl who has not yet got any pubic hair.' Among all those 'Voces repercussae' (Reverberating voices), Ekelöf has again included a refrain: '*Mádeia perimádeia*'[21] ('Well done, by Zeus, Oh yea by Zeus!'). In the final greetings by the boys, which is a counterpart of their initial greeting to

Victoria, Ekelöf has changed the authentic name, Noëte, to Sabina. The section ends, as it began, with the part of Saga, a *defixio*, only now the Latin text is written in the Greek alphabet.

Why did Ekelöf employ these Pompeian graffiti in his *Elegy?* Whatever the answer may be, the voices of the past were important to him in various ways. He may often have wanted to listen to the voices 'down below' more than to the loud voices of his own time, in which he did not feel at home. The informal tone, the spontaneous quality in these scribblings, appealed to him. What then, was his motive in including a large number of grave-inscriptions in the remaining Latin part of the *Elegy?*

These grave-inscriptions originate in different social groups and different provinces of the Roman Empire. It is obvious from Ekelöf's manuscripts that his inclusion of this vast number of quotations was not a whim: he copied or studied about two thousand grave-inscriptions and then selected some to fit together as he wanted them to appear in his *Elegy.* The 'parts' have been added by Ekelöf: 'Conservi, Conservae / Pueri, Puellae et Infantes' (Slaves, bondwomen, boys, girls and children), who all cry:

> Tene me ne fugia
> Tene me ne fugia
>
> Hold me or I shall escape
> Hold me or I shall escape

Ekelöf was fascinated by the strong pessimism expressed in lines like:

> Nunc mors perpetua(m)
> libertatem dedit
>
> Now death
> gave eternal freedom

In Latin, this statement is as eloquent as if it had been composed by a Lucretius, Ekelöf said. All those formulaic 'Dis Manibus. Hic iaceo', to the good gods, 'the gods under the world' – as Muriel Rukeyser translated – with their mention of the year, month, day, even hour of the departed one's life – all this seems to have touched the poet, in its naivety. He empathized with the simple ancient people who considered death a prelude to a happier life, a *dies natalis*, a kind of birthday to a new existence. Ekelöf's concern with death is as intense as is his concern with life. If his assimilated quotations, in general, are anything to go by, he relied much more heavily on sayings of the dead than those of the living. One can perhaps infer that he had more use for their 'voices' than for living voices. The 'outsider' Ekelöf, the individualist, more often than not sought his support among the 'greater majority' (to quote Petronius) than among the living.

The section ends with a reminder:

> Vos superi
> bene facite
> diu vivite
> et venite!

which Ekelöf read as:

> You who live on earth
> after me
> do good deeds
> and live a long life
> and come
> i.e., down to us dead.

It is a rare occasion indeed when he employs such a blatantly moral statement as that! On the next left page, he placed his own drawing of a strange-looking creature nailed upside-down to the saltire. It is hard to determine whether he is alluding to Spartacus or Peter.

The Latin part is concluded by another *defixio* which is from Carthage. It consists of the riveting of race horses in *quadrigas*, teams of four horses each. The original, as Stolpe observed, has a picture of a circus with the *meta*, the conical column with signal flags serving as a turning post at each end of the Roman Circus; four horses circle the *meta* clockwise. As we can see, the names have been selected in such a way that they suggest the four elements. To some extent they correspond to the four elements in the Brinvilliers section on the facing page of the *Elegy*. By employing the *quadriga* Ekelöf introduced a new aspect of time into his poem, and by building the theme of the *quadriga* into four, he added great complexity by simple graphic design.

Clearly, Ekelöf did not support the Romantic view of Pompeii, as embodied in Shelley's *Arria Marcellina*, Madame de Staël's *Corinne*, or Bulwer Lytton's *The Last Days of Pompeii*; nor does he reflect Wilhelm Jensen's *Gradiva* in the presentation of snapshots from Pompeii. The destruction (metamorphosis) of the city and its people can be seen as a parallel to the permanent petrifaction that Archaeopteryx met in its flight.

Parallel to the Latin runs the English. The call of 'Μέγα 'Αλέξανδρε' (Méga Aléxandre) and 'Στατεῖρα μοῦ' (Stateîra moū), makes it clear that the transformations have led to Alexander the Great, with a suggestive mirror-motif. The 'sexy ditty' and the 'violation and abortion scene' (with minor characters from the eighteenth-century Swedish poet, Carl Michael Bellman's world) are linked together by a picture of an olive press from Pompeii. The marginal note, 'A fourth a fifth!' repeats frequent musical concepts or terms in the *Elegy*. It indicates, roughly, where the most hermetic part of the *Elegy* begins.

> Never step
> upon a crack
> or you'll break
> your mother's back   (lines 441–4)

are taboo-like admonitions, perhaps obsessions of a child. They are followed by a playful promise of

> tales
> broad as doorways
> long as flails   (lines 445–7)

the ensuing fulfilment of which is provided by seven summarized memorable dreams that the Swedish scientist, philosopher, and theologian Emanuel Swedenborg (1688–1772) took down for his *Dream Journal*. 'The naturalist suddenly realizes the irrational in his own intellectual life',[22] commented Ekelöf. 'Dreams like ringing from the deeps' (line 461) suggests common European folk tales in the ringing of bells, or bells that have sunk into the sea. Bells ringing from the deeps corresponds to the earlier ringing of bells from heights, i.e., from belfries. 'Oarfish inland-driven' (line 638) is a deep-sea fish, presumably symbolizing deeply hidden forces in the personality. 'Sea-creatures that gape over the ships' (line 468) are to be seen in maps and drawings, such as in *Carta Marina* by Olaus Magnus (1555). The scene then moves from Nordic waters to the Mediterranean, to Southern shores, where 'Lestrygonians' introduce the well-known myth in the *Odyssey*. It reminds us of the monster Cyclops – whose father was Poseidon, who makes an appearance in the *Elegy* – and the Lestrygonians, the gigantic cannibals (Book x) whose king feasted on one of the three men Odysseus had sent inland. While the two men fled, the Lestrygonians destroyed all ships except the one on which Odysseus sailed.[23] Ekelöf's reference is primarily neither to Book x of the *Odyssey* nor to chapter 8 of Joyce's *Ulysses*; he alludes to 'the famous antique fresco fragments in the Vatican'.[24] There are eight scenes in this unique fresco of the episode. Alinari's superb photograph no. 38029, *Distruzione della flotta di Ulisse*, is the best reproduction, but occasional reproductions of separate parts of the fresco can be found in, for example, B. Nogara's *Art Treasures of the Vatican*.[25] The reader should be able to perceive echoes of Homer's wallowing waves and sense something of the dangers and excitement of seafaring life.

> pigs that cry and try to speak:
> 'Have we not conquered?'   (lines 474–5)

suggests the sailing to the island of Aeaea, where Circe tapped half of Odysseus's crew with her magic wand, transforming them into talking swine. There follows the visit to Hades, the cremation of Elpenor, and a necessary sacrifice to Poseidon before 'The Man of Grief' (Odysseus)[26] can return home.

If, indeed, in the previous lines, the question was whether to 'eat or be eaten', as Bloom speculates, in the next, it is not giants eating men, but *lithophages*, 'stone-eaters', eating away at a god – Poseidon – making if not 'holes and swellings' at least 'holes' in his limbs. As a result of a shipwreck at sea, the statute of Poseidon was seen by the eyes of fish rather than humans until finally it was recovered from the Bay of Baia (the 'old china' just before the '1809' episode was recovered from a shipwreck in the harbor of Gothenburg, incidentally). It can now be seen at Pozzuoli (Puteoli). This drowned god has thus been created and salvaged by humans and brought not to a temple but to a museum where he can be looked at. In a sense this is creation in reverse. Even if the god somewhat resembles almighty Zeus, Amedeo Maiuri[27] is fully convinced that it is a Poseidon–Neptune statue:

> Lithophages in the deeps:
> Holes and swellings on the limbs of the god   (lines 476–7)

'The coral red tree of aerated blood –' suggests that the pattern of the circulation of blood in anatomy might remind us of a silhouetted image of a tree with branches and roots, or perhaps of corals, the trees of the sea. The pyre on the beach could be an allusion to 'Shelley's funeral pyre',[28] of which Trelawny wrote several accounts.

'Quick! Have you other lives?' (line 486) is a line that, in Ekelöf's own translation of Rimbaud's 'Mauvais sang', had been taken from *Une saison en enfer* ('Vite! est-il d'autres vies'?).[29] 'Can we reach across the sea to another reality via dream?' suggested A. Losman.[30] Others might want to interpret the line as a question of whether or not there is an after-life.

The voice crying from the tree's bark is that of the Dryad, the tree–nymph, who lost her life when the tree in which she lived was being cut down. Eurydice, the wife of Orpheus the poet, was the most renowned of the dryads; with his lyre he visited the underworld and nearly recovered her, a queen of the dead. The kid sucking the breast of a *panisca*, an inferior woodland deity representing Pan, can be seen in the Villa dei Misteri in Pompeii.

'The unicorn seeking refuge' (line 491) alludes above all to the first of the famous 'La dame à licorne' tapestries in the Musée de Cluny, Paris, and also to the equally famous Unicorn Tapestries in the Cloisters, New York City. The unicorn, according to legend, was the shyest of all animals and could be captured only by an innocent maid. If and when it encountered such a virgin, it would go to her of its own accord and piously settle itself on her lap, as it does in this poem.

The line 'O purity, purity!' (line 493) has a double meaning in Swedish where '*O*' can stand both for the exclamation 'O!' and a negating prefix 'im-', making it refer to 'impurity' as well as to the principle meaning, 'purity'. The line is another echo from *Une saison en enfer*, in which the last line of the poem 'L'Impossible' reads 'O pureté! pureté!'[31] The virgin motif has been explored extensively in Ekelöf's poetry.

The 'Fire Song' is partly a description and interpretation of the 'Garden of Delights' triptych (Prado, Madrid) by Hieronymus Bosch:

> Flames and these dancing
> fire-mills shifting
> obscure signals
> significant glances   (lines 496–9)

which are to be seen on the upper part of the right panel.

> Devils that fly on ladders
> high above the onlookers   (lines 510–11)

These lines also refers to Bosch. When the hellish visions recede, the concern of the 'I'-persona is with the ceremonies after his death. A connection is established with the funeral pyre (earlier) and the infernal fire by the afterthought:

> No, just be burnt to ashes.   (line 541)

The quotation that follows reiterates the cremation theme:

> Enfin c'en est fait,
> La Brinvilliers est en l'air
> de sorte que nous la respirerons![32]   (lines 551–3)

is from Mme de Sévigné's letter of 17 July 1676, and refers to an episode typical of the widespread belief in witchcraft and epidemic of poisonings prevalent in Europe and New England in the latter half of the seventeenth century. In the next scene, with the Greek Gorgon, water is again the chief element. When Perseus had composed himself, and had, with the help of gods (Hermes and Athena), fulfilled his pledge, the presentation of the Gorgon Medusa's head, he had mastered her petrifying stare and thus overcome death and at the same time become an overlord of death.[33] Many strands are woven together in this central poem of the Gorgon: as an octopus and a sea monster; the Gorgon as Alexander's cursed sister; the Gorgon as a form of the Great Goddess 'in her aspect as goddess of death' and the octopus as a human, because it carries on a philosophical monologue!

The 'Eleoûsa' in the Gorgon section is the Mother of God, depicted on a variety of Greek and Russian icons, in which the position of the child God differs considerably, but generally shown as the merciful one, i.e., the Eleoûsa, with her head lovingly tilted towards that of the child God. The entire scene is again a double exposure; 'reeds hardly grow by the Mediterranean shores, but rather at Mölna',[34] thus establishes a return to the opening of the *Elegy* in 'The return journey': 'The reeds bowing...

In spite of the fact that *A Mölna Elegy* was partially written during the World War II, there are only a few references to the war, one of them being,

> all of us floating here
> floating along
> O these carcasses that float
> that head into the reeds
> but rock uncertainly outside.   (lines 582–6)

Another is found in 'Marche funèbre':

> A flighty moment –
> and now the devil is in the belfry
> he who robbed us of our future   (lines 617–19)

Here 'the devil' stands for Hitler, according to the manuscripts. It is a slightly revised line from Rimbaud's 'Nuit de l'enfer' in *Une saison en enfer*.[35] If the citation of Chopin's Funeral March suggests the banality of *sorrow*, the reference to Hitler can possibly hint at the banality of *violence* and its impermanence. The red fever-ball – a childhood experience – corresponds to the slightly revised line from Desnos's 'Définition de la Poésie pour' (*sic!*), attributed to Max Ernst: 'la boule rouge qui bouge et roule', which is to be found in Rrose Sélavy (1922–3) in *Corps et Biens* (no. 125).[36] 'O saisons, ô châteaux!' is from Rimbaud's *Une saison en enfer* and deals with happiness. Ekelöf had translated the poem in his volume of French poetry, *From Baudelaire to Surrealism* (1934).[37]

'Leavetaking', which is less than the coda to be expected, re-introduces the 'same apple', thus reminding us of the continuing moment, while 'the front gable clock' speaks a line from *Finnegans Wake*.[38] The preceding line of that book, 'Gunnar's gustspells', apostrophizes the poet's own name and includes several references to theater (Schouwburg; Uplouderamain; Curtain drops), which may give us the associations to the 'Old Actor' (from the beginning of the *Elegy*).

One can read about 'rāgas and rāginis' in A. H. Fox-Strangways' *The Music of Hindustan*,[39] a book which had accompanied Ekelöf since his youth. These melodies are personified as fairies, mostly female, in Mogul miniatures, samples of which are to be found in the British Museum, where Ekelöf first saw them. 'A genius' introduces himself now as le Roquefort, now as le Brie, which are both, as Göran Printz-Påhlson has noted,[40] to be found in Rimbaud's poem 'Rêve', from about 1874. The jocular genius in the *Elegy* (and in 'Rêve') constantly seems to change identity and therefore fits the theme of metamorphoses. The genius may have a counterpart in one of the many spirits who earlier filed past in the *Elegy*. 'The disabled emanations (dancing)' parallel the lame elves' dance before the 'Park Scene'.

Ibn el-Arabi was one of Ekelöf's favorite authors, who speaks a single word in the *Elegy*: 'Labbayka!' which means 'At thy service!'[41] This word is part of the Mohammedan pilgrimage rituals, the essential sign of the consecrated state. The Thrush – a symbol for the poet himself – now silent with an upthrust beak, has found a place on the family heraldic armorial. The silent heraldic thrush could have served as a dignified emblem to end the *Elegy*, but in his remarkable mosaic of quotations, allusions, and reminiscences, Ekelöf apparently wanted to apostrophize Edith Södergran and Emanuel Swedenborg. We are fortunate enough to have Ekelöf's comments on these two quotations. He intimated that the mother (in the Södergran poem) soothes the child while they are waiting at the station. War is raging and along the roadbed are dead soldiers. The situation is not as yet dangerous, but it is precarious.[42]

The Swedenborg quotation is the last one in the *Elegy*. Here a mystic concerned with dreams had the final say. The word 'water' is mentioned twice and suggests other analogies and parallels in the *Elegy*, indeed, it begins with a water image and it ends with water. In the rhymed final lines, *time* is again the central theme. On the very last page of the *Elegy* the reader is saluted: *Vale viator!*, just as he was greeted with *Ave viator!* at the beginning of the long 'moment'. In a note Ekelöf wrote: 'a moment becomes timeless when the itinerant wanderer passes the gravestone and sees its *Vale!* and *Ave!* or the reverse...Such a fugue should be read both ways, [but] I have not reached as far as that in perseverance.'[43] Below the salutation *Vale viator!* is a picture of Archaeopteryx, the primitive bird whose fossil remains were discovered in the nineteenth century, in Bavaria.

It seems clear, then, that there are several kinds of unity in this complex poem. At one level, there is a unity akin to that of Strindberg's *A Dream Play*: there is an auditive focus, a 'dreamer', who is the centre of all the metamorphoses. The theme of 'Time' as transformation links all the sections, and, in a brilliant and original way, the notion of the moment as a simultaneity of transformations provides a solution to the problem explored by T. S. Eliot of striking a line for our own times through the past while maintaining and displaying the belief that 'the whole of the literature of Europe...composes a simultaneous order'.

NOTES

1 *BLM* (1946), 358. Ekelöf translated Gide's *Les Faux-Monnayeurs* into Swedish: *Falskmyntarna* (Stockholm, 1932), reprinted in 1962) (Forum-biblioteket, 127). Cf. Reidar Ekner, *Gunnar Ekelöf en bibliografi* (Stockholm, 1970). The idea of a *vertical section of time* may have originated in Gide, who also provides *A Mölna Elegy* with a central theme: 'in the past our future is determined'.

2 Note to me, November 1963.

3 Cf. annotation in a copy of *En Mölna-elegi* in the possession of Ekelöf's widow, Mrs Ingrid Ekelöf, Sigtuna. The manuscripts of *En Mölna-elegi* are to be found in the Manuscript and Rare Books collection of Uppsala University.

4 Leif Sjöberg, *A Reader's Guide to Gunnar Ekelöf's 'A Mölna Elegy'* (New York, 1973), p. 54.

5 *A Reader's Guide*, p. 55.

6 *Samlade dikter*, edited by Gunnar Tideström (Helsinki, 1950), p. 143, or pp. 51-2 in the 1962 edition.

7 E. Swedenborg, *Drömboken*, edited by Per-Erik Wahlund (Stockholm, 1952), p. 50.

8 Refers to the poem 'Mazeppa' in Victor Hugo's collection *Les Orientales* XXXIV (with its motto, 'Away-!-Away!' from Byron's 'Mazeppa'). *Oeuvres complètes de Victor Hugo, Poésies* (Paris, n.d.), II, 179.

9 Jan Christiaan Smuts, *Holism and Evolution* (New York, 1961; first published 1926). Cf. esp. Edmund W. Sinnott's Introduction, p. xiii.

10 *Dikter* (Stockholm, 1965), pp. 235–6.

11 *Selected Poems of Gunnar Ekelöf*, translated by Muriel Rukeyser and Leif Sjöberg (New York, 1967), p. 61.

12 '*Dorland's Illustrated Medical Dictionary* (24th edn, Philadelphia and London, 1965), p. 846.

13 Richmond Y. Hathorn, *Greek Mythology* (Beirut, 1977), p. 7.

14 Hathorn, p. 7.

15 Hathorn, p. 8.

16 Note on the Latin material, written (or dated) on 26 October 1963. Ekelöf probably refers to *The Common People of Pompeii* (Baltimore, 1939).

17 '*Latrin och kräkiska*. Det antika materialet i Ekelöfs *En Mölna-Elegi*.' *Rondo* (Stockholm), 1 (1961), 14ff. Stolpe's essay has been of great value to me, especially by identifying Ekelöf's sources.

18 Stolpe, p. 14.

19 Stolpe, pp. 14ff.

20 *Lexicon Petronianum: Ioannes Segebade et Ernestus Lommatzsch* (Lipsiæ, 1818), p. 217.

21 As Stolpe has noted, this cry or burden from a song was lifted from Petronius's *Cena Trimalchionis*, 52:9.

22 *Appendix*, *OoB* (Stockholm, 1956), p. 478.

23 Hathorn, pp. 392ff.

24 *Appendix OoB*, p. 478.

25 (New York and Bergamo, 1950), p. 230.

26 Hathorn, pp. 392ff.

27 *Campi Flegrèi* (Rome, 1949), pp. 40–1, with a reproduction of the salvaged statue.

28 *Appendix*, *OoB*, p. 478.

29 Rimbaud, *Une saison en enfer*, translated by Louise Varèse (New York, 1961), pp. 20–1.

30 'Kring En Mölna-elegi' (Göteborg, 1958), mimeographed essay, p. 22.

31 Rimbaud, pp. 74–5.

32 *Appendix*, *OoB*.

33 Hathorn, pp. 28ff.

34 *Argument*, *En natt i Otočac* (One night in Otočac; Stockholm, 1961), p. 80.

35 Rimbaud, pp. 28–9.

36 (Paris, 1930), pp. 30ff.

37 *Hundra år modern fransk dikt* (Stockholm, 1934), pp. 34–5.

38 p. 257, line 35.

39 (Oxford, 1914 and 1965). Cf. VI, 151–80.

40 *Appendix till Solen i spegeln* (Lund, 1960), p. 49.

41 G. E. von Grunebaum, *Muhammedan Festivals* (London and New York, 1958), pp. 28ff.

42 *A Reader's Guide*, p. 137.

43 In one of Ekelöf's copies of *En Mölna-elegi*, now in the possession of Mrs Ingrid Ekelöf, Sigtuna.

GUNNAR EKELÖF

A Mölna Elegy

Metamorphoses

Translated by
Muriel Rukeyser and Leif Sjöberg

Ave viator!

I sit on a bench of the past,
I write on a page of the past.
On Mölna September snows down in red leaves.
jetty October flows away in yellow leaves.
One stands with me staring, a lurid fool who plays
crazy-eyed into November while he plays
his wordless ballad for the deaf –

That was another season, when the legless sprang
and the fingerless played their guitars till they rang...

The institution for cripples rented the past last summer   10
for a few weeks of illusion for its captives:
Like pullulating pools the ancient echo-chambers

of most instructive and threatening examples,
of abortive larvae and lemures,
of twitching goose-stepping twisting grey chimeras.
And their amusements resembled the ballets
of clumsily manipulated dolls.
Now blankness here again and the same sadness
– or else another.
What do I care. My life stands still.   20

A flying moment robbed me of my future...

Wave song

Windrush and wavespray
Waverush and windspray
Waters' rush and winds
cool on the forehead and cheek –
solitary, and you
always on course:
An eternal *then* which is now
An eternal *now* which is past
Time arrested, flailed:
The sun nailed

30

on our bedlam spire
Silos and towers –

Windrush and wavespray
Waverush and windspray
Waters and these shifting
bellringing waving
winds – dancing, advancing:
Calling, recalling
as if the clouds were ringing   40
glissando over ice, wild grebe shouting
ice-ring round the horizon –

Waters and windspray.

The sun setting
The return   glows through fading
journey   greens...clucking of jetties
along the canal, graded
receding ebbing subsiding
wider the propellor's sucking
backwash...The reeds bowing...   50

The brant who paddle sideways...
And the fishing ones, half daft,
mute shadows laze in wonder
over a cork sucked under
a tarnished sheath that dances
with jellied pauses
after love-fests of summer:

Corno   Little Eros' armor...
– Toot of the ferry-boat horn
past leaning willows borne   60
in by the bridge –

Windrush and wavespray
waverush and windspray
spray of the roller's blow
cool upon cheeks and brow

He begins   isolation and I:
to transform   the selfsame or another
I or not I?
The future – now – the past
time running wild   70
years last for minutes
with a tail of yellow leaves
or time held

stockstill in the elms'
wetblack branches held –
Clotho cuts off the button...
Proud city –

I have an appointment with the past.
I stay here waiting and waiting for the past.
Old actor   I was just considering a memorandum
on the punctuality of ladies... – Victoria!
I belong alas also among your captives,
beside the victory chariot – Ha! – surviving captive:
(The sapphire on the little finger, raised,
mouth against crook of cane...)

A flying moment –

All of this in the season when the legless sprang
and the fingerless played their guitars till they rang

and the deaf heard it all
and the crippled did not fall   90
the blind came running to the call.

(curtain)

(dance of lame elves)

He falls asleep,
nodding

Trees of the park
(in unison behind him)

How he has aged since last time!

A blind window
(*on Mölna's gable*)

I saw him Lord knows how many years ago
as Prospero –   100

A mirror in the window

Now he is at most an old dandy
serving a life sentence on his island.

A drop
(*falls in the green barrel*)

Blink!

A blackbird
(*calls a warning in the park's silence*)

An apple

Thuds dully, bumps, lies dumb.   110

Mill-gnome
(*cap in hand*)

It's just like that at the mill, too...

Elf

(in the snowberry bushes)

It's just like that with our parts! Who were you?
Surely you were the punk?

Mill-gnome

Shame! Who were you yourself?
(reflectively) No, only one of the drunks,   120
so thoroughly that I really don't remember
who the hell I was! And you?

Elf

Of course I knew who I was...
                    (points at blackbird who hides in the bushes)
                                        Do you see that one?

Mill-gnome

So-what?

Elf

He too is transformed.   130

Mill-gnome

Hah! Do you think he used to be white?

Elf

I well know what he was...He used to sing,
I remember it clearly, high in a treetop,
so beautifully that one stood still and blushed,
or in the cornfield on a summer night
so that one stayed there at the open window,
but that was long ago, another cry,
I think it was a feeling only – something   140
that now is dead. Now he has only
his warning cry, but then he sang! Ah,
now in the spring my flowers are so small,
so very small! And these white berries,
who'll turn to look at them?

Mill-gnome

What rot! Surely they'll do for squeezing!

Snowberries

Pt. Pt. Pt.

Elf

(*hides her face, disappearing*)

My God! What has become of me!

Blackbird

(*escapes*)

Biedermeier sofa

(*in the club-pavilion, struts, three turns*)

Unheard-of! Unholy! Unimaginable!

Front gable clock

(*black clock-face with traces of gilt figures, the hands missing*)

Trr! Timeworn curses! My watchworks hurt!   160
Clockstroke!

Mill-gnome

(*cap in hand, sneaks away squinting to the mill*)

I swear it! It was only when I was stinking drunk.

Mirror at the window

(looks at him coldly, through a lorgnette)

Blind window

(as before, stares absently)

− But how can Prospero
be alive? And here?   170

Same drop

(down into the barrel)

Blank!

Same apple

Thuds dully, bumps, lies dumb.

Same wind in the trees

Away! Away!

Black bird

(is heard calling a warning at a distance in the silence of the park)

Then you wake, and hear to your amazement   180
like parrot-screeching from an old maid's apartment:
How-are-you? – Beautiful Laura, Laura...

And then a laugh, as from a used-up whaura;
How aaare you?

Aunt Grey

(*grave-faced, hairy wart on chin*)

How he has grown since last time!

Aunt Green

(*her hair an unreal henna-color*)

I remember him Lord knows how many years ago   190
when he was no bigger than that!

Tante Louche

(*strangely smiling, sees everything sidelong*)

How aaare you?

Thank you kindly. Splendid.
Really excellent.

Or bad, very bad!
(It does not matter what you say –)
Time has abandoned me long since.
It has deserted me   200
as I did time.
(A flying moment...)
And do you remember, remember
old china with seashells encrusted
– how long has it waited in the sealed-up room?
the painted Tula box filled with dried roseleaves
and a moist fragrance, the bulging wallpaper,
the curling-iron heater forgotten, the candles
gnarled as yellowing relics in the sconces
beneath Madam Mont-Gentil's portrait, a rara avis   210
at teatimes...

                           – I remember, remember...
1809
          That day when we could all breathe again
          and the city exulted. The weather so splendid, too,
          that ladies went shawled as to a fête in spring
          (toward which the inner warmth of pleasure led).
          The initiates (they were not a few) had gathered
          at Castenhof and sang the windows open
          and somebody handed out a glass of champagne
          in which to toast our freedom. You took it   220
          and drained it although your admirer
          was the Royal Governor...

– And do you remember
old china with seashells encrusted,
– how long has it lain in the green depths? –
a carved calabash, the shell of a sea-turtle,
the Indian hammock, its complicated plaiting
and the slaves' song from the muggy middle-deck
so like the underworld when one stood in the fresh air
and heard the roar of the sails?   230.

                    – Yes, I remember
1786   a night on circa one degree north latitude.
The sky stood clear and in godlike majesty.
On the horizon was seen the wellknown light
which emanates from all the myriad beings
with which the ocean is so richly endowed.
I promenaded on deck with the first mate
when suddenly in the east we saw a great star
which increased every second in greatness.
I reported to the captain who soon came up,   240
gave orders to summon every man on deck
to reef the sails, heave to and lash the rudder.
And then the star or meteor burst open
into a thousand rays or with the speed of thought
over the ship the rushing of these rockets
that covered the whole horizon with a shining
so dazzling that you could have seen a hair
if one had been hanging from the masthead!

Just then arose a hurricane, so violent
that we dreaded the capsizing of the ship   250
and soon after such an abundant rainfall
that all the water vessels could have been filled
with what washed over the deck in a few moments.
This phenomenon lasted hardly forty minutes.
Air and sky cleared, the stars grew visible,
the wind the same. The sails set.
The watch was relieved and allowed to turn in
and the ship proceeded on the same course as before.
But in the clarity of night was heard again
now slack, now strong, as in rhythmically varied
   choruses   260
locked in, below decks, the singing of the slaves...

    So I feel
in the depth of my midriff these dead:
The air I breathe is clogged with all the dead,
the thirst I drink is mixed with all the dead,
they are my hunger and they are my food:
I die their life, they live my death.

    Then you remember too
a summer afternoon of unspeakable closeness
mindless hammering from the plate-workshop   270
and somewhere far away on empty streets

a sideless wagon clattering on cobblestones
but as if in a surge of silence...All were gone
out to the country...And the red ball,
the high fever-ball, dazzling and inflamed,
came rolling over you, in one moment
of intolerable speed and in the next unendurably slow.
And the window's slant suncross on the floor
came relentlessly crawling closer to the bed.
And the wagon came clattering on cobblestones   280
without ever once stopping...
To the linden woods
they had all gone, or to the country.

– Yes, I remember
the meadow with the mushrooms under the oaktrees
the big oaks,
and as reward for hic haec hoc and avoir être
one hamper packed for a fête champêtre
and our games, mostly at forfeits
where Arrasmiha presided beside   290
Camilla, after milking –

And do you remember the lindens, the old lindens?
Monsieur Petter and Cousin at the locked gates,
the high locked gates?

Tittle-tattle in the attic boxroom,

the big boxroom,

by the foxes,

the little foxes,

spoilers of vineyards –

His left hand rests under my head   300

and his right arm doth embrace me –

And do you remember the junipers on the hill

the tall junipers?

You drilled them as if they were soldiers.

And do you remember the boulders, the big boulders?

You gave names to them all.

– I remember:

Even time has its vineyards.

How risky though their harvest-times,

how unpredictable!   310

And then I remember the hours clocked, the long hours

   clocked

the ticked minutes, minute minutes tocked,

slowly lockstepping, slowly

shoulder-borne –

I remember the seconds, the dropped moments

or the held, riveted ones. I remember
Time,
I carry it in me,
I bear it in me like a rock, a child of stone,
complete and unborn –   320

MANTISINA
TRIPODARTTIISP.ATI
PVTIIRIIII
ITNIII
DISTIIIIN IIVTA
PS.PININNITIS
TIIIIVASII
IKTIIINI
STINN
IVNKT
SINBOPINIS

Saga

Atracatetracatigallara
precata egdarata
hehes celata
mentis ablata
dii iferi
vobis comedo
si quicqua sanctitates habetes
Malcio Nicones oculos
manus dicitos bracias uncis
capilo caput pedes femus venter
natis umlicus pectus mamilas
collus os bucas dentes labias
mentus oclus fronte supercili
scaplas umerum nervias ossu
medulas venter mentula crus
quastu lucru
defico in as tabelas
Rufa Pulica manus detes
oclos bracia venter mamila
pectus osu medulas venter
crus os pedes frontes
uncis dicitos venter
umlicus cunus
ulvas iliae Rufas Pulica
defico in as tabeles
Atracatetractigallara
precata egdarata
hehes celata
mentis ablata

239

Μέγα
'Αλέξανδρε

– Behold, I am King over all that has gone before
and prince over myriads of those gone under.
September snows down in red leaves,
October flows away in yellow leaves
I reign over the abysses of these captives,
who have held back in staying immature
and within a being, still higher, still captive.
September snows down in red leaves.
October flows away in dead leaves.
Always fare on! Call me the backward one,   330
a vestige of one latent from the start,
a moment riveted out of some event
which only in its wholeness can account for
my actions.
Sept. Oct.
Sext. Oct.
Thus I unlatch the latches and unbolt the doors.
Thus in vain I step out of mirrors
into mirrors,
I myself see in endless mirror-series   340
how unalterably and alienated
I leer –

Pueri

*Victoria, vale, et ubique vis
suaviter sternuitis!*

Carmen
faeculare

Pathici

Regulo feliciter quia verpa est!

Puellae

*Fonticulus pisciculo suo
plurma salut!*

On a cornelian
crawling into
his shell
a snail
looking like
a priapus
Over him glitters
a star

Pueri

Sabina, felas! No belle faces.

Puellae

Fortunate, linge cunu!

Στατεῖρα
μοῦ
    – You are the Princess of the unassimilated,
yourself unassimilated, filled with the aborted,
yourself a prisoner within some bigger being
from whom you shall have your seeing.
Sept. Oct.
Sext. Oct.
– You expect metamorphosis without action?
– I expect only from metamorphosis   350
strength for action.
Sept. Oct.
Sext. Oct.
– You seek in the eternal the rational?
– I seek in the temporal the irrational.
September snows down in red leaves.
October flows away in yellow leaves.
November is the one you go to beg with
– a shabby gaudy pimp –
December is the one you go to bed with.   360
At one a.m.
a sharp one came.
January is the one who filled your belly out.
February the one who stilled your mouth.

Omnes

Tuttu sodales hic ad exemplar
felant Stabianas puellas.

Puellae

Fortunate, animula dulcis,
perfututor!

Pueri

Me, me mentulam linge!
Destillatio me tenet!

Pathici

Qui verpam vissit
quid cenasse illum putes?

Pueri

Diced nobis Sineros
ut merdas edatis —

Baucis

(recocta vino
trementibus labellis)

Futuitur cunnus pilossus
multo melius quam glaber.

Two o'clock came
he does the same.
In the month of March, at five
does he drive.
Sleighbells ringing.
He stamps snow off in the hall.   370
Eight, and again the mountain bringing
forth a mouse.
The month when you are fooled, April,
fool you he will.
One o'clock
a young cock.
By cinq heures, the time of the tea-dance,
this goat can prance.
Then at six
more complex tricks   380
but not yet! wait,
let's fly at eight.
Two o'clock came
he does the same.
At midnight, by the gate deep in the wood
a piston tight in your cylinder stood.
Three was cried
he came outside.
Ten, in a hotel room at the beach you'll find
a sunburnt couple doing 69.   390
At one o'clock
this young cock.

Voces repercussae
(ceventinabiliter arrurabiliter
inclinabiliter irrumabiliter)

*Hic ego, cum veni, futui
deinde reddi domi.*

*Scordopordonicus hic
bene fuit quem voluit.*

*Sum tua, aeris as. II.
Lahis felat, as. II.
Felix felat, as. I.*

*Siquis hic sederit
legat hoc ante omnia:
Siqui futuere volet
Atticen quaerat, bellis moribus.*

On a sardonyx
Eros riding
on a priapus
his reins
hang slack

*Amet qui scribet
pedicatur qui leget
qui opscultat prurit
pathicus est qui praeterit
ursi me comedant
et ego verpam qui lego*

Over the picture: TEXNH
Under: THΔE

(cunnuliγγeter inclinabiliter
ceventinabiliter)

Omnes

Μάδεια περιμάδεια

Philemon

*Turtur Baucis caca
ut possimus bene dormire*

Don't forget five p.m.:

Press the button! –

Ensign Morian

(*in*)

Cajsa Stina, Mother Bobbi

(*they curtsey*)

Where are you, breastchild,

in the mill, stonechild?   400

Yes, you'll find –

Mind!

Never step

upon a crack

or you'll break

your mother's back!

Got him?

– Got him?

The bum,

hold tight!   410

et pedicare natis candidas
gelasinos tuos, cunnu tibi fricabo
diciti adiuvabunt pruriginem.

Baucis

(cachinnum edens)

Veneria Maximo mentla exmuccavt
per vindemia tota
et reliquet putr. ventre
mucei os plenu.

Puellae

Ubi me iuvat asido.

Pueri

Sabina, lumen, vale, vale, usque vale!

Omnes

Μάδεια περιμάδεια

On a cornelian seal
Priapus
with the crupper
of a lion
He holds
a shell
in his grip
His head is raised
Over him flutters
a butterfly

Σαγα

ἀδιουρο περ μαγνουμ δεουμ

ἐτ περ ἀνθεροτας

ἐτ περ ἐουμ κουι ἀβετ

ἀρχεπτορεμ σουπρα χαπουθ

ἐτ περ σεπτεμ σθελλας

οὐθ ἐξ κουα ὁρα οχ comποσουερο

Ah ça!
My dear!
No nonsense here!
Ergot does it and
    ergot is sure
Castor is faster
Leave a deposit!

Drat,
catch the rat!
Sucking child, stone child
got him?
– Got him.
Jack of sacking,
Jack of dust,
Jack of spiderwebs
first and last,
without the gism for a spasm,   420
not worth a piece of string:
Winding winding
chains of brains.
Burst your cyst
straining at the mill
spasm where you get him
Take hold
with a broom!
Hold that,
that's the rat!   430
Water is the membrane,
Manjack the millstone
spindrift the grist.
Roll with the water,
moan with the mill
Stone child, sucking child
got him?
– Got him

Ah ça!
My dear!
No nonsense here!
Castor is faster
Ergot does it and ergot
is sure
A fourth a fifth!

νον δορμιατ Σεξτιλλιος Διονισιε φιλιους
οὐραθουρ φουρενς
νον δορμιατ νεκουε σεδεατ νεκουε λοκουατουρ
σεδ ἰν μεντεμ ἀβιατ με Σεπιθμαμ ᾽Αμενε φιλια.
οὐραθουρ φουρενσ ἀμορε ἐτ δεσιδεριο μεο
ἀνιμα ἐτ χορ οὐραθουρ
Σεξτιλι Διονισιε φιλιους ἀμορε ἐτ δεσιδεριο μεο
Σεπτιμες ᾽Αμενε φιλιε.
του αοὐτεμ Αβαρ Βαρβαριε Ελοεε Σαβαοθ
Παχνουφυ Πυθιπεμι
φαχ Σεξτιλιουμ Διονισιε φιλιουμ νε σομνουμ χονθινγαθ
σεθ ἀμορε ἐτ δεσιδεριο μεο οὐραθουρ
οὐιιους σιπιριτους ἐτ χορ χομβουρατουρ
ὀμνια μεμβρα θοθιους χορποριс Σεξθιλι Διονισιε φιλιους.
σι μινους δεσχενδο ἰν ἀδυτους ᾽Οσυρις
ἐτ δισσολουαμθεν θαπεεν
ἐτ μιτταμ οὐθ ἀ φουλμινε φερατουρ.
ἐγὼ ἐνιμ σουμ μαγνους δεχανους
δει μαγνι δει Αρχαμμαχαλαλα. . .ε

Conservi, Conservae
Pueri, Puellae & Infantes

Tene me ne fugia
Tene me ne fugia
revocas me regione
prma Aurelio.
Foras muru exivi
Tene me quia fugi
reduc me ad Flora
ad tosores.
Ptronia dicor
Tene me quia fugibi
et revoca me ad domum

Stag's head

joint to joint, Jack.

...Slack!   440

Never step

upon a crack

or you'll break

A fourth a fifth! your mother's back,

So, shall, you come, to hear, tales

broad as doorways

long as flails

long as streams,

short as dreams

long as the chains of coachmen's reins   450

long as long Horn Street

Of youth and the house of Gustavus.

Of Venice, about the beautiful Palais.

Of Sweden, about the white sky of heaven

Of Leipzig, about him who lay in boiling water.

About him who fell collared into the pit.

About the King who gave the priceless gift in a hovel.

About the farmhand who wanted me to get out.

About my delights lying in bed at night.

Jetsam on the beaches of sleep   460

Dreams like ringing from the deeps

Oarfish inland-driven

Grief's soft leviathans

with their closed eyelashes

dangerous even in sleep

because of glances that cannot be concealed

Theodotenis
ad domnum meum
Vitalione.
Tene me quia fugibi

Nunc mors perpetua
libertatem dedit.

———

Dis Manibus Sacrum
Iacet sub hoc signino
dulcissima Secundilla
quae rapta parentibus
reliquit dolorem
ut tan dulcis erat
tanquam aromata
desiderando semper
mellea vita.
'Αρωμάτι τᾶυτα
Tene me quia fugi

Dis Manibus Sacrum
M. Ulpius Firmus
anima bona superis reddita
raptus a nymphis:
Ulpius Nymphicus.
Tene me quia fugi

Dis Manibus. Hic iaceo
infelix Zmyrna
puella tenebris
December pater et
Ianuaria mater
b.m.f.

beneath those eyelashes!
Sea-creatures that gape over the ships
and the Lestrygonians who destroy them
in wonderful colors   470
weathered, half obliterated
People rushing at random
speared wild boars
or pigs that cry and try to speak:
'Have we not conquered?'
Lithophages in the deeps:
Holes and swellings on the limbs of the god
watered reflections rippling over his face
waves advancing beautifully from Naxos
to break at the red palace in Mycenae   480
Hearts excised, torn to pieces
Coral red tree of aerated blood –

A pyre reeks on the beach!
A man stands there with a heart in his hand!
He squeezes it:
Quick! Have you other lives?
The voice that cries from the tree's bark
at the axe-bite
speaking at the point of being cut down
The kid sucks at the breast of the fauna   490
or the unicorn seeking refuge

Ut dulcis flos filia
breviter frunita anima
ut narcissus, ut rosa.
Tene me ne fugia

Καταχδονίοις θεοῖς
Calytyce Pupia.
Tene me quia fugi

Dis Manibus Sacrum
Nimphydia miserina
vixit anno uno
mensibus VIII
diebus XX
noctu una
orabus IIII.
Tene me quia fugi

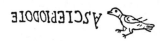

O nefas quan floridos
cito mors eripis annos
Tene me ne fugia
Tene me ne fugia

Cogitato te hominesse   Serpent and star
et scito: moriendust
Vale

Vos superi   A Dutch door
bene facite   with iron rings
diu vivite
et venite!

Tene me ne fugia

in the virgin's lap
O purity, purity!

Fire song

O firerush and glow spray
Glow rustle fire spray
Flames and these dancing
fire-mills shifting
obscure signals
significant glances
blinking red beacons   500
Tornadoes that pluck
flames like locks of hair
tongues that lick
spires and towers –

Glow rush fire spray
Fire rush glow spray
Fire mills seeing
Fire dogs peeing
on fire-trees
Devils that fly on ladders   510
high above the onlookers
unconscious of the fire's threats
those who have beshatten

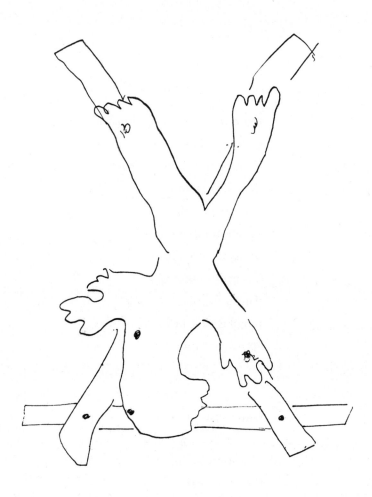

us in the year of years
How have they seen fit
to see fire? Fire that endures
fire that swinks and sweats?

They see it as grisly
but it is heavenly
Hell, it is heavenly –   520
Certainly the fire is grisly
but truly truly
Hell where the others live
is the sad
world of the burnt-out –
Shit!

Fire rush and glow spray
Glow rush and fire spray
Flames and those circling
windmills signalling   530
fire glances signifying
lightings splitting
network of golden branches
on the retina
Fire through every pore
Skin gleaming bleeding
gold –

Sidereus
    Piropus
        Inpulsator
            Igneus
                META

Exsuperus
    Omnipotens
        Animator
            Aquila

Venator
    Arenarius
        Noctivagus
            Augur

Oceanus
    Castalius
        Tiberis
          Imber

No, let me be cast into the sea
without cannonball, without banner
slowly disintegrate integrate   540
No, just be burnt to ashes
and cast into the sea
That way shall I drown also in the air
The smoke shall have carried me over lands
The lightest element of me rest in the stratosphere
The average part of me lie as manure
in every man's garden
while the heaviest shall sink to the bottom   ·
and melt into the midpoint of all things
and the subtle part shall fly like spores   550
to kindle new life. Enfin c'en est fait,
La Brinvilliers est en l'air
de sorte que nous la respirerons!

No, let me live
even if it be below humanity
The least vestige of life is better than this frightfulness
whatever it is, and *that* nobody knows!

Γοργώ

Be damned to you
damned and tabu, that is, sacred
May you bide alone 560
Unblest like
the octopus in the deeps
the rapacious
the hungering
the one whose eyes go hungering
devouring

That white thing on the headland, say
the shimmering on the headland, say
whiteness in my eye
floating along the horizon 570
The white thing on the headland
its seeming a gull, say
on the headland, white white –
its seeming
Eleoũsa, ringing

Wherefrom,

Mother –

Yes, wherefrom have you borne me

wherefrom have you borne me

my hunger is my strength   580

my evil is my good

all of us floating here

floating along

O these carcasses that float

that head into the reeds

but rock uncertainly outside

Uncertainly rocking

wavesplash windspray

windrush wavespray

Waves and flames
Flames that fused
earth and air to wholeness
O purity purity!
All that never came to be
All that led to nullity –
Waves that glittered
Waves of which I used to think:
You are a way to the world
As far as desire you bear us

But it never begins –   600

—————

Shy dodging in the hedge
twilight, spring, a sweet thrush
He has lost his singing
and can only cry warning –

—————

The sun in perpetual sunset
Fire-clouds shifting flaunting
beyond reach burning images
O holy clouds! –

—————

A desolate wind from the city

Marche   and nearer, further   610
funèbre   the bells' burden, swinging fifths
– it's burning! it's burning! –
of the dead march:
We lived – just then!
We live now not at all,
we shall live – for the first time!
A flighty moment –
and now the devil is in the belfry
he who robbed us of our future,
robbed us of our past   620
The red fever-ball which makes me reel
rolls, tumbles over, rushes
Fever that slowly
makes a vault of me, rushing
dizzying
rolls me, over me,
dizzy – – –
– la boule rouge qui bouge et roule –
time arrested, aroused...
And over again...   630
And over again...

And once again the banal development
in slow procession, slowly borne
with teardrenched trembling maidenhair
the sorrow of women, the whitest lilies:
Sob, sob, sob!
You black birds:
You were singing just then!
You are not singing now,
you shall sing – for the first time!   640
O saisons, ô châteaux!
O willows on the banks, O Babylon!
Happy he who taketh thy little ones
and dasheth them against the stones!

Leavetaking   But you are not at all the avenger
at once one of the many

and one of the few:
Neither nominated nor nominator
neither numerator
or common denominator: 650
Your formula is the stroke between
seldom and never,
you have it written on your forehead:
The same one and still another
Your innocence is greatest in disgrace
– then it emerges, indestructible –
your voice is at its most clearly audible
while you are silent...The journey
you make as a passenger
not as a dispatcher 660
potent precisely in your impotence
certain in your uncertainty!
For neither as station-master nor as lineman
do you have anything to do with
this, the parallel
train tracks' infinity.

The wheels spin and spin,
fools stand and cheer and grin
at every station.
The train goes further 670
without arriving at milder
zones.

The sun each moment nailed
time arrested and flailed
without circumference becoming center,
without black becoming white...

Puzzle, puzzle and puzzle
till you are puzzled double
by both the old and new,
both one and two.   680
Then all your waiting is past:
something grey beside you at last,
it finally stands there – you!

Same apple
Thuds dully, bumps, lies dumb.

Front gable clock
(face altered by stroke)

When the h, who the hu, how the hue,
where the huer?

Rāgas and Rāginis
(slowly circling)

690

A genius
Je suis le Roquefort...

Disabled emanations
(dancing)

Apple, papple, barries, charries
one and two, one and two:
out goes y-o-u...

Same genius
Je suis le Brie etc.

700

Ibn el-Arabi

Labbayka!

The thrush
(heraldic bird; silent, immobile,
with its beak up)

— — — — —

Be still my child, there is nothing
all is as you see: forest, smoke and the flight of the railroad tracks.
Somewhere far away in a distant land
there is a bluer sky, a wall with roses
or a palmtree and a warmer wind —   710
and that is all.

— — — — —

— I left Oehlreick
and there was deep water in the road
but at one side it was shallow, a pathway —
I went to the side,

thought I should not walk in the deep water

– thought a rocket struck loose up across me,

that sprayed a shower of sparks of beautiful fire:

love for the sublime.

Perhaps. 720

From the past's rarely
through now's midway barely
to the future's still less
still more rarely

Vale Viator!

PART III
Essay reviews

Goethe in English

MICHAEL HAMBURGER

There are many reasons for the failure of Goethe's work to establish itself in the awareness of a large English-speaking public even to the degree that Büchner's work, say, or Rilke's, or Kafka's has done in this century. The lack of canonical translations, comparable in durability to the Schlegel–Tieck Shakespeare versions, is a symptom rather than a cause. It points not only to the special difficulty of translating Goethe but to fundamental differences in kind between even his major works and the plays of Shakespeare. For all his classical affinities and his aspirations to classical status, Goethe was modern enough, and rash enough, to describe his *oeuvre* as 'fragments of a great confession' – in an auto-biographical context, admittedly, but with the result that the significance of this *oeuvre* has too often been looked for not where it ought to lie, within the confines of each work, but in the history and entelechy of his person; and that person, like the totality of his productions, was elusively protean, with a range that can be appreciated only by prolonged study. Hence T. S. Eliot's notorious misjudgement of Goethe as one who 'dabbled both in philosophy and poetry and made no great success of either' – the misjudgement of a critic who believed in the impersonality of art. Hence, too, my recollections of being 'taught' Goethe's poems, in Professor Boyd's Blackwell edition, as though their primary function and *raison d'être* had been to document Goethe's successive love affairs. How unlike Shakespeare, of whose person we know so little, and need to know even less!

To a considerable extent the difference is one of approach and interpretation; but not entirely. Even a reader wholly unacquainted with Goethe scholarship and the long history of his work on the two parts of *Faust* would have to be insensitive not to be conscious of the stylistic discrepancy between those passages of Part I going back to the *Urfaust*

273

and those – like the *Zueignung, Vorspiel, Walpurgisnacht* and *Walpurg-isnachtstraum* – that were added at later periods on grounds that have less to do with their literary or dramatic effectiveness than with Goethe's personal development and changing attitudes to the original conception. In other words, those later additions take the risk of breaking the unity of the tragic work that Goethe associated with his *Sturm und Drang* phase, for the sake of a larger and heightened unity not fully attained or communicable except in relation to the sequel, Part II; or, if we prefer, in relation to Goethe's personal development and growing intellectual scope.

A translator intent on rendering the complete text of Part I – as Randall Jarrell[1] did, unlike MacNeice and Stahl before him – has to bridge that discrepancy, as well as the distances, formidable enough, between two eras, two languages, two cultural and historical complexes. (A cursory collation with the German text revealed the omission of only one line in Jarrell's version.) MacNeice had the sheer metrical skill undoubtedly needed for these intricate transpositions. Jarrell, his widow tells us in an essay appended to the translation, also had the devotion to Goethe's work that should have qualified him for the most exacting demand of all, to recapture the unprecedented, rhapsodic freedom of the original, a freedom not only of dramatic structure but of rhythmic modulation from speech to speech, sometimes from line to line. It is the expressive rightness of the modulations that holds the work together, despite its variety and range. If we want a counterpart of that range in the English poetry of Goethe's time, we cannot find it in the work of any one poet; that is why a translator, too, needs to combine the capacities of both Shelley and Byron, but also of Burns, Crabbe and even Landor, with a Wordsworthian directness thrown in.

Jarrell seems to have been after such freedom when he decided that 'anything that wants to rhyme can'. At the same time, though, he chose what Mrs Jarrell calls 'metered verse' – as though the rhythmically irregular *Knittelvers* (not to mention the smoothly formal octets of the *Zueignung*) did not depend on rhyme to be verse at all. For all the good those 'metres' do Jarrell's version he might just as well have opted for honest prose, as Barker Fairley did in his recent translation. His other possibilities were to master Goethe's prosody, adapting it very closely, or to devise verse forms that do not look or sound like Goethe's verse, but render its movement, its urgency and its pungency. According to his widow, again, 'the tone and language he used are neither imitation German nor imitation English, but plain English intended for readers and playgoers'. Such plain English would still have had to be either good prose or good verse; and it would have had to be capable of conveying the shifting modes of the original, from cynical coarseness or epigrammatic acerbity to the starkest pathos and the most delicate lyricism. Jarrell's version does maintain an even, rather neutral, plainness that could be acceptable to readers or audiences with no expectations based on the original text; and even that is a respectable achievement. Yet it fails in lyrical passages like the *Chor der Engel*, as in the classical virtuosity of the Dedication and Prologue. Jarrell's *Song of the Rat* and *Song of the Flea* are much more successful (with a corresponding resort to rhyme). His *King in Thule* is spoilt by the last stanza, as are the *Walpurgis Night's Dream* and Robert Lowell's version, contributed to Jarrell's unfinished text, of Gretchen's spinning song, where the concluding 'gone' is not only elliptically ambiguous but out of key with the naive directness of the rest.

On the level of semantic faithfulness Randall Jarrell's version is generally reliable, though 'the point that bans me' (p. 73) is not an accurate, or intelligible, rendering of 'die Spitze, die mich bannte'. A hardly understandable squeamishness may be responsible for the rendering of 'Und Kopf und H–' as 'head and tail' (p. 184). It is on the level of diction and vocabulary that Jarrell ought to have taken greater liberties than he did. His diction can be as colloquial and slangy as MacNeice's in places, but rarely with MacNeice's zest, where zest is called for. Elsewhere, and especially over the least earthy passages, Jarrell can lapse into lifeless archaism, like 'man's weal, man's woe' (p. 85).

As far as playgoers are concerned, Jarrell would have been wise to omit those scenes, like the *Walpurgisnachtstraum*, which belong to the larger framework of the complete and definitive text, since most of the philosophical and satirical allusions would be lost, in any case, on an audience not familiar with both parts of the play. That applies to the majority of potential readers also, given the lack in this book of elucidatory comment and notes.

If one may still posit the existence of a 'common', general or educated reader – and that has become very doubtful – what he or she badly needs in the English-speaking world is a substantial selection from Goethe's works of all periods, with generous introductions and commentaries that would enable him or her to trace the threads – not only biographical – linking one phase, one area of Goethe's wide concerns, to another. It is shocking to reflect that no such edition of Goethe's work in English is available – only necessarily inadequate one-volume compilations like *The Essential Goethe* or Stephen Spender's paperback *Great Writings of Goethe*, together with an unending succession of separate translations that partly replace, or displace, partly duplicate their predecessors, but never create a solid basis for an understanding of Goethe's work, and biographical or critical studies that refer to works not even available in translation. Present conditions, true, are anything but favourable to an ambitious enterprise of that kind; but subsidies are available for countless projects neither as central nor as long overdue.

David Luke's new verse translation of Goethe's *Römische Elegien*[2] could serve as a model for such an edition, for not only his introduction and notes but the translation itself show his grasp of what a contemporary English reader needs to know in order to respond to this particular work. In Goethe's case at least, some knowledge of the genesis of a work may have to be assumed before that work can be liberated from its biographical and historical occasion. David Luke provides the knowledge, without overrating its relevance, and is then free to make his version both true to the spirit of his text and consistently lively. Since he appreciates the indivisibility of meaning and form in poetry, he remains close to Goethe's adaptation of classical elegiac metre, though without pedantry, and without forgetting the differences between the two languages and the three poetic traditions, including the Latin, that converge and diverge in his field. With a single exception,

> Fetching water, and Mars snatched her up into his arms (II, 16)

his accentual elegiacs flow smoothly and strongly, even to an ear unaccustomed to caesuras or incapable of assimilating more than two unaccented syllables between stresses.

Luke's diction strikes a happy balance between classical decorum and the colloquial, often ironizing, informalities of the original. His vernacular can be brilliantly appropriate, as in the lines:

> If one must choose between mist of the north and a host of
> Hard-working southern fleas, give me fleas any day! (XV, 3–4)

There are many such felicities, and only one line that jolted this reviewer for reasons of style or diction, yet might not have done if the German text did not face the translation. In rendering

> Fehlet am Wagen ihr nicht, der nach der Oper sie bringt

as

> Drives to the opera now, fetched in a smart-looking coach

Luke has introduced an intimation of showiness that strikes a wrong note, sacrificing plain statement, if not decorum, either to colloquialism or the demands of the metre; but that is a small flaw in a sensitive, highly intelligent and resourceful translation.

As in his Penguin selection of Goethe's poems with prose translations, Luke has gone out of his way to do justice to Goethe's full range; in this case, by reminding his readers that these poems began as Goethe's *Erotica Romana*, and by including the usually banned elegy *XIV a*. That, too, is a step in the right direction, towards a Goethe not only unexpurgated but stripped of all solemnities other than his own.

NOTES

1 *Goethe's Faust. Part I.* An English translation by Randall Jarrell (Faber, 1978).
2 *Goethe's Roman Elegies*, translated by David Luke (London, 1978).

Reason and ritual in Greek tragedy
On René Girard, *Violence and the Sacred* and Marcel Detienne, *The Gardens of Adonis*

RICHARD GORDON

On 8 September 1978 *Le Monde* ran an *entretien* with René Girard in consequence of the publication in France of his latest book, *Des choses cachées depuis la fondation du monde* (1978). That book, and the recent publication of *To Double Business Bound: Essays on Literature, Mimesis and Anthropology* (Johns Hopkins University Press), confirm Girard's ambition to turn literary criticism into cultural analysis. The semioticians, of course, have a similar ambition, but Girard will have none of that, as he will have no trendy Marxism: his cultural pessimism feeds on grander revelations from the late Romantics, from nineteenth-century anthropology and Freud himself. The disinterested reader of his remarks to Christian Delacompagne in *Le Monde*, noting their engaging blend of pretentiousness and vacuity, may well wonder what all the fuss is about. But Girard is a sign of the times. Hired, as it were, by the bad conscience of atheism, he has embarked on a predictable *bricolage* designed to block up gaps in a singularly inadequate symbolic set. Religion is no longer simply bosh, but a naive protection against the permanent threat of intestine violence. Without religion, we are permitted to perceive that truth, but find ourselves in a crisis, forced to choose between 'absolute violence' and its 'absolute renunciation'. The *bricolage* consists in a ransacking of 'great literature', anthropology, psychology and even theology so as to reveal this tremendous secret, a revelation which itself commits us to an existential choice.

The fortuitous appearance of this English translation of Girard's earlier presentation of his theses (published in Paris in 1972) in the midst

* René N. Girard, *Violence and the Sacred* (*La Violence et le sacré*), translated by Patrick Gregory (Johns Hopkins University Press, Baltimore and London, 1977). Marcel Detienne, *The Gardens of Adonis* (*Les Jardins d'Adonis*), translated by Janet Lloyd (Harvester Press, Hassocks, Sussex, 1977).

of the current debate makes a critical examination of his view of religion opportune. And although I am mainly concerned with his view of Greek tragedy, which has a central place in the argument, I begin with his views about primitive religion. And since my view of Greek tragedy is partly indebted to the group of French scholars, in the Centre de Recherches Comparées sur les Sociétés Anciennes in Paris, to which Marcel Detienne belongs, a review of his *Gardens of Adonis* may serve better than anything else to sharpen the point against Girard.

Before I outline Girard's thesis, two points are worth making, one briefly, the second at greater length. The first concerns 'great literature'. Inasmuch as a theory of religion simultaneously involves a theory of cultural crisis, the insights of greater writers have for him a privileged position – a position he is prepared to assert with some vehemence:

Le fait que certains rois sont sacrifiés et que certains victimes se voient traitées de façon 'royale' ne constitue qu'une aimable curiosité, un paradoxe amusant, mais dont il faut laisser le méditation aux esprits brillants et legers, tel William Shakespeare sagement enfermé dans quelque ghetto littéraire, sous la garde des dociles oncles Tom de la critique qui répètent tous en choeur, chaque matin, que la science c'est bien beau mais que la littérature c'est mieux encore parce que ça n'a absolument rien à voir avec la réalité.[1]

(p. 418F)

In itself, of course, such a view is unexceptionable, so long as the great writers indeed have the perceptions attributed them – a problem we shall return to later.

Beyond great imaginative writers, however, Girard has been most heavily influenced by three men, all of the late nineteenth and early twentieth century. One, of course, is Sir James Frazer, who, wiser than he knew when he likened himself to a chameleon,[2] has become a kind of universal father, 'notre maître à tous'.[3] The debts go deeper than Girard's guarded acknowledgement of Frazer's prodigious industry and intuitive good sense might suggest (pp. 123, 317). In spite of many differences in both drift and self-confidence, Girard appears almost as the remythologist of Frazer's remythologies – perhaps incvitably in a book whose ambition is to uncover the hidden origins of primitive religion.[4] For each, primitive culture occupies a timeless space, con-demned to the wheel of ritual re-enactment of aboriginal occurrences. The development of a legal system plays for Girard much the same role that 'science' played for Frazer in distinguishing 'primitive' from 'civilized'.[5] They share an effective belief in Tylorian 'survivals' which makes it possible for them both to use information derived from contemporary primitive peoples (Girard uses a good deal of contemporary ethnography) in order to speculate upon the remoter practices of all mankind.[6] Although Girard remarks adversely at one point on Frazer's rationalism, he shares with him a rationalist assumption that social institutions, and above all religion as a set of ritual practices, 'have been originated to function as they do',[7] or at any rate as he claims they do.

More telling perhaps than any of these damaging methodological assumptions is Girard's curious imaginative dependence upon Frazer, a dependence which itself links Girard with so many other modernist pessimists.[8] Some of the high dramatic moments of *The Golden Bough*, the innocent scapegoat (*The Scapegoat*, pp. 252ff), the tragic cycle of royal murder (*The Dying God*, chapter 2), the Aztec sacrifice (*The Scapegoat*, chapter 7), provide the very heart of Girard's view of religion. Both see a fundamental relation between their concern with religion and a modern cultural crisis; a tremulous sharing of John's apocalyptic mantle produces in Frazer: 'We appear to be standing on a volcano which may at any moment break out into smoke and fire to spread ruin and devastation among the gardens and palaces of ancient culture wrought so laboriously by the hands of many generations',[9] and in Girard: 'In the evolution from ritual to secular institutions men gradually draw away from violence and eventually lose sight of it; but an actual break with violence never takes place. That is why violence can always stage a stunning, catastrophic comeback' (p. 307).[10] Both believe that modern society is sapped by superstition and arrogance (though of different kinds), but that true insight into primitive secrets is only possible in the modern world. And although their conception and comprehension of violence are very different, they have each a characteristic image of suffering – one might almost say that what the Priest-King of Nemi was to Frazer, Oedipus, the hero of Sophocles' play, is to Girard.[11]

But the choice of characteristic image also marks a distance. 'Oedipus' signifies an explicit debt not to the Freudians, whom Girard repeatedly castigates with pertinence,[12] but to a Derridian Freud, always most interesting where he seems least sure. By a deliberate *jeu d'esprit*, the most generally condemned of Freud's works, *Totem and Taboo*, is held to anticipate many of Girard's choice themes: the affectivity of religious practice (p. 196), the 'strange duality of sacrificial custom' – its quality as 'a transgression both culpable and obligatory' (p. 196), the need for unanimous participation in the rites (p. 198). Of course all these themes are to be found in Freud because they are also to be found in Wundt, Robertson Smith and Frazer, all of whom believed, with Girard, that sacrifice plays the same role in all primitive religions and must therefore be traced back to identical origins.[13] But Freud himself contributes two further theses: that to be true, a genetic account of religious ritual must be grounded in a real and historical act or acts; and that religious acts are acts of collective pathological emotion. An adequate theory of the origin of religion is to be found in the psychic conflict between desire and authority. The same fundamental passions exercise all human beings, who are forced to replicate aboriginal occurrences in spite of the fact that human societies betray the most astonishing detailed differences in their other cultural products and styles. After all, if we look high enough, the sky above is an undifferentiated blue.

This emphasis upon the collective nature of primitive religion links Girard's interest in Freud to the third of his Modern Masters, Durkheim. Again the debt is explicit, and again Girard's claimed role is that of articulator of the Master's valid insights (pp. 306–7). This Durkheim, though, is not the Durkheim interested in cosmology and classification, nor even the Durkheim who sundered the sacred from the profane, but Durkheim the symbolist, who argued that the vital issues of collective life are projected into symbols around which, and through which, rules and values are both generated and confirmed.[14] For the symbolist, religious actions are always other than the actors believe them to be. The actors' own statements about their intentions must be interpreted by reference to statements made by the sociologist about the absolute demands of an hypostatized society. Without this common factor, we are told, cross-cultural comparison and generalization would be impossible. Religious behaviour 'cannot be based upon an illusion'; divinity is an illusion, but society is not; so all religious actions and statements must be referred to the latter. This fallacious argument is termed by the Durkheimians 'taking religion seriously'.[15] And no one takes religion more seriously than Girard.

With these points in mind, let us turn to Girard's thesis in *Violence and the Sacred*, although much of what he says will be familiar to those who have read his peculiar little book on Dostoevski or his *Mensonge romantique et vérité romanesque*.[16]

Before religion was cultural crisis; and before crisis was social order. That primitive order is best understood as a melody, a system of differences commanded by a single differentiating principle, that of non-reciprocity. In this Genesis, the Garden of Eden is the time before the birth of Hegelian mimesis and violence, its chief mourner Ulysses in *Troilus and Cressida*, 'O when Degree is shaked...'. The place of the Fall is taken by the appearance of Violence, by which Girard means not simply crime, or even vendetta, but the destruction of the differences between individuals and so of their identity. To become human involves imitation of another human being, which in turn involves competition for that other's object(s) of desire. Mimesis coupled with desire leads automatically to conflict. The end of that conflict, as it spreads, is the subjective cancellation of all differences between the antagonists, by means of a process (pp. 159–61) which is notably unclear. They become 'doubles'. This seems to be simultaneously in the nature of things yet also 'wrong'. When this process is reduplicated throughout a society, a situation is created in which all violence is polarized into an hallucinatory vision of evil which is arbitrarily projected upon a single human victim, *le victime émissaire*, the arbitrariness of the choice reflecting the arbitrariness of the objects of desire. In the beginning, apparently in all societies which knew or know sacrifice, this unfortunate was pulled to pieces. The origin of sacrifice lies in this literal and historical *sparagmos*.

The reaffirmation of Degree obtained by this cathartic experience had such an effect that a series of replications, both literal and metonymic, were developed as the most satisfactory device to avoid a repetition of the original conflict – scapegoat rituals, human sacrifice, animal sacrifice: the eating of the flesh of such victims is to be understood as the 'devouring' of human violence. Such victims must be socially marginal in order to maintain the delicate fiction by which religion clouds the collective memory of what truly happened. The whole of religion derives ultimately from these substitutions, rituals of all kinds, myth, festival, and a great deal besides. Religion then is an essentially conservative social institution, a means of negating change, which is always seen as threatening Degree.[17] In the long run, law puts an end to the necessity for this mystification, which ultimately withers away; but not to human self-delusion about violence. Ours is an age without religion, but also without Degree. Our individualism is false, our intellectuals purblind. As Artaud, Thomas Mann and Bergman have seen, our culture is bubonic.

'Old ffreindes are best: King James used to call for his old shoes, they were easiest for his ffeet.' So too, Girard grounds his cultural pessimism, so fashionable now as to be an academic pastime, in old theories about religion. And, at least in the French version (Patrick Gregory's translation is unconscionably dull), he does so with an intelligence and panache that win admiration. But intelligence and panache are not enough. To quote another of John Seldon's witty observations: 'All confesse there never was a more learned Clergie. no man taxes them with ignorance, but to talke of that is like ye fellow yt was A great wencher, he wished God would forgive him his Lechery and lay usury to his charge. The Clergie have worse faults.'

In what follows, I discuss briefly a number of the most important failings of Girard's theory. As criticisms, they imply, but only imply, a very different series of approaches to religion, which I have no space to elaborate but which seem to me much closer to the spirit of Detienne's inquiry than to that of Girard's.

1. Although Girard gains some advantage over other Durkheimians by employing an explicit psychological theory, he cannot, and indeed scarcely attempts to, show that the pattern of human competitive response perfectly fictioned in Dostoevski's *The Double* (1846) is universal rather than the effective creation of a particular historical moment. The attempt to use Greek tragedy for that purpose, must, as we shall see, be one of the most tendentious parts of the book (pp. 47–63, 69–78). Like so much else, we have to take it on trust, without there being any particular reason for doing so. The complaint that social change threatens traditional distinctions (read privileges) is as old as Odysseus' attack upon Thersites, or even Hammurabi's Law Code, and cannot be elevated into a philosophy of existence; any more than Heidegger's notion of violence can be turned into sociological analysis.[18] The evident philosophical problem in uniting 'phenomenological' violence with actual deeds of violence is not solved at all by Girard's endlessly ambiguous handling of the term 'violence'. And even if we take the word in a non-psychological sense, as he seems to in the first part of the book, it is by no means evident that it is the intolerable fear of internal violence that works the engine of religious substitution. Rather, so long as violence of a certain kind is deemed 'normal' it may be entirely tolerable – even necessary to a social system. The backward communities of Corsica still practise a virulent form of vendetta founded upon the notion of honour. To die in one's bed is dishonourable; and since one of the rules is that women are not directly involved in the exchange of deaths, the economic life of the communities can proceed relatively undamaged by the men's preoccupation with killing each other. In other words, permitted violence – and there is no *a priori* limitation upon its intensity – may be a form of meaning. Doubt and anxiety arise only when the boundary between permitted and illicit violence is threatened, as often in sixteenth-century urban or sub-urban witchcraft cases in Europe, doubts which provoked a series of reinterpretations of witchcraft itself, first among lawyers and doctors, more gradually among philosophers and divines.

2. We may use the case of witchcraft to make a wider point about social rules. In one form or another, witchcraft is found all over the world, though not of course in every society. But almost invariably, it is associated with particular forms of physical and moral deviance, such as red eyes, squinting, staring, ugliness, deformity, excessive beauty, excessive prosperity, extreme poverty, quarrelsomeness, excessive friendliness, old age, marginality of many kinds. Accusations are not confined to people who possess such characteristics, but almost all societies pattern their view of the 'everyday' witch upon quite explicit infringements of norms. At one level, the existence of such stereotypes negatively sanctions a multiplicity of possible deviations; at another, the existence of such deviants provides a crucial linkage between what we would call the 'natural world' and the social order, thus providing explanations for selected instances of 'disorder'. If there is any 'primitive' institution intimately connected with violence, it must be witchcraft – which Girard never once mentions. And the mass of rules which surround both the exercise and the experience of such evil power, to say nothing of its frequently casual nature, is surely sufficient reason to deny both Girard's thesis of 'mystification' and his appeal to affectivity as the crux of religious action. Fear of witchcraft does not lead to 'irrational' action, as the rules betray: the nearest one gets to mass hysteria in relation to witchcraft are the so-called 'witch-finding movements' since the 1920s in Africa, which are a response to colonial intrusion and the legal abolition of witchcraft.

Girard pays the price, then, for picking up that side of the false dichotomy between emotion and intellect which Lévi-Strauss left him; and under the guise of playing fair with the savage, returns to that comforting nineteenth-century evolutionism which rocked the primitive in the bosom of passion.

3. By a curious, if not uncommon, *petitio principii*, Girard's entire argument takes it as unarguably obvious that the heart, and therefore the origin, of religion is to be found in the practice of sacrifice. The unstated organic metaphor glares; and it is instructive that there is not a single archaeological reference in the book.[19] But then, contemporary primitives are a sort of fossil... That sacrifice might be more profitably considered a member of a wider class of offerings, though important because of its employment of a living mediator; that the rules for such a wider class of offerings may be related to the rules for redistributive economic activity; that most ritual activity may be 'pragmatic' and not cathartic; that we need a dynamic rather than an essentially static model for religious activity, which might involve reference to cognitive

structures beyond – none of this, the familiar baggage of most current social anthropology, has any interest for Girard. 'Generations of modern intellectuals, insofar as they were not atheists – that is, fools who pretended to know what no man can know – have been taught by Kierkegaard, Dostoevski, Nietzsche, and their countless followers inside and outside the existentialist camp, to find religious and theological questions "interesting".'[20] Impeccably modern for once, Girard neatly inverts the late-Victorian fascination with the heart of darkness. Without sacrifice there could be no civilization, without ritual death there could only have been hatred. Gratuitous death made everything possible. The Spanish bull-fight, so dear to French intellectuals of the thirties and forties (Girard has many links with Bataille), has finally made it to the centre of things. More peripheral and less organic minds might, however, prefer to sketch a theory of sacrifice from some such proposition as this:

In traditional Kwakiutl belief the animal skin memorialized a creature that had allowed itself to be killed in fulfilment of a compact . . ., as among Eskimos, for reciprocal benefits, which would sustain the permanent circulation of life: The animals sustained mankind; mankind would sustain them. From this point of view, which is not merely that of the Kwakiutl, but of most American Indians, the animal pelt could be no mere trophy of a killed beast, and its circulation could not serve the narrow interests of men alone. The logic of a doctrine of reciprocal relations, not to mention of primordial identities between men and animals, dictates the assumption that the animal skins and other valuables are also represented as forces in the system of circulation. Exchange involves not men alone, but also the beings represented by the so-called 'currency' of exchange.[21]

4. Girard's commitment to a univocal geneticism leads him, in company with his older models, into a further difficulty. Blankly unhistorical, he is forced either to deny change (primitives oscillate between the extremes of post-cathartic *tristitia* and 'sacrificial crisis') or to evaluate it, in this case dystopically. To put the problem in the mildest way, there must be something odd about a theory of religion which has no evident interest in, or capacity to account for, universalist and salvationist religious activity, and can only conceive of them as degenerative (they think too much?). There must also be something wrong with a theory which claims to account for the astonishing variety of religious practices over the world by feebly referring to their common failure to succeed in an alleged common purpose – the recapturing of an original act of generative unanimity (p. 302). By explaining a set of religious practices entirely outside the framework of expressed intentions and implicit evocations within which it has meaning for its believers, we have

evidently succeeded only in showing nothing but that we are different from them and like to think ourselves cleverer.

Girard constantly claims that he is not a reductionist. But it will be evident that his very notion of what an explanation of religion would look like is itself utterly reductionist. For geneticism is not history; and functionalism nothing but a metaphor in drag: the tired props that sustain so much cultural 'analysis' will not take one far in the understanding of something difficult like religion. A properly historical understanding of religious practice must begin with competent ethnography, and link a discourse about power with one about cognitive categories. Both discourses, in any continuing society, are without closure; any one moment represents an historical development within each discourse, at least part of which can in principle be traced by means of linguistic analysis, informants' statements, actual relationships, the shape of cultural borrowing. Whether, between this kind of theoretical statement and the multiplicity of actual religious institutions and practices, there lies a 'middle level' of the kind represented by Girard's work seems to me highly problematical; and certainly not to be taken for granted. And if such a level exists, it would not look like *Violence and the Sacred*.

5. The notion of religious 'deviance' is now commonplace in ethnography.[22] But Girard has no place for it in his scheme of things. For him, all rituals are 'straight' (and equally deluded). He relates them hierarchically in a pedigree: first human sacrifice, then animal *sparagmos*, then ritualized animal sacrifice, then degeneration into festivals or anti-festivals. Of course all this is straight out of the nineteenth century, based on the unavowed evolutionary principle 'oddest: earliest', and we do not need to take it very seriously. But one of Girard's principal props, quoted by him from Freud's quotation of Robertson Smith's quotation of a very poor seventeenth-century edition,[23] is the description by St Nilus the Elder of a pre-dawn sacrifice and *sparagmos* of a camel by the Arabs of the desert between the Red Sea and Arabia proper, as practised in the fourth century A.D. Robertson Smith, Freud and Girard have all found in this account precious illumination concerning the true and original nature of sacrifice. It is particularly useful to Freud and Girard because Robertson Smith's inventive translation removed it from what little context Nilus gave it, and neither felt it necessary to do any research upon pre-Islamic Arabian religion. According to St Nilus, a pure white camel was forced onto its knees, while the participants walked round it three times chanting a hymn to the Morning Star. While they were still

chanting, one of the chieftains or a respected priest cut the camel's *tenon* (which usually means the hock) and drank the blood. The rest of the men (women were excluded from participation in most rites) rushed forward and devoured the raw flesh they hacked off with their swords. For Girard, of course, this camel is merely a substitute for a man,[24] just as the whole sacrifice is just a re-enactment of an aboriginal mob-murder: 'In the Sinai sacrifice the camel is bound like a criminal and the crowd is armed; in the Dionysiac *diasparagmos* the victim is not bound and the attackers have no weapons. But two constants remain: the crowd and the mad rush at the victim' (p. 199).[25] Now one of the points noted by S. A. Cook in his edition of Robertson Smith's *Lectures*[26] is that, at least in the Hebrew tradition, all sacrifices specifically eaten *with blood* involved animals strictly taboo in ordinary life – pig, dog, mouse, vermin in general. In other words, we have neither textual motive nor general reason to take the eating of raw flesh outside the context of other 'normal' rules for sacrifice and suppose it to be 'early'. It is simply that different modes of sacrifice can co-exist in different ritual contexts. We certainly may be confident, from other information about the Arabs which Girard did not trouble to discover, that in the fourth century A.D. this camel sacrifice was not 'normal'.[27] And Nilus provides several instructive details which Robertson Smith omitted: distinctions were made between hide, flesh and guts – they seem to have been tackled by different groups; and all trace of the victim had to have disappeared before the sun rose – Nilus stresses the efforts they had to make to consume the bones in time. And the key may be that this was a special sacrifice, undertaken, according to Nilus, if the preferred beautiful war-captives were not available for sacrifice. At any rate, if the Morning Star referred to is to be identified, as is most likely, with Al-'Ouzza, the ordinary camel-sacrifice to her involved the digging of a special pit, the *ghabghab*.[28]

To confirm that, of course, one would need far more detailed evidence than we are ever likely to possess about normal pre-Islamic Arab sacrificial codes – and alimentary codes, animal-classification codes, *espace religieux* besides. For it is precisely in such relationships that the 'meaning' of ritual for the actors is established. Girard's 'historical' thesis, derived from the compulsory evolutionism of the late nineteenth century, is in truth about as historical as the etymologies of Brugmann and the 'historical linguists', without being derived from a rigorous model. For the thesis is derived not from some chronological marking but from an *a priori* assumption that human sacrifice, because repugnant to developed sensibilities (in the ancient world as well as in the modern), must be earlier than animal sacrifice. The point about 'deviance' serves to suggest that we have rather to do with rules and goals: different goals demand different rules. To draw a schematic contrast, while 'normal' cult draws tighter the bonds of reciprocity and obligation, 'deviant' cult bursts them, temporarily shattering the usual rules and rearranging relationships. If we cannot imagine a human society without rules, we cannot imagine one without deviance.[29] From that perspective, Girard's 'history' is both gratuitous and without motivation.

As a theory of religion, then, Girard's book is like British Leyland: it is hard to produce the goods with antiquated machinery. It has the utterly predictable demerits of its pedigree; its tone of brilliant self-confidence is the fruit merely of wide reading with a closed mind. Like so much contemporary meta-writing, it has little, either of interest or profit, to offer us.

My narrower concern, however, is with Girard's theory of tragedy, and his reading of Greek tragedy in particular.[30] Rather like Camus,[31] he sees tragedy as the literary expression of a cultural pendulum-swing. The mythological 'moment', which corresponds to the preservation of distinctions and the effective suppression of violence, is incapable of tragic insight. The existence of tragedy is itself evidence of a renewal of the 'sacrifical crisis': 'if a tragic poet touches upon the violent reciprocity underlying all myths, it is because he perceives these myths in a context of weakening distinctions and growing violence' (p. 65 and cf. pp. 42ff). Such an insistence allows him to distance himself from Gilbert Murray, Jane Harrison and the other Cambridge ritualists, who thought that the structure of tragedy was itself based upon ritual (p. 95). But for Girard, tragedy is anti-mythical – precisely because it offers a first approach to the decipherment of the 'méconnaissance protectrice' (p. 375F = p. 271) of the true nature of the sacred which it is the function of both ritual and myth to effect (p. 244; cf. p. 64, 84). For that reason, Sophocles (p. 206), Shakespeare, and to a lesser degree Euripides are Girard's truest antecedents in the task of decoding the nature of religion.

In spite of its prescience, however, tragedy fails to penetrate to the heart of the violent secret: it is too close to the mystification of myth – its very performance 'constitutes a sort of rite, the shadowy similitude of the religious experience' (p. 290). Aristotelian *katharsis* is to be taken as the spectator's simultaneous (if eventual) rejection of the tragic hero as wholly 'other' (the sacrificial phenomenon), and his gratitude for the rules which protect him from reciprocal violence. 'Every true work of art...promotes prudence and discourages hubris' (pp. 291–2).[32] The central interest of tragedy, however, is its capacity to represent the process of the creation of the 'monstrous double', the point at which all social differentiation disappears (p. 292). As quasi-ritual tragedy merely perpetuates the frail balancing-act that is religion; as vision of the truth it can be wantonly destroyed by its host culture (in this case, presumably fourth-century Athens, p. 296).

Nothwithstanding Girard's increasingly expansive invocation of tragedy, on which Morris Weitz has surely said enough, this theory certainly looks as though it is rooted in an historical experience, and therefore escapes the obvious, and proper, strictures one would wish to make against ordinary essentialists theses. Nevertheless this is an odd version of history. The only evidence offered for a 'sacrificial crisis' in fifth-century Athens is the fact of tragedy itself – for it is the 'function' of great writers to discern such things. Pale history indeed, that discerns the *demonstrandum* by means of an *a priori* truth; paler still, in that we are offered a 'cultural' theory of tragedy which makes no attempt to link the uniquely public role of Athenian tragedy not only to the democracy but not even to the individual competition for honour by which the genre is stamped just as it subjects it to critical examination. But that is not the kind of involvement, or the kind of marginality, in relation to Athenian society that Girard has stomach for. The only permissible factors are myth, sacrifice and the scapegoat. And it is that delimitation of the inquiry that renders Girard's reading of Greek tragedy, hailed by Carl Rubino as 'unorthodox [but] consistently perceptive and never less than brilliant',[33] utterly superfluous, in that it renders, *per absurdum*, far more of that tragic drama opaque and 'unreadable' than it could ever hope to illuminate. 'Fine Witts destroy themselves with their owne plotts...; they comonly doe As the Ape that saw the Gunner putt bullets in the Canon & was pleas'd with it & hee would bee doeing soe to[o], att last hee putt himselfe into the peece, & so both Ape & Bullet were shott away together.'

In furthering his argument that tragedy restores 'violence to mythological themes' (p. 64), Girard uses four Athenian tragedies in particular.[34] In considering each of them in turn, and in mounting order of importance to his argument, I hope both to indicate a judgement of his 'reading' and to suggest the outlines of a truly 'cultural' account of fifth-century tragedy, one which deliberately abandons the usual paraphernalia of the literary criticism of tragedy in favour of an historical understanding that does not mouth the cant of universality.

It is obviously crucial to Girard's argument that he establish the existence, and characterize the quality, of the 'sacrificial crisis'. Scenes from Athenian tragedy constitute his major evidence. The crisis comes about, or rather, is in evidence, when the institutions of sacrifice and the 'differences' they maintain decay. An example of such decay is to be found, according to him, in Euripides' *Herakles* (pp. 39–41): 'the real subject of the play is the failure of a sacrifice, the act of sacrificial violence that suddenly *goes wrong*'. The tendentiousness of 'real subject' is obvious – no such simple synopsis of the play is possible, for it densely intertwines a whole series of tragic subjects (in the sense that they are repeatedly found to be discussed in Athenian tragedy): the nature of the distinction between friends and enemies, the ambiguity of violence, the proper placement of the 'hero' on the frontier between the divine and human worlds, the relation between human sense-making and 'reality' insofar as that is constituted by the divine order, the coherence of the traditionally clear distinction between *aretè* and *kakia*, etc. Against that we may set the pallid comment by Girard: 'Euripides' *Herakles* contains no tragic conflict, no debate between declared adversaries' (p. 39–40).

At any rate, the 'sacrificial crisis' is supposed to be betrayed first by Lycus's attempt to offer Herakles' wife Megara and his children as sacrificial victims. There is no supporting line reference; nor could there be one, for none exists. Megara and the children are gathered as suppliants at the altar of Zeus to escape Lycus's violence; Lycus, like a truly lawless tyrant, intends to ignore their right to divine protection by burning them to death (240–46), in order to protect himself from their vengeance in the future for his murder of Creon (165–9). Lycus allows Megara and the children into the palace to put on the clothes of death (329–32); after the first *stasimon*, they return 'wearing the garments of the dead' (442–3), and Megara breaks into her own, and her children's, death-lament – the breakage of code here (*others* are supposed to perform the task) meets Lycus's breakage of the suppliancy code.[35] And she begins with an utterly apposite and ironical metaphor taken from sacrifice: 'Who is the priest, who the disemboweller...? The victims here are ready to be led to Hades' (451–3). The image is evoked, of course, by the juxtaposition of the themes of death and an altar. The whole point lies in the unstated reference to the 'corrupted sacrifice' theme used most notably by Aeschylus in the *Agamemnon*.[36] The perversion of the privileged ritual means to collective *dikè* necessarily creates the reverse of *dikè*, *adikia*; to expose the perversion is itself a means to compel the gods to take notice. Megara's use of the image, in other words, rests upon the assumption that a divine, the traditional, order exists and will be effective in the long run against Lycus's impiety. Yet the play, as it continues, makes it equally explicit – though in a manner ignored by Girard – that such an order does not exist. For after Herakles has saved his wife and children, Euripides introduces on to the stage, for the privilege of the spectators alone, an extraordinary scene between Iris, one of the gods' messengers, and Lyssa, the goddess of madness. She is reluctant to harm Herakles – she knows he is innocent, just as the human beings know he is – but is compelled by Iris in a savage quip: 'Hera has not sent you down to show your sanity' (857), to drive him mad. So Herakles' killing of his children and his wife at the altar with his traditional 'culture-hero' weapons, the bow and the club, has nothing to do with the notion of sacrifice, as Girard would have it (p. 40); the killing has no 'ritualistic origins'. Rather, just as Herakles' ravings ironically recapitulate his past achievements,[37] so, inversely, this successful murder at the altar of suppliancy ironically doubles the unsuccessful murder by Lycus.[38] The crux, though, is not that Euripides has dimly perceived the 'sacrificial crisis', but that the gods have explicitly been shown to be other than everyone imagines them to be. The trouble lies not with men, but with the gods, as the dialogue between Theseus and Herakles at the end confirms – which constitutes itself an ironical commentary on the traditional reflections of the chorus in the second *stasimon* (655–72). Euripides combines a critique of traditional conceptions of divinity with an assertion of the possibility of true friendship between men. To accept Girard's reading is to ignore the substance of the play. No sacrifice has 'gone wrong': such sacrificial motifs as there are exist precisely because the audience knows the difference between true sacrifice and these murders: his denial of suppliancy defines Lycus's tyranny; her sending of Lyssa defines Hera's injustice.

A similar partiality marks Girard's use of his second example in this context, Sophocles' *Trachiniae*, another play about Herakles. In Euripides' play, Herakles is a true culture-hero; but here he is a brutal and sexually aggressive monster. To win back his love, his ageing wife, Deianeira, sends him a sacrificial robe smeared, as she thinks, with a 'love-philtre' given her by the centaur Nessus as he lay dying, killed by one of Herakles' poisoned arrows.[39] For Girard the fact that Herakles is killed by the poisoned robe, his killing of the messenger Lichas and Deianeira's suicide, evidence the violence that stems from a failed sacrifice – it is the heat of the sacred flames which activates the poison.

That much at least is true (765–71): the question is whether it proves Girard's point. I doubt it. At one level, the play is the enactment of the coming to pass of an oracle from Zeus at Dodona, which foretold Herakles' death – at this point in the turning of the years (155–74): it is then no coincidence that Herakles was sacrificing to Zeus at Kènaion (753), or that his first words are 'O Zeus' (983), or that Herakles' corpse is to be burned on mount Oeta where sacrifices are made to Zeus (1191–2), or that the play's last word is 'Zeus' (1278). The sacrifice at Kènaion does not fail: its 'true' purpose, in Zeus's plan, is to kill Herakles, as Herakles finally realizes – he knows what has to be done on Mount Oeta (1164–78). One of the play's central themes is that of revelation, therefore, a theme intimately related to that of light versus darkness; sometimes the light of day brings happy news (203–4) – albeit ambiguous; sometimes the power of the sun reveals hidden secrets (the tuft of wool impregnated with Nessus's poisoned blood burns in its heat, revealing to Deianeira the truth of what she has done: 672–718). In burning the wool, the sun reveals truth; homologously, the heat of the fire which causes the robe to tear at Herakles' flesh, the fire sacred to Zeus, reveals another truth, finally realized by Herakles: that this is the time for his own literal burning in another sanctuary of Zeus, Mount Oeta. It also reveals to him the working of reciprocity – of equal exchange: as he gave death to Nessus, so the dead Nessus gives death to him; as Eròs consumed him (354–5), so he is consumed by the gift of Eròs (441f., 577); as he destroyed the hearths of others, his own hearth gives him back death – gifts in this play are never what they seem. And likewise, the order of Zeus, which all this reveals, is not what it seems, but deeper, denser and more difficult than traditional piety comprehends.[40]

Having established the reality of the 'sacrificial crisis', Girard argues that it can only be resolved by the arbitrary selection of a surrogate victim; and he believes that Sophocles' *Oedipus Tyrannos* offers us insight into that braking mechanism (p. 67). Briefly, in what is essentially yet another variant upon a traditional critical theme in relation to this play, Girard argues that Thebes is suffering a 'sacrificial crisis' symbolized (and concealed) both by the parricide/incest and by the plague: both are understood to create equality where there should be difference (pp. 74–6). This crisis is enacted in the play by the scenes involving Oedipus, Creon and Teiresias, who are revealed as undifferentiable: 'Each of the protagonists believes that he can quell the violence; at the end each succumbs to it. All are drawn unwittingly into the structure of violent reciprocity – which they always think they are outside of...' (p. 69). In this conflict Oedipus is defeated – it could have been one of the others – and Creon and Teiresias succeed in deflecting the burden of guilt for the growing collective violence upon him (pp. 77–8). 'If the community is to be freed of all responsibility for its unhappy condition and the sacrificial crisis converted into a physical disorder, a plague, the crisis must first be stripped of its violence. Or rather, this violence must be deflected to some individual – in this case, Oedipus' (p. 77). Oedipus is therefore a true scapegoat, the arbitrarily chosen repository of climactic violent reciprocity, whose function is to provide the delicious ignorance of the truth about human violence which all primitive communities yearn for (p. 82).

All this seems to me not only inherently implausible but utterly wrong. Instructively, Girard bids us to ignore the second part of the play:

If we eliminate the testimony brought against Oedipus in the second half of the tragedy, then the conclusion of the myth, far from seeming a sudden lightning flash of the truth, striking down the guilty party and illuminating all the mortal participants, seems nothing more than the camouflaged victory of one version of the story over the other, the polemical version over its rival – the community's formal acceptance of Tiresias' and Creon's version of the story, thereafter held to be the true and universal version, the verity behind the myth itself. (p. 73)

No doubt we could all do some very beautiful criticism if we were free to rewrite our texts. Oracles, the old servant, the shepherd, Oedipus's own activity in uncovering his identity, all these are dispensable for Girard; Creon, attacked by Oedipus for conspiring against his throne, comes to have the 'same version' as Teiresias, who ultimately announces Oedipus's patricide and incest; Laius' act in disposing of his son is supposed to be one of 'anger' (p. 69). Violence there may be in the play, but the major violence is Girard's own against it. The heart of the matter, no doubt, is the refusal to distinguish between play and myth – strikingly attested by Girard when he tells us that it all really happened: 'The Thebans – religious believers – sought a cure for their ills in a formal acceptance of the myth, in making it the indisputable version of the events that had recently convulsed the city and in making it the charter for a new cultural order...' (p. 83). I would note only that the earliest version we know, in Homer (*Od.* 11. 271–80), specifically says that Oedipus did not leave Thebes but continued to rule there. It seems to me obvious that we cannot discuss 'the' myth, we can only discuss Sophocles' version of it. And what that version does is to explore a fundamental problem of Greek theodicy, the intelligibility of suffering.[41]

Sophocles contrives a situation in which one truth, the evident innocence of Oedipus, seems to be maintainable only at the cost of denying one of the central guarantors of the intelligibility of experience, oracles, and so in effect, the religious system itself. On the other hand, to insist upon the validity of the oracles, as Teiresias does, is in effect to deny what had, by the fifth century, come to be seen as a necessary aspect of the notion of guilt, namely intentionality. It is a fundamental part of the process of fifth-century law that a defendant be guilty or not guilty. But in this case act and intention are at variance: Oedipus was running away from his supposed parents in Corinth when he killed his father. He is therefore both guilty and not guilty, an ambiguity paralleled in the play by the forced juxtaposition of *daimòn* and the theme of Oedipus's free action. By insisting equally on the older conception of objective guilt – in using the theme of the plague and human/animal infertility – and on the newer conception of personal intention, expressed in the elaborate emphasis upon what Odeipus 'knew', Sophocles neatly probes the coherence of fifth-century legal and religious ideas.[42] Oedipus's ambiguity in legal terms reverberates, at the level of family relationships, membership of the city, knowledge and ignorance, blindness and sight, emotion and reason. He is ambiguous in relation to all these conventional and reassuringly 'real' oppositions – there is nothing arbitrary in his isolation. For a man to fall outside the structure of categories in terms of which the Greeks organised their experience of both the civic and the natural worlds, was to be forced into one or other of the only other major categories remaining: beast or god. And in the *Oedipus at Colonus*, though it was written much later, Oedipus duly is presented first as a beast, transiently as a citizen, finally as *heròs*. Inasmuch as Sophocles here provides an answer to his major question in the *Oedipus Tyrannus*, the intelligibility of suffering, he bypasses other traditional Greek theodicies precisely because they were all too simple to meet this case, precipitated by and only interesting at a relatively precise point in the fifth century when the tug of both old and new was vividly perceptible – even if we grant that the possibility of such a theodicy was inherent in the version of the myth Sophocles chose to elaborate: 'redundant' theodicies abound in complex myth-structures. The familiar Sophoclean theme of mutability, which of course presupposes a different theodicy, is made finally intelligible only by setting the arbitrariness of Oedipus's fate directly in relation to his heroization.[43] We must assume that this answer had not occurred to Sophocles when he wrote the *Oedipus Tyrannus*, which thus takes on the character of a *Problemstellung*, while the very writing of the later play suggests his dissatisfaction with the tentatively offered traditional theodicy which supported the earlier one.

It is characteristic of Girard's approach that he is forced to manipulate the givens of the plot so as to reconcile them with his view of the myth which lies behind. It is thus that the oracles become not privileged links between two worlds but counters in a game of political scapegoatism; and thus that the arguments between Creon and Oedipus, Teiresias and Oedipus become merely the verbal equivalents of the fight between such enemy brothers as Eteocles and Polyneices (p. 71). Each of the participants shares equal responsibility for the sacrificial crisis, because each of them 'participates in the destruction of a cultural order' (p. 71). Not only does this view ignore the way in which the quarrel with Creon produces the first glimmerings of doubt in Oedipus's mind (730ff.) – just at the point at which Jocasta prematurely exults in the failure of the original oracle to Laius (707–25); it also ignores the verisimilitude of Oedipus's reaction both to Teiresias and to Creon. Granted that the play begins with Oedipus's assurance of the truth of a whole series of interrelated propositions about his status and identity, which are one by one revealed to be the opposite of the truth (hence the consistently ironical play in the first part of the drama), it is the part of a reasonable man – and Oedipus is above all reasonable – to explain Teiresias's outburst in a manner consistent with those fixed propositions.[44] Girard's analysis simply fails to register that they are all false, and that they are discovered to be false by Oedipus whose rational deductions arrive finally at the same point as Teiresias's inspired certainty. The opposition between reason and revelation is discovered to be as false as the opposition between innocence and guilt.[45]

Girard's use of his fourth major example taken from Greek tragedy, Euripides' *Bacchae*, seems to me no less unsatisfactory (chapter 5, pp. 119–42). Having traced a connection between carnival and the sacrificial crisis ('The fundamental purpose of the festival is to set the stage for a sacrificial act that marks at once the climax and the termination of the festivities', p. 119), Girard introduces the 'antifestival', whose intention is 'to reproduce the beneficial effects of violent unanimity while abbreviating as much as possible the terrible preliminaries – which, in the case of the antifestival, are perceived in a negative light' (p. 122). Dionysiac religion conforms to the type of the antifestival; the *Bacchae* itelf is, in part at least, an account of the original bacchanal, in the context of the original sacrificial crisis: while Oedipus is an image of a ritual pattern, the scapegoat–*pharmakos* pattern, Pentheus images the actual original sacrifice of the victim of collective violence. The myth of the *Bacchae* thus preserves a unique truth about the origins of religion, divinity and arbitrary cathartic violence. It is merely unfortunate that Euripides did not quite grasp the significance of his material: 'The "problem of the *Bacchae*" would never have arisen if Euripides had fully acceded to the violent origin of the rite, the playing out of violence, and had acknowledged the generative act of unanimity preserved by the rite, lost in the onslaught of reciprocal violence and recovered through the mechanism of the surrogate victim' (p. 137). Once again, in the name of 'theory', an adequately dense reading of the play is abandoned in favour of a number of points which seem to support Girard's thesis, but which need not be understood in the way in which he chooses.

Thebes at the beginning of the play is gripped by a sacrificial crisis, as Pentheus lucidly sees (p. 127). All social distinctions have been erased, sexual differences abolishes; the presiding genius of this cancellation is Dionysus, who appears as god, man and beast, all three, and who incarnates the violence of collective action (pp. 132–3). It is his plan which will save the threatened community by choosing the innocent Pentheus for collective dismemberment: 'Peace and harmony now return to Thebes, which will henceforth honour the god in the manner ordained by him' (p. 130). Dionysus claims legitimacy 'not from his ability to disturb the peace but from his ability to restore the peace he has himself disturbed...Divine intervention is transformed into legitimate anger against a blasphemous hubris, which, until the crucial display of unanimity, seemed to implicate the god himself' (p. 134).

It is of course obvious once again that the heart of our problem is to know whether Girard is talking about some 'original' myth upon which Euripides' play is calqued, or about the play preserved to us. Girard seeks to slide away from the problem by referring to Euripides' oscillation between 'audacity' and 'timidity' which prevented him from performing fully his proper tragic task of pulling the mythic veil from the heart of violence (p. 137). The critic can simply note that Girard's 'summary' of the play is factually false: 'reading' becomes 'dreaming'. To begin with, there is in Euripides' play no suggestion that Thebes returns to peace and harmony after the intervention of Dionysus. His malignity against his primary victim, expressed already in the prologue, continues against other relatives of his mother Semele, namely Agave, her other sisters and Cadmus. Indeed, if a fragment of Dionysus' lost speech in the last scene is correctly to be linked with Herodotus 5.61, the Cadmaeans, the original inhabitants of Thebes, were all to be exiled.[46] Hardly good evidence for 'peace and harmony'. Again, so far from thanking the god for his benefits, Cadmus responds to Dionysus' laconic justification for what he has done ('Violence was done to me, a god') with the retort: 'It is fitting that the gods should not equal mortals in their anger' (Dodds 1347–8). Dionysus' violence is vengeful, not cathartic, as he announces in the prologue (23–42); and in view of the ending, his 'When I have put things to rights here' (49) is utterly ironical.[47]

It must surely be clear that Euripides did not even dimly perceive the task or insight Girard ascribes to him. And it seems to me that we can understand better what he was trying to discuss in the *Bacchae* by taking into account not some imaginary 'history' of Thebes but the relation between Dionysiac cult, and other similar cults, and the dominant religious norms of fifth-century Greece in the manner suggested by Marcel Detienne.[48] For although by the fifth century B.C. the worship of Dionysus had to some extent been integrated into the dominant norms, it remained in principle marginal. I stress once again that Girard's theory of the 'primitiveness' of Dionysiac worship is a mere product of nineteenth-century evolutionism, which cannot be confirmed by the chronological marking of the evidence. The alternative is some form of structural analysis. From such a perspective, it is immediately obvious that one of the special features of Dionysiac cult was its emphasis upon ecstasy, a religious goal quite at odds with the goals of normal cult (the contrast is of course far too schematic, but will do for our purposes). The achievement of ecstasy was accomplished by the breakage of codes of decorum, sexual norms, spatial norms and sacrificial norms upheld by 'normal' cult. This fundamental contrast duly appears in Euripides' play, which is characterized by a complex series of oppositions, which are the 'limits' of its discourse: oppositions between culture and nature, domesticity and hunting, reason and possession, cleverness and insight, boundedness and freedom, law and anarchy, and many others. Oxymoron perfectly characterizes the gulf between normality and ecstasy: the god's cult is *ponon hedun, kamaton t'eukamaton* (66–7: literally, 'sweet toil and good-weary weariness') – especially striking in a culture in which there was no dignity in labour.[49]

But escape into that antinomian world of ecstasy is utterly ambiguous, for it is simultaneously superhuman and subhuman: the women of Thebes perform miracles (704–11), attesting their divinity, but they are also, by that very token, animals (731). And it is precisely the order of the *polis* which defines itself between those two possibilities. Pentheus is right: there can be no reconciliation between the world of the *polis* subtended by traditional sacrifice, and this other world which is simultaneously divine and bestial. The opposition is of course not complete – not as complete as Pentheus makes out – wine, love and pleasure are all goods of the *polis* too (770–4); and Pentheus's own readiness to be deceived confirms the ambiguity of these comforting oppositions. But it is Euripides' purpose to question the adequacy of the multiple oppositions in terms of which not only Sophists in the late fifth century tended to found the coherence of their experience of the world. And, whatever its role in Dionysiac myth, for him the death of Pentheus is nothing but a crime, the point at which the god's vengeance is simultaneously fulfilled and recognized for what it is: ecstasy gives way to lamentation, as ecstasy always does.[50] So far from Euripides' having dimly perceived the truth about the necessity of arbitrary violence but recoiling from it, it seems to me that we have an utterly coherent and highly intelligent probing of a completely different problem, the relation between two antithetical strands in Greek religion which were nevertheless to be found side-by-side in the fifth-century *polis*: in Euripides' own day the threat of Dionysus himself had been absorbed – but what of Bendis?

Cadmus's response to Dionysus at the end of the play is appropriate only in terms of one of the common classical theodicies, which deemed the gods to play fair, modelling themselves on (changing) human conceptions of justice. It was one of the parts of Greek tragedy to question such a theodicy, to make use of myths which suggested a more difficult and sometimes darker pattern of divine action, myths which emphasized the arbitrary quality of the gods' power. Here, as elsewhere, Euripides' admission of that traditional tragic purpose is tempered by the irony with which not only Pentheus, but also Dionysus, is treated, that irony which undercuts cant even when it issues from a god's mouth. No one here is outside the tragic action, least of all the speaker of the prologue. For he speaks not the elementary language of the religious life, but the new language of self-interest.

These detailed arguments against Giraud's understanding of specific tragedies take us back to his theories about tragedy in general, or at any rate about Athenian tragedy. 'Antimythical' such tragedy surely is not, even in Girard's terms: so far from discerning a disappearance of distinctions, many tragedies proceed by demonstrating the inadequacy of the oppositional categories which formed the basis of much Greek thinking. Apparently fixed opposites melt into each other, the hidden is revealed, law becomes violence, the barbarian Greek, the victim the pursuer. Such dissolutions cannot be understood, I would argue, without remarking a correlative insistence in Athenian tragedy upon the existence, both explicit and implicit in myth, of a wider range of theodicies than could be privileged in the ordinary practice of 'civic' religion. It is obvious that even simple societies possess a range of theodicies; and increasing social complexity tends to generate more: the range of the 'thinkable' increases. One of the ways in which Athenian tragedy produces its specific effects is precisely by confronting the existence of such alternative theodicies. In effect, tragedy performs the opposite function of the *bricoleur*: while he uses the débris of the old to shore up the new, tragedy draws attention to disjunctures in symbolic sets, to the cracks in cosmologies, to the incoherence of current understandings of motive, responsibility and causation.

Nor is the reason for such anxiety far to seek. The Athenian tragedians faced, not a society which threatened to extinguish 'Degree' (for all the complaints of the oligarchs), but one which had been forced rapidly to face the cognitive consequences of the democratic revolution of 508–507 B.C. Now it is not usual to speak of the 'cognitive consequences' of that revolution. Yet there is an important point here. For the democratic revolution forced an increasingly sharp confrontation between the complex and unsystematized traditional version(s) of 'the way things are' and the relatively determinate body of rules and practices embodied in the decisions of the *ekklesia* (assembly) and the other institutions of the democracy, bound as these were to new perceptions of proper social relations and tolerable economic activity, and so, at a deeper level, to the fundamental problem of individual identity. The most articulate, but by no means the most important, expression of these tensions is the work of the fifth-century Sophists;[51] but we would do well to note how the dilemmas of tragic heroes also reflect them. The 'old' new criticism has for too long legitimated the traditional domination of philology and belle-lettrism in the study of Athenian tragedy.

Girard's attempt to 'place' Greek tragedy fails precisely because it is inadequately historical – indeed time for him has no significance whatever. Certainly his attempt to confer special status upon the achievement of Sophocles and Euripides is utterly misplaced. Their 'relevance' lies not in a supposed perceptiveness of the eternal problem of 'violence', but, if anywhere, in their exemplification of the necessity of doubt about those things which others believe to be most certain.

The initial reception of Marcel Detienne's *Jardins d'Adonis* (first published in 1972) was favourable. It was prefaced by an enthusiastic résumé by Jean-Pierre Vernant, then at the École Pratique (IVe Section) and now professor at the Collège de France, who has long worked closely with Detienne on the study of Greek myth. It was also received with a sort of relief by reviewers. Detienne's articulate brilliance combined with the structuralism of Lévi-Strauss (who also liked it) seemed to have laid bare the logic of the myth of Adonis, which had troubled ever since the general abandonment of Frazer's dying–rising god schema and the failure to replace it with anything better.[52]

The argument was accomplished and ingenious, and pursued with a relentless clarity. Frazer failed to understand the significance of the myth because he concentrated his attention exclusively upon Adonis himself. What he did not notice was that Adonis' mother is called Myrrha (Myrrh). If we look at myths and tales about the collection of spices (of which myrrh is just one, of course) in the Greek world, we find that they also involve the sun; and that relates them clearly to the notions dryness and purity. For that reason we find spices used in the Greek world to mediate 'vertically' between men and gods – they are used in sacrifice. The association can be revealed also by examining the ideas of a 'deviant' group, the Pythagoreans, which are yet structured in the same way. But this 'vertical' axis must be joined by a 'horizontal' one: spices, and especially perfumes (a closely linked category) mediate between human beings. They bring together those who are normally apart. Perfumes are then particularly associated with seduction (as in the myth about Myrrha) and adultery. The figure of Adonis is the figure of the arch-seducer. But because this precocious sexual activity is found in one who is so young, it is met by a 'corresponding' premature impotence and then death. This complex of ideas figures in the festival of Adonis, the *Adonia*, in which a 'garden' is cultivated, which precociously sprouts and then withers in the heat of summer. The festival seems to have belonged primarily to the unmarried women who were no longer children. As such, the *Adonia* can only be understood in contrast to the Athenian festival of married women, the *Thesmophoria*, in which Demeter, the goddess of corn, was worshipped above all. So we find in the contrast between the festivals a contrast between marriage and seduction, cereal-culture and non-agriculture, fecundity and sterility. The worship of Adonis is to be related to a generalized male fear of excessive female sexuality (associated with the hottest part of summer), and can be seen as a kind of cultural 'comment' on enduring tensions between legitimate wives and concubines or other 'illicit' sexual partners.

In 1974, however, Giulia Piccaluga published a slashing review in which she called attention to Detienne's arbitrary selection of the available evidence, his suppression of elements which do not fit his theses, and his constant habit of employing the need for a 'full reading' to depreciate the work of others in the same field: 'questo non è "leggere", neppure leggicchiare; è un arbitrio isolare alcuni motivi dal vivo di un contesto, niente di piú' (p. 39).[53] Now it is unfortunate that Detienne has not responded to this critique; for to show, as he has, that Giulia Piccaluga's own theory about Adonis is inadequate is not of itself to rebut her remarks.[54] The heart of the problem lies in the validity of a non-structuralist critique of a structuralist analysis: to say that Detienne has misrepresented the 'facts' is of course to say nothing, since the 'facts' are produced by the model being used. Piccaluga's criticisms are not of the model at all, and may be said to fall into the category of the 'naively empirical'; indeed, it is not at all clear to me that she knows what she thinks of the model itself.[55] For underlying her critique is a familiar muddle about structuralism, the assumption that the model must either be fully explicit, 'locatable' somewhere; or else be merely conjured up by the investigator. The old false choice between God's Truth and Hocus Pocus that bedevils positivist attacks upon structuralism will get us nowhere. At most one could say that Detienne might profitably have exended his model, in particular so as to deal with the tradition about Adonis as a hunter, and with those which assign him a parentage other than Myrrha. Such an extension might well have threatened the coherence of his analysis.[56]

One's first doubt, then, is whether the structural account in *The Gardens of Adonis* is as total as Detienne claims; that is, whether the model is sufficiently complex. But a deeper doubt concerns the very conception of 'structure' with which he is working. At times it seems to be closed and determinate, as when he dismisses later elaborations of the Phoenix myth as 'ideology' (p. 142 n. 147 = p. 68 n. 2F); at others, for example when he discusses the structure of Pythagorean ideas, quite open-ended. What exactly distinguishes these two kinds of elaboration of underlying structures? There is at least a hint of opportunism here. Beyond that of course we must note the tendency to reify the notion of structure, to think of it is a sort of vital template which turns out imaginative products all marked with the same copyright. In dealing with the relation between myth and society it is insufficient to declare that one has discovered a privileged structure without taking into account the endless possibilities of 'interference' – particularly in a 'hot' society. As Edward Ardener remarks, 'Human minds can use, as comparative experience shows, any evident structural regularity upon which to build the most unexpected and varied semiotics.'[57] There may well be, and in this case there probably are, several (fragmentary) structures combined and dissociated in countless acts of *bricolage*.

For the most difficult question of all concerns the kind of coherence which one can legitimately demand of a mythic, or a ritual, structure. Does a determinate series of codes, or of oppositions, ever constitute a group of myths or rituals in such a way that we can firmly discriminate between 'essence' and 'ideology'? What exactly are the costs of heuristically pretending that a single structure underlies a given myth-sequence or ritual? Now that Dan Sperber has given us what must be accounted a complete critique of the validity of a linguistic model of symbol-structure, what more proper alternatives are there?[58] The importance of Sperber's work is that it allows us to accept that traditional thought can be both 'systematic' and lacunate, that it may contain endless deviance and inconsequence, and that 'levels' of speculation about the natural world may be linked in many ways. Above all, it allows us to reintegrate actors' models (i.e. conscious models) into a form of structuralism and so escape Lévi-Strauss's mannered intellectualism. Sperber's notion of 'evocation', though not yet a full theory, does not infringe Detienne's project at all: it merely serves to make it adequately complex.

In this special case of Greek myth, there is another problem, recently highlighted by Jack Goody.[59] He has persuasively argued that the possibility provided by literacy of making lists tends to produce oversimplifications of actual beliefs, not only among modern students but even within the society in question. It is by now a commonplace that one of the characteristic forms of argument among the pre-Socratics in Greece involved the use of polar categories;[60] and it is now recognized that the same applies to a great deal of classical discourse. The problem for the structuralist student of Greek myth and the codes into which it is integrated is to judge the extent to which this characteristic pattern of elite discourse, accentuated by the predominance of a common educational structure, organized and re-presented the body of myths and rituals in such a way as to render them only too amenable to a Lévi-Straussian structural analysis. We must then treat with considerable reserve, if sympathy, Detienne's claim that the 'parallelism between the categories operative in the rational thought of the fifth and fourth centuries on the one hand and the principal concepts underlying the mythical material on the other' is 'remarkable' (p. 131). I would say, rather, that given the nature of our sources for both the codes and the myths, the parallelism is entirely predictable.

But to say all this is neither to damn Detienne's enterprise in *The Gardens of Adonis*, nor to espouse some form of the history of religions; though we may regret the bare presentation of this translation to the English-speaking world, where it will almost inevitably suffer the incomprehension typified by Peter Walcot's review in the *Journal of Hellenic Studies* of Detienne's later book, *Dionysos mis à mort* (1977).[61] Collectively, the members of the *Centre* to which he belongs have contributed more than anyone in the past twenty years to the study of the relation between myth, religion and society in archaic and classical Greece. As a tentative sketch of the structure of the Olympian pantheon and of its ramifications within paradigmatic codes, Vernant and Detienne's *Les Ruses de l'intelligence*, now translated into English, is unsurpassed.[62] No one has shown more clearly than Vernant the crucial significance of Hesiod as an Archaic intellectual in synthesizing and articulating the 'unconscious' structure of Greek cosmogonic and sacrificial ideas for his own culture and time.[63] Though unsystematic, Vernant and Vidal-Naquet's book on Greek tragedy represents one of the few attempts to inquire into the nature of Athenian tragedy's representation of, and confrontation with, the society of Athens at a level which is other than banal.[64] In perhaps the most difficult area of all, Pierre Vidal-Naquet, and now his associate Nicole Loraux, have done more than anyone, save Louis Gernet, to tease out the relationships between characteristic patterns of archaic and classical thought, written historical documents, and actual institutions.[65] Of this group, Detienne is the most Lévi-Straussian; one may say that he defines the margin of their collective attempt to steer between the dominant positivism of classical studies and the neo-Stalinism characteristic of another group of French classicists associated with Pierre Lévèque. To put it perhaps over-harshly, Detienne offers a form of idealism against which they must all react. And for me, idealism is not a dirty word.

Finally, let me suggest what is perhaps implicit in all this, that insofar as both religion and tragedy constitute meanings within their culture, they are both amenable to the same kind of treatment, whether we call it post-Lévi-Straussian (but still anthropological) structuralism, historical cognitive sociology or the history of *mentalité*. That does not, of course, mean that they are not amenable also to other approaches, which may, among other things, highlight the differences between them. What must be excluded, however, is the pseudo-historicism offered by Girard, subtended as it is neither by an explicit model of the relationship between symbolic set and social structure nor by an awareness of the diversity of possible meanings generated within a single religion. The kindest remark one can make to him is that he would have done better to have admitted the mythical status of his 'history' – the sort of admission that Freud came to make in *Beyond the Pleasure Principle*. For there is no 'secret' at the heart of religion; it is neither pathological nor does it 'wither away'; it is not even, except for the most simple-minded, a single category. And even as myth, the thesis is as pared of significance as most aetiologies. Let John Seldon have the last word: 'Religion is made a Juglers paper, now 'tis a horse, now 'tis a Lanthorne, now 'tis a Boate, now 'tis a man. To serve ends Religion is turn'd into all shapes.'[66]

NOTES

1 This passage is omitted from the American translation (p. 301). Indeed, there are so many slight omissions and additions that the translation almost counts as a new edition, though we may regret that Patrick Gregory has adhered to Girard's unaccountable practice of omitting line references in literary, and especially dramatic, quotations.

    Girard's claim here is a familiar one with him: see *Deceit, Desire and the Novel: Self and Other in Literary Structure* (Baltimore, 1965), p. 3: 'A basic contention of this essay is that the great writers apprehend intuitively and concretely, through the medium of their art, if not formally, the system in which they were first imprisoned together with their contemporaries'; and *Dostoïevski: du double à l'unité* (Collection La Recherche de l'Absolu) (Paris, 1963), pp. 35–59.

2 R. Angus Downie, *Frazer and the Golden Bough* (London, 1970), p. 111.

3 Luc de Heusch, *Le Roi ivre ou l'origine de l'état* (Paris, 1972), p. 14 (a Lévi-Straussian analysis of African sacral kingship). The most forthright, if barbed, recent appreciation of Frazer must be I. C. Jarvie's: 'Frazer was a comparative sociologist and a great one; great because of his scope and explanatory power, his exhilarating antireligiousness and his fine English style. That what he says is false does not detract from him at all' (*The Revolution in Social Anthropology* (London, 1964), p. 33).

4. 'But if we do not always agree with [earlier scholars'] concepts we approve of their quest: to fathom the hidden meaning of primitive religions and to establish their essential unity' (p. 197) – a marvellously nineteenth-century project.

5 'It is significant that sacrifice has languished in societies with a firmly established judicial system – ancient Greece and Rome, for example, In such societies the essential purpose of sacrifice has disappeared. It may still be practised for a while,

but in diminished and debilitated form' (p. 18). Indeed, on the following page, the possession of a judicial system serves to distinguish 'civilized' societies from 'primitive' ones *tout court*. The Barotse would be flattered; as for traditional judicial systems, a reading of S. van der Sprenkel, *Legal Institutions in Manchu China* (London, 1962), for example, might have disabused Girard of his grosser misconceptions.

6 Tyler did not of course invent the notion of 'survivals', although he gives that impression in *Primitive Culture* (2nd edn, London, 1873), I, 16. See John Burrow, *Evolution and Society* (Cambridge, 1966), pp. 240–1.

7. S. E. Hyman, *The Tangled Bank: Darwin, Marx, Frazer and Freud as Imaginative Writers* (New York, 1962), p. 212.

8. See J. B. Vickery, *The Literary Impact of the Golden Bough* (Princeton, 1973).

9 'The Scope of Social Anthropology', in *Psyche's Task* (2nd edn, London, 1913), p. 170.

10. Indeed, Girard is evidently more pessimistic still about modern intellectual and cultural life: see for example his remarks on pp. 108, 205–6, 238–40.

11 Cf. Hyman, *The Tangled Bank*, p. 439: '*The Golden Bough* is not primarily anthropology, if it ever was, but a great imaginative vision of the human condition.' Girard's book reveals the same uncertainty of purpose, I think.

12 For example, pp. 184–5, 189–90, 194–5, 201, etc.

13 Cf. Paul Ricoeur, *Freud and Philosophy* (New Haven, 1970), pp. 198–208.

14 As usual, Robert Towler, *Homo Religiosus: Sociological Problems in the Study of Religion* (London, 1974), pp. 62–84, is instructive.

15 A full critique of the Durkheimian thesis is offered by John Skorupski, *Symbol and Theory* (Cambridge, 1976), Part I, especially pp. 18–35; note too his critique on pp. 51–2 of another of Girard's central texts, Godfrey Lienhardt's study of the Dinka.

16 See note 1 above (*Deceit, Desire and the Novel* is the English translation of *Mensonge romantique* [1961]). G. has himself resumed his theory in 'The Plague in Literature and Myth', *Texas Studies in Literature and Language* (special issue on Myth and Interpretation), 15 (1974), 833–50; other sympathetic résumés may be found in some reviews of the French edition, in *Critique*, 303–4 (1972), 716–28 (Pierre Pachet) and in *MLN*, 87:7 (1972), 986–98 (Carl Rubino), for example (I have not seen the large study of G. and Deleuze by Eugenio Donato announced by Rubino).

17 Girard's thesis might then be seen as an original variant, in very different terms, of Mircea Eliade''s proposition that all religion seeks ultimately to negate history; the kindest statement one can make about Eliade has been made by Leszek Kołakowski, 'Mircea Eliade: Die Religion als Paralyse der Zeit', in *Geist und Ungeist christlicher Traditionen* (Stuttgart, 1971), pp. 140–9, but perhaps the truest by Ivan Strenski, 'Mircea Eliade, some theoretical problems', in *The Theory of Myth: Six Studies*, edited by Adrian Cunningham (London, 1973), pp. 40–78.

18 See J. Derrida, 'Violence et métaphysique: essai sur la pensée d'Emmanuel Levinas', in *L'Ecriture et la différence* (Paris, 1967), pp. 117–228.

19 At least Walter Burkert in *Homo Necans* (Berlins, 1972), in many ways an equally essentialist book, makes some attempt to use archaeological evidence to justify his view of the primordial centrality of sacrifice in religion.

20 Hannah Arendt, 'Angelo Guiseppe Roncalli', in *Men in Dark Times* (London, 1970), p. 67.

21. Irving Goldman, *The Mouth of Heaven: an Introduction to Kwakiutl Religious Thought* (New York London, 1975), p. 124.

22 I. M. Lewis, *Ecstatic Religion* (Harmondsworth, 1971). By 'deviance' I mean more or less institutionalized religious goals alternative to those offered and legitimated by 'normal' practice.

23 p. 199, quoted from Freud, *Totem and Taboo* (*Standard Edition*), *p. 138. Those less used to the methods of modern scholarship may find the passage, from St Nilus's third Narratio*, in Migne, *PG* 79, col. 613, though it has suffered a number of mutilations by the time it reaches Girard's text.

24 Curiously enough, although he had no means of knowing it in view of his source, Girard is quite right about this: at the beginning of the passage, Nilus says explicitly that this sacrifice was only undertaken if there were no human captives to sacrifice. But of course the fact is of no service to Girard, for whom the substitution would have to be unconscious, part of the *méconnaissance protectrice* which protects primitives from an understanding of what they do.

25 The discrepancies between this sentence and the version of Nilus given above, which makes reference neither to binding nor to an altar, are due entirely to Robertson Smith's text and translation.

26 W. Robertson Smith, *Lectures on the Religion of the Semites: the Fundamental Institutions* (1889; 1894; 3rd edn, by S. A. Cook, London, 1927), p. 343 and n. 3.

27 Sacrifice in Central Arabia (to which the Saracens of Greater Sinai seem to have belonged culturally) normally involved cooking; and normally one only drank the blood of a camel when threatened with death by lack of water in the desert: see, for example, G. Ryckmans, *Les Religions arabes préislamiques* (2nd edn, Louvain, 1951), pp. 10–13.

28 Ryckmans, p. 24.

29 See further, p. 298 below and note 48.

30 He has also produced a theory of comedy from the same premisses: 'Perilous balance: a comic hypothesis', *MLN*, 87:7 (1972), 811–26.

31 For example, in a lecture given at Athens in 1955, translated as 'On the Future of Tragedy', in *Lyrical and Critical Essays* (New York, 1968).

32 Girard is fond of such essentialist remarks; cf. 'Perilous balance', p. 825: 'There is something profoundly subversive in all true comedy.'

33 In his review, *MLN*, 87:7 (1972), 994. Let me, in passing, record a certain distaste for Rubino's sneer at a predictable sort of objection likely to be made against Girard's theory 'from certain segments of the intellectual world, especially the Anglo-American intellectual world' (p. 993). The plea that one is misunderstood has been heard once too often.

34 Euripides' *Herakles*, Sophocles' *Trachiniae* and *Oedipus Tyrannus*, Euripides' *Bacchae*, though he does make passing reference to one or two other plays. I agree with Rubino (p. 996–7) that it is odd that Girard should have made no use of Aeschylus' *Oresteia* – it would have lent itself well to his habitual 'reading' strategy.

35 On suppliancy codes in Greece, see J. P. Gould, 'Hiketeia', *Journal of Hellenic Studies*, 93 (1973), 74–103; and on rules for the ritual lament, Margaret Alexiou, *The Ritual Lament in Greek Tradition* (Cambridge, 1974), pp. 5–7, 10–14.

36 Froma Zeitlin, 'The motif of the corrupted sacrifice in Aeschylus' *Oresteia*', *TAPhA*, 96 (1965), 463–508, with the postscript, 97 (1966), 645–53; P. Vidal-Naquet, 'Chasse

et sacrifice dans l'*Orestie* d'Éschyle', in J.-P. Vernant and P. Vidal-Naquet, *Mythe et tragédie en Grece ancienne* (Paris, 1972), pp. 135–58.

37 J. C. Kamerbeeck, 'Unity and meaning of Euripides' *Herakles*', *Mnemosyne*, 4: 19 (1966), 1–16; pp. 12–13.

38 Girard observes (p. 41): 'The murder of Lycus is presented in the Euripides play as a last "labor" of the hero, a still-rational prelude to the insane outburst that follows. Seen from the perspective of the ritualist, it might well constitute a first link of impure violence.' Not at all. Since no one in the play makes the slightest connection between the killing of Lycus (seen by the chorus as just, 809–14) and the anger of Hera (which is explicitly 'unjust': Lyssa, 854, 856), what right has the critic, ritualist or not, to argue otherwise; unless, of course, 'ritualism' is merely a cloak to give us the right to say whatever we wish about a given text with no responsibility of control?

39 Here, as elsewhere, Girard's summaries are quite unreliable (pp. 41–2). For example, his 'shirt of Nessus' is a complete fiction, and Herakles' supposed impurity as a returning warrior an unwarranted interpolation.

40 Some of the best recent studies of the play are by Charles Segal, who brings out the relation between many apparently disparate themes: see *L'Antiquité classique*, 44 (1975), 30–53; *Yale Classical Studies*, 25 (1976), 141–72; *Dionisio*, 45 (1971–4).

41 I use 'theodicy' here in the Weberian sense, as developed, for example, by Peter Berger, *The Social Reality of Religion* (London, 1969), pp. 53–80; also published as *The Sacred Canopy* (New York, 1969).

42 For a similar presentation of the problem, see J.-P. Vernant, 'Ébauches de la volonté dans la tragédie grecque', in *Mythe et tragédie*, pp. 43–74.

43 As usual, John Jones, *On Aristotle and Greek Tragedy* (London, 1962), pp. 166–77, 200–14, is perceptive. On the thematic parallels between *Oedipus Tyrannus* and *Oedipus at Colonus*, see B. Seidensticker, 'Beziehungen zwischen den beiden Oidipusdramen des Sophokles', *Hermes*, 100 (1972), 255–74.

44 See, for example, M. W. Champlin, '*Oedipus Tyrannus* and the problem of knowledge', *Classical Journal*, 64 (1969), 37–45; Brian Vickers, *Towards Greek Tragedy* (London, 1974), pp. 501–9. When Oedipus discovers the truth, he freely admits that he wronged Creon (1420–1).

45 Cf. R. L. Kane, 'Prophecy and Perception in *Oedipus the King*', *TAPhA*, 105 (1975), 189–208, though he does not see that the oppositions are cancelled.
   Two further points should perhaps be noted:
   (1) Oedipus' status as *king* is not crucial to Sophocles' version, though it becomes so to those who read into it a treatment of the 'divine king' motif. As I read it, Oedipus' kingship is for Sophocles nothing more than a given which he chooses not to change. After all, how many of the characters in a typical collection of Greek myths, such as Apollodorus' *Bibliotheca*, are *not* members of royal houses?
   (2) There is no stress at all in the play upon the saving of Thebes, which G.'s theory requires so strongly that it becomes for him a 'fact' about the play. Sophocles concentrates entirely at the end upon Oedipus' personal fate; and Thebes is not exactly Biarritz in *Oedipus at Colonus*, either.

46 See Dodds' edition (2nd edn, Oxford, 1960), p. 58, with pp. 234–5; also Jeanne Roux, *Les Bacchantes* (Paris, 1972), I, 217–19. The passage of Herodotus puts the exile of the Cadmaeans during the reign of Laodamas, son of Eteocles – that is, long after the present incident. By suppressing this, as he seems to do, Euripides contrives

to suggest that the exile of the people of Thebes is part of a present punishment.

47 Especially in view of his next-reported exploits, at Argos, where much the same thing happened (Apollodorus, *Bibl.*, 3.5.2).

48 See 'Ronger la tête de ses parents', in *Dionyos mis à mort* (Paris, 1977), pp. 135–60, and his brief presentation of the wider aspects of the problem in 'La viande et le sacrifice en Grèce ancienne', *La Recherche*, 75 (February 1977), which is an outline of the thesis of a forthcoming book, *La Cuisine du sacrifice*. Although I find the thesis in need of nuance, it is defensible as a series of rough contrasts.

Briefly, Detienne sees the Dionysiac *sparagmos* in relation to normal Greek sacrificial and alimentary codes. Whereas normally the animal's edible flesh was separated from the fat and the bones, and eaten after the sacrifice 'proper', we find in Dionysiac myth, and vestigially in ritual, the motif of human/divine flesh, not cut up with the proper sort of knife but torn apart, and eaten not cooked but raw. It is this complex of ideas which suggests to Detienne that Dionysiac cult is 'deviant'.

49 Jeanne Roux, *Les Bacchantes*, II, 263–4, rightly points to the relation here between oxymoron and salvation.

50 A rather similar view, which insists upon the sex-reversal motif but not upon Euripides' critique of the subtending polarities, is to be found in Charles Segal, 'The Menace of Dionysus: Sex Roles and Reversals in Euripides' *Bacchae*', *Arethusa*, 11 (1978), 185–202.

51 See recently, Friedrich Solmsen, *Intellectual Experiments of the Greek Enlightenment* (Princeton, 1975), though I have little sympathy with the overall perspective he adopts.

52 None of the reviewers in the classical journals were committed structuralists, but all welcomed the book with varying degrees of warmth.

53 'Adonis e i profumi di un certo strutturalismo', *Maia*, N.S. 1: 26 (1974), 33–51. Several of the reviews in classical journals made some of her points, but none combined them into a critique of this kind.

54 'Les malheurs de la chasse', in *Dionysos mis à mort*, pp. 64–77. Both in that book, however ('Les Grecs ne sont pas comme les autres', pp. 17–47), and in 'La mythologie scandaleuse', *Traverses* (September 1978), one can see the outlines of his reply.

55 It is at any rate evident that the editor of *Maia*, Antonio La Penna, intended that the review should be seen as a triumphant vindication of positivism: 'la dimostrazione petrà riuscire utile a quanti di noi si lanciano sull'ultima moda, senza spirito critico, per mostrarsi aggiornati' (p. 33).

56 One criticism Giulia Piccaluga does not make, but which ought to have been made, concerns Detienne's evident difficulty in assigning evidence to specific paradigmatic codes – I found myself often suspecting him of what one might call 'transformational reclassification'. This common problem in structuralist analyses might repay treatment along the lines of Tony Trew, 'Theory at Work', *University of East Anglia Papers in Linguistics*, 6 (1978), 39–60.

57 'Introductory Essay: Social Anthropology and Language', in *Social Anthropology and Language* (ASA Monographs, 10), edited by E. Ardener (London, 1971), pp. ix–cii at p. lxxxii.

58 *Le Symbolisme en général* (Paris, 1974), translated as *Rethinking Symbolism* (Cambridge, 1975).

59 *The Domestication of the Savage Mind* (Cambridge, 1977).

60 Cf. G. E. R. Lloyd, *Polarity and Analogy* (Cambridge, 1966; 2nd edn, 1971).

61 *J.H.S.* 98 (1978), 188. As for this English version of *Les Jardins d'Adonis*, which received the Scott Moncreiff Prize, Mrs Lloyd has, as usual, done her job admirably. It is however furnished with an absurd number of misprints, muddled diagrams, and indeed mistakes, for some of which, such as 'Kinras', 'Philichorus', 'Athanaeus', 'Souda', she must take responsibility.

62 Paris, 1974. The English translation is published by Harvester Press (1978), which has in hand a number of other books by members of the group, to appear within the next couple of years.

63 See especially, 'Le mythe hésiodique des races, essai d'analyse structurale' (1960) and 'Le mythe hésiodique des races: sur un essai de mise au point' (1966), in *Mythe et pensée chez les Grecs* (3rd edn, Paris, 1971), I, 13–41, 42–79; 'Le mythe prométhéen chez Hésiode', in *Mythe et société en Grèce ancienne* (Paris, 1974), pp. 177–94; 'Sacrifice et alimentation humaine à propos du *Prométhée* d'Hésiode', *Annali della Scuola Normale Sup. di Pisa*, Classe di Lettere e Filosofia, 3rd series, 7: 3 (1977), 905–40. The two last are to appear in English in *Religion, Myth and Society in Ancient Greece*, edited by R. L. Gordon (Cambridge, forthcoming).

64 *Mythe et tragédie en Grèce ancienne* (Paris, 1972). An English translation is to appear next year.

65 P. Vidal-Naquet: note especially, 'The Black Hunter and the Origin of the Athenian Ephebeia', *Proceedings of the Cambridge Philological Society*, 194 (1968), 269–92; 'Esclavage et gynécocratie dans la tradition, mythe et l'utopie', *Recherches sur les structures sociales dans l'Antiquité classique*, Introd. Cl. Nicolet (Paris, 1970), pp. 63–80; 'Valeurs religieuses et mythiques de la terre et du sacrifice dans l'Odyssée', *Annales ESC*, 26 (1970), 1278–97; 'Le cru, l'enfant grec et le cuit', in *Faire l'histoire*, edited by J. Le Goff and P. Nora (Paris, 1974), III, 137–68; 'Bêtes, hommes et dieux chez les Grecs', in L. Poliakov, *Hommes et bêtes, Entretiens sur le racisme* (Paris, 1975), pp. 129–42; 'Plato's Myth of the Statesman, the Ambiguities of the Golden Age and of History', *Journal of Hellenic Studies*, 98 (1978), 132–41. Several of these are to appear in Gordon (n. 63 above), often with alteration and additions.

Nicole Loraux: 'L'interférence tragique', *Critique*, 317 (1973), 908–25; and 'Sur les races des femmes', *Arethusa*, 11 (1978), 43–87. A mass of work by the students of this group awaits publication.

66 I should like to thank Elinor Shaffer for her comments on an earlier draft of this review.

The longest way with the dissenters
A review of Donald Davie's Clark Lectures

ELINOR SHAFFER

Donald Davie's signal services to eighteenth-century poetry, especially those reaches of it now most deeply sunk in critical and readerly disfavour and neglect, have an honourable history of a quarter of a century behind them. In books like the brilliant *Purity of Diction* and *Articulate Energy*, in anthologies such as *The Late Augustans* and *Augustan Lyric*, in numerous articles and in his own verse, Davie has urged the case for poets between Pope and Wordsworth. He has never written in a spirit of mere scholarly antiquarianism or idiosyncratic connoisseurship; his primary concern has always been for poetry in Britain today, a concern one would not hesitate to call impassioned except that the Davie of *A Gathered Church* would find the word distasteful.[1] He has always spoken as a modern poet, sifting the poetry of the recent and the distant past, in English and in other languages for a viable tradition, a viable style. The recent collection of his essays of the past two decades, *The Poet in the Imaginary Museum*,[2] reminds us of his finely felt and precisely understood enthusiasm (another word he would today reject) for Pound and Eliot, for Wallace Stevens, Robert Graves, Charles Tomlinson, and latterly Thomas Hardy.

These impulses are still powerful in *A Gathered Church*: the neglected poets Isaac Watts and John Wesley are again defended, as part of a formative religious culture that reached a larger public than any of the more renowned poets of their time, and as representatives of what Davie is pleased to call neo-classicism, a conservative, Augustan poetry of Dissent. Doubtless he is right to feel that eighteenth-century Dissent (and indeed eighteenth-century religious feeling altogether) has been too much denigrated in favour of the radical Dissent of the seventeenth century, whose devotees have of late been conspicuous in tracing the continued saving, subterranean activity of the Muggletonians and the

Ranters throughout the century, emerging triumphantly in Revolution and Blake. The central tradition was not this, Davie is concerned to say, but the mature, accommodating Dissent which carved out a place for itself very near, though still excluded from, the Establishment. The values of simplicity and sobriety served not only nascent capitalism, as Weber and Tawney long ago assured us (here Davie wonders about the role of the country congregations), but also an aesthetic ideal and a genuine poetic accomplishment. Speaking as a Baptist (born) and a neo-classicist (made), Davie organizes these sensible paradoxes into a tradition for himself and for modern English poetry; if there is a reminiscence of Eliot's construction of a tradition, it is only deliberately to underline the contrast to Eliot's imperial American claim to the whole of European poetry, the whole of the imaginary museum. The firmly and primly limited ideal sorts oddly with the brilliant volatility of Davie's thought and his reckless juggling with the history both of religion and of literature.

Conservative Dissent is surely of great historical importance, and deserves sober and persuasive advocates. But Davie has gone so far that he has bereft the very 'neo-classicism' he has defined of any major literary representatives whatsoever. The more receptive one is to Isaac Watts's brand of poetic Dissent ('We are a Garden wall'd around, /Chosen and made peculiar Ground'), the less one can forbear to see how much Blake inherited from him (as has long since been amply shown): but Davie is concerned to cut off the heir without a penny. Davie associates Blake with the 'excesses' of Wesleyan worship, with 'religious sentiment perverted, and doctrine coarsened out of recognition' (p. 53); he was 'not a hero of the democratizing of Scripture, but a martyr to it' (p. 54). Blake is made responsible for the 'enthusiasm' which Davie wants to see as the source of Philistinism, and labelled 'a homegrown hot-godspeller' (p. 60). This skewed judgement, this language is unforgivable, whatever the provocation in recent Blake studies. Blake was no Methodist (no more was he a Ranter); and indeed, many who supported the American and the French Revolutions were as 'Augustan' a set of Dissenters as one might ask. (But then, Davie cannot accept the Unitarians into his fold either, for they are (forsooth) too intellectual for him. He even goes so far as to offer another, conflicting account of the rise of that Arnoldian bogeyman Philistinism which lays it all at the door of the Unitarian *philosophes* who 'queered the pitch' for the rest by being too advanced in enlightenment (p. 131).) 'Dissent has its snobberies', Davie reminds us; and in saying nothing of Milton (even in his eighteenth-century incarnations, which would have required no reference to the public-house radicalism recently attributed to him by Christopher Hill), and by consigning Blake quite falsely and needlessly into the willing hands of the most extreme radical Dissent, Davie has left himself a poetic orphan. 'Revisionism' can go no further.

How far these dubious polemics have led Davie from his own best insights is most poignantly illustrated by his suppression of his previous generous (and accurate) tributes to Christopher Smart as the greatest poet between Pope and Wordsworth (though we might prefer to say 'between Pope and Blake'). Davie's selections from Smart, including that splendid poem, 'A Noon-piece, or the Mowers at Dinner', and the full text of 'A Song to David' (of which only a mutilated version appears in Helen Gardner's *Oxford Book of Religious Verse*), established the 'disconcerting grandeur' of this poet. But Smart's personal disorders have led to his being classed with the Romantics, and, as John Holloway has perceptively pointed out in his fine *Blake: The Lyric Poems*, only Smart, among the writers of hymns for children, conveyed the quality of innocent joy which Blake was to make his own (as opposed to the minatory and coy didacticism of Watts, Wesley, Mrs Barbauld, and all those who wrote 'for' rather than 'of' innocence). So in *A Gathered Church* Davie's only mention of Smart is to dismiss him for the 'laxity and vapidity' of his complexly inwoven version of Psalm 90 compared with Watts's insistent four-line simplicities.

If Davie sacrifices poetry to polemic, he also sacrifices religion to it. The terms in which a latter-day poetic non-conformist like Lawrence is likewise excluded from *A Gathered Church* turn back on and undercut even the case Davie has made for conservative Dissent. The grounds of his dismissal of Lawrence as a writer is that that the sacrament of the Eucharist may not have been celebrated at Eastwood. The Congregational Chapel therefore was not 'a centre and arena for *worship*, for the enactment of the ultimate mysteries' (p. 94). Lawrence must, accordingly, have been 'crippled from the first, and throughout his life, from having been born to, and reared in, a religious community that had lost its bearings and reneged on its inheritance' (p. 95). But how can the partaking of the Eucharist be made the measure of Dissenting religious observance? And Davie applies this private 'Test' throughout the book: Robert Hall is praised for his restatement of the doctrine on Easter Day, 1800 ('when there were just six communicants in St Paul's Cathedral'). Later, R. W. Dale is praised as 'the only prominent dissenting minister to hold by the full uncompromising doctrine of the Eucharist in the second half of the (nineteenth) century', in contrast to Matthew Arnold's 'emasculated theology' (p. 82). And we hear, ominously, of William Hale White that 'there is no reason to suppose that he took the Lord's Supper much more often than William Blake did' (p. 98). An unsavoury recipe for Dissent emerges: a Calvinism which would allow Dissenters to subscribe to very nearly all the Thirty-Nine Articles, and social accommodation. Are these not just the reverse of the qualities that have made Dissent valuable? – continuing theological innovation, and steadfast refusal of accommodation – indeed, in the famous phrase despised by Arnold, 'the dissidence of Dissent and the protestantism of the Protestant religion'. What is still less savoury is that Davie should attempt to associate theological rigidity and social accommodation with poetry. I have written at length elsewhere of the new senses of 'myth' which were vital for both religion and poetry in this period. Davie's use of the Eucharist in these contexts is a degradation of the touchstone method of criticism that Arnold at his best used flexibly and sensitively, as it is a degradation of the ritual itself.

Doubtless the provocation is great to sink both Blake and Lawrence, for Lawrence has surely been overrated, and Blake is well on his way to becoming the major Romantic poet, and no longer assimilable to 'late Augustanism'. We should all have been in Davie's debt, had he claimed Blake for his own, as central to Dissent and to late Augustanism, in a magisterial piece of criticism fit to set beside E. P. Thompson's splendid essay on Blake's 'London', which speaks so eloquently for the radical interest.[3] But finally it is with Leavis's great tradition that Davie's defiantly minor tradition begs for comparison, Leavis's affirmation of an authentic native non-conformism. Here it suffices to point out that George Eliot too is passed over in *A Gathered Church* with a few words – the literary figure who more than any other gives the lie to his thesis of the unrelieved decline of Dissent in the nineteenth century, culminating in that disgraceful Eastwood where the Eucharist 'may' not have been celebrated. As Davis writes in his latest collection of poems, in 'Depravity: Two Sermons':

> But the hoopoe whoops
> Always inside, and rancorous. Rancour! Rancour!
> Oh patriotic and indignant bird![4]

In a postscript to his fine essay, 'Hardy's Virgilian Purples', Davie noted that the recent spate of work on Hardy seemed impelled by a wish to prove that Hardy provides a viable insular alternative to the international 'modern Movement', and that he himself was 'quite out of sympathy with that sort of endeavour'. What excited him, he records, is the evidence that 'Hardy proceeded in a way not wholly different from Pound's, say, or Joyce's, or (I could have added) Eliot's' (*Essays*, p. 235). Why, then, has he abandoned, in *Thomas Hardy and British Poetry*, as in *A Gathered Church*, this more generous and productive view? Perhaps part of the answer lies in a passage in 'The Imaginary Museum' (1957): 'the modern style in poetry...precludes formal perfection...A poem by Dryden enjoys a kind of formal beauty and completeness that (we have got as far as this) no truly modern poem *can* enjoy' (pp. 55–6). Davie got as far as this by an illegitimate extension of the situation of the poet in the imaginary museum, namely, that he must be aware of the world's poetry converging upon him at all times with alternative styles, alternative modes of experience, and must, therefore, give notice of this overtly, by breaking the illusion, if only for a moment, by transgressing the convention. But of course it is a nonsense to say that such awareness, even such overt formal recognition of it, precludes formal perfection, either of at least some traditional kinds or of a new kind. Davie has argued himself, again quite needlessly, into a backwater.

Surely the way forward lies not through Davie's extravagant and sterile 'Little Englandism' – nay, 'Factional and Fractional Englandism' – but through that acute critical cosmopolitanism in the service of English poetry which Davie has represented throughout most of his career. Even if it be true that 'English poetry has committed itself to the status of being not more than a marginal pleasure, a deliberately and self-confessedly provincial utterance', paradoxically it cannot maintain itself even in these reduced circumstances without continued immersion in and comparison of itself with poetry still aspiring to a 'universal language', that exotic poetry once celebrated by Davie in James Joyce, in Hugh MacDiarmid, and in Ezra Pound's *Cantos*.

The very name of Pound, however, recalls the variety of embattled positions assumed towards that poet in the history of modernism, in which even the staunchest defenders of 'new bearings' could damn Pound; and Davie's own multifarious and fertile changes of attitude towards him seem to epitomize that history. Not only in his books on Pound (*Poet as Sculptor*, and the Fontana *Pound*), or in *Thomas Hardy and British Poetry*, but in a series of essays – no name is mentioned more often than that of Ezra Pound in 'The Imaginary Museum' – Davie invokes Pound for a startling range of effects. Now he uses Pound's

distinction between imagism and symbolism to display Eliot as a
symbolist of the order of Valéry; now he gives yet another reading of
'Hugh Selwyn Mauberley' and the predicament of British culture; now,
in a charming essay, 'Towards a Pedestrian View of the Cantos' (1972),
he follows in Pound's footsteps on his walking tours from Poitiers to
Aubeterre-sur-Dronne, and suddenly the *Cantos* become a topographical
poem in the style of Dryden's contemporaries. The flag of Pound has
never waved over one land only. Davie, as so often, renders, with the
history of his own opinions, the history of the period. After all, the notion
of 'canon', like that of genre, has been subject to an invasion which has
shaken the connotations of permanence and stability that attach to them;
like genre, which may no longer be rooted in nature, whether according
to Aristotelian or Goethean metaphysics, so the literary canon may have
more to do with circulating libraries than with aesthetic value. If the
reminiscence of stability is still conveyed by them, it is through the
kaleidoscopic rapidity with which new canons, like new genres, appear
and fade away. The comparison of Davie's Dissenting canon with Eliot's
tradition or with Leavis's is after all misleading: for while they still
aspired to 'high seriousness', and courted comparison with Coleridge,
who in a phrase ('Dryden and Pope are classics of our prose') created
and celebrated an authentic change of sensibility, Davie's is rather a
cantankerous jeu d'esprit, a brilliant piece of canon-making for a day
which epitomizes criticism in our time. In that light, Davie's canon, his
dissent from Dissent, is not a curious aberration but a familiar if not
wholly reassuring sign of his (and our) critical life.

NOTES

1 Donald Davie, *A Gathered Church: The Literature of the English Dissenting Interest,
   1700–1930* (Routledge and Kegan Paul, 1978). The Clark Lectures 1976.
2 Donald Davie, *The Poet in the Imaginary Museum: Essays of Two Decades*, edited
   by Barry Alpert (Carcanet, 1977).
3 E. P. Thompson, '"London"', in *Interpreting Blake*, edited by Michael Phillips
   (Cambridge, 1978).
4 Donald Davie, *In the Stopping Train* and other poems (Carcanet, 1977).

Books received

(The inclusion of a book in this list does not preclude a review on this or a later volume.)

Adams, Robert. *After Joyce*. Oxford University Press, 1977

Allmand, C. T., ed. *War Literature and Politics in the Late Middle Ages*. Liverpool University Press, 1977

Atkins, John. *Six Novelists Look at Society*. John Calder, 1977

Bayley, John. *An Essay on Hardy*. Cambridge University Press, 1978

Bloch, R. Howard. *Medieval French Literature and Law*. University of California Press, 1978

Bogumil, S. *Rousseau und die Erziehung des Lesers*, Herbert Lang Verlag, 1978

Bouissac, Paul. *Circus and Culture. A Semiotic Approach*. Indiana University Press, 1976

Bungert, Hans, ed. *Die amerikanische Literatur der Gegenwart*. Reclam, 1977

Bush, Clive. *The Dream of Reason. American Consciousness and Cultural Achievement from Independence to the Civil War*. Edward Arnold, 1977

Cairns, Christopher. *Italian Literature*. David and Charles, 1977

Cernuda, Luis. *Selected Poems*. Translated by Reginald Gibbons. University of California Press, 1978

Clements, Robert J. and Gibaldi, Joseph. *The Anatomy of the Novella. The European Tale Collection from Boccaccio and Chaucer to Cervantes*. New York University Press, 1977

Close, Anthony. *The Romantic Approach to Don Quixote*. Cambridge University Press, 1978

Close, R. A. *English as a Foreign Language*. Second edition, Allen and Unwin, 1977

Coopland, G. W., ed. *Letter to Richard II, a Transcription and Translation of 'Epistre au Roi Richart' by Philippe de Mézières*. Liverpool University Press, 1977

Davie, Donald. *A Gathered Church*. Routledge and Kegan Paul, 1977

In the Stopping Train (poems). Carcanet Press, 1977

Poet in the Imaginary Museum. Carcanet Press, 1977

Detienne, Marcel. *The Gardens of Adonis. Spices in Greek Mythology*. Translated by Janet Lloyd. Harvester Press, 1977.

Doulis, Thomas. *Disaster and Fiction: Modern Greek Fiction and the Impact of the Asia Minor Disaster of 1922*. University of California Press, 1978

Eco, Umberto. *A Theory of Semiotics.* Macmillan Press, 1978

Erzgräber, Willi, ed. *Moderne englische Lyrik.* Reclam, 1976

Esslin, Martin. *Antonin Artaud.* John Calder, 1976

Finnegan, Ruth. *Oral Poetry, its Nature, Significance and Social Context.* Cambridge University Press, 1978

Fischer, Hermann, ed. *Englische Barockgedichte.* Reclam, 1971

Fokkema, D. W. and Kunne-Ibsch, Elrud. *Theories of Literature in the Twentieth Century.* C. Hurts and Co., 1978

Fowler, Roger. *Linguistics and the Novel.* Methuen, 1977

Furst, Lillian. *Counterparts.* Methuen, 1977

Garber, Frederick. *Thoreau's Redemptive Imagination.* New York University Press, 1977

Girard, René. *Violence and the Sacred.* Translated by Patrick Gregory. John Hopkins University Press, 1978

Goethe, J. W. von. *Roman Elegies.* Translated with an introduction and notes by David Luke. Chatto and Windus, 1977

Gray, Richard. *The Literature of Memory, Modern Writers of the American South.* Edward Arnold, 1977

Gumpel, Liselotte. *'Concrete' Poetry from East and West Germany. The Language of Exemplarism and Experimentation.* Yale University Press, 1976

Hamburger, Michael. *German Poetry 1910–1975.* Carcanet Press, 1977

Hardwick, Charles S. *Semiotic and Significs: The Correspondence between Charles S. Pierce and Victoria Lady Welby.* Indiana University Press, 1977

Hawkes, Terence. *Structuralism and Semiotics.* Methuen, 1977

Hermassi, Karen. *Polity and Theatre in Historical Perspective.* University of California Press, 1978

Heninger, S. K. *Cosmographical Glass. Renaissance Diagrams of the Universe.* Dawson Publishing, 1977

Homburger, Eric. *The Art of the Real. Poetry in England and America since 1939.* Dent, 1977

Hönnighausen, Lothar. *Grundprobleme der englischen Literaturtheorie des neunzehnten Jahrhunderts.* Wissenschaftliche Buchgesellschaft, 1977

Janz, Curt Paul. *Nietzsche.* Carl Hanser Verlag, 1978

Levin, Samuel R. *The Semantics of Metaphor.* John Hopkins University Press, 1978

Lamont, William, and Oldfield, Sybil, eds. *Religion and Literature in the Seventeenth Century.* Dent, 1977

Link, Franz, ed. *Amerikanische Lyrik von 17. Jahrhundert bis zur Gegenwart.* Reclam, 1974

Lodge, David. *The Modes of Modern Writing. Metaphor, Metonymy and the Typology of Modern Literature.* Edward Arnold, 1977

McHugh, Roland. *The Sigla of 'Finnegans Wake'.* Edward Arnold, 1977

Mendelson, Edward, ed. *The English Auden.* Faber and Faber, 1977

Middleton, Christopher. *Bolshevism in Art.* Carcanet Press, 1978

Mukařovský, Jan. *The Word and Verbal Art.* Yale University Press, 1977

O'Flaherty, James C., ed. *Studies in Nietzsche and the Classical Tradition.* University of North Carolina Press, 1977

Oral Tradition. Literary Tradition. A Symposium, edited by Otto Holzapfel. Odense University Press, 1978

Parrinder, Patrick. *Authors and Authority.* Routledge and Kegan Paul, 1977

Prescott, Anne Lake. *French Poets and the English Renaissance*. Yale University Press, 1978

Regosin, Richard L. *The Matter of My Book. Montaigne's Essais as the Book of My Self*. University of California Press, 1978

Sebeok, Thomas A., ed. *A Perfusion of Signs*. Indiana University Press, 1977
 ed. *Sight, Sound and Sense*. Indiana University Press, 1978

Tatlow, Anthony. *The Mask of Evil. Brecht's Response to the Poetry, Theatre and Thought of China and Japan*. Peter Lang, 1977

Tzara, Tristan. *7 Dada Manifestoes*. Translated by Barbara Wright. John Calder, 1977

Skilton, David. *The English Novel*. David and Charles, 1977

Watson, Garry. *The Leavises, the 'Social' and the Left*. Brynmill Publishing Company, 1977

Webb, Timothy. *The Violet in the Crucible, Shelley and Translation*. Oxford University Press, 1977

Weinberg, Kurt. *The Figure of Faust in Valéry and Goethe*. Princeton University Press, 1976

Williams, Raymond. *Marxism and Literature*. Oxford University Press, 1977

Periodicals received

Cahiers roumains d'études littéraires (Editions Univers, Bucharest), 1 (1976), Comparatisme et actualité

The Canada Mongolia Review (University of Saskatchewan, Saskatoon), 3:2 (October 1977)

Canadian Review of Comparative Literature (University of Toronto Press for the Canadian Comparative Literature Association), Winter 1974 and Fall 1977

The Comparatist Journal of the Southern Comparative Literature Association (University of Tennessee), May 1977 and May 1978

Eco. Revista de la Cultura de Occidente (Buchholz, Bogotá, Colombia), December 1977

Glyph (Johns Hopkins Textual Studies, Baltimore and London), 1977

Kris. Kritik, Estetik, Politik (Stockholm), April 1978

Mosaic. A Journal for the Comparative Study of Literature and Ideas (University of Manitoba Press), 8:4, On the Rise of the Vernacular Literature in the Middle Ages; 10:2 Faerie, Fantasy and Pseudo-mediaevalia in Twentieth-Century Literature; 10:3 Shakespeare Today

Neohelicon. Acta Comparationis Litterarum Universarum (Mouton for the Hungarian Academy of Sciences), 1/2

The New Review (London), August 1976: Anti-psychiatry Issue; Summer 1978: The State of Fiction – a Symposium

New Universities Quarterly (Blackwells, Oxford), Autumn 1977, Spring and Summer 1978

Nietzsche-Studien. Internationales Jahrbuch für die Nietzsche-Forschung (de Gruyter, Berlin and New York), 6 (1977)

Poetics (North Holland Publishing Company, Amsterdam), September 1977

PTL. A Journal for Descriptive Poetics and Theory of Literature (North Holland Publishing Company, Amsterdam), 1977

Synthesis. Littérature Histoire Arts (Bulletin du Comité National de Littérature comparée, Bucharest), 55 (1977)

Bibliography of
comparative literature in Britain

The bibliography has been compiled by Dr Paula Clifford (Reading). It is based in the first instance on information supplied by the members of the British Comparative Literature Association, and by respondents to a wider inquiry. Although entries have been checked against the British National Bibliography, it is not possible to claim completeness or guarantee accuracy in every case. There is no section on translation and translators, as work in Great Britain is already covered by the bibliography of translations in the *Yearbook of Comparative and General Literature* edited by Henry Remak (Bloomington, Indiana). The headings used are those of the full annual bibliography, discontinued in 1971, in the *YCGL*, which were adapted from Fernand Baldensperger and Werner P. Friedrich, *A Bibliography of Comparative Literature* (Chapel Hill, North Carolina, 1950). We should like to thank Professor Ulrich Weisstein, editor of the *YCGL* bibliographies, for his generous advice.

In this bibliography, place of publication is London unless otherwise stated. In the case of the university presses the place of publication is omitted.

1975

I. COMPARATIVE, WORLD AND GENERAL LITERATURE

Black, M. *The Literature of Fidelity*. Chatto and Windus
Brooks, H. F. *The Use and Abuse of Literary Criticism*. Birkbeck College
Craig, D., ed. *Marxists on Literature: an Anthology*. Harmondsworth, Penguin
Culler, J. *Structuralist Poetics*. Routledge and Kegan Paul
Daiches, D. and Thorlby, A., eds. *Literature and Western Civilisation*, vol. 4, *The Modern World I: Hopes*. Aldus Books
Duggan, J. J., ed. *Oral Literature: Seven Essays*. Scottish Academic Press
Fowler, R., ed. *Style and Structure in Literature*. Oxford, Blackwell
Gassner, J. and Quinn, E. *The Reader's Encyclopaedia of World Drama*. Methuen
Goldman, L. *Towards a Sociology of the Novel*. Translated by Alan Sheridan. Tavistock Publications
Hardy, B. *Tellers and Listeners: the Narrative Imagination*. Athlone Press
Jeffares, A. N. 'Commonwealth Literature in the Modern World'. In *Commonwealth Literature and the Modern World*, edited by H. Maes-Jelinek. Brussels, Marcel Didier

Jones, P. *Philosophy and the Novel*. Oxford University Press

Martin, G. D. *Language, Truth and Poetry*. Edinburgh University Press

O'Flinn, P. *Them and Us in Literature*. Pluto Press

Poole, R. 'In the Beginning was the Word: George Steiner's *After Babel*'. *Books and Bookmen* (June)

Righter, W. *Myth and Literature*. Routledge and Kegan Paul

Sayce, R. 'Die Definition des Begriffs "Stil"'. In *Romanische Stilforschung*, edited by H. Hatzfeld. Darmstadt

Seymour-Smith, Martin. *Guide to Modern World Literature*. 4 vols. Teach Yourself Books

Steiner, G. *After Babel: Aspects of Language and Translation*. Oxford University Press
   Extraterritorial: Papers on Literature and the Language Revolution (first published 1971). Harmondsworth, Penguin

Ward, A. C. *Longman Companion to Twentieth Century Literature*. Second edition, Longman

West, A. *Crisis and Criticism and Selected Literary Essays*. Lawrence and Wishart

II. THEMES AND MOTIFS

Gatt-Rutter, J. 'Calvino Ludens: Literary Play and its Political Implications'. *Journal of European Studies*, 5, 319–40

Harrison, B. *Henry Fielding's 'Tom Jones': the Novelist as Moral Philosopher*. Sussex University Press

Martin, G. D. 'Racism in Genet's *Les Nègres*'. *Modern Language Review*, 70 (July), 517–25

Smeed, J. W. *Faust in Literature*. University of Durham Publications

Topsfield, L. T. *Troubadours and Love*. Cambridge University Press

Wells, D. A. 'The Wild Man from the *Epic of Gilgamesh* to Hartmann von Aue's *Iwein*: Reflections on the Development of a Theme in World Literature'. New Lecture Series, Queen's University, Belfast

III. LITERARY GENRES, TYPES AND FORMS

Aers, D. *Piers Plowman and Christian Allegory*. Edward Arnold

Bacarisse, P. 'Sà-Carneiro and the "conte fantastique"'. *Luso-Brazilian Review*, 12 (Summer), 65–79

Barnes, G. 'The *riddarasögur* and Medieval European Literature'. *Medieval Scandinavia*, 8

Boulton, M. *The Anatomy of the Novel*. Routledge and Kegan Paul

Howard, R. 'Contradiction and the Poetic Image'. *Minnesota Review* (Fall)

Kermode, F. *The Classic*. Faber

Klein, H. M. 'Molière in English Critical Thought on Comedy to 1800'. In *Molière and the Commonwealth*, edited by R. Johnson *et al.* Jackson, University Press of Mississippi

Marshall, J. H. 'The Transmission of Troubadour Poetry'. Inaugural Lecture, Westfield College

Noble, P. S. 'Kay the Seneschal in Chrétien de Troyes and his Predecessors'. *Reading Medieval Studies*, 1, 55–70

Rance, N. *The Historical Novel and Popular Politics in Nineteenth-Century England.* Vision Press

Roberts, Patrick. *The Psychology of Tragic Drama.* Routledge and Kegan Paul

Thomson, G. *Marxism and Poetry* (first published 1947). New edition, Lawrence and Wishart

Wicker, B. *The Story-Shaped World: Fiction and Metaphysics.* Athlone Press

Wilson, C. *The Craft of the Novel.* Gollancz

IV. EPOCHS, CURRENTS AND MOVEMENTS

Bullen, J. B. 'George Eliot's *Romola* as a Positivist Allegory'. *Review of English Studies*, 26, 425–35

Davies, M. C. 'La notion de modernité'. *Cahiers du 20e siècle* (Paris), 5, 9–30

Driscoll, R. *Symbolism and Some Implications of the Symbolic Approach: W. B. Yeats during the 1890s.* Dublin, Dolmen Press

McMillan, D. '*Transition*', the History of a Literary Era. Calder and Boyars

V. BIBLE, CLASSICAL ANTIQUITY

Murdoch, B. O. and Benskin, M. 'The Literary Tradition of Genesis: Review of J. Evans, *Paradise Lost* (1968)'. *Neuphilologische Mitteilungen*, 76, 389–403

Shaffer, E. S. '*Kubla Khan*' and the Fall of Jerusalem. The Mythological School in Biblical Criticism and Secular Literature 1770–1880.* Cambridge University Press

VI. INDIVIDUAL COUNTRIES

Goetinck, G. *Peredur: a Study of Welsh Tradition in the Grail Legends.* Cardiff, University of Wales Press

Heywood, C. 'The Criticism of African Novelists and their Narrative Sources'. In *Commonwealth Literature and the Modern World*, edited by H. Maes-Jelinek. Brussels, Marcel Didier

Perry, N. 'French and English Merchants in the Eighteenth Century: Voltaire Revisited'. In *Studies in Eighteenth-Century French Literature presented to R. Niklaus*, edited by J. H. Fox, University of Exeter Press

VII. INDIVIDUAL AUTHORS

Almansi, G. *The Writer as Liar. Narrative Technique in the 'Decameron'.* Routledge and Kegan Paul

Asmundsson, D. R. 'Frederika Bremer in England'. Ann Arbor, Xerox University Microfilms

Bassnett-McGuire, S. 'Textual Understructures in J.-L. Barrault's *Rabelais* and Tom Stoppard's *Rosencrantz and Guildenstern are Dead*'. *Comparison*, 1, 102–40

Bullough, Geoffrey. *Narrative and Dramatic Sources of Shakespeare*, vol. 8, *Romances*. Routledge and Kegan Paul

Fletcher, D. 'Aaron Hill, translator of La Morte de César'. *Studies on Voltaire and the Eighteenth Century*, 137, 73–9

Fletcher, J. *Claude Simon and Fiction Now*. Calder and Boyars

'The "Intimacy of a Horror": the Tradition of Wilson Harris's *Palace of the Peacock*'. In *Commonwealth Literature and the Modern World*, edited by H. Maes-Jelinek. Brussels, Marcel Didier

Ghertman, S. *Petrarch and Garcilaso. A Linguistic Approach to Style*. Thamesis

Gunny, A. 'Pope's Satirical Impact on Voltaire'. *Revue de littérature comparée*, 49, 92–102

Harrison, R. B. *Hölderlin and Greek Literature*. Oxford University Press

Hunt, Tony. 'Herr Ivan Lejonriddaren'. *Medieval Scandinavia*, 8, 168–86

Kennedy, A. K. *Six Dramatists in Search of Language: Studies in Dramatic Language*. Cambridge University Press

Levin, H. *Ezra Pound, T. S. Eliot and the European Horizon*. The Taylorian Lecture for 1974. Oxford, Clarendon Press

McMillin, A. B. 'Byron and Venevitinov'. *Slavonic and East European Review*, 53 (April), 188–201

Murdoch, B. O. 'Fritz Reuter und Scholem-Aleichem'. In *Fritz Reuter Gedenkschrift*, edited by H. C. Christiansen. Amsterdam

Osborn, M. 'Classical Meditation in *The Wanderer*'. *Comparison*, 1, 67–92

Pechter, E. *Dryden's Classical Theory of Literature*. Cambridge University Press

Ritchie, J. M. 'Georgian Names in Bertolt Brecht's *Der kaukasische Kreidekreis:* a Note'. *New German Studies*, 3, 48–52

Singh, G. 'Dante and Pound'. *Critical Quarterly*, 17, 311–28

'Pound and Cavalcanti'. In *Essays in Honour of John Humphreys Whitfield*. St George's Press

Truman, R. W. '*Lazarillo de Tormes*, Petrarch's *De remediis adversae fortunae* and Erasmus's *Praise of Folly*'. *Bulletin of Hispanic Studies*, 52, 33–53

Tysdahl, B. J. 'Byron, Norway and Ibsen's *Peer Gynt*'. *English Studies* (Amsterdam), 56

Waidson, H. M. 'Auden and German Literature'. *Modern Language Review*, 70, 347–65

Waidson, H. M., and Holmes, T. M. 'The Shakesperean Strain'. In *The German Theatre*, edited by R. Hayman, Oswald Wolff

Weightman, J. 'Ibsen and the Absurd'. *Encounter*, 45

Worth, K., ed. *Beckett the Shape Changer: a Symposium*. Routledge and Kegan Paul

VII. LITERATURE AND THE OTHER ARTS

Merchant, P. 'William Carlos Williams and Brueghel'. *Comparison*, 1, 52–66

Meyers, J. *Painting and the Novel*. Manchester University Press

Paulson, R. *Emblems and Expression: Meaning in English Art of the Eighteenth Century*. Thames and Hudson

Redwood, C. 'Delius and Strindberg'. *Music and Letters*, 56

1976

I. COMPARATIVE, WORLD AND GENERAL LITERATURE

Cluysenaar, A. *Introduction to Literary Stylistics*. Batsford

Cox, R. F. 'Five Theses on Literary Education in the University'. *Hermathena*, 121

Di Fidio, O. 'Marxism and Literary Criticism'. *Association of Teachers of Italian Journal* (March)

Esslin, Martin. *An Anatomy of Drama*. Temple Smith

Fletcher, J. 'Comparing the Literatures: or, What Happens when the American Dream is Celebrated on Opposite Sides of the Fence'. *Comparative Literature Studies*, 13, 116–31

'Literature and the Problem of Evil'. *Theology*, 79, 274–8 and 337–43

Jeffares, A. N. 'Literatures in English'. *Contemporary Review* (May), 264–8

'The Literatures of the Commonwealth'. In *Povijest Svjetske Knjizenosti*. Zagreb, Mladost and Stvarnost

Padley, G. A. *Grammatical Theory in Western Europe, 1500–1700: the Latin Tradition*. Cambridge University Press

Patrides, C. A., ed. *Aspects of Time*. Manchester University Press

Prawer, S. *Karl Marx and World Literature*. Oxford University Press

Rowley, B. A. 'Die Entwicklung der Germanistik in Grossbritannien und Irland anhand britischer Antrittvorlesungen'. In *Jahrbuch für Internationale Germanistik*. Bern, Herbert Lang, 342–51

Shaffer, E. S. Essay Review of Michael Foucault, *L'Archéologie du savoir*. *Studies in the History and Philosophy of Science*, 7 (Autumn), 269–75

Steiner, G. *After Babel: Aspects of Language and Translation* (first published 1975). Paperback edition, Oxford University Press

Wellek, R. and Warren, A. *Theory of Literature* (third edition, 1963). Harmondsworth, Penguin

Zéraffa, M. *Fictions: the Novel and Social Reality*. Translated by Catherine Burns and Tom Burns. Harmondsworth, Penguin

II. THEMES AND MOTIFS

Bradbury, M. 'The Denuded Place: War and Form in *Parade's End* and *USA*'. In *The First World War in Fiction*, edited by H. M. Klein. Macmillan

'Dangerous Pilgrimages: Transatlantic Images in Fiction, 1'. *Encounter*, 47 (December)

Dronke, P. *Abelard and Heloise in Medieval Testimonies*. University of Glasgow Press

Fletcher, D. '*Candide* and the Theme of the Happy Husbandman'. *Studies on Voltaire and the Eighteenth Century*, 161, 137–47

Fletcher, J. 'Cultural Pessimists: The Tradition of Christopher Priest's Fiction'. *International Fiction Review*, 3, 20–4

Hunt, T. 'Fatality and the Novel: *Tristran, Manon Lescaut* and *Thérèse Desqueyroux*'. *Durham University Journal*, 68 (2), 183–95

Klein, H. M., ed. *The First World War in Fiction. A Collection of Critical Essays*. Macmillan

'The Natural Hero, the Lowest Common Denominator and the Wounded Heart: Variations of the Everyman Figure in the War Novels of Franconi, Williamson and Wiechert'. *Comparison*, 2, 19–72.

Murdoch, B. O. *The Irish Adam and Eve Story II*. Dublin, Commentary

Pickup, I. 'Réquisitoires contre le Code pénal dans le roman sous la monarchie de Juillet'. *Revue de science criminelle et de droit pénal comparé*, N.S. (April–June)

III. LITERARY GENRES, TYPES AND FORMS

Dronke, P. 'Learned Lyric and Popular Ballad in the Early Middle Ages'. *Studi Medievali*, 3rd series, 17, 1–40

Katz, M. R. *The Literary Ballad in Early Nineteenth-Century Russian Literature*. Oxford University Press

Martin, G. D. 'Masterful Images Because Complete, or, Icon and Ison'. *Comparison*, 4, 3–41

Scott, C. 'The Limits of the Sonnet: Towards a Proper Contemporary Approach'. *Revue de littérature comparée*, 50, 237–51

Shields, H. '*The Grey Cock*: Dawn Song or Revenant Ballad?'. In *Ballad Studies*, edited by E. B. Lyle. Cambridge, D. S. Brewer, 67–92 and 185–204

Victorian Melodramas: Seven English, French and American Melodramas. Edited and introduced by J. L. Smith. Dent

IV. EPOCHS, CURRENTS AND MOVEMENTS

Boyle, N. 'Review of *The Secularization of the European Mind in the Nineteenth Century* by O. Chadwick'. *Cambridge Review*, 98, 149–52

Bradbury, M. and McFarlane, J., eds. *Modernism*. Harmondsworth, Penguin

Furst, L. R. *Romanticism*. Second edition, Methuen

Minta, S. M. J. 'A Problem of Literary History: "Petrarchism" in Early Sixteenth-Century French Poetry'. *French Studies*, 30, 140–52

Newton, J. and Bettinson, C. D. 'The Legacy of Naturalism in *Les Caves du Vatican*. *Neophilologus*, 60, 200–6

Parrinder, P. '*News from Nowhere, The Time Machine* and the Break-up of Classical Realism'. *Science-Fiction Studies*, 3 (November) 265–74

Scott, C. 'Symbolism, Decadence and Impressionism'. In *Modernism*, edited by M. Bradbury and J. McFarlane. Harmondsworth, Penguin

Shaffer, E. S. 'Das Bild der Natur in der romantischen Naturphilosophie'. *Jahrbuch für Internationale Germanistik*. Bern, Herbert Lang

V. BIBLE, CLASSICAL ANTIQUITY

Allen, L. *John Henry Newman and the abbé Jager. A Controversy on Scripture and Tradition*. University of Durham Publications

VI. INDIVIDUAL COUNTRIES

Allen, M. J. B. and Calder, D. G., trans. *Sources and Analogues of Old English Poetry: the Major Latin Texts in Translation*. Cambridge, D. S. Brewer

Clifford, P. M. 'The American Novel and the French *Nouveau roman*: Some Linguistic and Stylistic Comparisons.' *Comparative Literature Studies*, 13, 348–58

Devereux, G. *Dreams in Greek Tragedy: an Ethno-psycho-analytical Study*. Oxford, Blackwell

Dronke, P. 'Peter of Blois and Poetry at the Court of Henry II'. *Medieval Studies*, 38, 186–235

Haugen, E. *The Scandinavian Languages*. Faber

Molesworth, R. *An Account of Denmark as it was in the Year 1692*. Copenhagen

Stanford, W. B. *Ireland and the Classical Tradition*. Dublin, Alan Figgis

   'Monsters and Odyssean Echoes in the Early Hiberno-Latin and Irish Hymns'. In *Latin Script and Letters*, edited by J. J. O'Meara and B. Naumann. Leiden, Brill

Wollstonecraft, M. *Letters Written during a Short Residence in Sweden, Norway and Denmark*. Lincoln, University of Nebraska Press

VII. INDIVIDUAL AUTHORS

Alexander, M. 'On Ezra Pound's "Seafarer"'. *Agenda* (Winter), 110–26

Allen, L. 'French Intellectuals and T. E. Lawrence'. *Durham University Journal*, 68, 52–66

Bullen, J. B. 'Fra Bartolommeo's Quest for Obscurity'. *English Language Notes*, 13, 206–9

Ewbank, I.-S. 'Shakespeare, Ibsen and the Unspeakable'. Inaugural Lecture, Bedford College

Five Norwegian Poets. Lines Review (Edinburgh), 55–6

Fowler, F. M. 'Goethe's "Faust" and the Medieval Sequence'. *Modern Language Review*, 71, 838–45

Gunny, A. 'Problems of Assessing English Literary Influences on Voltaire'. *Comparison*, 3, 88–108

Gurr, A. 'Third-World Drama: Soyinka and Tragedy'. *Journal of Commonwealth Literature*, 10, 45–52

Hugo, Victor. *Littérature et philosophie mêlées*. Edited by A. R. W. James. 2 vols. Paris, Klincksieck

Ives, M. C. 'Pope's *Windsor Forest* as a Possible Source of Romantic "Waldeinsamkeit": a Suitable Case for Investigation'. *Comparison*, 3, 65–87

Knowlson, J. 'Beckett and John Millington Synge'. *Gambit International Theatre Review*, 7 (22), 65–81

   'Voltaire, Lucian and *Candide*'. *Studies on Voltaire and the Eighteenth Century*, 161, 149–60

Mackillop, C. D. and Hopkins, D. W. 'Immortal Vida and Basil Kennett'. *Review of English Studies*, 27, 137–47

McCobb, A. 'Aaron Bernstein's *Mendel Gibbor*: A Minor Source for *Daniel Deronda*'. *English Language Notes*, 14, 42–3

Pilling, J. 'Beckett's *Proust*'. *Journal of Beckett Studies*, 1

   Samuel Beckett. Routledge and Kegan Paul

Poole, R. 'A Philosophy for Today? Isaiah Berlin's *Vico and Herder*'. *Books and Bookmen* (July)

Redfern, W. D. 'Giono, Ponge and La Pierre'. *La Revue des Lettres Modernes*, 468–73; *Jean Giono 2*, 113–36

   'Vallès and the Existential Pun'. *Mosaic*, 9, 27–39

Riley, E. O. 'Cervantes and the Cynics'. *Bulletin of Hispanic Studies*, 53, 189–205

Singh, G. 'Montale e Leopardi'. *Misure Critiche*, 3 (18), 5–21

Thomas, N. L. 'Werther in a New Guise: Ulrich Plenzdorf's *Die neuen Leiden des jungen W*'. *Modern Languages*, 57

Williams, D. 'The Role of the Foreign Theatre in Voltaire's *Corneille*'. *Modern Language Review*, 71, 282–93

VIII. LITERATURE AND THE OTHER ARTS

Honour, Hugh. *The New Golden Land: European Images of America from the Discoveries to the Present Time*. Allen Lane

Huysmans, J.-K. *Grünewald*. Translated by R. Baldick. Oxford, Phaidon (J.-K. Huysmans, 'The Grünewalds in the Colmar Museum', was first published in *Trois Primitifs*, Paris, 1905)

Ritchie, J. M. 'The Theatre of German Expressionism and the Visual Arts'. *New German Studies*, 4, 23–9

Wetherill, P. M. 'Poetry, Painting and Reality'. *Forum for Modern Language Studies*, 12 (December)